James Crawford is a writer and broadcaster. His first major book, *Fallen Glory: The Lives and Deaths of History's Greatest Buildings* was shortlisted for the Saltire Literary Award for best non-fiction. His other books include *The Edge of the Plain: How Borders Make and Break Our World*, *Who Built Scotland: 25 Journeys in Search of a Nation*, *Scotland's Landscapes* and *Aerofilms: A History of Britain from Above*. In 2019 he was named the Archive and Records Association's first-ever 'Explore Your Archives' Ambassador.

Praise for James Crawford

The Edge of the Plain: How Borders Make and Break Our World

'Crawford's essays, through vivid accounts of historical episodes and contemporary problems, illuminate how the world acquired its current shape . . . Eye-opening'
Literary Review

'Excellent'
Guardian

Fallen Glory: The Lives and Deaths of History's Greatest Buildings

'Conveys superbly these absorbing tales of hubris, power, violence and decay'
Sunday Times

'Witty and memorable . . . moving as well as myth-busting'
Mary Beard, *Times Literary Supplement*

Scotland from the Sky

'A stunning combination of aviation adventure and historical detective work'
Press and Journal

'Crawford is a genuine, risk-taking adventurer'
Daily Express

Wild History

Journeys into Lost Scotland

JAMES CRAWFORD

First published in 2023 by
Birlinn Ltd
West Newington House
10 Newington Road
Edinburgh
EH9 1QS

www.birlinn.co.uk

Text and photographs copyright © James Crawford 2023

The right of James Crawford to be identified
as the author of this work has been asserted by
him in accordance with the Copyright, Designs
and Patents Act, 1988

All rights reserved. No part of this publication
may be reproduced, stored, or transmitted
in any form, or by any means, electronic, mechanical
or photocopying, recording or otherwise, without
the express written permission of the publisher.

ISBN 978 1 78027 786 8

British Library Cataloguing-in-Publication Data
A catalogue record for this book is available on
request from the British Library

Designed and typeset by Mark Blackadder, Edinburgh

Printed and bound by PNB, Latvia

Contents

Map	8–9
Introduction	10

Worked

Belnahua, Firth of Lorn	21
Cauldstane Slap, West Lothian	25
Fasagh Ironworks, Loch Maree	29
Ard Nev Deer Trap, Isle of Rum	35
The Fish Road, Loch Glascarnoch	38
Ben Griam Beg, Sutherland	45
Kirnie Law, Innerleithen	49
The Viking Shipyard, Isle of Skye	53
Ard Neackie, Loch Eriboll	57
Fethaland, Shetland	63
Ailsa Craig, Firth of Clyde	67
Sandwood Bay, Sutherland	73
Salisbury's Dam, Isle of Rum	79
Lassodie Village, Fife	83

Sacred

Callanish XI, Isle of Lewis	91
Viking Boat Burial, Swordle Bay, Ardnamurchan	97
Glencruitten 'Cathedral of Trees', Oban	101
Tigh na Cailleach, Glen Lyon	105

St Peter's Seminary, Cardross	111
Sgorr nam Ban-Naomha, 'The Cliffs of the Holy Women', Isle of Canna	119
Dun Deardail, Glen Nevis	123
Cathkin Park, Glasgow	126
Na Clachan Aoraidh, Loch Tummel	133
Jacksonville Hut, Rannoch Moor	137
Square Cairn Cemetery, Bay of Laig, Isle of Eigg	142
The Forest Pitch, Selkirk	149

Contested

Dere Street Roman Road, The Borders	155
Culbin Sands Poles, Moray	161
Clach na Briton, Glen Falloch	165
X-Craft Midget Submarines, Aberlady Bay	169
Cairn Cul Ri Albainn, Isle of Mull	173
Royal Observer Corps Monitoring Post, Kinbrace	179
Roman Signal Station, Rubers Law	183
The Atlantic Wall, Sheriffmuir	189
Inchkeith Island, Firth of Forth	193
North Sutor Battery, Cromarty Firth	201
John Randolph, Torrisdale Bay, Sutherland	205
Cramond Island, Firth of Forth	208
Garva Bridge, General Wade's Military Road	215
Ardoch Roman Fort, Braco	221

Sheltered

The Bone Caves, Inchnadamph	228
Peanmeanach, Ardnish Pensinsula	235
Cracknie Souterrain, Borgie Forest, Sutherland	241
'The Bothy', Isle of Staffa	247
Coire Gabhail, 'The Lost Valley', Glencoe	251
Hermit's Castle, Achmelvich	256
Shiaba, Isle of Mull	261

Contents

Northshield Rings, Eddleston	267
Mingulay Village, Outer Hebrides	271
The Sgurr, Isle of Eigg	277
Moine House, Sutherland	282
Mavisbank, Loanhead	289
Cove Harbour, Berwickshire	295
Tap O' Noth, Rhynie	301
The Shepherd's House, Pentland Hills	304
Postscript	309
List of Illustrations	311
Acknowledgements	315
Index	316

Worked

1. Ailsa Craig, Firth of Clyde
2. Ard Neackie, Loch Eriboll
3. Ard Nev Deer Trap, Isle of Rum
4. Belnahua, Firth of Lorn
5. Ben Griam Beg, Sutherland
6. Cauldstane Slap, West Lothian
7. Fasagh Ironworks, Loch Maree
8. Fethaland, Shetland
9. The Fish Road, Loch Glascarnoch
10. Kirnie Law, Innerleithen
11. Lassodie Village, Fife
12. Salisbury's Dam, Isle of Rum
13. Sandwood Bay, Sutherland
14. The Viking Shipyard, Isle of Skye

Sacred

15. Callanish XI, Isle of Lewis
16. Cathkin Park, Glasgow
17. Dun Deardail, Glen Nevis
18. The Forest Pitch, Selkirk
19. Glencruitten 'Cathedral of Trees', Oban
20. Jacksonville Hut, Rannoch Moor
21. Na Clachan Aoraidh, Loch Tummel
22. Sgorr nam Ban-Naomha, 'The Cliffs of the Holy Women', Isle of Canna
23. Square Cairn Cemetery, Bay of Laig, Isle of Eigg
24. St Peter's Seminary, Cardross
25. Tigh na Cailleach, Glen Lyon
26. Viking Boat Burial, Swordle Bay, Ardnamurchan

Contested

27. Ardoch Roman Fort, Braco
28. The Atlantic Wall, Sheriffmuir
29. Cairn Cul Ri Albainn, Isle of Mull
30. Clach na Briton, Glen Falloch
31. Cramond Island, Firth of Forth
32. Culbin Sands Poles, Moray
33. Dere Street Roman Road, The Borders
34. Garva Bridge, General Wade's Military Road
35. Inchkeith Island, Firth of Forth
36. *John Randolph*, Torrisdale Bay, Sutherland
37. North Sutor Battery, Cromarty Firth
38. Roman Signal Station, Rubers Law
39. Royal Observer Corps Monitoring Post, Kinbrace
40. X-Craft Midget Submarines, Aberlady Bay

Sheltered

41. The Bone Caves, Inchnadamph
42. 'The Bothy', Isle of Staffa
43. Coire Gabhail, 'The Lost Valley', Glencoe
44. Cove Harbour, Berwickshire
45. Cracknie Souterrain, Borgie Forest, Sutherland
46. Hermit's Castle, Achmelvich
47. Mavisbank, Loanhead
48. Mingulay Village, Outer Hebrides
49. Moine House, Sutherland
50. Northshield Rings, Eddleston
51. Peanmeanach, Ardnish Pensinsula
52. The Sgurr, Isle of Eigg
53. The Shepherd's House, Pentland Hills
54. Shiaba, Isle of Mull
55. Tap O' Noth, Rhynie

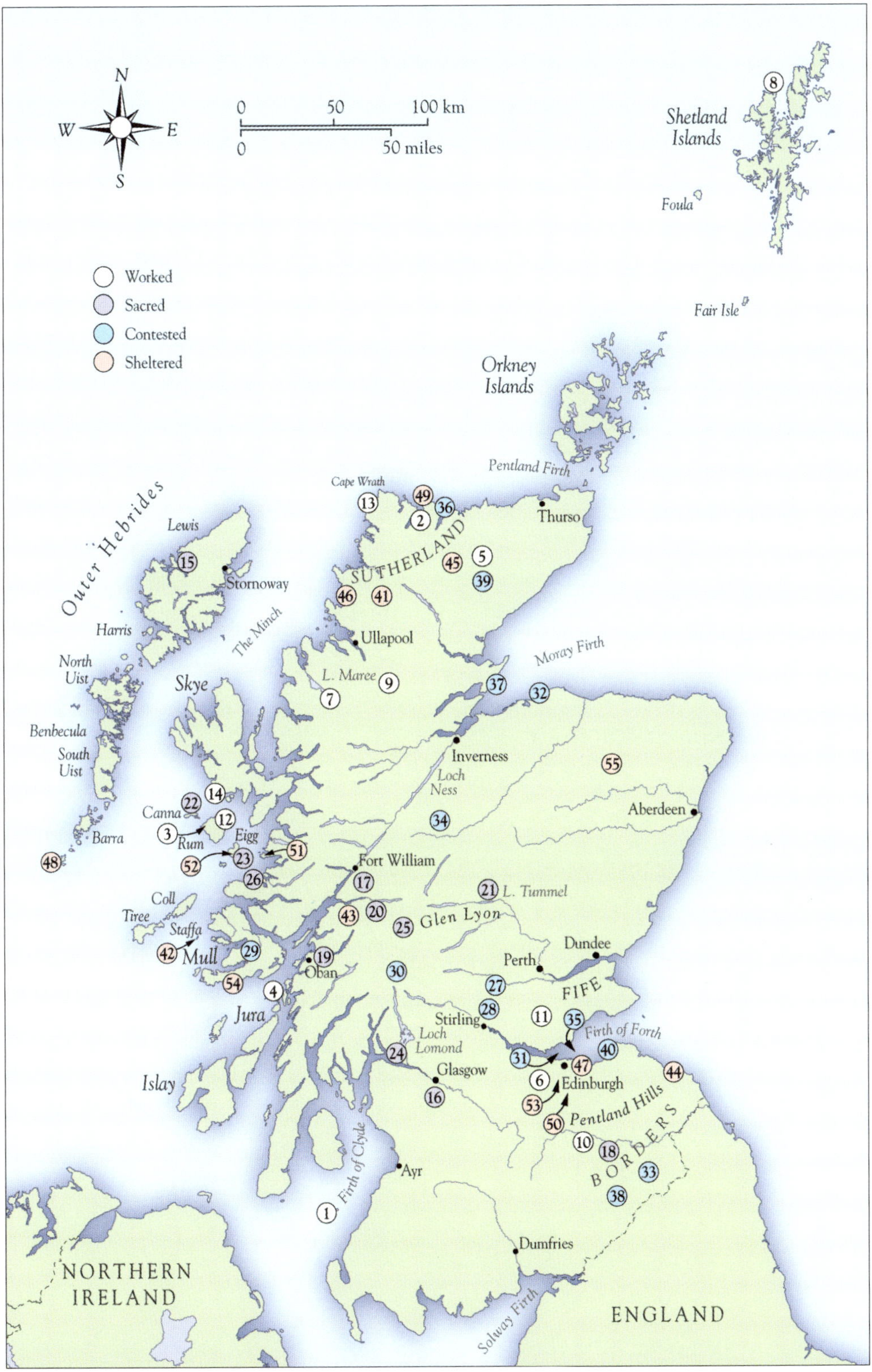
N
S
W
E
0
50
100 km
0
50 miles
Shetland Islands
Foula
Fair Isle
Worked
Sacred
Contested
Sheltered
Orkney Islands
Pentland Firth
Cape Wrath
Thurso
SUTHERLAND
Outer Hebrides
Lewis
Stornoway
Harris
The Minch
North Uist
Benbecula
South Uist
Barra
Skye
Canna
Rum
Eigg
Ullapool
L. Maree
Moray Firth
Inverness
Loch Ness
Aberdeen
Fort William
L. Tummel
Glen Lyon
Coll
Tiree
Staffa
Mull
Oban
Jura
Islay
Perth
Dundee
FIFE
Stirling
Firth of Forth
Loch Lomond
Glasgow
Edinburgh
Pentland Hills
BORDERS
Firth of Clyde
Ayr
Dumfries
Solway Firth
NORTHERN IRELAND
ENGLAND
1
2
3
4
5
6
7
8
9
10
11
12
13
14
15
16
17
18
19
20
21
22
23
24
25
26
27
28
29
30
31
32
33
34
35
36
37
38
39
40
41
42
43
44
45
46
47
48
49
50
51
52
53
54
55

Introduction

You scramble up over the dunes of an isolated beach. You climb to the summit of a lonely hill. You pick your way through the eerie hush of a forest. And then you find them. The traces of the past. The crumbling remains that our ancestors left behind; moss-covered, tumbledown ruins; giant, overgrown earthworks; a circle of forgotten stones. Perhaps they are marked by a tiny symbol on your map, perhaps not. There are no signs or plaques to explain their fading presence before you, nothing to account for what they once were – who made them or lived in them or abandoned them. Now they are merged with the landscape. They are being reclaimed by nature. They are wild history.

• • •

How can history be wild? Well, in one sense, it can't. Wilderness – true wilderness – means somewhere unaltered by human activity. Today, very few wild environments can be found anywhere on Earth. And arguably, even where they can, the scale and extent of human-influenced climate change has filled the very atmosphere, or seas, or soils around them. This is the product of the Anthropocene, the 'human time' – the name that has been given to our newest geological era, conceived to acknowledge that the presence and influence of people is no longer just something written *on* the surface of the Earth but has become woven irrevocably *into* the very fabric of the planet.

Scotland long ago lost any claim to true wilderness. Since the end of the last Ice Age, some 10,000 years ago, this land has been moved through, occupied, cut up, cut down, dug out, built on and entirely changed. No parts –

Introduction

even those areas that are perceived as the most 'extreme' or 'remote' – have been left untouched by people. What has happened to our landscape is an accumulation. Of interventions, of events, of life. It began with hunters stalking their prey north and killing and cooking on land that we now call Scotland. In the process they left behind simple piles of shells and bones in rubbish pits known as middens – fish bones, deer antlers, hazelnut kernels. The scorch marks of the millennia-old fires that they lit, the hearths that they gathered around, have persisted, in the depths of the loam, all the way up to the present day.

As time passed, these traces – so faint and fragmentary at first – built inexorably. Much was destroyed or erased or lost. But not everything. The *not everythings* from one era merged with the *not everythings* from another. The fires stopped moving, the walls around them grew solid, the accumulation intensified and accelerated. Ploughshares started to rip up the ground. Axes – and a colder, wetter, windier climate – began to clear the forests. Bit by bit, communities overspread the land, turning the wilderness to their own ends.

The result is that, today, we live entirely among the physical impression and presence of the past. Often it emerges in the shapes of our towns and cities; in the ways our fields look; in the bare reaches of our sheep-wandered hills and moorlands. Just as before, so much has been destroyed or erased or lost. But at the same time, the list of the *not everythings* from successive periods has grown vast. Some have even been afforded special status, segregated from the present to be offered up as preserved, curated ruins and tourist attractions; even adopted as national icons. A handful receive millions of visitors each year.

But the majority do not. Rather, they exist in a state of continually fading obscurity, spread out across those parts of the landscape which people once knew, but now, largely, don't. They are what this book is about. The uncurated and the ignored, the unfiltered and the abandoned. Those places that are not wilderness, but rather feel post-human: the shadows of people's lives in the landscape, sometimes growing faint, but still persisting. *They* are what I mean by wild history. History set adrift, let loose, let go. History, in some sense, set free. Just there: overgrown, overlooked – and increasingly untamed.

• • •

For a decade, I worked in an archive which, at the time that I came to join it, was exactly 100 years old. It was a slightly odd kind of an archive, with rather unusual origins – not least that, when it was first founded in 1908, it wasn't supposed to be an archive at all.

It had been established as a Royal Commission, tasked by King Edward VII with making 'an inventory of the Ancient and Historical Monuments and Constructions connected with or illustrative of the contemporary culture, civilisations and conditions of the life of the people in Scotland from earliest times to the year 1707'. Only a few years earlier, in 1882, Parliament had passed the first-ever Act for the preservation and protection of ancient sites and structures. That Act came with a list of those places throughout the UK deemed most important. A third of them were to be found in Scotland, but it still amounted to just twenty-one sites – a few stone circles, a handful of burial cairns. There wasn't even a single castle. Everyone knew that there had to be more: it was just that no one had ever been tasked with identifying them.

This job fell to Alexander Ormiston Curle, the Royal Commission's first Secretary, and its only full-time member of staff. The original intention was that he would carry out a desk-based study, compiling a master list from previously existing maps and accounts – but Curle and the six commissioners appointed to oversee his work were having none of it. In the first hour of their first meeting, held in Edinburgh in February 1908, they decided that 'it was essential that the Secretary should visit each county in turn with the object of personally inspecting each monument'.

By the summer, Curle was out in the field on his bicycle, navigating the quiet backroads of Berwickshire in the Scottish Borders, maps and measuring instruments strapped to his crossbar. On day three, he set off south from the village of Coldingham to arrive at a place called Habchester, marked on his Ordnance Survey (OS) map with the enigmatic title 'site'. 'I made use for the first time of my surveyor's staff and clinometer and found them most handy,' he wrote in his notebook, which he later titled *The Private Journal of a Wandering Antiquary*. What he was recording was the remains of a 2,000-year-old hillfort. 'Though one half has been entirely obliterated,' he said, 'it

Introduction

is still a most striking fort, with two ramparts.' While he humbly doubted the accuracy of his measurements, he resolved that they were, at least, 'better than the word "site"'.

Curle kept going with this first survey up until the beginning of November, travelling some 300 miles by bicycle – and, as he proudly recalled, only five times by horse and trap and twice by car. Of walking, he said, 'The number of miles I have tramped by moorland and meadow I have no reckoning of but they are many. It has never been anything but the most intense pleasure to me.' In the process, he visited and explored over 260 sites, seventy-one of which had never been recorded before. And, although he did not realise it at the time, all those journals full of scribbled accounts, observations and measurements, marked the beginnings of an archive.

A year later, Curle was in Sutherland in the far north of Scotland, working all summer and autumn in often harsh conditions. There, he wrote, 'The monuments and constructions of Sutherland were found to greatly exceed in number those previously known to exist.' His second report was three times the length of his first. Curle continued his relentless progress. By 1916, when the Royal Commission's work was suspended until the end of the First World War, he'd visited five of Scotland's twenty-five counties. At that rate, the Royal Commission was on course to finish its task sometime around the 1950s. Except, as Curle's Sutherland report noted, rather matter-of-factly, 'There still exist a certain number of objects which have not come under our observation.' So, in essence, even when the survey of a county was complete, it wasn't actually complete.

As the work began again after the war, and as the decades passed, the field notes and reports were increasingly supplemented by survey drawings, maps and photographs of sites. The 'inventory' of the places themselves continued to grow (as did the number of staff – although Curle had resigned as Secretary in 1913 to take up the position of Director of the National Museum of Antiquities, he had continued to assist with the Royal Commission's field surveys). But so too did all the material that went into creating and evidencing that inventory. The Royal Commission had become a kind of living archive. In capturing the traces of the human presence in the landscape, it was, in effect, reproducing itself – and the landscape – over and over again.

The parameters of what it was supposed to be recording kept changing too. During the Second World War, the threat of destruction from Luftwaffe air raids saw the date range for inclusion in the inventory shift by over a century, from 1707 to 1815, to ensure that it included Edinburgh's New Town. After the war, the remit of the Royal Commission was extended again, incorporating the archive of the Scottish National Buildings Record, which was set up in 1941 to make an emergency record of the nation's historic architecture. Before long, any date limit on what to record or collect was dropped completely. Soon, an organisation that had started by inspecting stone circles was moving into recording sites of heavy industry and modernist architecture – factories, foundries, steel works, high-rise tower blocks. The original Royal Commission wasn't even meant to be an archive, and here it was holding hundreds of thousands – and then over a million – photographs, maps, plans and drawings relating to almost every aspect of Scotland's archaeology and architecture.

The eccentricity of this archive was, in many respects, what interested me. My role there, put simply, was to make sense of the stories it contained and to find ways of communicating them to a wider public – who were almost entirely unaware of its existence. In the process, I developed an enormous affection for the idea that lay behind it, minted in that very first meeting in 1908: that the best way to truly understand the history of our landscape is to get out there and explore it yourself. That this idea had gradually evolved into an impossibly large, perfectly quixotic endeavour only increased its appeal.

The longer that I spent among the archive's shelves, negatives, boxes and plan chests – full of photographs, sketches, drawings and faded, handwritten notations – the more it put me in mind of a famous short story by the Argentinian author Jorge Luis Borges. Called 'On Exactitude in Science', it is just one single paragraph long, and describes a fictional empire where the art of cartography has attained such perfection that 'the Cartographers Guilds struck a Map of the Empire whose size was that of the Empire, and which coincided point for point with it'. Borges, in turn, had been inspired by Lewis Carroll's *Sylvie and Bruno Concluded*, in which two characters discuss how, in an unnamed country, they went from mapping six inches to the mile, to a mile to a mile. One character asks the other if they have used this map yet.

Introduction

To which the reply comes, 'It has never been spread out . . . the farmers objected: they said it would cover the whole country, and shut out the sunlight! So we now use the country itself, as its own map, and I assure you it does nearly as well.'

The archive of the Royal Commission, originating with Curle's journal, had grown so exponentially over the course of a century – and was rapidly in the process of duplicating itself into a mass of binary code through the process of digitisation (what one of Curle's successors as Secretary, Roger Mercer, called the archive's 'Big Bang' moment) – that it had begun to aspire towards the same 'exactitude' that Borges and Carroll described. The ultimate inventory of a nation, created by perfectly assembling a record of every physical aspect of that nation: the two constantly shifting and changing in lockstep.

• • •

It was my work in the Royal Commission's 'impossible' archive that inspired this book. Curle and those who followed him were involved in a process of reading and translating the tangible remains of the human impact on the landscape of Scotland: with the result that they found that impact everywhere, to such an extent that it seemed unfeasible to account for it all, even if that didn't stop them from trying. The story of their effort remains largely obscure and untold – and is reflected, too, in the enduring obscurity of many of the sites that they visited over the course of more than a century.

A few years ago, I began travelling out into the landscape to see some of these sites for myself. What follows is just a fraction of what is out there, a glimpse, if you like, into a whole world of 'wild' histories. This is a guide to those sites, but it is a partial and provisional one made up of a series of vignettes from journeys across the country to places that – with a handful of exceptions – see very little in the way of passing traffic.

They include a 2,500-year-old hole in the ground found on a lonely knoll in Sutherland, leading down into what may be Scotland's oldest surviving basement. Colossal ancient border markers delimiting the boundaries of long extinct kingdoms. Drowned roads and fading drove roads. Beached shipwrecks and rhododendron-choked modernist wrecks. Medieval deer traps and prehistoric cattle ranches. Lost valleys and lost villages. Pictish 'cities', Viking boat-burials, a shrine to the goddess of winter and a stone circle surrounding a three-millennia-old lightning strike. A Roman signal station, a concrete hermit's castle and the regrowing ruins of a cathedral made of trees. A moorland on the cusp of the Highlands that once served as a surrogate for Gallipoli. Five miles of beach and tidal sands studded with the bone-bleached uprights of over 2,000 wooden poles.

Largely, I was alone on these journeys, although sometimes I travelled with others. Like Curle, I did a lot of walking and cycling – although, I confess, rather more than just two trips in a car. And I photographed every single site, just as I found it, whether in sun or rain or frost or snow. I thought a lot about how to organise these sites, what information to include on how to reach them. Some are very easy to find and access. Others offer rather more of a challenge. In the end, I resolved to provide just one simple clue – a grid reference.

Each grid reference is your starting point. Locate it on an OS map, see how it has been rendered and translated into the curves and whorls of contour lines. From there, you can begin to build up a sense not just of this one point, but also of what surrounds it: first 'reading' the landscape, and then working out how to get from wherever *you are* to wherever *it is*. All these layers of preparation enrich the journey itself: the realisation of what you may have imagined previously only through the map, or experienced at a remove, through pictures and photographs, accounts written by other travellers from other times. Maybe you walk or cycle as you try to connect the abstraction of the grid reference to the reality of the mountains, hills, rivers and moorlands that surround you.

Once you reach the site, stop for a while, if you can, and watch how the landscape moves and shifts around it. Most likely, there will be no one else there. It is a process that offers up a particular intimacy with the landscape; and which allows you to commune, in whatever way you like, with a history of place. To think of what these sites must have been when first created, or used, or lived in; but also to reflect on their persistence, their ability to be both 'out of time' and still here, right in front of you, undeniable features of the modern world.

Perhaps more than anything else, this book is an invitation. An invitation

Introduction

to see for yourself just how much of the past still lives with us in the present. An invitation to explore the unexplored and make pilgrimage to the lost and overlooked. An invitation to 'use the country itself, as its own map' – and to see where it will take you.

• • •

The sites in this book are split into four categories – reflecting, in the broadest terms, how people have used the landscapes of Scotland over the millennia.

There are the remains of **worked** landscapes, tracts of Scotland that have been turned over, opened up and emptied out by those who sought to use the natural environment as a resource, whether for subsistence or for profit.

There are those places that, for reasons both known and unknown, have been marked out as **sacred**: spaces of ritual or worship, imbued with some sense of spiritual meaning, even if that meaning has long vanished.

There are the lingering traces of conflict, of **contested** earth, the marks left behind by wars, both recent and ancient, that reflect the seemingly eternal human capacity for fighting over space, driven by the desire to own and dominate territory.

And finally, and most simply, there are **sheltered** landscapes: dwellings and homes, from bare and simple bothies to now-ruinous Enlightenment visions of 'perfect' houses. The fading remains left by those who once chose to set down roots and carve out a life on one particular patch of soil or rock.

Think of these four categories as signposts to your journey into a lost Scotland: way-markers to our wild history.

James Crawford
Edinburgh, March 2023

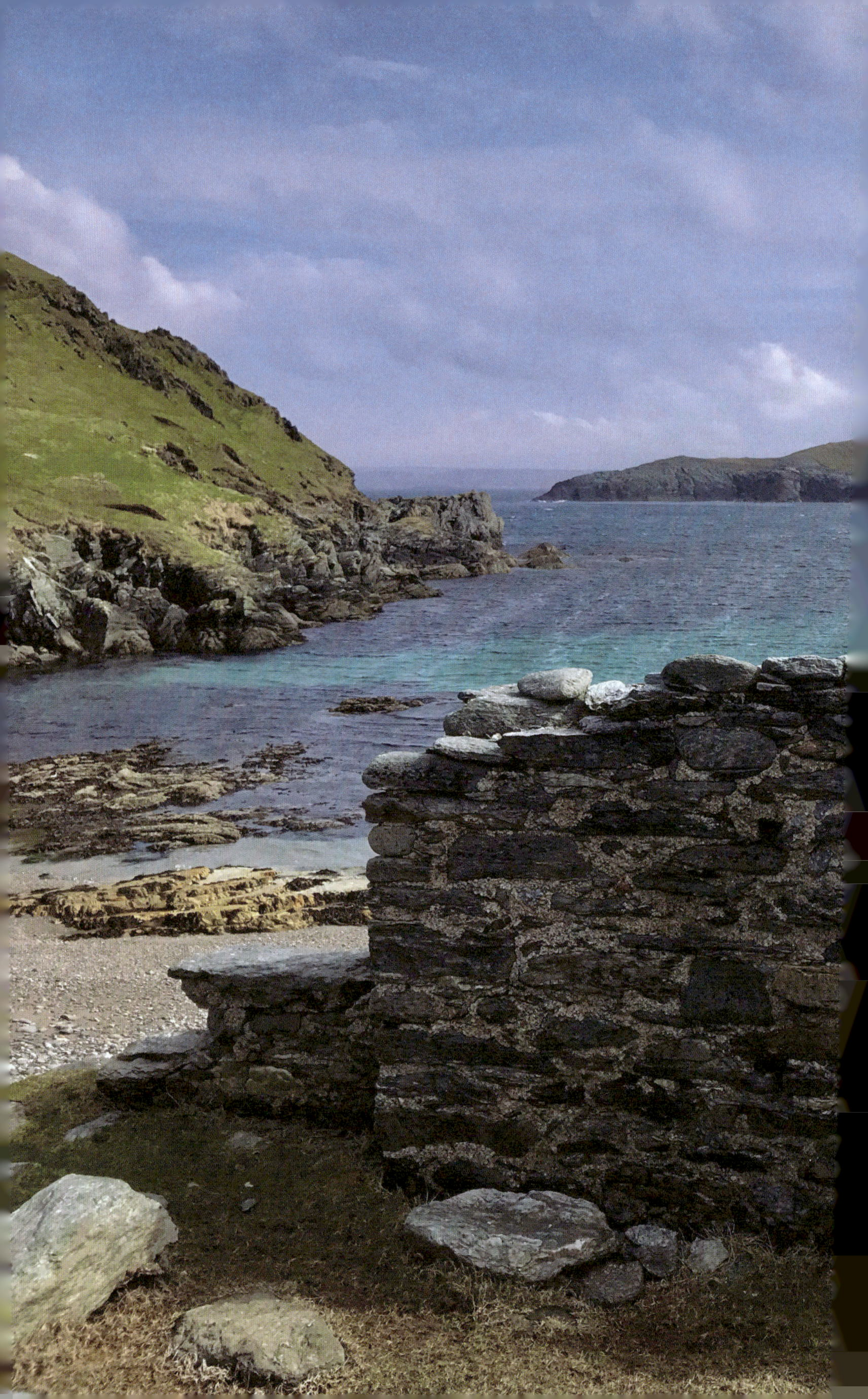

Worked

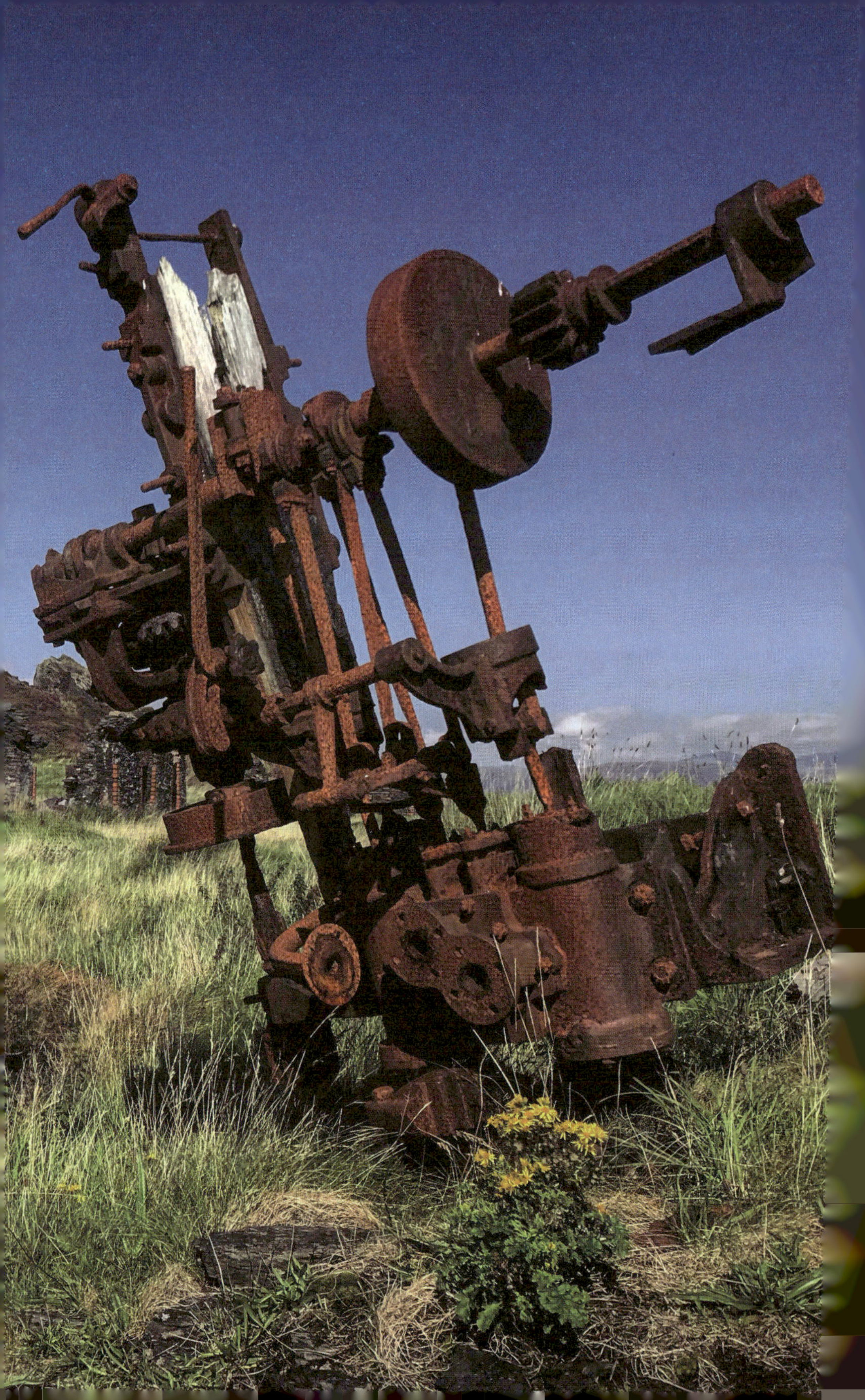

Belnahua, Firth of Lorn

NM 7130 1270

On the island of Belnahua, emptiness takes on an obvious, physical character. It is a hollow place. Even more specifically, a hollowed-out place. Absence defines it now. The people are missing, the cottages that they lived in stand in neat, ruined, roofless rows. But far more than that, large chunks of the island are missing too. For centuries, the fabric of this landscape was hewn away – chipped and cracked, battered down and blown up, to be taken elsewhere. Until, that is, there was no more left to take, and no one left to take it.

I had approached from the north-east, sailing away from the small jetty at Cuan to round the tip of the island of Luing. The sky was an unbroken blue, the water below it a rich navy, streaked white with flickering sunlight. Although there was almost no swell, a strong breeze was blowing in from the west, brushing the whole surface of the sea into tiny, persistent, fast-moving ripples.

Belnahua itself is little more than a ripple. It is only around 300 metres long and 200 metres wide, and its highest point, a solitary rock crag, reaches up just seventy feet. The rest of the island is a perfectly flat slab: a tiny, grass-topped pebble dropped right into a fast-flowing confluence of seas and oceans. The waters of the Sound of Luing, the Firth of Lorn and the Atlantic course around it. Or, when storms hit, as they often do on this part of the west coast, break right over the top of it.

There is no jetty now, no place to safely moor a boat, so I had to land by rib, jumping onto a ridge of black rock jutting out from the southern shore. The instant that you set foot on the island you are confronted by the reason for both its one-time occupation and its destruction. Slate. Fragments of it are everywhere, cracking and skittering underfoot. The beaches that surround the island are formed entirely of slate, and huge piles of it have accumulated in endless, precarious heaps above the shoreline.

The slate that makes up Belnahua – along with the series of other islands running in a seam down this stretch of the Argyll coast – began to be formed some 400 million years ago. Colossal geological shifts folded, compressed and heated layers of mud that had once lain on the bed of a shallow prehistoric sea. The result was the creation of a rich blue-black slate, everywhere flecked with little gleaming stars of iron pyrite, or fool's gold. Just like the seas that surround it, Belnahua slate has a distinctive rippled surface. As if even the rock here is windblown.

In effect, Belnahua became one giant island quarry. Slate was worked here from at least as early as the seventeenth century, but the real acceleration in the extraction process began at the end of the eighteenth century. At peak, over 200 people lived here – quarrymen and their families. There were workers' cottages and a schoolhouse, but all supplies, even drinking water, had to be brought from the neighbouring island of Luing.

Over the course of a hundred years, Belnahua's rock was worked down to the bone. It did not take long to find the main source of this slate. Walking just a few metres up from the beach, I came to a cliff edge. Below me was an expanse of turquoise water, so large that it took up maybe a third of the area of the island. This was no inland lake – or, at least, no natural one. The centre of Belnahua had once been a quarry, its slate rock scooped out, down to a depth of some sixty feet below sea level. Workers were constantly pumping water out of this great gouge of a hole. And then, when they left, there was nothing to stop the sea breaking in, or the rain filling it up. The result is a kind of doughnut island, surrounded by sea, but also with the sea at its centre.

Slate from Belnahua travelled the world. Roof tiles fashioned from its rock went as far afield as Nova Scotia. For a time, it was a place of incessant noise and movement – and dust. Great clouds of slate dust birled up from the quarry floor, coating the land and whipping out across the sea on the breeze. It so thickened the air that the women had to travel a mile south to Lunga to wash and dry their clothes and bed linen. The traffic of boats was constant, bringing people and food, unloading equipment and loading up quarried slate.

Belnahua, Firth of Lorn

Everywhere I walked on the island I found the traces of industry and activity. Along with the discarded slabs (slate quarrying was notoriously inefficient – for every usable piece that was produced, nine imperfect ones had to be thrown away) there was a mass of old machinery. Winding engines, the intricate cogs and pistons of steam-driven derrick cranes, boilers, the wheels and tracks of quarry carts. All had turned a russet orange with rust. Dandelions and pink thistles grew among them. The constant wind made the island's overgrown wild grass bend and sway around me in running waves.

No one has lived on Belnahua for over a century. The industry collapsed around the time of the First World War, and most of the workers were called up to fight. The quarries flooded beyond the point of ever being usable again. Yet, all the same, I felt a sense here of an abandonment that was at once total and strangely recent. Everything had been left behind exactly as it was. Handles ready to be cranked, cogs poised in the act of turning, piles of slate waiting to be lifted and loaded. It was as if the people had just walked out of their front doors one day and boarded a boat to the mainland, fully intending to return. Except no one ever did.

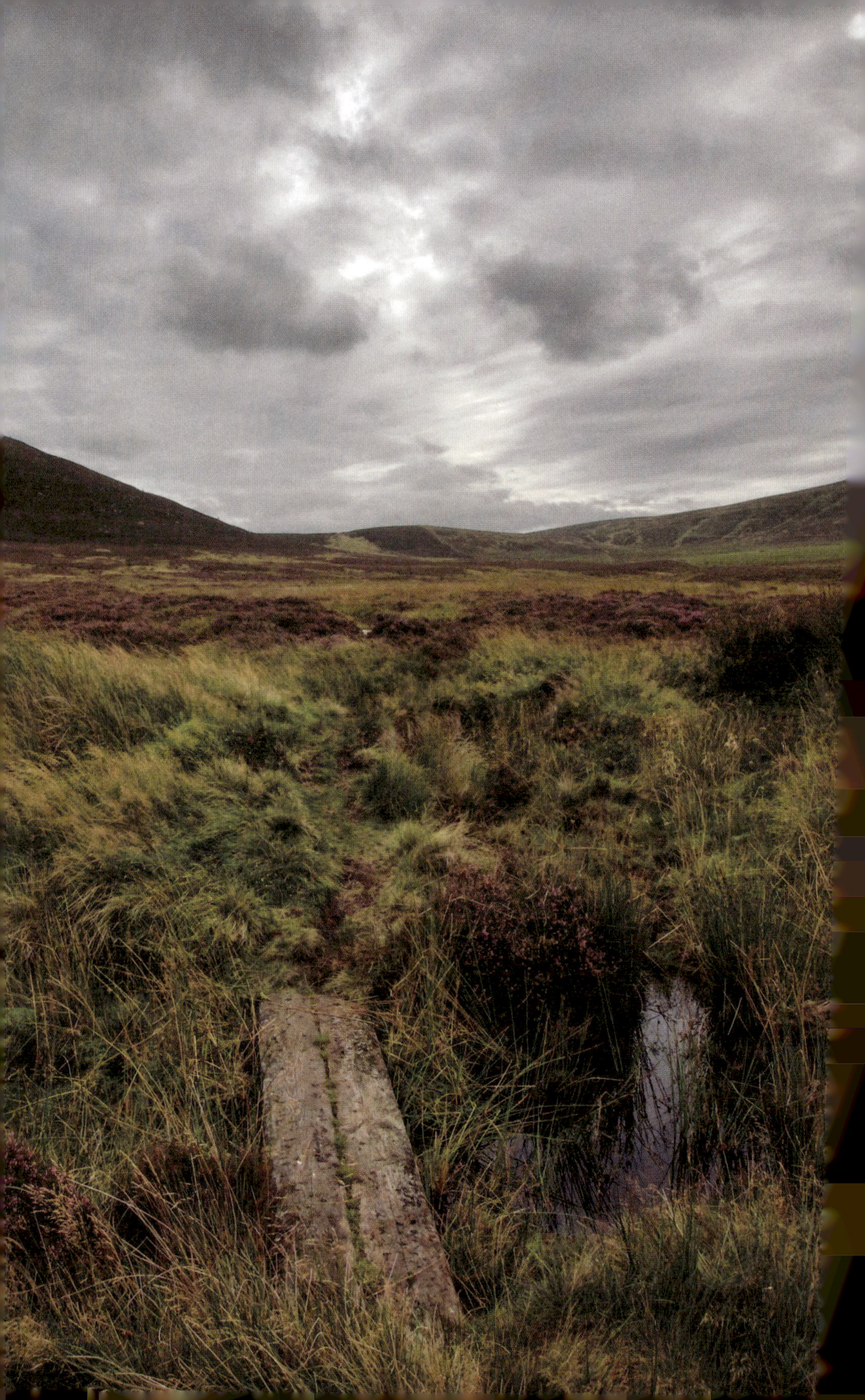

Cauldstane Slap, West Lothian

NT 1166 5877

The way ahead was faint, overgrown, sometimes hard to discern – but there was always just enough of it visible to lead me onwards. A hint in the bog and the mud. An impression that unrolled into the distance, punctuated by wooden planks which had been set in place to cross a series of tiny streams and burns. And while these traces of a path curved and oscillated, the general direction was still clear – heading just a fraction off due-south, towards a pass running between the twin hills of East and West Cairn.

People do still walk this route today, although not in great numbers. Its starting point is a tiny car park, hidden in trees opposite a disused quarry a few miles west of Edinburgh along the A70. The modern road here skirts the lower slopes of the Pentland Hills, avoiding their heights to run on into South Lanarkshire. The old path I was following, however, takes the opposite approach. Known as the Cauldstane Slap – 'slap' is the Scots word for 'pass', 'cauldstane' is simply 'cold stone' – it makes no detour, just cuts straight across the Pentland ridgeline, plotting a course through the middle. Go back just a few centuries and this boggy slope was, in effect, one of Scotland's main roads.

Most particularly, it saw the passage of cattle. Tens of thousands of them every single year. Many were on their way south, first to West Linton and Peebles, then all the way across the Borders to England. Some would have travelled hundreds of miles, leaving the Highlands to be sold and bought at the cattle markets of Crieff and Falkirk before continuing their journey. Others would be travelling back north, purchased in Linton and then driven for weeks or even months up to the glens. This movement back and forth would have been constant for hundreds of years – perhaps from as early as the fifteenth century, but certainly heavy and sustained in the eighteenth and nineteenth centuries.

In his landmark work *The Drove Roads of Scotland*, first published in 1951, A.R.B. Haldane described this route. 'To this day,' he wrote, 'the marks of animal traffic through the Cauldstane Slap can be seen in the soft broken ground to the east of the small burn which feeds Harper Rigg Reservoir.' The tenant of the local farm – whose family had worked this land for generations – told of seeing drovers using the Cauldstane Slap as late as the end of the nineteenth century, and that he had often heard his father and grandfather speak of how busy the route had been. The cattle, he said, passed just beside his farmhouse, so they would always try to make sure that their 'meadow hay' had been cut before the droves came – 'for the beasts went pretty much as they chose, and the drovers were none too careful in herding them'.

Often the herds would rest up for the night on the north side of the pass, waiting till dawn to set off on the high crossing between the two hills. The thousands of cattle would be 'stanced' in an irregular line leading for miles upslope, with the drovers sleeping beside them – while the owners (or 'topsmen') would be given beds in the farmhouse. The tenant told Haldane of how his father had once seen the cattle make their way here through an early autumn snow, with the white slopes 'reddened from the feet of the beasts, presumably worn by the hard roads which they must have used for part of their journey from Falkirk'. It is a potent, visceral image – the drove road drawn out across the landscape in a long line of blood.

The 'marks of animal traffic' that Haldane reported are long gone now. There was no pattern I could see in the grass and heather, no real trace of the centuries-long tread of hooves on the vegetation – or, at least, nothing beyond a general sense of a 'flattening' of the land, which could easily have been my imagination.

As I approached the pass a more solid path emerged, rocky underfoot, but still wet in places, often carrying sections of a stream downslope. It began to rise steeply to meet the saddle between the two hills, topping out at some 440 metres. Cloud had obscured the warm September sun with a mass of grey, and the wind had come on strong: as if it, too, was drawn to follow this route through the hills. From the head of the pass, I could look south over a wide expanse of high moorland, carpeted almost entirely in blackening heather. In the distance were the hills of the Tweed Valley. This place felt open, exposed, and yet, at the same time, hidden and isolated. I could see for miles. But in those miles, there was no sign of roads or buildings or towns or villages. There was just the line of the path, the way onwards, the way behind me – and nothing else.

Cauldstane Slap had the nickname – admittedly shared by many drover routes – Thieves Road. Robbers were reputed to have hidden in the dense heather here: 'cattle reivers' looking for opportunities to break animals off from the herd and escape with them into the hills. In his history of *The Water of Leith* from 1896, John Geddie quotes from a sixteenth-century source that 'the Slap' was used by the 'broken men' of the Borders, who had 'schakin all fear of God, reverence of the law, and regaird of honestie', to make raids from Eskdale and Liddesdale into the lands of the Lothians. Others came here to meet in secret. In 1684 a Covenanter preacher supposedly spoke to an assembled crowd – of perhaps as many as 200 men and women – from the natural pulpit of a rocky outcrop known as Wolf's Craig.

Drovers, topsmen, cattle, reivers, preachers, Covenanters and 'broken men'. Much has passed within, and passed through, Cauldstane Slap. Yet little has clung on. The mass movement of livestock was once one of the defining features of life in Scotland. As Haldane put it, 'There are few glens in the Highlands, even few easy routes leading to the South over moor and upland country, which have not known the tread of driven cattle.' To even attempt to map these tracks was, he said, a futile exercise because, 'through the very multiplicity of routes', you would soon arrive at a meaningless knot. All the same, on the ground itself, the years 'increasingly dim and obscure the mark and memory of the men and beasts that once travelled the drove roads'. Paths, when no longer walked, grow out. The physical remains of the lines dwindle and fade. The flattened earth rebounds. Eventually, even the landscape forgets.

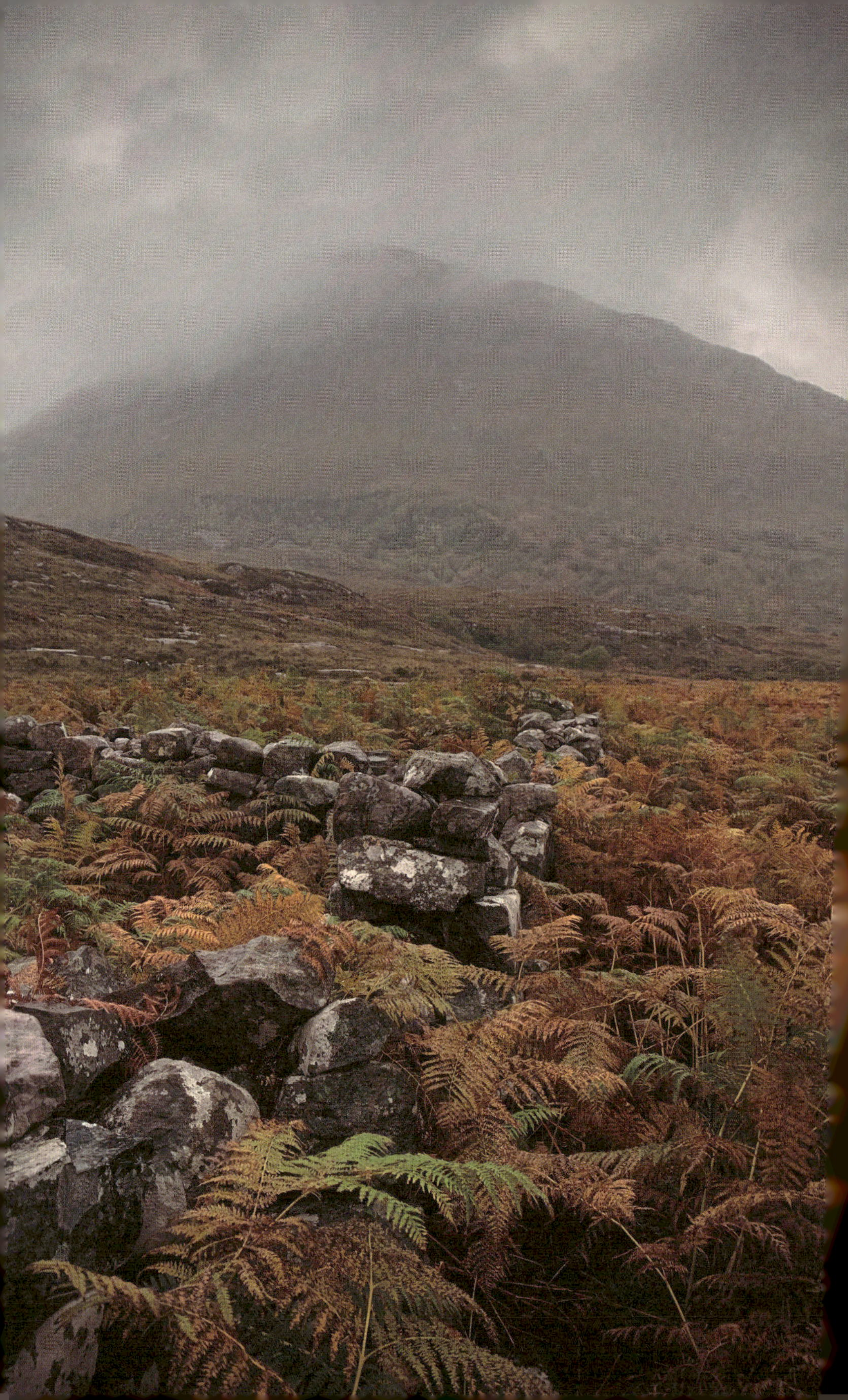

Fasagh Ironworks, Loch Maree

NH 0115 6542

The Fasagh river dropped down from Loch Fada, brimming over the lip of the steep-sided, natural reservoir formed between the towering peaks of Slioch and Beinn Tarsuinn. A small dam and sluice gate had been erected to control the waters, allowing them to well up and then be released when needed. The descent was steep and rapid, falling from Loch Fada's height of 300 metres down to sea level in less than three miles. The river fed into the great stretch of Loch Maree at its eastern end, slicing right through the middle of a flat fan of land. It was here, on its southern bank, that the channels were cut into the earth to divert its course to surround a small cluster of buildings.

Those buildings were fixated on extreme heat. Trees from the abundant forests on the slopes of Loch Maree were chopped down and their wood burnt to make charcoal. This charcoal was then heaped alongside quantities of iron ore in pear-shaped structures of stone and clay and kindled – using bellows often fabricated from sheep or goatskin – to temperatures of over 1,000°C. The river water was used as an essential coolant or lubricant. Then, as the ferocious fires intensified, the iron ore would turn molten, and suddenly *bloom* into life.

This is a process that had been known about for thousands of years – ironworking using 'bloomeries': small hearths that produce a spongy slag that can be beaten into shapes. At Fasagh, however, there were signs of a change. Not in the technology, but in the scale. Around the beginning of the seventeenth century, iron was being fashioned here continually and in great quantities. When the chemist and antiquarian William Macadam explored the site in the 1880s – at least 200 years after it had been abandoned – he wrote of how the whole place was 'surrounded by immense heaps of iron slag of the oldest black type'. He uncovered traces of buildings, the stone walls that contained the rediverted river, large tree stumps covered in 'molten matter, which has cracked the wood and flowed into the cavities, filling them up', along with large solid slabs of cast iron that had once been used as anvils.

I could find very little of this when I came to Fasagh. I had walked the two and a half miles from Kinlochewe to the north-eastern bank of Loch Maree on a day of incessant rain. There was no wind, and so the drops just fell straight down, in near silence. The landscape was saturated, swollen with moisture. A huge waterfall was cascading down the sheer grey cliffs forming the flank of Meallan Ghobhar and, at the point where the Kinlochewe River entered the loch, it had risen above its banks and flooded a swathe of the surrounding trees. The site of the old ironworks was covered almost entirely in tall, orange bracken. I walked around and across it, soaking myself in the process, looking for Macadam's walls and black slag, for any sign of the old water channels, or those tree stumps in their molten casings. But there was nothing – some barely discernable humps and bumps in the level of the land, mostly concealed beneath the undergrowth (or, perhaps more accurately, *overgrowth*). Time and nature had steadily erased this once bustling industrial landscape.

I crossed the Fasagh river by footbridge – it surged beneath me in a hissing torrent – and continued along the bank of the loch. On the northern half of the fan of land, I passed the large, rectangular walls of a sheep fold, their stones just visible above a sea of orange. Beyond that, the lochside became a wall of steepening cliffs, apart from one last flat shelf with a depression at its centre, containing a tiny lochan. Here and there among the grass and bracken were little clusters of boulders: the last traces of some twenty-three graves. In Gaelic, this place is known as Cladh nan Sussanach – 'the burial ground of the Englishmen'. Local tradition has it that outsiders – *sussanach*, English-speakers, either from south of the border, or perhaps simply Lowland Scots – came here to work the iron, and those that died were buried on this shore. The story also goes that the little lochan, now known as Lochan Cladh nan Sussanach, was where they threw their tools when the furnaces at Fasagh were finally abandoned.

Fasagh was not the only site of ironworking on the banks of Loch Maree.

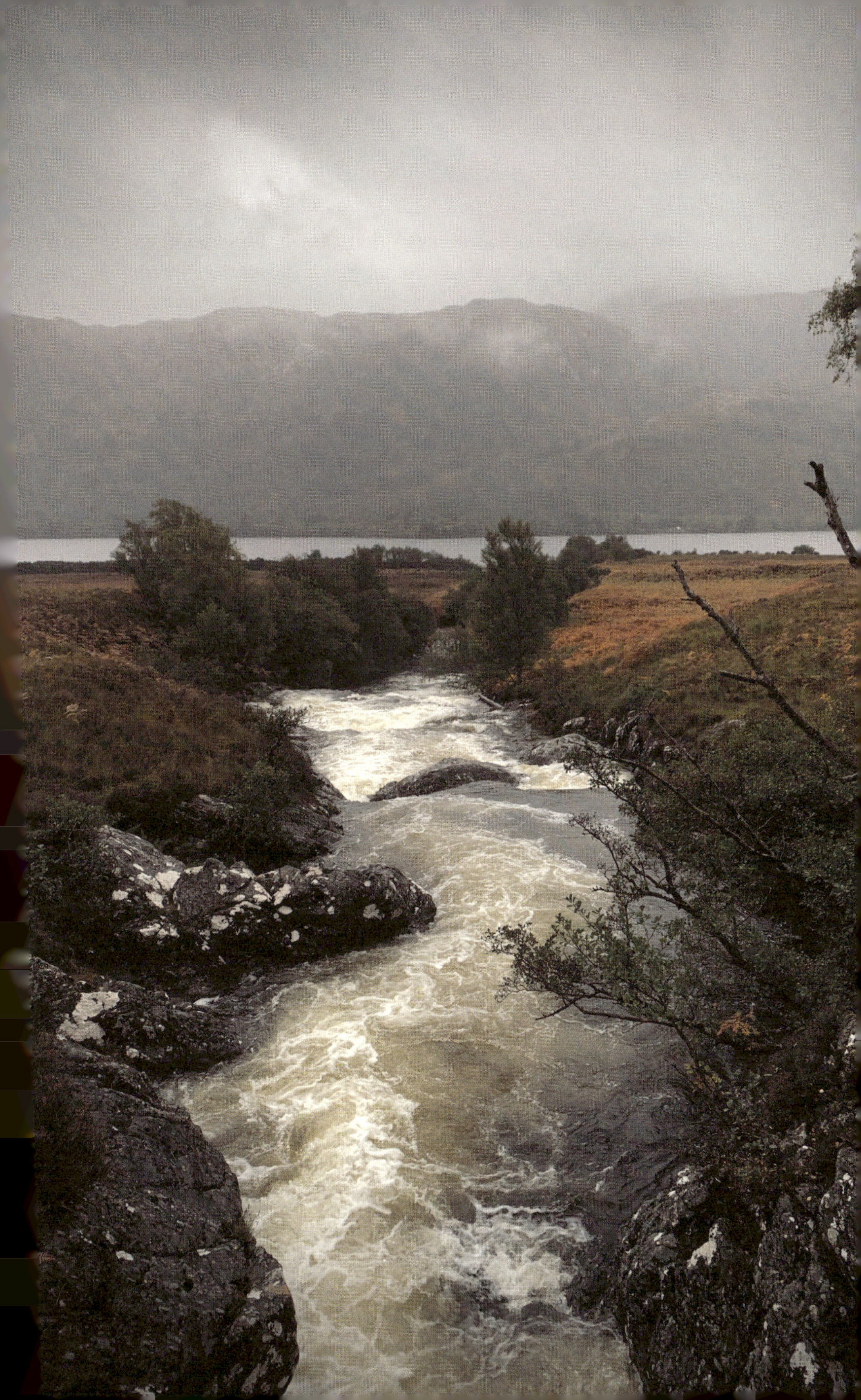

In fact, although extensive, it was also the most primitive. Just five miles to the north-west, surrounded by the forest of Letterewe, was the site of Scotland's first-ever blast furnace. Right alongside the fast-flowing Abhainn na Furneis – 'the burn of the furnace' – was a new innovation in the process of ironworking. The fires in bloomeries could not reach the melting temperature of iron, and so produced molten slag from which wrought iron could be extracted only by continuous reheating and reworking. Blast furnaces, however, could reach the required melting point for creating liquid iron, and could run constantly, so long as they were kept topped up with fuel. In 1610 a proto-industrialist, Sir George Hay of Nether Liff, was granted an exclusive commission by King James VI 'to make iron and glass within the said kingdom of Scotland' for a period of thirty-one years. Another blast furnace was built at the far north-western end of Loch Maree, at a place that became known as Red Smiddy.

For a time, iron production was relentless. Ores were brought by sea from Fife to the loch head at Poolewe, then transported on to the furnaces. The fires were stoked by charcoal created by felling and burning huge tracts of the trees that covered the entire northern shore of Loch Maree. The devastating impact of ironworking on the environment had already long been recognised – royal prohibitions in both Scotland and England, going back to Elizabeth I, had been issued to prevent, as one Scottish edict put it 'the utter want and consuming of the said woods'. But with the ban lifted on Loch Maree – and Loch Maree alone – the pace of cutting and burning was astonishing. At peak, Hay's ironmaking venture, and the furnaces of Letterewe and Red Smiddy, were consuming upwards of 300 acres of forest a year. Forges fashioned the liquid metal on site, in particular casting cannons, which were being traded both within Scotland and abroad.

The work continued at pace for over a decade and then, all of a sudden, seemed to be snuffed out. Reports suggest that by 1624, the furnaces had gone cold. Hay had transitioned from industry to politics – becoming Scotland's Lord High Chancellor – and had seemingly lost interest in his venture on Loch Maree. Some accounts suggest that production continued, much scaled back, up until the 1660s; but either way, the industry had moved on. Ironworking would return in the eighteenth century, in the colossal foundries and furnaces of the Central Belt, but its origins in the far north-west High-

Fasagh Ironworks, Loch Maree

lands would largely fade from memory. Just some obscure names on the map – the furnace burn, the sassenach graveyard, the rock of the iron and the hill of the mine – and clusters of, mostly overgrown, rivers of slag.

    I watched the ceaseless rain patter in a static buzz on the surface of the lochan behind the burial ground. And I wondered if those tools from Fasagh – a heap of 400-year-old hammers, tongs, billows and anvils – still lay somewhere beneath its waters.

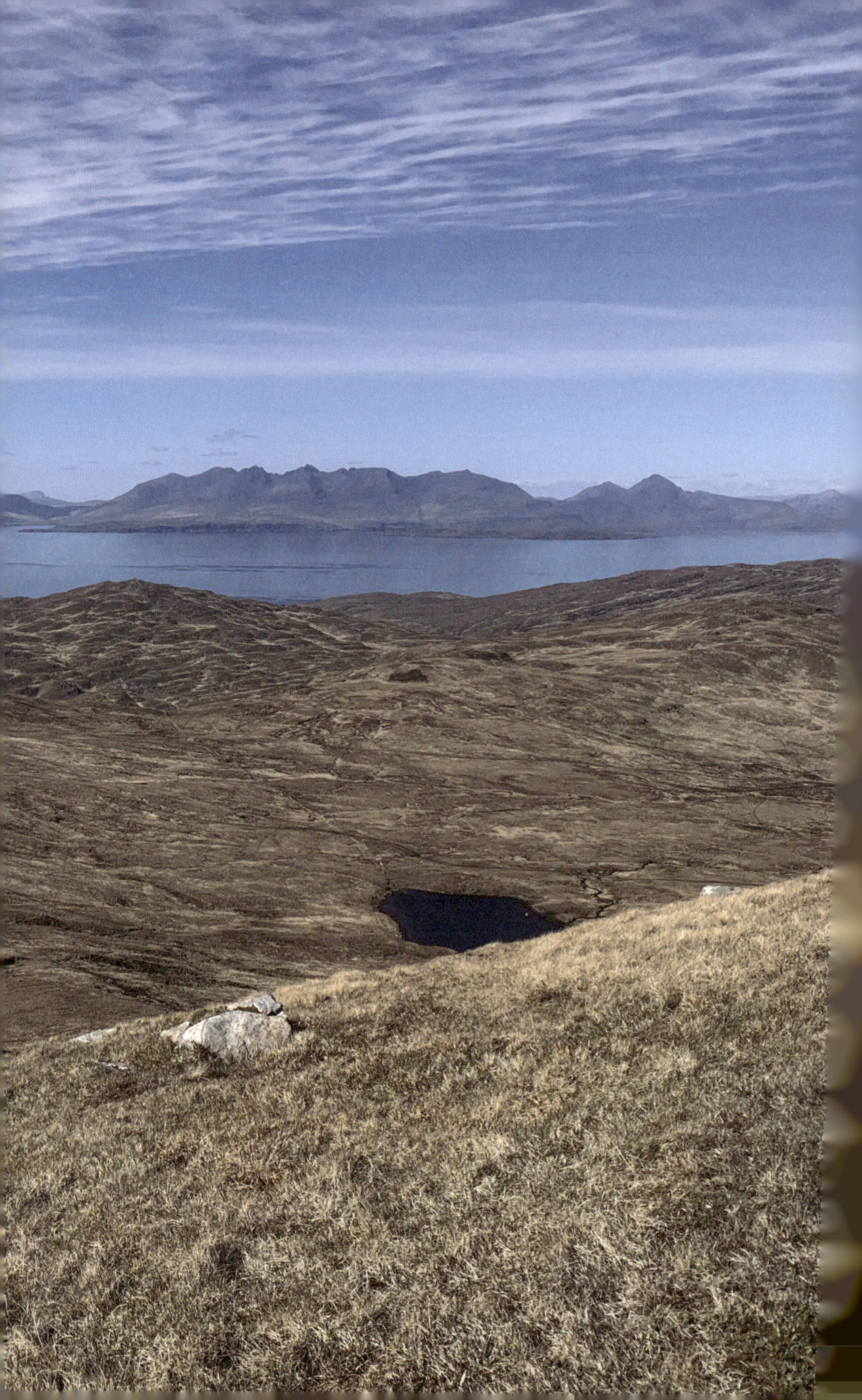

Ard Nev Deer Trap, Isle of Rum

NM 3418 9928

The first sign of the trap was a line of stones, curving up the hillside. I could see it coming into view long before I reached it, appearing in the distance as I crossed the small plateau of ground linking the lower slopes of Ard Nev to the tight valley of Glen Duian. On the ground, it began as a smattering of small boulders, giving out to fields of scree – hard to define as anything, really. But after another half-kilometre, the rocks cohered: a solid wall emerged from the heather, in places so substantial as to rise above my head. Clearly man-made, it could, perhaps, be mistaken for a boundary marker, or the remnants of some old drystone dyke. Except that on one side it was pressed right up against the almost-sheer slope of the mountain. This wall wasn't built to *divide*, but to *enclose*.

There is a second wall too, following the contours across the glen, just beneath the summit of another mountain, Orval. These two walls both start far apart down in the valley, but as they approach the high saddle of land between Ard Nev and Orval, at around 1,500 feet up, they come closer and closer together, until there is just a few metres between them. At this point it is clear that you are arriving at a bottleneck – nearing the business end of a giant, landscape-sized funnel.

It had taken another half hour of walking to reach the saddle. It rolled upwards and then began to drop down sharply, like a cresting wave. Suddenly, unfurling ahead of me was a remarkable view. First was the jagged black line of the Skye Cuillins. This was followed by a sea of polished blue, flat and pristine. And then, finally, came the land directly below me, the empty stretch of rocky moor that makes up the north-eastern corner of Rum. I moved to rest on a slab of stone breaking through the grass on the precipice of the saddle, just where the ground began to dip down at an increasingly sharp angle. And that was when I saw it right in front of me – a creamy-white deer antler, five points branching out from an elegant curve of bone.

The timing and the location of this find was almost laughably appropriate. The walls I had been following up to this spot had once been used to corral the island's wild deer in their hundreds and thousands. The people of Rum had chased them up this glen. Unable to escape over the walls, the deer would have reached the saddle. And then, in a frenzy of fear and panic, with the ramparts pressing in around them, they ran on – perhaps falling and tumbling at this point – down the other side, where the rocky funnel finally met in the endpoint of a circular enclosure. There, one by one, they were slaughtered.

No one knows quite when this deer trap was first built. Perhaps it was medieval, perhaps far older than that. When an English clergyman, Edward Clarke, came to Rum in 1797, he was shown a 'rampart of stones erected along the side of the mountain' that led to a 'pit' surrounded by more stones. And in this pit, he was told, 'the hunter stationed himself with his gun', to await the arrival of the frantic animals. The trap had seemingly remained in use until, just ten years before Clarke's visit, deer 'became perfectly extinct on Rum'.

As I sat high up on the saddle, I turned the antler over and over in my hands. It was no relic, but must have been shed just days earlier, by the island's current population of deer. The animals have returned to Rum. And in far greater numbers than the people.

'How strange a cycle!' wrote the ethnographer and geologist Hugh Miller, when he came here in the later nineteenth century, to find a place largely devoid of both deer *and* humans. At that exact time, the whole island was being offered for sale 'and it was on the eve of being purchased by some wealthy Englishman, who proposed converting it into a deer-forest'. Miller could only shake his head at the irony.

'Uninhabited originally save by wild animals,' he wrote, Rum 'became at an early period a home of men, who, as the grey wall on the hillside testified, derived, in part at least, their sustenance from the chase . . . they reared herds of cattle and flocks of sheep, – their number increased to nearly five hundred souls, – they enjoyed the average happiness of human creatures in the present imperfect state of being.'

Ard Nev Deer Trap, Rum

Then they, too, were removed from their home by a landowner. 'Cleared off to the backwoods of America,' as Miller put it, 'the descendants of men who had chased deer' on Rum's hills, and who 'regarded this place indisputably as their own'. And so the emptied island was to 'return to its original state as a home of wild animals where a few hunters from the mainland might enjoy the chase for a month or two every twelvemonth, but which could form no permanent place of human abode. Once more a strange and surely most melancholy cycle!'

A shepherd who witnessed the moment that the people of Rum were 'carried off in one mass' described how 'the wild outcries of the men and the heart-breaking wails of the women and their children filled the air between the mountainous shores of the bay . . . They went wailing away across the stormy sea: and the wild hills of their native isle will see them no more for ever.'

The last people were removed in 1828, and Miller had come to Rum four decades later, to find an island that mixed a harsh beauty with an unmistakable air of desolation. He described a moment as evening fell, with a light that 'was clear, calm, golden-tinted' so that 'even wild heaths and rude rocks had assumed a flush of transient beauty and the emerald green patches of the hillsides, barred by the plough lengthwise, diagonally, and transverse, had borrowed an aspect of soft and velvety richness, from the mellowed light and broadening shadows'.

Everywhere the traces of people still remained – their houses, their townships, their farms and their ploughlands. The long, snaking walls of their deer traps. To Miller, the shock of absence was palpable. 'All was solitary,' he wrote. And the island was a ghost: 'It seemed as if man had done with it forever.'

Not forever. The people are back, around two dozen of them fringing the shore of the main bay at Loch Scresort. The deer, maybe a thousand or more, run in herds through the emptied glens and the ruins of the communities who once lived there. 'How strange a cycle!'

The day was tipping into evening as I strapped the antler to my backpack and began walking again, the light that same clear gold that Miller had described. I followed the long line of deer trap back downhill, until the stones split and scattered and faded away to nothing.

The Fish Road, Loch Glascarnoch

NH 2964 7353

In the late eighteenth century, John Knox, a Scottish philanthropist and one-time London bookseller, embarked on an extensive tour of the Highlands and Islands. Knox was a committed 'improver'. He looked at northern Scotland and saw it 'lying almost in a state of nature: the riches of its shores, though more important to great national purposes than the mines of Mexico and Peru, were scarcely sought after'. Its people were 'frequently exposed to famine', had 'no means of employment' and, as a result, 'were rendered torpid by idleness'.

This was a place, he lamented, that had been ignored for too long by a modernising world. Just look at the roads alone. Even the most basic infrastructure was lacking, he said. Beyond Inverness, 'no roads have been formed; communications between the two seas are nearly cut off, intercourse and traffic between man and man, are rendered impracticable'. As a result, 'through a considerable part of the year the inhabitants of each respective glen or valley may be considered prisoners strongly guarded by impossible mountains on one side, by swamps and furious torrents on the other'.

Of course, Knox had a solution. Specialist engineers, at least 500 soldiers and 'an equal number of Highlanders' – working for 'seven or eight pence per day' – could plot new routes through the landscape. These professionally built roads would, Knox concluded, 'bring the inhabitants of the West, the North, and the Eastern shores nearer to each other', ensuring that 'new schemes of trade would be formed'.

Crucial to all of this was fish. The seas off the north-western Highlands – and the waters in and around Loch Broom, in particular – were thought to be abundant with massed shoals of herring. There was product to be caught, and profit to be made, in transferring it to the large towns and cities to the south and east. Except, as Knox experienced, and as a military report had put it a few decades earlier in 1755, the route which did exist between Loch Broom and Inverness was 'reckoned amongst the worst in the Highlands of Scotland, being mountainous, rocky and full of stones, and no bridges on the rivers, so that nothing but necessity makes strangers resort here and for the great part of the year it is almost inaccessible'.

Today, you can make this journey – of a little less than sixty miles – by following the A835. Beyond the Conon Bridge, at the point where the Conon River feeds out into the Cromarty Firth, the modern route sits almost exactly on top of the old road. Or, at least, one of the old roads. Knox's account, first published in 1786, was dedicated to the 'noblemen and gentlemen' of an organisation founded in the same year – the British Fisheries Society. Created for the purpose of 'Extending the Fisheries and Improving the Sea Coasts of the Kingdom', the society was soon funding major infrastructure projects across the country. By 1790, survey work was underway for a 'Fish Road' connecting Dingwall – and by extension Inverness – to the shores of Loch Broom. And on those shores was an entirely new settlement: the port of Ullapool.

The British Fisheries Society didn't just stop at building roads. They built whole villages and towns too: conceiving, designing and constructing them from scratch. For Ullapool they identified a square fan of flat, low-lying land near the mouth of Loch Broom which they believed offered the perfect base for a deep-sea Atlantic fishing station. The town was already completed in 1790, a tiny stamp of urban geometry amid the unruly Coigach landscape. The road that ran to it, however, would not be ready for another seven years. And a decade after that, it had fallen into disrepair.

By this time, the Chief Engineer for the British Fisheries Society was Thomas Telford. Commissioned by the government to work with the society to 'find the most commodious and productive stations for the Fishery of both Herrings and White Fish', he was, at the same time, tasked with surveying, and then constructing or improving, the entire transport network of the Highlands. This work would take decades – and, of course, included the not inconsiderable task of slicing the whole country in two to create the Caledonian Canal – and it wasn't until the 1830s that Telford was able to turn his attention to the crumbling Ullapool Fish Road. As the Loch Broom parish account put it in 1835, 'About 40 years ago a road was constructed at great expense from Dingwall to Ullapool . . . But the line chosen was so absurd and the execution so wretched that the road has been for many years back not only useless but dangerous to foot passengers and riders on horseback, and to wheel carriages almost impassable.' Telford's improved route was completed by 1840.

To drive it now is to experience very much the same landscape as two centuries earlier, when the original road was first built. You pass through the steep-sided forest valley of Strathgarve in the shadow of the great, humped ridge of Ben Wyvis. The road twists and turns to mirror the course of the Alltan Dubh – the Black Water – and climbs steadily higher and higher. Telford's road and the A835 remain as one, passing over Black Bridge and straightening out through a landscape of bog and scattered glacial erratics.

Wild History

Until, at the point marked by the whitewashed buildings of the Aultguish Inn, they split dramatically apart. The modern road curves away up onto the slopes of the valley side, while the old road suddenly reappears and runs on, dead straight, to hit the immovable concrete base of the Glascarnoch Dam.

Here is a nexus point, where two massive projects of landscape and social engineering meet. The British Fisheries Society's attempt to transform and improve the Highlands collides with the colossal hydroelectric power schemes of the mid twentieth century. Completed in 1957, Glascarnoch Dam turned this river valley into a huge loch, seven kilometres long and two kilometres wide, that flooded houses, farms – and a whole stretch of Telford's road.

I came in late summer, in the middle of a long and unusually dry spell of weather. From the relative heights of the modern road, the view down to Loch Glascarnoch offered a bizarre sight. The water level was incredibly low, exposing a grey, lunar landscape of bare rock and mud. Running right through it – for miles – was the drowned Fish Road. I parked at the western end of the loch, clambering down through a tiny copse of trees to the exposed loch bed. After a hundred yards or so of rock and bog and black, rubbery silt, I was able to put my feet on the Fish Road.

I started walking along it back eastwards, the road running arrow straight ahead of me. Soon the rock and the bog gave way, and the road was surrounded entirely by that glutinous black mud. The tarmac surface was in remarkably good condition, however – strong and solid and barely cracked at all. Ahead were two uprights either side of the road which resolved, as I came closer, into the walls of a bridge. Built of dressed stone, they appeared near-perfect. Unbroken, unmarked. Almost, it seemed, as good as new.

This bridge had once been accompanied by a milestone – although that could no longer be seen. From here, it was eighteen miles further to Ullapool, fourteen miles back to Garve. You can find the bridge marked on the old first-edition OS maps from the late nineteenth century – which show that it was built to cross a small tributary leading into the River Glascarnoch. With the water levels so low, that tributary was suddenly running again. Its waters cut down through the silt to meet the wall of the bridge on one side and passed beneath it, presumably through a still-buried arch that I could not see. On the road went, until it passed out of sight as it began to turn around

The Fish Road, Loch Glascarnoch

an outcrop of land in the distance. A single boulder, a little larger than fist-sized, sat on top of one of the walls, as if placed there by a passer-by.

The bridge was a secret revealed. Perhaps it would be here for just a few days or weeks. Soon the rains would come again, the water would rise, and its walls would disappear beneath the waves. Would it remain submerged for generations this time? How long, I wondered, before anyone else would walk across it again?

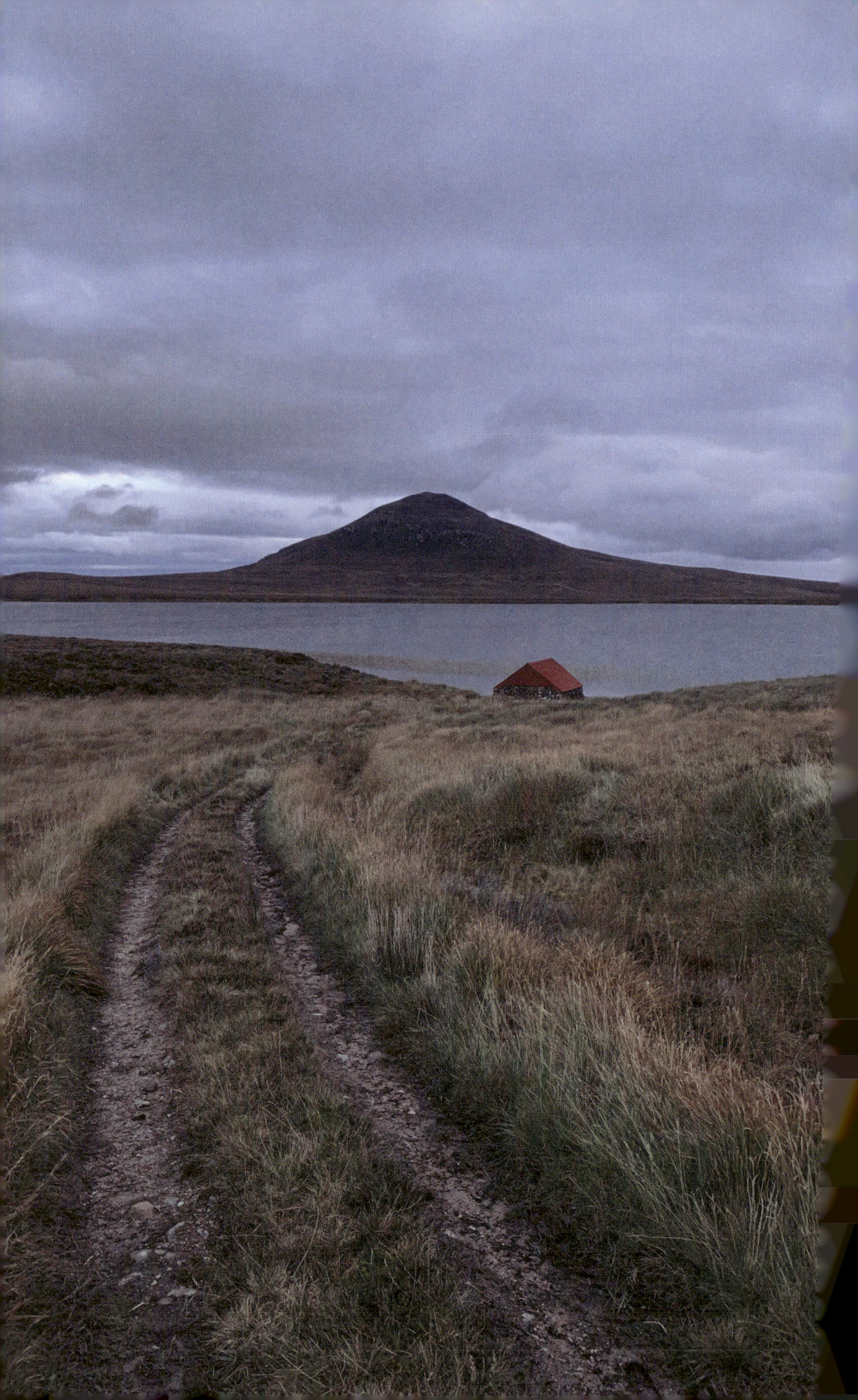

Ben Griam Beg, Sutherland

NC 8310 4110

It was early evening as I walked up the muddy track that skirts the lower slopes of Ben Griam Mor. The wind had dropped and there was a stillness to the land. A few miles behind me, off to the south-west, towards Loch nan Clar and the long hump of Ben Klibreck, rain was falling. It formed a solid, visible column, but it did not seem to move or shift in any direction, just held on to that one, same spot. Ahead of me, the sky was clearing, revealing patches of pale blue, fringed by sun-yellowed cloud. Silhouetted on the hillside, a watchful group of deer had gathered, moving to keep their distance as the path curved eastwards to take me towards them. Soon the second mountain appeared: a big black pyramid, rising above a wide red prairie of moss and deer grass. Ben Griam Beg – Ben Griam Mor's companion on this otherwise flat plain.

The shared name Griam may come from the Old Norse word *grima*, meaning 'masked' or 'hooded'. A guide to Sutherland placenames, produced by the Gaelic Society of Inverness in 1892, said of the pair that 'when a cloud wraps one in its passage, the other soon puts on its mourning robe, as if from sheer sympathy. They would, to the poetic imagination, appear like two mourners . . . the two mountains of gloom.'

The summits of Ben Griam Mor and Bern Griam Beg are only two miles apart, and their lower slopes run into each other, so that their bases touch. Alongside them are two small lochs – the circular pool of Loch Coire nam Mang, and the larger, kidney-shaped stretch of Loch Druim a' Chliabhain. The track came to an end on the banks of this first loch, passing alongside an old stone boathouse – which appeared to have been fitted with a new, pillar-box-red roof – to follow a narrow concrete pier that ran on for a few metres before slipping beneath the water. A little further out, a line of tall yellow reeds rose above the surface, framing the view out towards the shadowy face of Ben Griam Beg.

Even from this distance, I could see the walls. Above the steep black cliffs on the western face of the mountain, known as the Eagle's Crag, was a long thin line of grey. It continued around the southern flank, dropping a little in height, and then disappearing out of sight. Above it, more grey lines were scattered, all much shorter than the first, like scratches on slate. As I moved closer, picking my way around the spongy bank of the loch, some of them even resolved into circles: a series of enclosures, or pens. These were not shapes formed by fallen scree, but deliberate – and monumental – building works.

The longest of the lines runs for 500 metres, often over a metre wide, and two metres tall. Although now broken and tumbledown in places, much of it still remains intact, its large blocks of lichen-covered sandstone forming a wide perimeter surrounding dykes and enclosures, artificial terraces and another large wall, which encircles the craggy summit of the mountain. To this day, no one quite knows what went on here. Ben Griam Beg has the characteristics of a hillfort – which, with a summit of 580 metres and views that stretch as far as the Orkney Islands, makes it the highest in Scotland – but its ramparts seem fragmentary and incomplete. There are no clear signs of settlement, particularly on the enclosed area of the summit, but the traces of construction are everywhere. Some archaeologists suggest that it was a great pen for livestock, a prehistoric cattle ranch and summer pasture where the herds were brought each year. There is even some evidence of possible field systems – that people may once have farmed the slopes of the mountain.

According to this last theory, that could make the activity here very old indeed. Even attempting to cultivate this higher-altitude land would have likely required the warmer, drier conditions that prevailed in Scotland over 3,000 years ago, going back as far, perhaps, as the second millennium BC. The possibility exists that a community of herder-farmers once used Ben Griam Beg and were, in the end, forced to abandon it by climate change. Generation after generation may have built and maintained its walls and enclosures, then, over the course of centuries, watched the weather turn, slowly but surely; watched more and more storm clouds blowing in from the west; felt the air cool, and the frost and snow come earlier and stay longer each season; saw the soils grow damper and begin to slip down the slopes; found roots rotting and decaying in the wet ground; noticed the slow, inexorable spread of the peat, the dark pools forming all across the plain below, to suck at herders' feet and the hooves of their cattle.

It is apt that the only extensive survey of Ben Griam Beg, led thirty years ago by archaeologist Roger Mercer and a team from Edinburgh University, experienced what he described as 'adverse' weather conditions while working up on the mountainside. 'The weather deteriorated steadily through the day,' he wrote. 'The mountain was shrouded in cloud and mist which ultimately brought visibility down to about 20 metres and the wind rose to a velocity where it was difficult not to be pushed from one's feet . . . The mountain top is, indeed, today a terribly hostile environment.' Mercer, in the end, was sceptical of prehistoric farming on its slopes. 'The extreme remote and exposed situation,' he concluded 'probably indicates a temporary refuge of man and beast under threat of attack, rather than a permanent settlement.'

By the time I passed the second loch and began to climb towards the first long perimeter wall, the light had deteriorated sharply. The sun had not long set, but it was autumn and a cloud bank had gathered to the west, obscuring the already fading sky. There was no path, and the ground was threaded everywhere with boggy streams and burns – the Gaelic word for these tiny channels is *feith* – meaning 'vein' or 'sinew'. In the gloom, these watery veins were getting harder and harder to spot. I had no option but to turn back, just making it to the red-roofed boathouse and the far end of track before the darkness really set in.

As soon as I turned on my torch, the rest of the landscape disappeared – there was only the pool of light on the path in front of me, and the tiny, distant twinkle of the Garvault House hotel, where I had parked my car. After a while, I could hear movement in the blackness. A rustling in the heather not too far away. A muffled snorting became a sort of groaning roar. A stag was watching me from somewhere in the dark, following me across his territory. He kept pace with me all the way down the hill, until I crossed the final farm gate. I stopped there, shone my torch in a wide arc behind me. But by then he was nowhere to be seen.

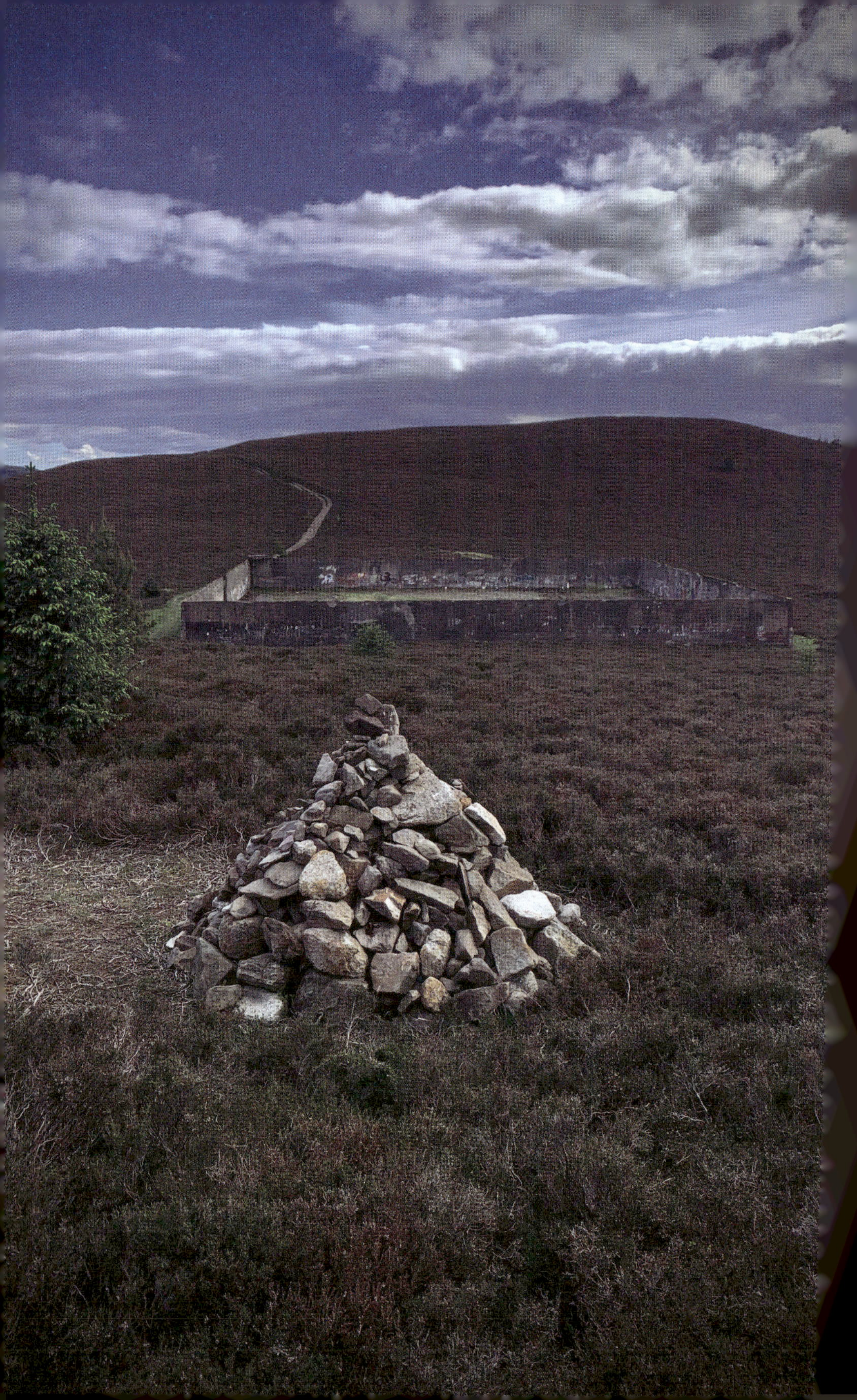

Kirnie Law, Innerleithen

NT 3484 3869

The four walls were each sixty metres long and four and a half metres high, forming a square that enclosed a huge, empty space on a flat saddle of land between the summits of two hills. The hilltops were part of a humped ridge-back, surrounded on three sides by tall plantations of Sitka spruce and swathed entirely in heather – the one exception being the bare ground inside the square of walls. It was evening, still early in the summer, but the heather was already shading from brown into a dusky purple.

    I had walked there from the west, just beyond the point where the valley of the Leithen Water feeds into the River Tweed, following a dusty track as it wound up through steep slopes of dense forest. It had been a still, hot, sunny day. Mountain bikers slogged past me heading upwards on the track, then, once they were high enough, disappeared into the trees. Every so often a shout, the rasp of wheels on rock, or a screech of brakes, echoed out through the corridors of spruce. This swathe of plantation on the very southern stretch of the Moorfoot Hills is called Caberston Forest – although bikers know it as 'the Golfie'. It's home now to a network of 'wild' or 'natural' bike trails (given names like Repeat Offender, Flat White and Waterworld) that are steep, rooty and unauthorised. The trails are cut, maintained – and abandoned – by the bikers themselves, threading narrow and illicit routes, some known only to a select few, through the trees.

    The main track only broke clear of the spruce canopy near the top of the ridgeline, almost 1,500 feet up. I had emerged out of the forest's dimness to see a bright, open sky, with one side of the walled square almost directly in front of me. It had a starkly monolithic quality: a great slab of grey concrete, massive yet inexplicable in its hilltop setting, rising above the sea of heather.

Wild History

The track continued straight on to its base, to the point where the west wall met the north wall. The surface of the concrete was cracked and flaking, and daubed here and there with graffiti, but it remained resolutely solid. I walked its perimeter, round to the eastern side now. It was there, exactly halfway along, that I found the only breach in the whole structure of the square – a yawning gap, fringed by spines of rusted rebar, where one entire three-metre-wide section had been demolished.

This gap now formed a kind of entrance portal, or gateway, that added to the strange, sculptural quality of the site. Walking through it was not unlike walking into the hushed space of a temple, the acoustics like an echo chamber, the sound of my footsteps bouncing around from wall to wall and back again. The reality, however, is that the deliberate creation of this hole in the eastern side – made by using explosives – marked the end of this structure's purpose. When originally built, just over a century ago, it had been fabricated as a sealed container. The base of the square was a massive sixty-metre-square slab of concrete, nine inches thick and containing a latticed mesh of steel reinforcements. The outer walls varied in thickness from eight inches at their tops, to twenty-one inches at their bottoms, and they were 'tied' into the base with more steel, to create a cantilevering effect. This was to ensure that they could cope with the strains of the specific load that they had to bear: no less than three and a half million gallons of water.

The real significance of this square was to create an artificial tank – a reservoir – for Scotland's first-ever pumped-storage hydroelectric scheme. Work had begun in 1919 and was completed by 1922. To get all the materials to the hilltop site, the long line of a funicular railway was built to run up the steep southern slope of Kirnie Law from the village of Walkerburn, 1,000 feet below on the banks of the Tweed. Some 400 tons of cement, 100 tons of steel reinforcement and 3,000 tons of aggregate were hauled upwards. At the same time, a twelve-inch steel water pipe was laid out in a trench dug into the ground leading south from the reservoir to a square concrete 'surge tower' just below the summit of Kirnie Law. From there it changed into a nine-inch pipe that ran in a direct straight line, down the steepest part of the hill, to two textile mills in Walkerburn, owned by the firm of Henry Ballantyne and Sons.

First built in the mid nineteenth century, the mills had operated on natural waterpower from the Walker Burn and the Tweed. This new scheme was devised to both improve efficiency and increase the power available. The old mill's breast wheels produced some 110 horsepower, but the owners wanted to increase to a capacity of 450 horsepower. During the day, high pressure water would rush down the pipeline from the reservoir (which took over 132 hours to fill from empty) to a Pelton turbine with its own generator, which would convert the flow into electricity. Then every night, when the mills closed and fell silent, the process would be reversed, and the surplus energy was routed through low-pressure turbines to pump the water all the way back up again.

This process continued for over twenty-five years, the pipes managing the flow up and down in an endless closed circuit, the water levels inside the concrete square rising and falling like the tide – sinking low by the onset of evening, brimming again come the morning. It was only in the late 1940s, when the mills were connected to the National Grid, that it fell out of use. The sudden abundance of 'mains' electricity saw the pumped-storage system, and its elevated, millions-of-gallons reservoir, abandoned. The final step was to blow a single hole in its side to ensure that it could never fill up again; or burst its seams to flood the village and the valley below.

What remains now is a curious monument to the speed of technological change – from cutting-edge system to obsolescence in just a few decades (with the irony that its renewable energy properties fit very well with the demands of our twenty-first-century world).

I climbed up a stony path through the thick heather to the top of Kirnie Law. The sun broke through the drifting clouds and hit the square below me. Its walls cast hard black shadows, with that one angular break for the missing section, the ad-hoc doorway. From above, in the heavy contrasts offered by the low light, it looked once again like a kind of modernist temple. There are rumours that people have sometimes come up here in large numbers, brought speakers and sound systems, filled the square with music and dancing. Not so different, perhaps, to the sites of rituals and celebrations that once crowned hilltops millennia earlier, in the Bronze and Iron Ages. As if that act of enclosing a space, for whatever purpose, has always offered an irresistible draw. See a wall in an open landscape, and you can't help but wonder what it is for, and what is waiting on the other side.

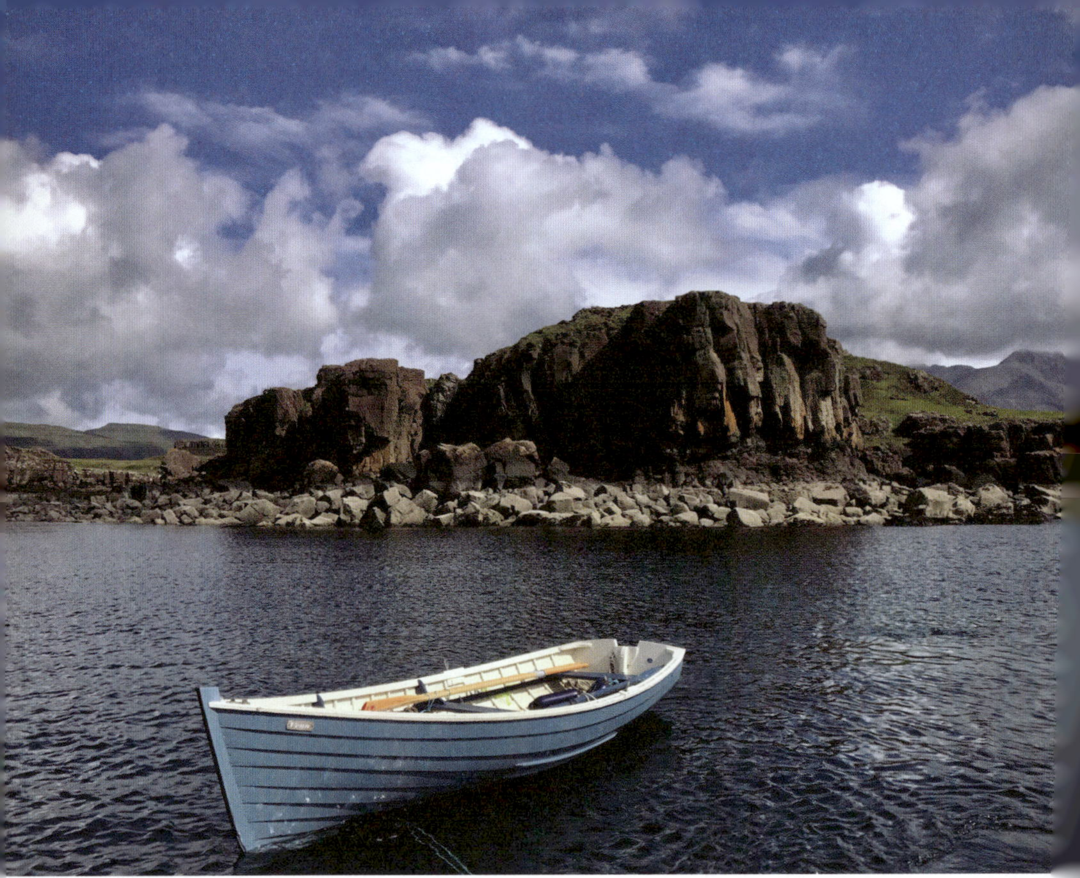

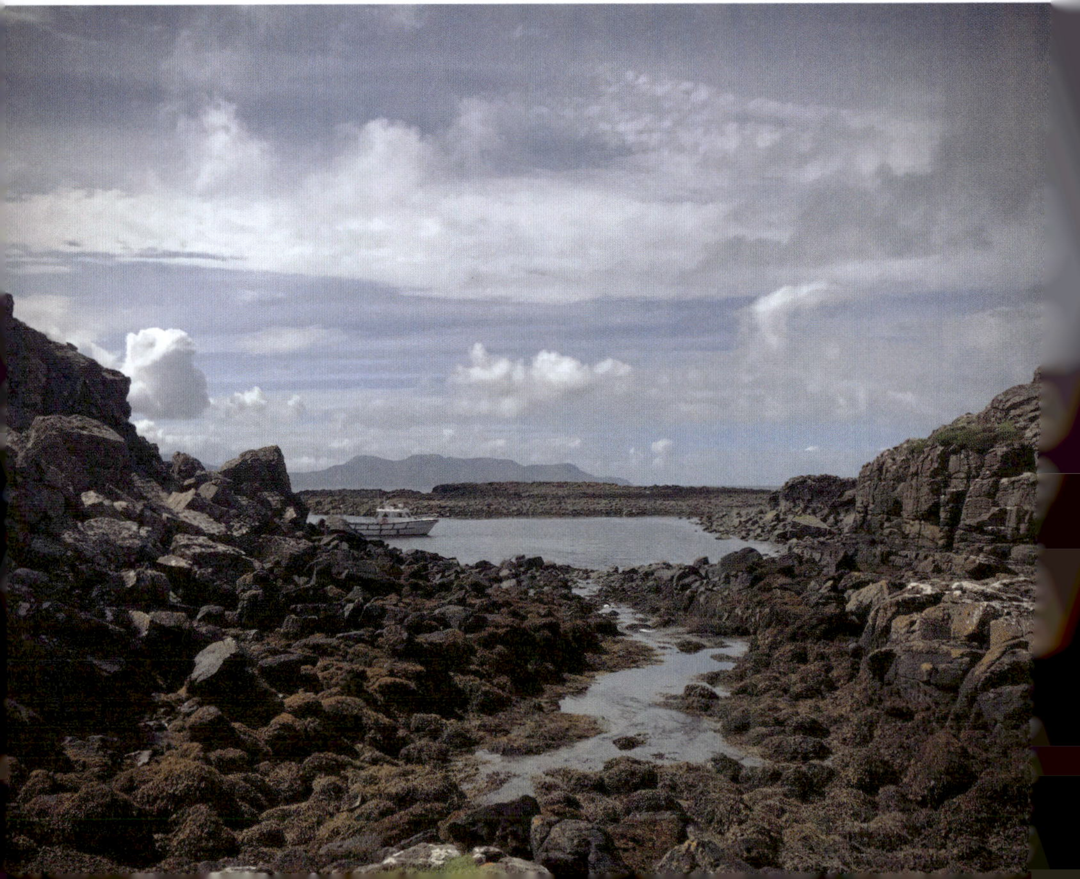

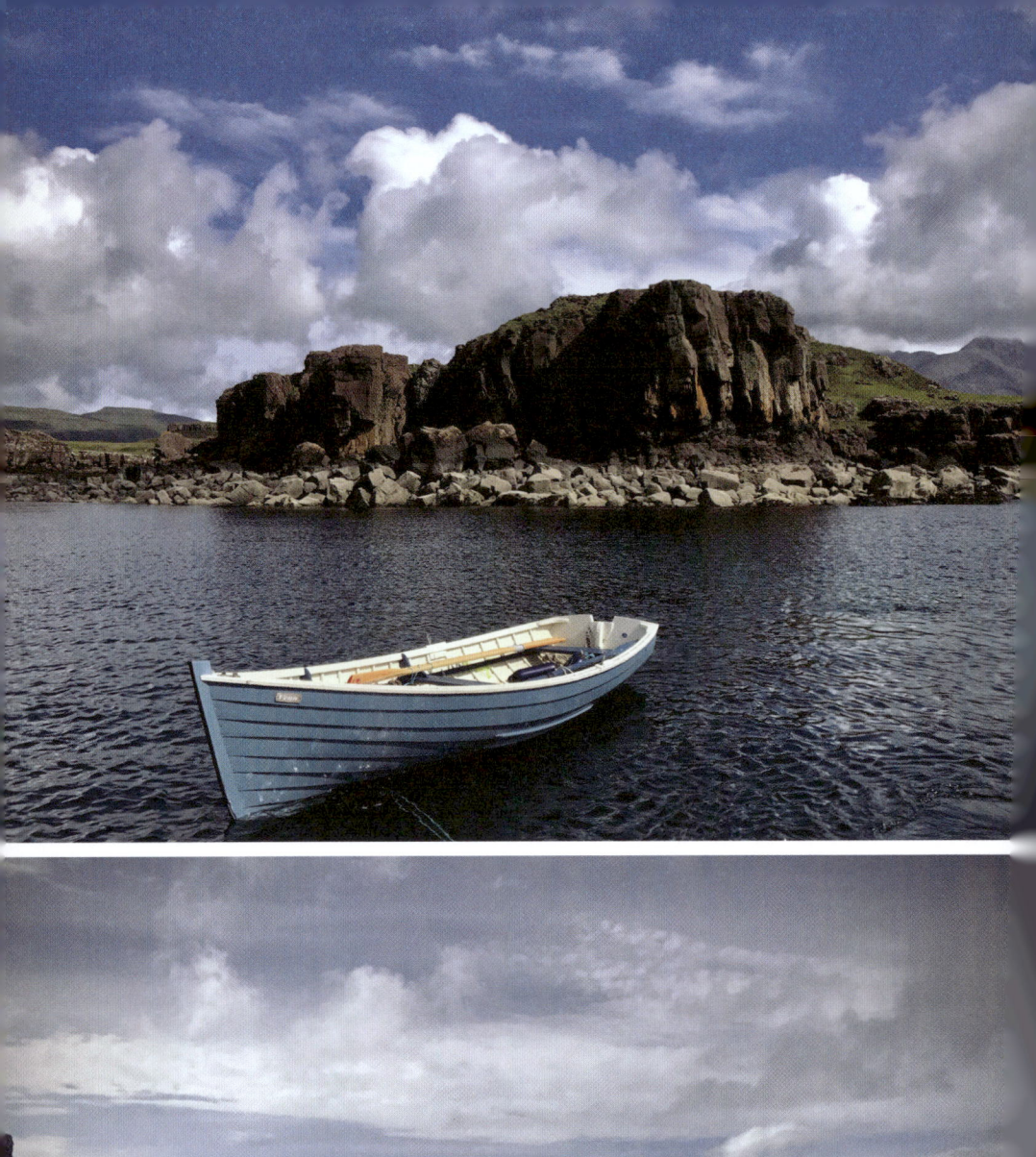

The Viking Shipyard, Isle of Skye

NG 3929 1639

I arrived at the tip of the Rubh' an Dunain peninsula early on a summer's morning and did not leave again until nearing sunset. I had come by boat, heading west from the stone jetty at the tiny hamlet of Elgol and sailing through the waters of Loch Scavaig and the Soay Sound. The peninsula reaches out in a near-perfect triangle from the south-western corner of the Isle of Skye: a flat wedge, its base set right at the foot of the serrated ridgeline of the Cuillin mountains, that recedes to a point, gesturing almost directly west towards the Atlantic Ocean. At its tip, there is a notch in the land, like a hole worked into a flint blade, that forms an irregular circle of water known as Loch na h-Airde. Running directly from that loch to the sea is a narrow, curving channel, just over 120 metres in length.

I tracked alongside the peninsula's southern edge: four miles of towering cliffs, many of them over a hundred metres in height, that only taper downwards as the land runs out. A flat outcrop of dark, volcanic rock formed a natural breakwater and we dropped anchor there, facing directly into the channel. The mountains rose up behind the shore, at once distant and looming. Their summits were obscured by huge, cotton-ball puffs of cloud, while the rest of the sky was perfectly clear. A pod of curious seals slipped their heads up above the water beside us. It was just after nine o'clock in the morning, but the sun was already hot.

I covered the short distance to land by rowing boat. It was low tide, the outflow channel reduced to a thin trickle running between piles of black rocks and orange seaweed. The boulder field narrowed but continued, leading right through the middle of a grassy shore, and I followed its trail all the way up to Loch na h-Airde. The loch was gathered in a little depression, not much more than 200 metres wide and surrounded by low, rocky terraces covered in wild grass. Undisturbed by the faint breeze, its surface was a solid veneer of dark blue.

In the year 2000, a retired local doctor, David MacFadyen, was walking the shoreline on the western side of the loch. A dry spell of weather had left the water levels unusually low and, as he looked across the reeded fringe to the exposed loch bed, he spotted an upright arm of wood. Digging it carefully out of the silt, he realised that it was man-made: a single piece of solid oak, fashioned into an elongated rib shape, with notches cut into each end. What he had found was a crossbeam, used in traditional boatbuilding to connect floor timbers to a hull. Subsequent radiocarbon dating revealed that it was at least a thousand years old.

I have seen this crossbeam, where it is now held, in Skye's Museum of the Isles. The preservation of the wood is remarkable. Although it has split and cracked along its grain – creating a series of shallow wrinkles and furrows – its overall shape has been retained perfectly. Archaeologists think that it once belonged to a kind of clinker known as a faering: a six-metre-long, four-oared vessel that originated in western Scandinavia. A Viking boat.

Over time, more timbers emerged from the loch bed, one from an even larger clinker, perhaps ten metres long. There was no doubt that these boats had been built for distant travel, for navigating across oceans. Which begged the question – what were they doing buried in the mud of a shallow, inland loch?

As morning drifted into afternoon, the tide turned. Rising water was beginning to flow rapidly over the rocks in the channel. What had looked like a dry, rocky stream bed began to transform before my eyes. The inrushing sea formed a hard black line, tendrils of now submerged seaweed waving like hands just below its surface. I sat for a time, maybe an hour, just watching. There was something transfixing about the way the watercourse pulsed and stirred under the tidal current. Minute by minute, it became increasingly obvious that the stones filling the channel were not placed naturally. They were walls. While they had largely disintegrated on the eastern bank, on the western side they remained solid and true. What I was looking at was a canal.

From perhaps as early as a millennium ago, boats had been travelling up and down this canal. After the timbers were discovered, marine archaeolo-

The Viking Shipyard, Skye

gists came to dive in the shallow waters of the loch, identifying the traces of stone-built quays at the head of the channel. Excavations on the shoreline uncovered the remains of two dry docks – known as nausts – where boats were pulled up onto land for repair. The traces of buildings – boathouses, store houses, living quarters – began to emerge all around the lochside.

Today, Rubh' an Dunain is not easy to reach. It is a four-mile walk along a lonely track from the nearest road: an eight-mile round trip. It is cut off from the rest of Skye by the towering rock wall of the Cuillins. Travel by foot and there is no doubting its remoteness. It is a site that only makes sense when viewed from the sea.

For a time, almost certainly for many hundreds of years, it would have been a place of constant activity. Ships coming and going. The incessant noise of repairs and construction, the chopping of wood and the hammering of nails. Simply by widening and bolstering the loch's outflow channel – and then adding a sluice gate to control the water level – the Vikings had engineered this natural landscape to create a perfect harbour and shipyard. For many generations, people used this peninsula, living almost their entire lives between land and sea. To them, its future abandonment would have seemed inconceivable.

I left as evening approached, the summer sun partly obscured by a haze of high cloud, the sky turning a mix of pale yellow and purple. Hauled the rowing boat down from one of the old nausts and into the now brimming canal. For just a few metres, I rode the pull of the tide down the channel. How long since any other boat had last done the same? And then I was clear, oars gripping the water, prow aimed due south, heading towards the distant silhouettes of Rum and Eigg, and the open sea.

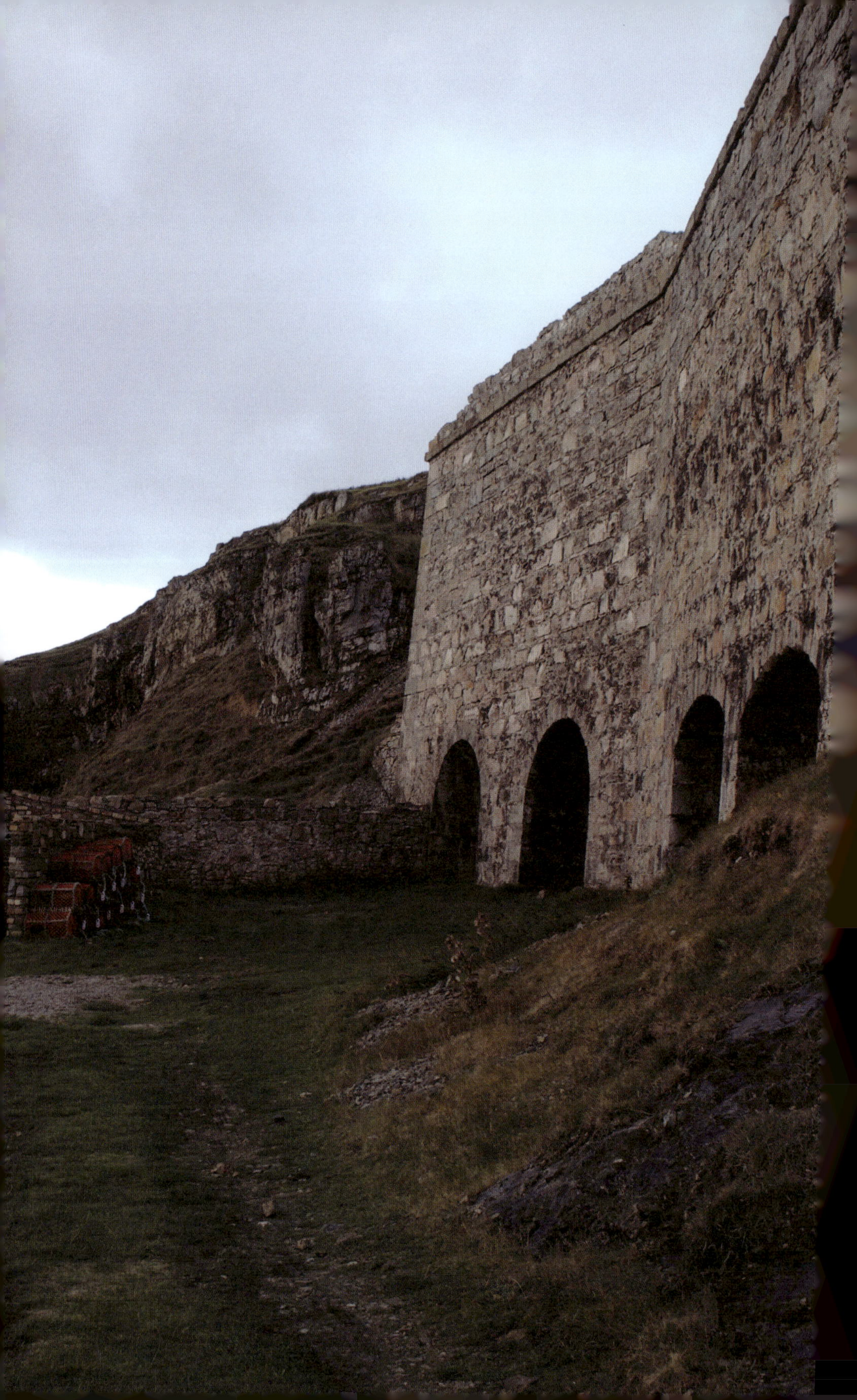

Ard Neackie, Loch Eriboll

NC 4467 5962

On a small promontory jutting out from the eastern bank of a ten-mile-long, deep water sea loch on the far northern coast of Sutherland, there is a brief flash of architectural monumentality. What looks like a section of giant, curved wall seems to emerge directly from a cliff face – as if it has been carved, like a relief sculpture, out of solid rock. This wall only runs for a short distance but is almost as tall as the cliff that surrounds it, reaching up some fifteen metres in height. There are four doorways, or portals, at the base of the wall – large, shadowy archways that appear to lead deep inside the promontory. But, given that they are almost entirely surrounded by water, there is nowhere really for them to go. Running directly away from these archways, out into the loch, is a long, narrow stone pier.

I had come from the west, driving from Assynt through the lonely valley of Strath Dionard to the Kyle of Durness. There the road met the northern coast, tracked it eastwards, then soon bent south again, to follow the deep cut of Loch Eriboll back inland. It was late October, and heavy rain showers were arriving in waves. Every so often a pale sun would break through, shining silver down the long surface of the loch. Then rolling clouds would extinguish it once again, turning the morning light into a grey, semi-darkness, and the water into a wind-rippled black, like a seam of solid rock.

On the eastern bank, the road climbed higher above the loch. After a few miles, the promontory came into view. From a distance, it could easily be mistaken for an island, except for a tiny spit of sand and shingle, a thin white thread, that attached it to the land. A track branched off the main road to lead down towards the beach. I parked at the top of it, beside a fence and a drystone wall, and began walking.

Wild History

At the base of the spit sat two modern, static caravans. A line of wooden telephone poles ran down the hill to stop halfway along the grass fringe that separated the two curving beaches. Two small fishing boats were in the bay, one roped against the pier, the other bobbing at anchor a few metres offshore. As I moved closer, I was able to make out the word THIEF spray-painted in block capitals on the red hull of the first boat. Where the beach rose up into the promontory, there was a dilapidated, two-storey house, its slate roof still intact, but its walls turned a pale grey with streaks of damp. Beneath that sullen, bruised sky, and against the looming backdrop of that huge stone wall, the whole place felt at once lived in and desolate, like it was squatting among the fragments of some ancient, abandoned ruin.

I followed the track to stand beneath the wall. It was built of dressed stone and remained in remarkably solid condition. From here, I could see that it wasn't curved but hinged – two walls that joined together at a slight angle. Those arched portals were, however, just a few metres deep and led to nowhere. There was a path that ran around the side of the wall to climb the cliff face. I scrambled up it, only to be confronted by a deep cleft in the rock. A whole chunk of the promontory had been hollowed out by quarrying, to create a gouged depression now filled with water. Another track led on to the top of the wall. Following it, I came upon four gaping holes. Concentric circles of stone, now partly overgrown with grass, formed deep shafts that dropped downwards, almost all the way to the base of the cliff. It wasn't a giant wall that had been built here, but four giant chimneys. Or, rather, four giant kilns.

A little over a century ago, thick clouds of acrid smoke would have billowed, near constantly, out of those holes – an alien fragment of urban industry transplanted into this northern landscape. The setting, in practical terms, was ideal. The whole promontory was a massive block of limestone. Once the kilns were built, the quarried rock only had to be taken a few yards before being loaded into the deep cylinders. The fuel sat at the bottom, lying on a metal grate, with the limestone then added on top. Alternating layers of fuel and rock were then stacked up until the whole thing was full. At the base of the kiln, in those archways, was a hearth and what was known as the 'draw hole'.

Once lit, the fires would heat up to temperatures of over 900°C, turning

Ard Neackie, Loch Eriboll

the calcium carbonate of the limestone into calcium oxide: known as 'quicklime', 'unslaked lime', 'lump lime' or, most simply, just 'lime'. As the fuel burnt down, the ash and lime were brought out of the draw hole and more layers added on top. It was a process that could, conceivably, go on without ever stopping – limited only by a lack of fuel, or rock, or people to load at the top and unload at the bottom. Boats came in from the sea to dock at the pier, bringing coal and coke to feed the furnaces (which may also, at times, have burnt the local peat) and then taking away the lime as it emerged from the kiln's four archways.

The process of lime production had been known about since Roman times, but the industrial and agricultural revolutions drove an enormous increase in demand. Lime was used in everything from construction and ironmaking to textiles, cosmetics and even lighting (the phrase 'limelight' comes from lime's use in making theatre stage lights). But most of all, it had become an essential ingredient in farming. Ploughed into the soil, lime could reduce acidity – a particular problem in Scotland, with its wet climate and abundance of decaying organic matter – substantially improving the supply of nitrogen to crops. Writing at the end of the eighteenth century, the Scottish agriculturist and economist James Anderson went so far as to say that lime was 'the basis of all essential improvements in this country'. Driven by that need to combat that natural soil acidity, it was said that Scotland used more lime per acre than anywhere else in Europe.

Thousands of kilns were constructed all across the country. From small 'field' kilns and 'clamp' kilns operated by individual farmers on their own land, to larger, industrial 'draw' kilns, just like the one built here at Loch Eriboll. They were, in a sense, the most numerous physical symbols of Enlightenment in the landscape – monuments to the application of knowledge and science. And the lime that they produced – that white, calcined, powdery rock – seemed like nothing less than the distilled essence of the modern world.

Perhaps inevitably, the scale and extent of this lime industry could not last. The stone did not run out, but it gradually became harder and more expensive to extract. As lime production was even more heavily industrialised in the twentieth century, the fires of local lime kilns quickly died out. Many kilns were demolished or abandoned, leaving behind strange brick ruins, consumed by the undergrowth on the rocky edges of farmlands.

    I stood on the summit of the promontory, above those four dark chimneys, and watched the clouds gathering again to the south. As the sun was obscured the sky turned a pale purple and the wind arrived in strong, cold gusts. Down below, in the crook of an old stone storehouse, were neat piles of buoys, fish crates and lobster pots. Waves began to beat against the far side of the stone pier and the boat anchored out in the bay bobbed wildly. Suddenly, the rain came on hard. I climbed quickly back down the path, to the foot of the kiln, and took shelter in the first archway. I sat for a while, in the space where the hot lime had once dropped and the perpetual fire had burned, and waited for the shower to pass.

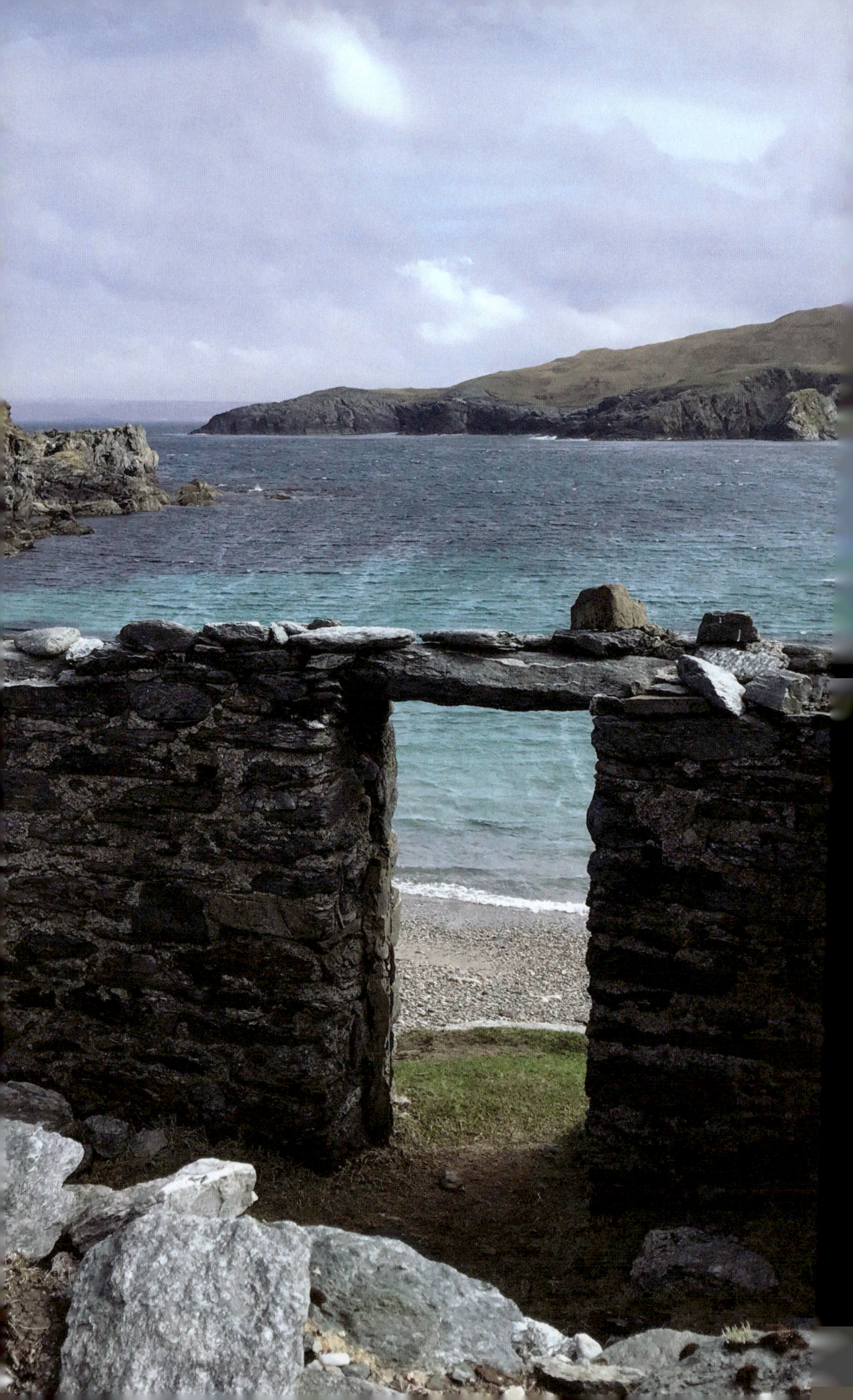

Fethaland, Shetland

HU 3750 9427

Through the gate, the path led up into the hills. All around, the grass was sparse and yellowed, and everywhere stones were poking up, breaking the skin of the land. A strong, relentless south-westerly was blowing. After twenty minutes, the sky, solid grey at first, was almost completely clear. I stood to watch the whole dark cloudbank shift at great speed away over the horizon. As I reached the top of another rise, I saw my destination – the very last stretch of Shetland Mainland, the Isle of Fethaland. The path ran down past a roofless old farm building towards an isthmus: two bright concaves of shingle beach laid out back-to-back, one facing the North Sea, the other the Atlantic Ocean. Beyond the isthmus was a final wedge of land, sloping down from tall cliffs on its western side to meet the sea on the east. At the highest point was the bright white box of a lighthouse beacon.

Groups of sheep watched me pass, some clustered for shelter behind stone dykes, but all giving me hard, inquisitive stares. The sun was high and bright as I walked down the last few hundred metres of moorland, the water in the bay a bright, inviting turquoise. On the grassy strip between the beaches was a jumble of twenty or so ruined drystone houses.

A community lived here once, not that long ago. Fethaland – from the Old Norse for 'fat land', or 'rich pasture' – was Shetland's busiest 'haaf', or deep-sea fishing station. In the nineteenth century, over sixty boats operated out of here – six-oared, open wooden boats called sixareens, built in the traditional Norse style. It was work for the summer months, with fishermen venturing forty or more miles out to sea to spool out seven-mile-long lines for cod, ling and tusk. What started as subsistence work became a major industry. Fish were cured, split open and dried on this beach, then packed for export to foreign markets. Go digging a little in the shingle and you can still find the fish bones. There were houses for each of the crews, seven men per boat, and these buildings were roofed with wood and turf, which was removed at the end of each season to avoid damage from winter storms. The industry collapsed in the last decade of the nineteenth century, however, rendered uneconomical by competition from advanced commercial fishing. By the start of the twentieth century, Fethaland was all but abandoned.

I sat down inside one of the roofless houses, framing my view out through the doorway to the waves lapping on the beach. Bright wildflowers sprouted from its empty window frames and half-collapsed lintel, garlanding the ruins in yellows and purples. A visitor in 1822, Samuel Hibbert, described a bustling, noisy site 'with all the disorder of a gypsy encampment'. It was hard to imagine as I sat there. It felt like the houses had been abandoned for longer than a century. There was just the wind and the calls of the sheep and the gentle breaking of the tide. Everything at Fethaland was crumbling steadily away – erosion and the elements taking buildings and beaches all at once. It is a place that deals in extremes of time, not moments. In this area you can find some of the oldest stones in the world – quartzites and schists and Lewisian gneiss. Great, wave-smoothed boulders lay all over the beach, their crystalline veins glimmering in the sunlight. Fethaland lies on the collision zone of two 500-million-year-old continental shelves – an accident of geology that allowed the fisherman access to the deep, abundant seas that they called the Far Haaf. Until others came here, and the old ways grew too dangerous, and the money went away.

I headed up to the lighthouse beacon on the towering cliffs on the northern side of Fethaland. It was lifted in by helicopter in the late 1970s – to aid tankers navigating into the vast Sullom Voe oil terminal, built twenty miles to the south. The automatic beacon was spinning round and round in its glass casing, ready to come on once the light dimmed. I kept on up to the very tip of the land. Nesting gannets wheeled below me, loud adult calls mingling with the high piercing cries of their young chicks. Buffeted by the wind, I glanced over the final precipice, down fifty or sixty metres to a rocky geo. I was shocked to see the huge white body of what looked like a sperm whale bobbing in the swell. It was rolled on its side, clearly dead, with a solitary seagull standing on its body, pecking absently at the flesh. It was a

Fethaland, Shetland

mournful sight. Once, though, it would have been a bonanza for the Fethalanders – blubber, bone, skin. And, of course, oil.

I walked back to my car, into the wind, head-on to strong gusts for the hour or so it took to return. I drove south and the sun cut in and out of the clouds, lighting up moorlands and hillsides and the innumerable lochans that drifted past. There was a stark, petulant beauty to it all.

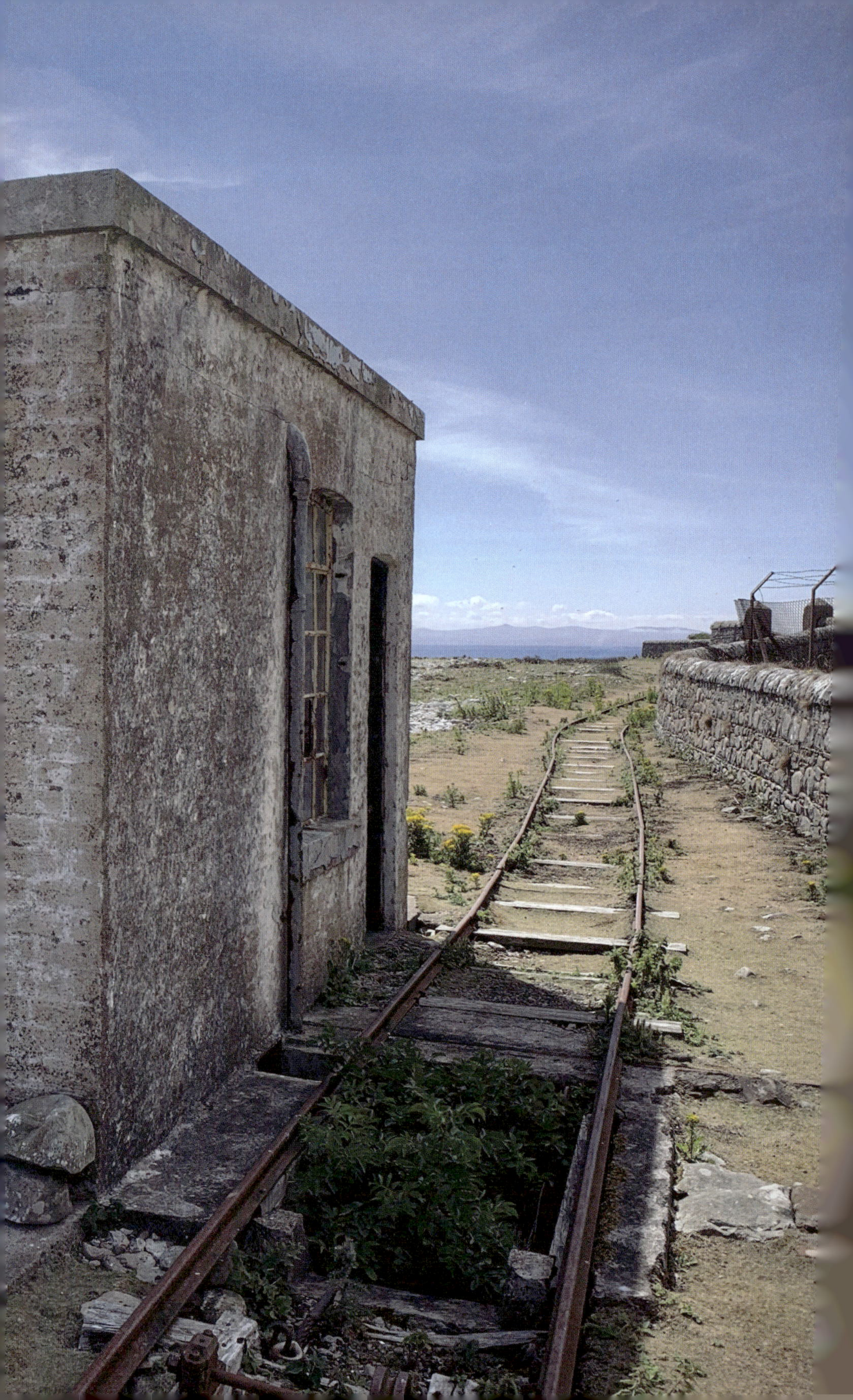

Ailsa Craig, Firth of Clyde

NX 0216 9974

The railway track was crimson with rust and its wooden sleepers weathered white as bone. Weeds sprouted up all along the line: an ankle-high avenue of pink thistles and yellow ragwort. The track passed right alongside a tiny, square building. Bricks that had once been red were bleached a pale pink, and the glass was smashed in almost all the individual panes of its white-framed windows. It looked like a waiting room for a ghost train. On the other side of the track was a drystone wall and, beyond that, two massive round holes that had once held a pair of gasometers. The gasworks building was behind them, its roof reduced to a skeleton of curved metal beams.

I walked the rails as they curved away past another building – a small cottage, also roofless. The rails began to drop down towards a shoreline of granite boulders, then continued out along a dilapidated pier that sloped gently into the sea, disappearing beneath the water. I stood on the pier, looking outwards from an island that is constantly being *looked at*. Set eight miles off the Carrick coast, where the Firth of Clyde meets the Irish Sea, it is a place that has always been more imagined than visited, a kind of permanent anchor for the entire westward view: the Ailsa Craig.

'In the distant horizon,' wrote the geologist John MacCulloch in 1819, the island 'forms an object peculiarly striking, from its unexpected magnitude in the blue haze, and from the decided and sudden manner in which it rises from the sea.' The result, he continued, is that 'it presents a solitary feature in Scotland, rather reminding the spectator of the volcanic islands of the distant Pacific Ocean'. MacCulloch circled Ailsa Craig in a boat but did not land – reasoning that to set foot on it meant no longer being able to see it. The shores, he said, were so narrow that to walk them would 'afford no view of the magnificent scenery that towers above them', while climbing to the summit of the island offered 'no sight of the perpendicular faces which constitute its most striking features'. Better instead, he thought, to keep his distance, sailing past the cliff faces to study their rock formations and scattering the island's many residents – its innumerable nesting seabirds – in the process. In taking flight, they became, MacCulloch said, like 'a cloud in the atmosphere which bears a striking resemblance to a fall of snow, or the scattering of autumnal leaves in a storm'.

At that time, the only obvious sign of any human presence at all was the abandoned ruin of what he described as 'an ancient tower of strength', set halfway up the south-eastern slope of Ailsa Craig's single, massive hilltop – a structure built in the sixteenth century, first to offer a site for Catholic worship and a potential staging post for a Spanish invasion of Scotland, then seized and fortified as a bulwark against that same invasion. What habitation the island had seen over the centuries was intermittent and temporary: the site of a monastic hermitage, a haven for religious refugees, a hideout for smugglers. Some fifty years before MacCulloch's visit, the naturalist and traveller Thomas Pennant landed on the island, finding 'the ruins of a chapel, and the vestiges of places inhabited by fishermen who resort here during the season for the capture of cod, which abound here from January to April'. Apart from those basic shelters – and the castle, which he sat beneath to eat dinner and drink water from a nearby spring – there was nothing.

In the mid nineteenth century, the owner of the island, Sir Archibald Kennedy, the second Marquess of Ailsa, employed a gamekeeper to help prevent the poaching of seabirds by passing ships. Described as the 'Keeper of Ailsa Craig' in the 1861 census, he lived with his two sons in a cottage built on the island's one flat stretch of land: a spit of boulders and bare grass on its eastern shore that had been formed by the sea tides and sediment coursing round its sides from the west. Two decades later, his tenancy was taken over by Andrew Girvan and his family: son Matthew, daughter Barbara and nephew Archibald. Andrew's profession was given as 'fisherman', but Matthew and William were described as 'curling stone dressers'.

From at least the beginning of the nineteenth century, rock from the island had been used to supply stones for curling. A sport that had been played for centuries on frozen ponds or rivers – using any kind of vaguely

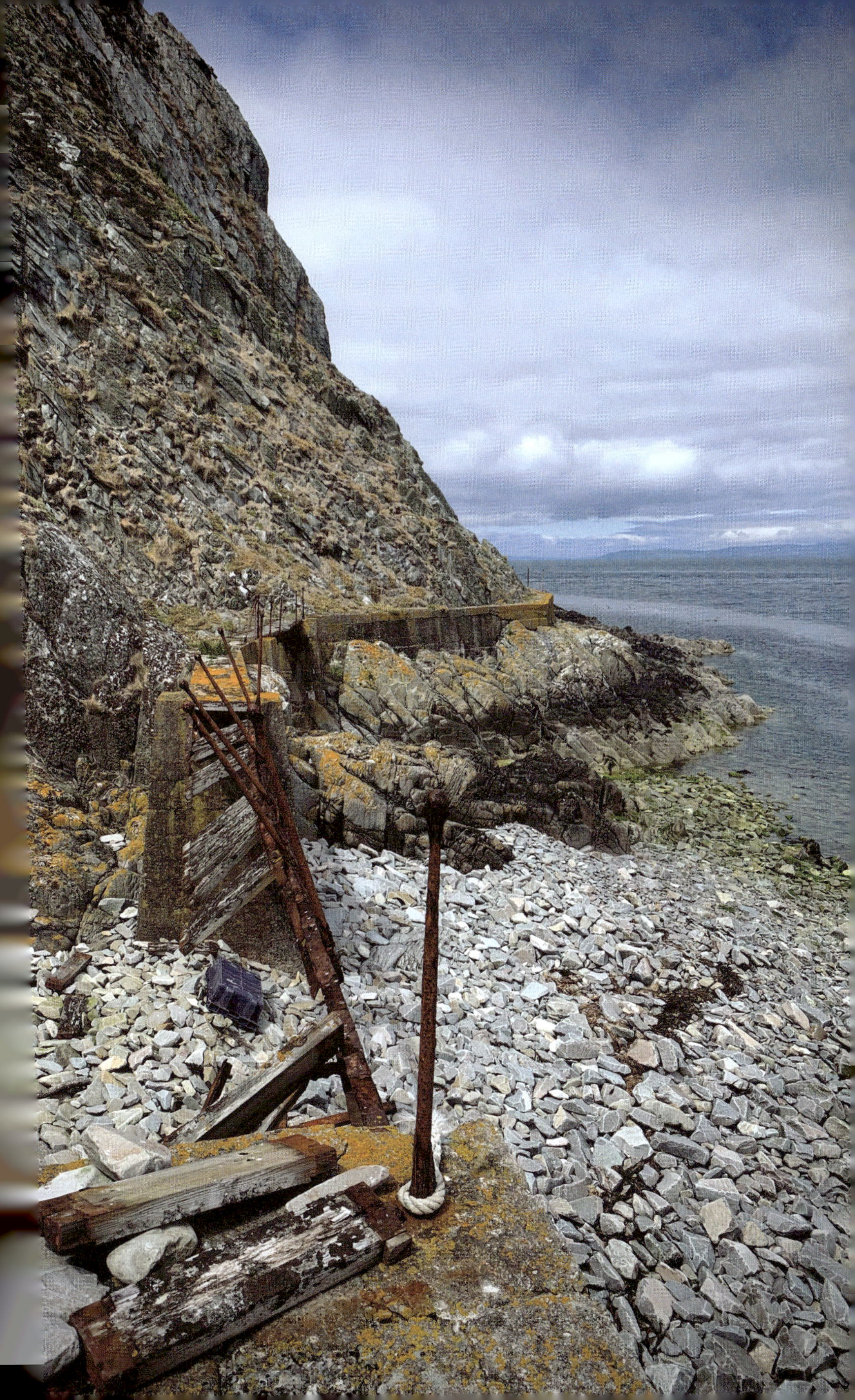

round or ovoid boulder that could slide across the ice – was becoming increasingly organised and competitive, requiring the standardisation of playing materials. Curling stones needed to be produced to a set size and weight. And Ailsa Craig, with its abundance of two specific types of granite – common green, and the very rare blue hone – was seen as the perfect source.

For decades, the Girvans operated a tiny, family quarrying operation, living in that solitary cottage by the sea, producing round blocks of granite known as 'cheeses', which they'd supply to Kays of Mauchline, a local Ayrshire business that fashioned them into finished curling stones. By the latter part of the 1880s, however, they were no longer the only people on the island. A spate of shipwrecks had prompted the construction of a lighthouse, along with two giant 'fog sirens' – twenty-foot-tall, conical, concrete 'trumpet houses', set at the northern and southern points of the island. Powering the horns required a gasworks to be built, with Crossley engines sending compressed air through hundreds of metres of iron piping to generate the long, loud siren blasts.

Industrial quarrying arrived on the island in 1907. The Ailsa Craig Granite Company leased a section of land on the south coast for large-scale extraction. Their interest wasn't in curling stones, however, but rather in removing massive sections of the cliff face to supply aggregate for road building. It prompted Neil Munro, journalist, critic and author of the *Para Handy* stories, to report that the whole of the west of Scotland was 'roused with indignation' at the possibility of Ailsa Craig 'being checked incontinent by soulless quarrymasters'. Not just one, but two narrow-gauge railways were built: the first to transport coal and oil from the pier to the gasworks and lighthouse; and then a 'mineral line', which ran from the southern cliffs all the way past the lighthouse to a 'quarry pier' where crushed stone could be loaded on to boats for transportation.

This business failed within little more than a decade, struggling to wring any profit from the high costs both of operating on the island, and of transporting the rock away from it. For a time, the quarry workers brought the population up to forty-nine people, but by the 1920s it was back to just the lighthouse keepers and the Girvan family. The Girvans continued to chip away at the cliffs to make curling cheeses – averaging up to ten a day, and sometimes as much as 1,400 a year.

Ailsa Craig, Firth of Clyde

I had gone in search of the blue hone granite quarry, on the far eastern coast of the island, following a – largely wrecked – concrete walkway originally built to reach the northern foghorn. It was a warm summer day, with only the lightest breeze. The island's population of young herring gulls was not long hatched, and the debris of empty, abandoned nests was everywhere. The cries of the adults grew louder and more agitated the further I moved around the coast. Sections of wooden bridges on the walkway had rotted away to nothing, so I continued across the bouldery shoreline.

The face of the quarry wall emerged in the distance, and soon I was climbing over great geometric slabs of cut rock, an ocean of old cheeses – either discarded because of flaws, or perhaps just waiting to be collected and removed. Kays of Mauchline still come here, every ten years or so, to harvest more rock – pulling a boat up to moor it just below the quarry wall and spending a week or more loading it with thousands of tons of fallen granite to take back to their factory. The blue hone is, it seems, unique – Ailsa Craig is the only place in the world where you can find it. And, in the finished curling stone, it forms the crucial connection to the ice: the only part of the stone that actually touches the surface of the rink. These little pieces of Ailsa Craig have travelled the globe. Curlers keep logbooks of the stones used in different rinks across the world – how well they slide, how much they turn. Which amounts, in effect, to a record of the continuing migration of this island's stone. A kind of ancestry of extraction.

The gulls began to protest my presence more aggressively. Every so often there was a rush in the air around my head. Winged shadows crisscrossed the ground. It was, I decided, time to retreat from the quarry. I moved past the piles of rusting, abandoned machinery to make my way back to the broken walkway. The gulls quietened, and now the only sound was the click and clack of the shifting sea of granite boulders beneath my feet.

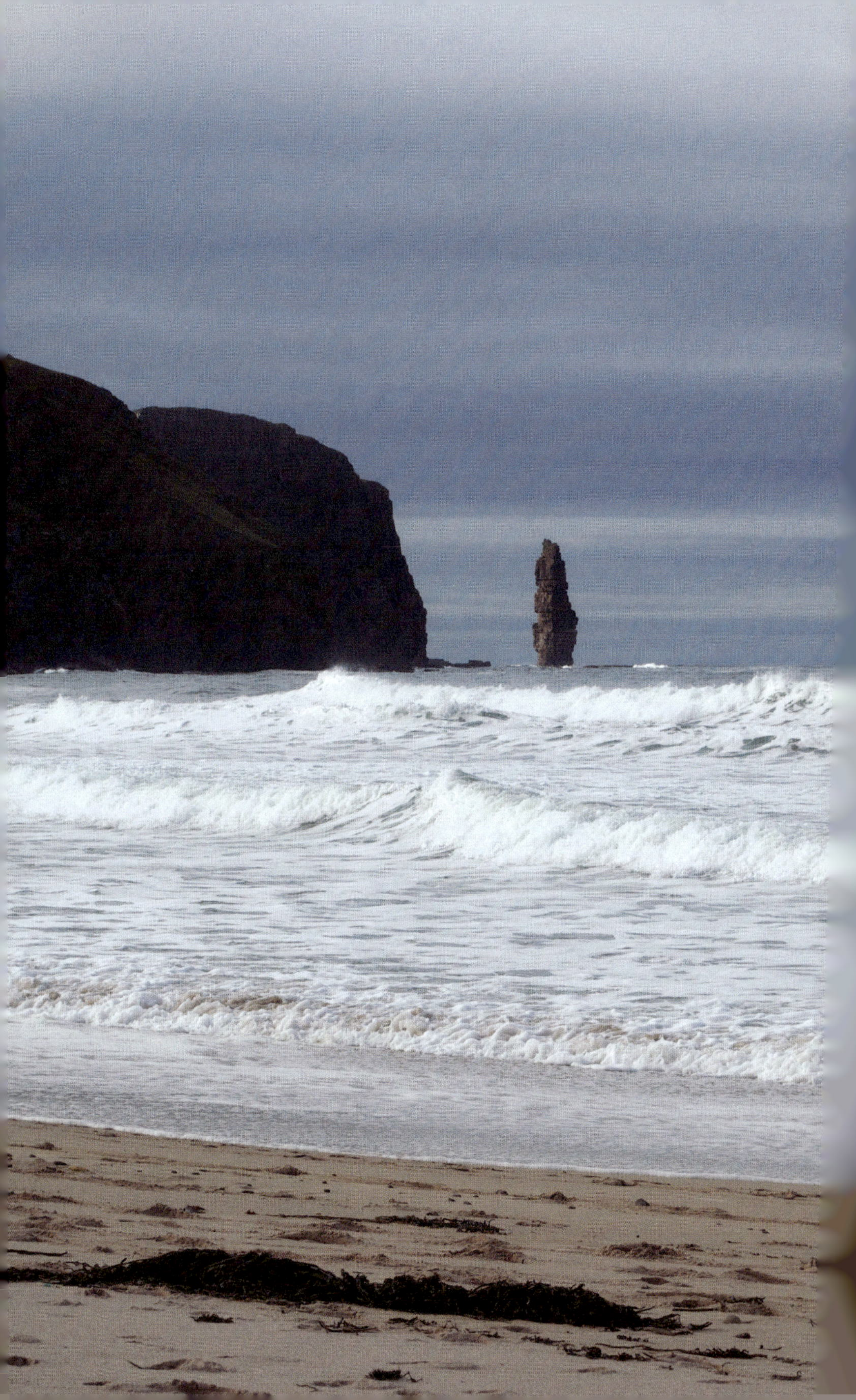

Sandwood Bay, Sutherland

NC 2202 6411

Sandwood Bay is an old place. Quite literally. In Gaelic, it was known as Seannabhad – *seann* for 'old', *abhad* for 'place'. This name, in turn, may be derived from the Old Norse *sandvatn* – 'sand water'. It is an apt description of this landscape, with its oddly geometric rectangle of freshwater loch, enclosed at its northern end by a mile and a half of empty beach that faces on to the relentless waves of the Atlantic Ocean. Travel some 500 or so miles northwards across that ocean and you can find another s*andvatn:* a striking, crystal-blue lake right in the middle of Iceland. The name also occurs – at what may be its origin point – in a handful of lakes in southern Norway. Sandwood, it seems, was visited, and perhaps even settled, by Vikings. But the paucity of other Norse placenames in the north-west of Sutherland suggests that, if those visitors did stay, it was not for very long.

Today, Sandwood Bay is celebrated for its isolation: billed as the 'most remote' beach on the British mainland, it has long been a place of pilgrimage for those seeking 'wilderness' and adventure. The rebranding of large stretches of the nearest main road – the A838 – as the 'North Coast 500', with Sandwood listed as one of its main attractions, has, however, brought a steady influx of new visitors to the old place. The once lonely four-mile trek across the boggy moorland of Strath Shinary has become rather less solitary in recent years.

Given the dramatic nature of the location, it may seem self-evident that the *seann* in Seannabhad was intended to convey some sense of the ancient, or the timelessly elemental. But this would be to misconstrue the Gaelic meaning. In fact, rather than noting the absence of people, it was about recalling their presence. Sandwood was described as an 'old place' because it was where people *used to* live.

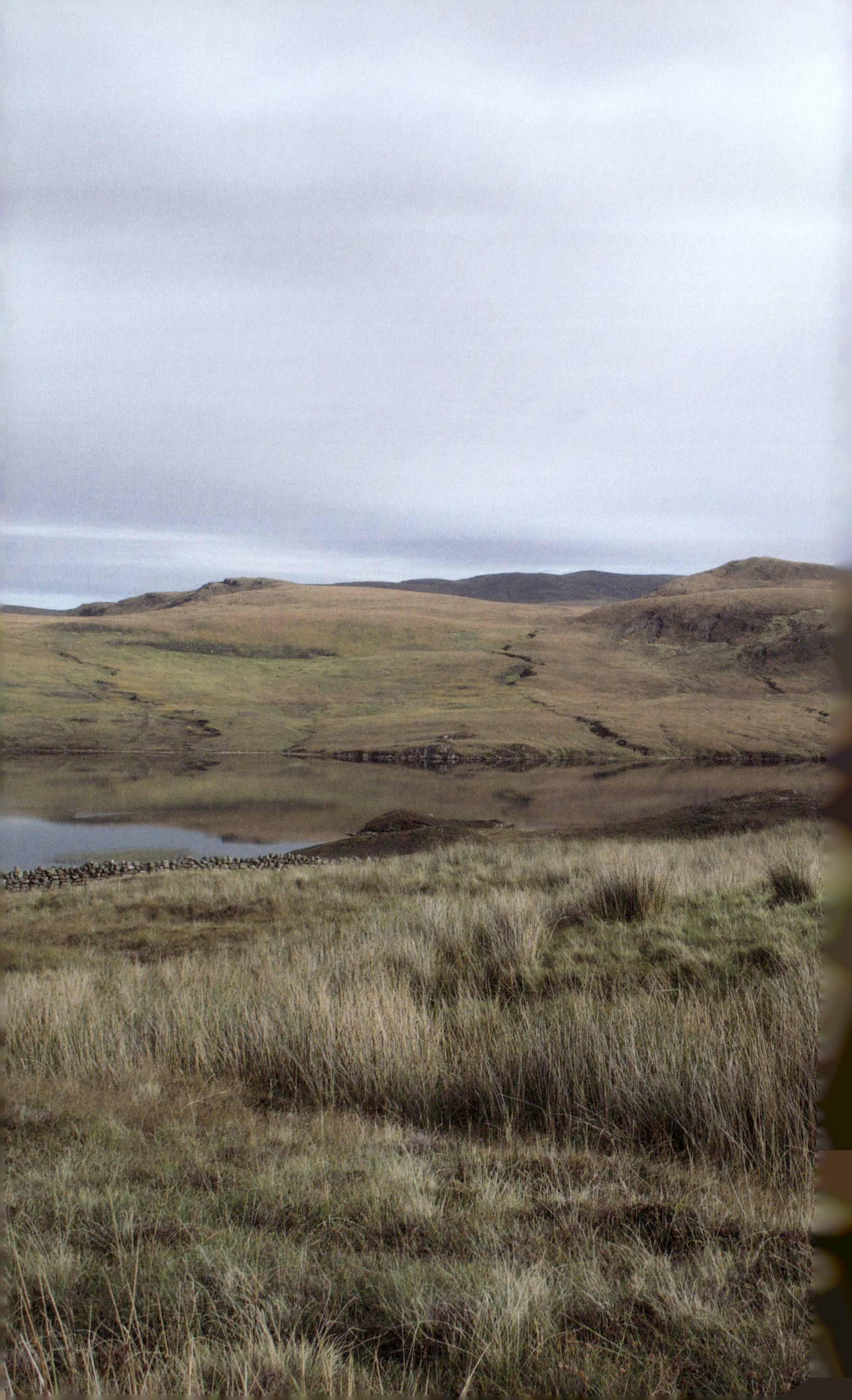

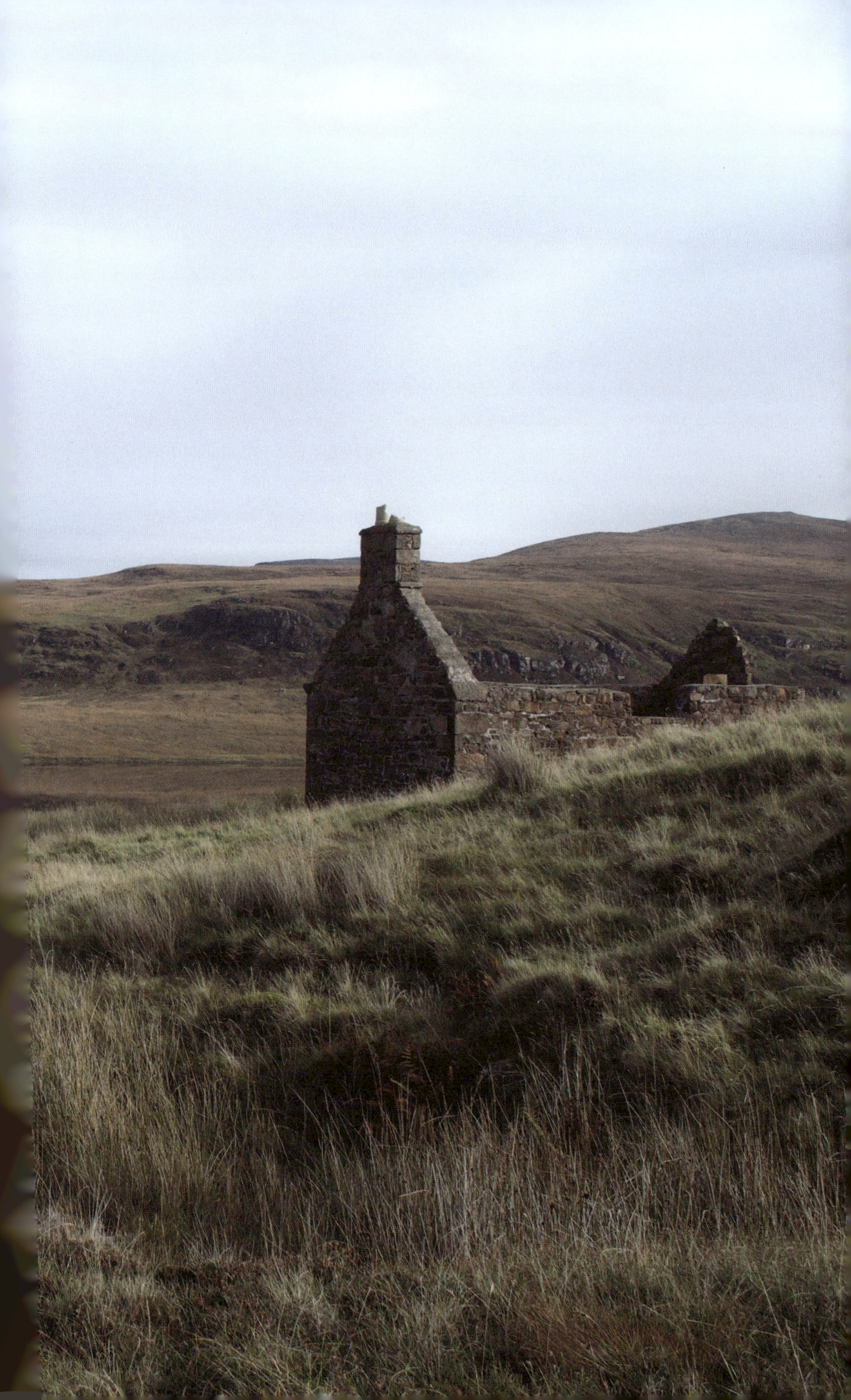

Wild History

Some lingering traces can still be found, just off the track that leads to the beach, on a hillside that overlooks the north-western banks of the loch. I had walked there on a perfectly still October day, picking my way across a wet, spongy slope of peat and heather towards the roofless shell of a house. It was nestled a little in the landscape, backed up against a slope that dropped down steeply to a burn before rising up again into a rocky outcrop. Below it, the loch was glass-flat, mirroring the hills on the opposite shore so perfectly that it was almost impossible to tell where the water began.

Drystone walls still divided the land here – there were two large enclosures in the front of the house, and one segment of wall running perfectly straight all the way down to the lochside, like a boundary line. I watched as sheep trotted nimbly through the makeshift gates created where the stonework had collapsed. Follow Sandwood Loch back to its southern end, and then trace a course up the Srathain river that flows into it, and you will find ruin after ruin. Abandoned sheep enclosures, the ankle-high footings of shieling huts, the ghostly outlines of long-gone homesteads. A little further up the moor behind me was Loch a' Mhuilinn: 'the loch of the mill'. The faint lines of cultivation terraces could still be seen running across the green sward on the hillside above the beach.

The building I was standing in was the last to be abandoned. It was not, however, a symbol of the community that had once lived here. Rather, it was the opposite. Sandwood, as with so many other rural townships across Sutherland, was struck by the potato blight of 1846. The landowner's response was to judge the generations-old farming system here economically unsustainable and to remove every family and replace them with sheep. This house, dating from the end of the nineteenth century, was built as the shepherd's cottage.

Quite how long people had inhabited Sandwood before that point is unclear. Certainly for many centuries. The geographer Timothy Pont included it – as 'Sandwatt' – on his sixteenth-century map of Scotland. His annotations complimented the region's 'good tak of herring' but bemoaned the swarms of 'black flies seen soaking men's blood', and warned that this part of the country was 'Extreem Wilderness' roamed by 'Many Wolfs'.

This tendency to label landscapes as, at once, inhabited *and* 'extreme wilderness' has long persisted. It exposes the innate subjectivity of the work

Sandwood Bay, Sutherland

of the early cartographer-explorers – a subjectivity which still lingers in the popular imagination today. As the mapmaker Joan Blaeu put it in his seventeenth-century 'atlas' of Scotland, this region of Sutherland was 'the farthest shore'. But *farthest* from what?

Admittedly, if you want to conjure up an ideal image of a 'farthest shore', then there are few candidates better than Sandwood Bay. I walked down and away from the shepherd's cottage, across the massive dunes at the head of the loch and on to the beach. Despite the near absence of any wind, the waves breaking in front of me were huge, towering. They ran and crested for miles, propelled inwards by a hungry swell, and when they hit the shore, they burst in a slick foamy rush over the pale-pink sands. The sheer size and power of them was startling. Their constant breaking filled the air with a mist of sea spray that, with no breeze, just hung like a faint gauze across the sky. Out to the west of the bay, standing like a last marker post before the open reaches of the ocean, was Am Buachaille, a 200-foot-high sea stack of Torridonian sandstone. If this isn't wild, you might ask, then what is?

All the same, I was not alone on the beach. Maybe a dozen other people were there. A family eating lunch among the dunes. An old couple walking the tideline with an excitable Border collie. A young couple in hiking gear I overheard speaking in French. A group of three middle-aged women running down to the sea in swimsuits and woolly hats. High up on the cliffs overlooking the bay was a figure in silhouette, and rising from his feet came the tiny black speck of a drone. There was life here again on the 'farthest shore' – albeit fleeting and transitory.

I looked out to sea as the sun broke through the high cirrus clouds and lit up one side of Am Buachaille. The stack's name is a symbol of life here too. In Gaelic, it means 'the herdsman', someone who watches over a place and its people. A herdsman always needs a herd. I walked back across the dunes and behind me the waves crashed and a woman, one of the 'wild' swimmers, let out a scream – of shock or delight? – as she waded into the cold Atlantic water.

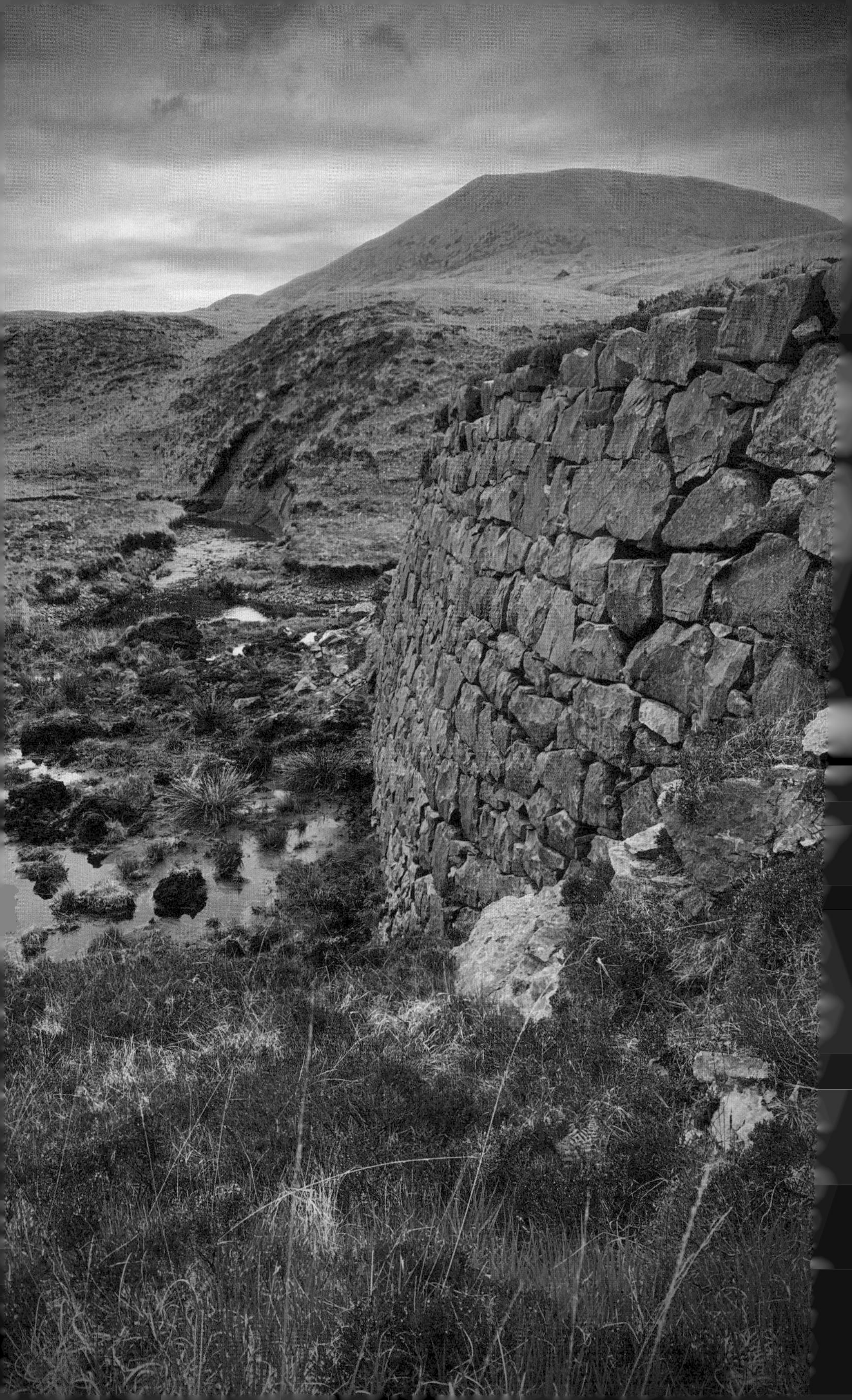

Salisbury's Dam, Isle of Rum

NG 3670 0005

There is no real road on the Isle of Rum. What starts as a stretch of dusty ground, leading away from the large concrete slipway on the southern shore of Loch Scresort, deteriorates, after just a few hundred metres, to a narrow, rocky, potholed track. This track continues on to the interior of the island, winding slowly upwards along the valley of the Kinloch River. It reaches its highest point – at around 800 feet – near the very heart of Rum, overshadowed on one side by the slopes of Ard Nev, and looking out on the other across a patchwork of small lochs towards a dark, imposing ridgeline of mountains. These are the Rum Cuillin, a series of peaks formed out of volcanic gabbro, the highest of which, Askival, tops out at over 2,500 feet. Taken together, they present a jagged silhouette of black rock, a monstrous jawbone, studded with sharp, hungry-looking teeth. The landscape here presses in on you, like being grasped in a rough, sinuous embrace. A little further on, however, and the Cuillin ridge begins to taper back downwards, the track gradually drops in height, and suddenly the view opens out to the Atlantic Ocean.

 I had stopped on a rounded promontory, overlooking a run of flat coastal land that ended in a wide semi-circle of shingle beach. The remains of buildings were outlined in grey stone on the grassy sward above the shore, and at that moment a herd of red deer, eighteen of them, were trotting through the ruins.

 This was what remained of the township of Harris, once one of the largest settlements on the island: a home, at its peak, to near enough a hundred people, spread across fifteen families. Along with the rest of Rum's population, they were cleared off the land in 1828 to make way for 8,000 Blackface sheep. Within less than two decades, however, this enterprise in sheep farming had collapsed. And so, in 1845, the island began another transformation. Purchased by a wealthy English aristocrat – the Marquis of Salisbury – the entire landscape was to be repurposed as a vast sporting estate.

Those deer down below me were, at least in part, a legacy of Salisbury's vision. Even before the people were removed from Rum, the deer had been wiped out, hunted to extinction. And so new herds were transported from the mainland, hundreds upon hundreds of animals let loose in the hills, oblivious to the role they had been brought here to play.

I followed this one herd as they made their way from the banks of Loch Long – its thin sliver of dark water set in almost the exact centre of the island – until they dropped out of sight in the steep-sided valley of Glen Harris, only to reappear again on the raised beach of the ruined township. I was perhaps a kilometre away from them, but they knew I was there, various of their number stopping stock-still to peer up at me across a stretch of abandoned ploughlands.

After a time, I made my way back along the track, to the north and east, to a spot near the headwaters of the Kinloch River. It was here that Salisbury's son, the Viscount Cranborne, had attempted to re-engineer the island's river system. Rum's major drawback as a sporting estate was its lack of salmon. While the moors and mountains offered a brooding, sublime backdrop for stalking, the prospects for salmon fishing were poor. Salmon need relatively deep water to travel from the sea to their spawning grounds, but, quite simply, the island's rivers just weren't big enough. Cranborne's solution was to make them big enough. He chose a site, just to the south of Loch Long, where he believed that the main tributary of the Kilmory River could be blocked and rediverted into the Kinloch River, which ran out to sea at Loch Scresort.

I found this construction just a little off the track, down a slope of dense heather and wild grass. Although hidden at first by the dipping land, its true scale soon became clear: a huge curving wall, easily six metres in height, formed of solid blocks of pinkish sandstone. It ran out, tall and imposing, straight across the river valley. Until, that was, it came to an abrupt and rather dramatic halt. Only around half of the wall remained: thirty metres of it, bending out from the eastern bank of the river. The final stretch, which would have joined it to the western bank was, however, gone completely.

Closer, I could see that it was not just one wall, but two, with a channel running between them, like a castle rampart. I climbed down into the channel, choked with heather and errant bits of stone, and followed it along until the whole structure clearly gave way. Here, the rubble, overgrown with grass, formed a narrow, sloping path, which allowed me to walk down to the riverside. There was something almost comical about the contrast between the scale of the dam and the modest size of the river. The water now met the base of the still surviving wall and simply bent around it, through the gap left by the collapsed stones.

Construction was said to have taken perhaps as long as a year, with hundreds of men and materials brought to Rum from the mainland, at a cost of some £1,700 – the equivalent of £250,000 in today's money. When the dam was first completed, the water built up against it, just as planned: running off through a channel cut for 300 metres through the rock to divert it into the Kinloch River to the east. You can imagine the viscount's reaction, that superhuman sense of entitlement – that he had managed to take a landscape and bend it to his will. Except the landscape had other ideas. It took just two days for the whole western side to collapse – all that effort, literally washed away in an instant.

The ruins of the dam are, perhaps more than anything else, a monument to hubris. A reminder that nature, and the environment, cannot always be so easily manipulated. All the same, Rum today remains a place altered forever both by human interventions and by human absence. Designated as a National Nature Reserve in 1957, it is now a crucial haven for wildlife – colonies of Manx shearwaters, red-throated divers, otters and even, in recent years, white-tailed sea eagles. Over a thousand red deer walk its hills and glens, and graze among its landscapes of abandonment. But if it is a wilderness now, it is a managed, and contrived, one. An ecosystem which, just like Salisbury's dam, remains in part, and in pieces.

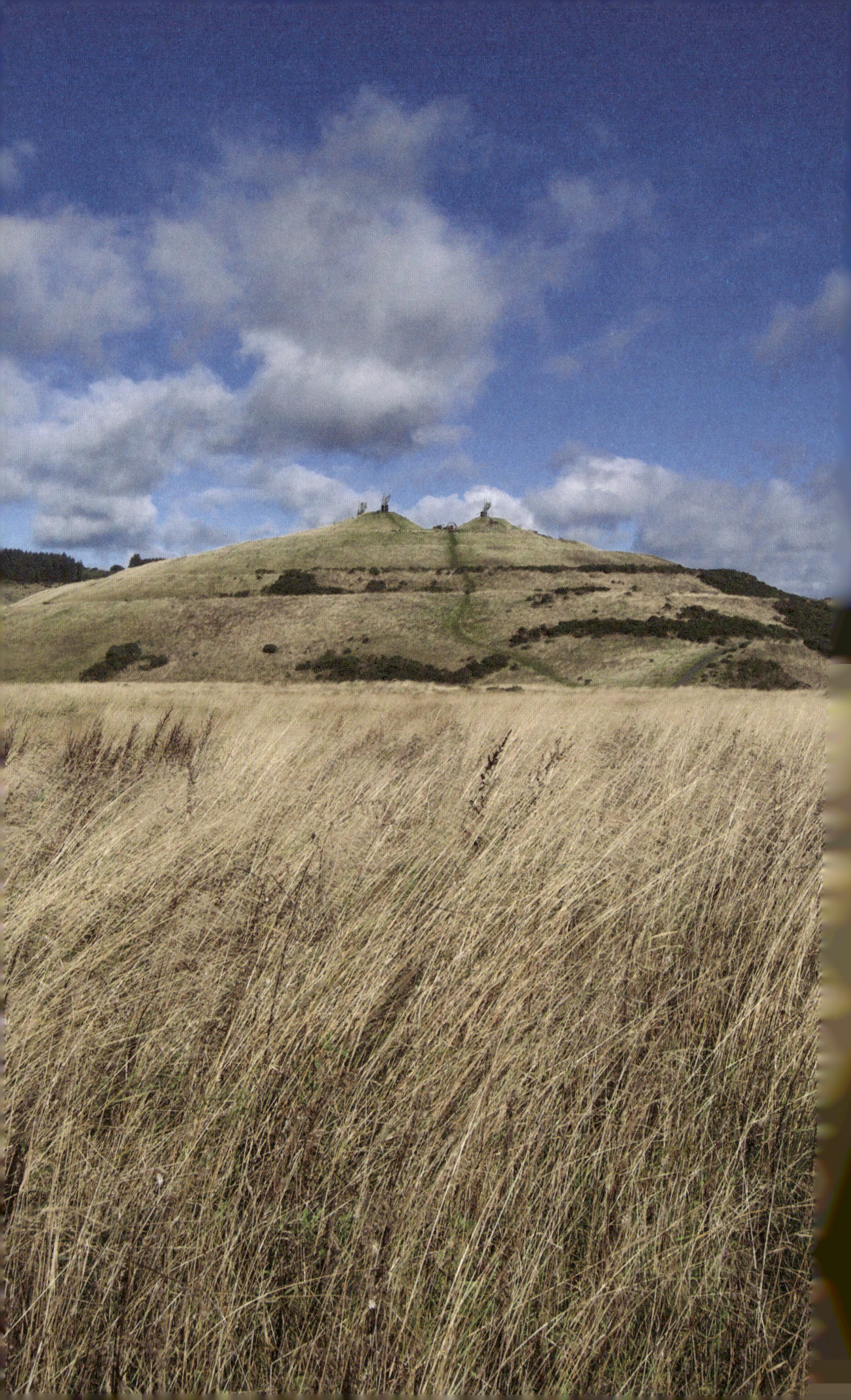

Lassodie Village, Fife

NT 1315 9253

Some ghost towns are cast to type: rows of empty houses; desolate roadways leading to nowhere; weeds and plants cracking the stones of roofless ruins. They are consumed by stillness and the silence which accumulates wherever the evidence of human activity still lingers, but the humans themselves are gone. The *other* kind of ghost town – the *true* ghost town, if you like – leaves no relics, no remains. It has not simply been changed or abandoned by the passage of time. Rather, it has been erased completely. Lassodie, just four miles to the north-east of Dunfermline, is one of those places.

Look for it on old maps and it is an apparition: there and then gone again. On the first-edition OS map, drawn in the mid nineteenth century, it exists in name only – a farmhouse, already said to be in a 'ruinous' state, nestled among woodland and surrounded by a great patchwork of agricultural lands. It is not until the second-edition map, completed in the early 1900s, that it suddenly appears, fully formed: long lines of houses, built either side of a curving road running for several hundred metres.

Known as the 'Rows' – both 'Old' and 'New' – these houses continued into what was called Fairfield. Together, they formed the brand-new village of Lassodie. Along with them came a large schoolhouse, the Free Church of St Ninian's, shops, a post office, a pub, a village hall and a football pitch. Just to the east was the West of Fife line of the North British Railway. Two branches led off it to cut right through the centre of the village, each one splitting again, multiple times, to join up with a series of holes in the ground: Lassodie's pitheads.

It was coal that brought the people and the community here. The first pits were opened at the beginning of the 1860s, prompting the construction of the original line of houses that became the Old Rows. As successive seams were exhausted, more holes were sunk in the land to the west, and the settlement grew and expanded. By 1893, the last pits – numbers ten and eleven – were established just alongside the schoolhouse. At the start of the twentieth century, the population of Lassodie had grown to over 1,400, with a school roll of some 250 pupils. At peak, the workers were producing upwards of 1,300 tons of coal every day, loading it onto the endless procession of wagon trains passing in and out of the village.

Of course, it is in the very nature of extraction that boom will turn, almost in an instant, to bust. From the beginning of the 1920s, the decline was sudden and rapid. Soon only three pits – four, ten and eleven – were still producing coal, but operations at the latter – which was the deepest, sinking down some 120 fathoms – were suspended due to large accumulations of water within the tunnels. Workers gradually began deserting the village, moving on to other collieries and leaving empty homes behind them. Many of the houses were already showing structural problems – cracks in the walls and ceilings caused by subsidence as the mines hollowed out the earth below.

In May 1931, the owners of the Lassodie Colliery posted a notice that the pits were to be closed immediately. As a result, the employment of the remaining 300 workers was terminated, and they were given just fourteen days' notice to leave their homes. A report in the *Dunfermline Press* – headlined 'Probable Disappearance of Village' – noted 'a strange calm resting over the place' in the wake of the announcement. With no work to do, some miners were fishing for trout from the banks of the nearby Loch Fitty, while others were playing football on the village's marshy – and famously grass-free – pitch. In among the houses, the reporter found groups of men assembled to discuss what the future might hold.

'Employment at Lassodie has been so steady for years,' he wrote, 'that the miners probably do not fully realise that operations at the colliery have come to an end.' One man said that he'd not had more than four days without work in the last four and a half years – and those days had been due not to a shortage of coal, but to a shortage of wagons to transport it away. Despite this, the rumours were circulating – to the disbelief of the villagers – that the colliery company was already planning to demolish their houses.

Thirty years later, in 1961, another reporter for the *Dunfermline Press*

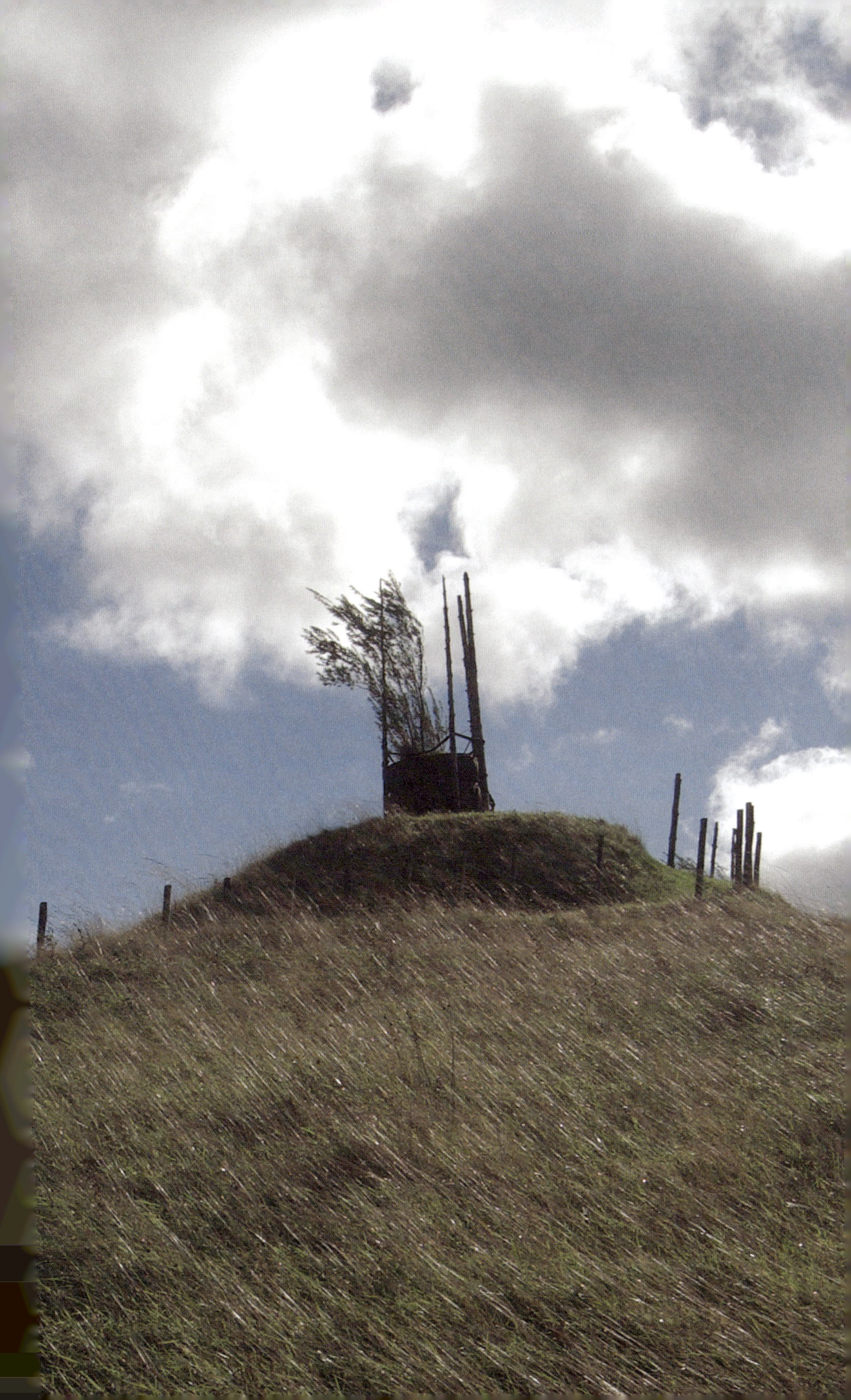

returned to the site. 'Wandering beyond Loch Fitty, I found myself close to where the mining village of Lassodie had once been. Although not a native, I had known the village in my youth, and now found it hard to realise it was no more. I looked round, but apart from some bricks that had once supported the gable end of Fairfield and a broken lintel sunk deep in the grass, there was no indication anywhere that the village had ever existed.' For a time, some residents had clung on to their homes, in defiance of the eviction notice and court orders of removal, but this had only delayed the inevitable. By the 1940s, all of the buildings were gone.

Even this, however, was not the end of the erasure of Lassodie. The miners of the 1930s had bemoaned the closures because they said there was still so much coal here. In the 1960s, new extraction companies came to claim that coal, turning the whole site into an enormous open-cast mine – which they named St Ninian's, after the old village church. Machinery tore open the earth to get to the seams, eradicating not just the last faint traces of the former village, but all of the land on which it had once stood. These works continued, on and off, all the way up to 2016.

Another half-decade later, I made my own way 'beyond Loch Fitty' to where 'Lassodie had once been'. It was a bright morning at the very end of September. Past the far eastern shore of the loch, a tiny stretch of broken tarmac led to a metal gate. On the other side of the gate, a track of bright-green grass cut across a wide open plain of tall, pale-yellow reeds. Looming over it all was one giant, geometric mound topped by three small, barbed summits. It was an entirely artificial hill, created from the vast heaps of spoil left behind by the open-cast mine.

The American artist Charles Jencks had been commissioned to shape this abandoned space into a colossal piece of landscape art – called the 'Fife Earth Project' – with a series of spiralling mounds being built to surround a loch cut into the shape of Scotland. The work was never completed, however, and what remains is a strange mixture of half-finished artwork and industrial wasteland. Signs at the gate warned of CCTV, drone surveillance and sink-holes. But already large swathes of gorse and heather grew on the black earth here, now heaped up or smoothed out on top of the footprint of the houses of what had once been Fairfield.

As I crossed the plain, a grey heron flew low over my head. In the distance, two buzzards wheeled high in the air. Approaching the foot of the mound, I disturbed a roe deer, which broke cover and ran at speed down a slate-grey track, not once looking back. A gravelled path curved around the mound to reach the summit, but a second route, walked into the grass, led straight to the top. There I found pieces of rust-red mining machinery arranged to form a long avenue running between those three separate barbs, each of which was topped with a tree planted in a ring of rubber tyres, surrounded by bare, bone-grey pine trunks. The effect, presumably intentional, was of some kind of primitive, post-apocalyptic totem poles.

To the north, far down below in the deepest chasm left by the mine works, was the new loch – more kidney-shaped than Scotland-shaped. Its shores were coal-black, but hundreds – perhaps even thousands – of wild birds were clustered on its waters. To the west was a second mound, not as large as the first, but still surrounded by the same spiral pathway. It sat right on top of the houses of the New Rows and Lassodie's old school.

In 2021 the site was acquired by an organisation called National Pride, which aims to turn its 900 acres into what they call an 'eco-therapy and wellness park'. Their masterplan envisages a spa, wildlife observation pods, a technology centre and accommodation units surrounding 'bio-diverse ecology sanctuaries'. Houses may return here, for the first time in nearly a century.

All the same, apart from a solitary dog-walker far off in the distance, I didn't see anyone else. There was something uncanny, almost eerie, about this place: old industry's ghostly residue. A feeling persisted that my presence in the wildening spoil of what was once Lassodie was somehow illicit, or an intrusion. It is a sense that may prove hard to overcome – for people, at least. I saw that deer again, or maybe it was a different one now, down in the valley between the mounds. It stood still for a few moments, as if it could sense I was watching. Then it turned and ran off to the west, down the arrow-straight path of what had once been a railway line.

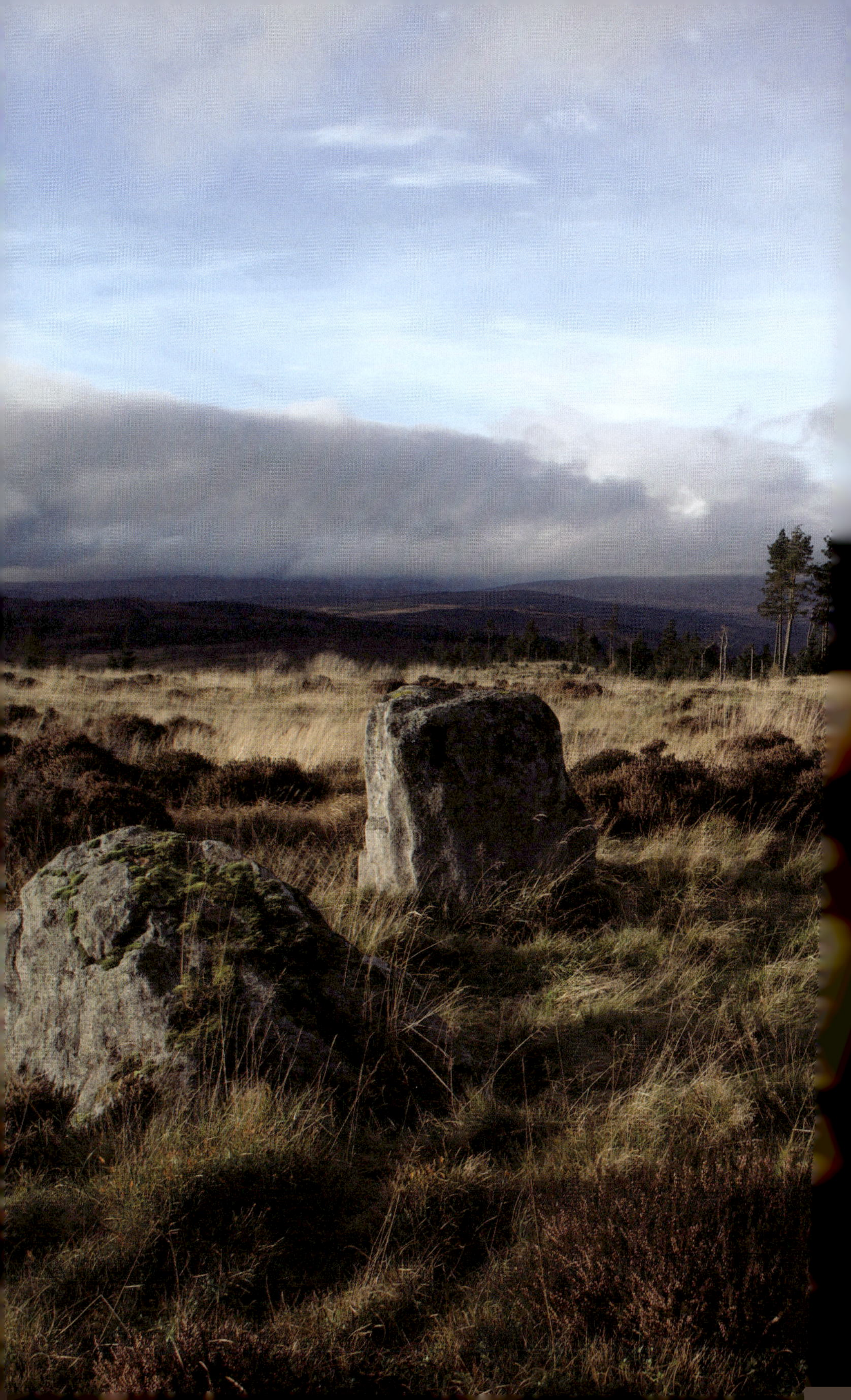

Sacred

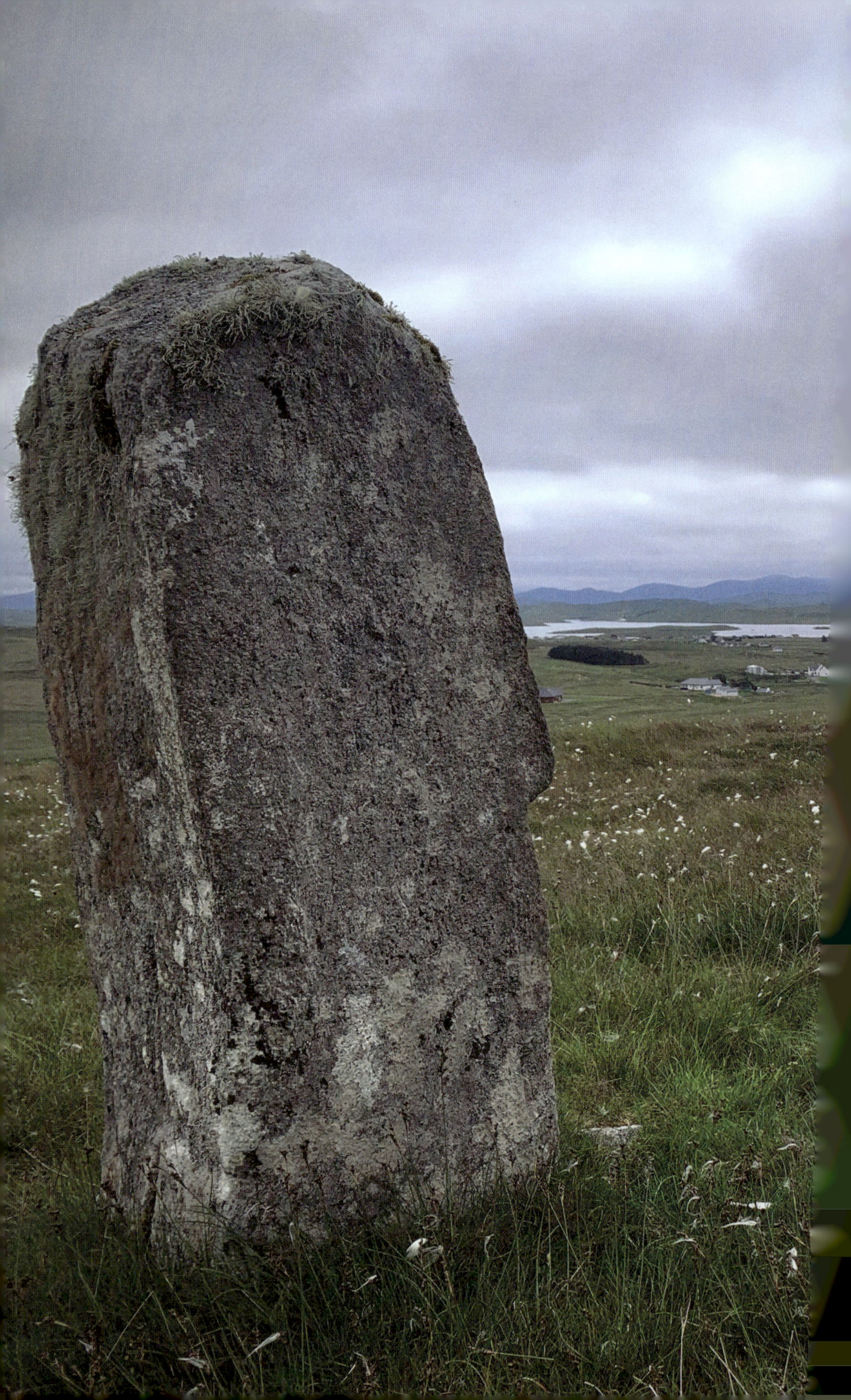

Callanish XI, Isle of Lewis

NB 2223 3569

Think of the soil that has built up over much of the bedrock of Scotland as being like thin skin over bone. Do almost anything to it and it leaves a mark, a permanent impression, like a wrinkle on your face. The traces of someone simply digging into the earth 2,000 years ago can still be visible today – a memory, if you like, preserved physically, tangibly, in the landscape. That is, of course, if you can still see the soil.

Around 1000 BC, Scotland's climate became wetter and cooler, encouraging the growth and spread of peat – its accumulated mass of partially decayed vegetation building up in acidic bogs and wetlands, sometimes in layers that are now several metres deep. Where peat has thrived – in the north of the country, and the Western Isles in particular – many of our ancient landscapes have been largely submerged. Those wrinkles are hidden away.

It was late July and I had come to the Isle of Lewis to meet Richard Bates, Professor of Earth and Environmental Sciences at the University of St Andrews. Over the past few years, Richard and his team of researchers have been spending their summers on Lewis, using geophysical survey techniques – especially electromagnetic and geomagnetic probes – to, in effect, *see through* the peat. Peeling away its obscuring mass and then, just possibly, finding and mapping those lost landscapes.

It was a still, overcast day as I drove across the flat boglands between Stornoway and Loch Roag, a large sea loch on the island's western coastline. Just a short distance before reaching its frayed, inundating shore, I turned off onto a single-track road that climbed steadily uphill past a smattering of farmhouses before crossing a cattle-grid and continuing on towards a stretch of open moorland. After a few hundred yards, I pulled into a square of scrub ground alongside the shell of an abandoned barn, now repurposed as a sheep enclosure, and climbed out of my car.

Richard was waiting for me a little way back down the road. A lean, avuncular Welshman with a grey-white moustache framing an easy smile, he was wearing the slightly incongruous outfit of a battered baseball cap and an extravagantly patterned Aran jumper. After a quick greeting, he was soon leading me up a steep slope pierced with shards of Lewisian gneiss, their grey knucklebones poking out through the earth. In between these rocky uprisings, the ground held the soft, springy mass of deep layers of peat – mercifully dry after several days of warm air, high pressure and no rain. Around a kilometre from the roadside, and some thirty metres above it in vertical height, the land briefly levelled out to a flat shelf carpeted with wildflowers and a mass of white-tipped bog cotton. Near the centre of this plateau was a single standing stone, a metre and a half tall and covered in pale green moss and thick patches of grey-white lichen. This is what is known as Callanish XI.

The name will, very likely, be familiar. Callanish is one of the most iconic Neolithic sites in the world – comprising an eighty-metre-long avenue of stones leading on to a circle of stones surrounding a huge, five-metre-high central monolith. The whole monument is erected on a rounded knoll surrounded by water and flat land. Once buried in over a metre and half of peat, its true scale was only revealed to the modern world in the middle of the nineteenth century. Today, this 'first' Callanish – numbered as site I – receives over 30,000 visitors a year. Its pull is so strong that many don't realise that it is just one part of a whole ritual landscape, a series of standing stones and burial cairns and stone circles all constructed in this same small area some 5,000 years ago. Callanish XI, for instance, is so ignored that the passage of feet has not even worn a path up to its high vantage point.

Such obscurity does not, however, necessarily equate to significance. As Richard pointed out to me, this is the only site to offer uninterrupted views to every other location in the Callanish landscape. We looked out from it almost directly south, with the great swathe of Loch Roag off to our right, running out north-west to the Atlantic Ocean. Water was everywhere in view, pools and lochs and lochans. A reminder that Lewis's ancient terrain is *twice* drowned – by the expanding peat, and by the rising seas. Callanish I was most prominent, up on its rocky plug; and beyond, shimmering blue-grey

Callanish XI, Lewis

in the distance, were the mountains of Harris, with the ridgeline known as the Cailleach na Mointeach, 'the Sleeping Mother', laid out in her peaceful, permanent slumber.

While only one stone stands here today, Richard's research has revealed that this may not always have been the case. 'We did see things beneath the peat,' he told me: what he called the 'signatures' of possible stones toppled over and buried in the ground. 'We don't absolutely know. We'd have to dig to be sure. But the signatures we get back are exactly the same as the signature for this one remaining standing stone.'

He showed me the visual readout of the geomagnetic survey. It was rendered in monochrome, with darker patches – tending from grey into black – representing areas of high electrical magneticity. Overlain on an aerial image of the site, there was the clear impression of a series of shadowy shapes forming in a pattern with the one remaining standing stone. Perhaps as many as thirteen hard black marks. The traces, it seems, of a lost stone circle.

These 'signature' results alone would have been a significant discovery. But they paled in comparison to something else on the readout: a huge anomaly, emerging from almost the exact centre of the ring of stones. Richard described it to me as a 'black cross', but I saw it more as a heavy, line-drawing of an eagle taking flight, head raised, wings aloft.

'In my career,' he said, 'I've only seen anomalies like this in very dry places like deserts. And they are formed by lightning strikes. Huge lightning strikes onto the ground.'

The geomagnetic survey was able to pick up the traces, left in the rock, from the electrical impact of a strike. But even more remarkable, here at Callanish XI, the lightning must have hit the ground *before* the arrival of the peat. As Richard explained to me, 'If it's wet ground, saturated ground, that just dissipates all the electricity. You don't get a signature.'

Given that the peat only began to spread and grow at the beginning of the first millennium BC, it means that Richard has discovered clear evidence of lightning hitting the earth here at least 3,000 years ago.

'Was the stone circle here,' Richard asked, 'and for some reason right at the centre there was a strike? Or did the strike happen, and somebody saw it and decided this was an important place, so let's build a stone circle around it?'

For as long as antiquarians and archaeologists have been uncovering and researching stone circles, they have been speculating on the reasons for their construction: as sites of arcane ritual; as primitive calendars; as devices for tracking the sun and moon or reading the stars. Richard's discovery had offered up a new theory. That they were built to either commemorate, or even call down, great bolts of electricity. Stone circles as ancient lightning rods.

Certainly, as I stood up on that plateau and looked out over the swathe of Lewis's landscape, I found myself increasingly seduced by the logic. And, whether this was the true answer or not, there was an undoubted thrill to stand on the exact spot of an ancient lightning strike. To look up at that grey summer sky and imagine a different time, thousands of years in the past, as a column of light screamed down from the clouds to hit the earth *right here*. Our wonder at the elemental power of nature has not dimmed between then and now.

    Richard's work continues. One 'anomaly' at the centre of a stone circle could always just be coincidence. But find another, and that coincidence tips over into a purpose. Further geomagnetic surveys are underway at more Callanish sites: Richard and his team engaged, quite literally, in the search for lightning striking twice.

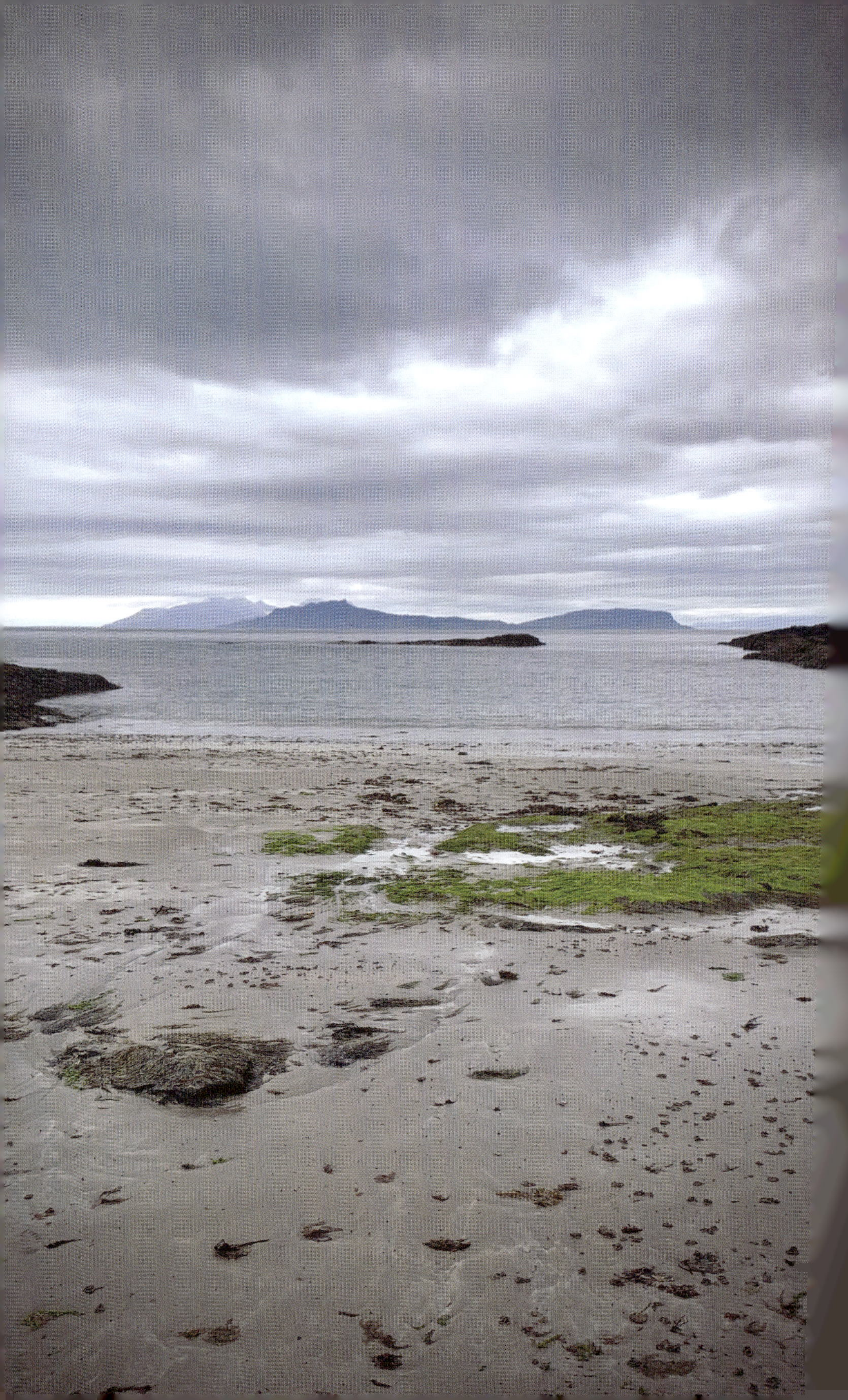

Viking Boat Burial, Swordle Bay, Ardnamurchan

NM 5459 7078

I approached the bay just as the captain and his crew would have done a thousand years earlier: sailing south, with the peninsula straight ahead, rising in silhouette like a great rock wall across the water. *Their* boat had been wooden, powered by oar and sail. Mine, on the other hand, was propelled by the constant, metronomic thrum of a diesel engine. Ten centuries separated us, but the fundamental elements of the landscape we passed through – the mountains, the coastline, the sea – had not really changed at all. Our view was their view.

The light had an unusual quality to it. High, grey clouds, lit by an early-summer sun, seemed to coat everything with a metallic-blue tinge. There was no wind, and the sea was calm. As our boat carved through the flat waves, they looked almost viscous, parting around the bow like liquid mercury.

The peninsula – our destination – was Ardnamurchan, its long finger of land pointing out almost directly west, towards the Outer Hebrides and the Atlantic Ocean. Near its tip is a great circle of mountainous rock, the last traces of a caldera, the crater left behind by a 60-million-year-old volcano. The legacy of this geological past is a rocky coastline, jagged and uneven, full of submerged reefs but also natural harbours, which cradle shallow, sheltered beaches of pale white sand.

Sometime around the tenth century AD, a group of Vikings landed on one of these beaches – at a place known as Swordle Bay. (The name itself is derived from the Old Norse for 'green valley'.) Once there, they dragged a boat up to a grassy shelf set just above the shoreline. And then they began to dig.

Wild History

First, they carved out a long channel, big enough to fit their boat. Then within the boat, they placed the dead body of one of their crew. Once in position, with the head facing west, they arranged possessions all around – a sword with a silver pommel and a hilt fashioned from bone, a drinking horn, pottery from the Hebrides, a bronze ring pin from Ireland, a whetsone from Norway. Stones were then laid over the body, and on top of those were placed a shield and a spear. Finally, more stones and earth were piled up to seal the grave.

I made my own landing on Swordle Bay, transferring from our boat to the beach by rubber dinghy, with a pod of three curious dolphins cresting the water alongside. The tide was out, making the beach into a long, narrow strip, bordered on either side by straight rocky outcrops. After pulling the dinghy up through the waves, I walked over the wet sands and climbed onto that same shoreline. Just a few metres further, in a little field of buttercups and seagrass, I came across an oval of rough stones, around three metres long and perhaps a metre and a half wide.

It was an unprepossessing feature, and it would have been very easy to ignore or dismiss. Indeed, the archaeologists who first came to investigate this bay in 2011 thought initially that it was just debris deposited by a farmer clearing small boulders from his fields. Until they began to look a little closer and discovered the fragments of hundreds of metal rivets – all laid out in that same oval pattern. The last traces of that buried boat.

This discovery was the first complete Viking boat burial ever found in the British Isles. Boat burials were rituals reserved only for individuals of the highest status – chieftains, or great, ocean-going adventurers. When the archaeologists came to excavate the mound, all that remained of the body were several teeth and a fragment of an arm bone – but it was enough for laboratory testing to discover that it was a man, and that he originally came from a coastal village in Norway. We can only speculate as to how he ended up in a grave set on Scotland's Atlantic seaboard. But perhaps even more remarkable is that he was not alone. His burial was, in fact, just one of a number of monuments to the dead created here, going back almost 6,000 years.

On a hillock just above the Viking grave, there are the remains of a stone cairn, built around 4000 BC, with an internal chamber that was found to hold

Viking Boat Burial, Swordle Bay

human remains. Over time, different people had been interred in the cairn – the charred fragments from cremations, tightly bound bundles of bones. And then finally, a thousand years after it was first constructed, a single, complete body was laid inside, along with pieces of pottery. This last burial saw the cairn sealed for good. Around 1800 BC, however, and just a few metres away, a new tomb was built. Again, a single body was placed inside, with a necklace fashioned from jade beads – a sure sign of far-flung trading connections.

Clearly there was something special about this bay, something that kept bringing different people here, over an exceptionally long period of time, to commemorate their dead. Standing there at that moment, overlooking the beach and the still waters to the north-west, that 'something' did not seem too hard to discern. Far more than today, the lives of our ancestors, both ancient and recent, were connected intimately to the sea. Bays like Swordle were gateways, bridging points. The way to reach the rest of the world.

I walked away from the grave, back across the sands to the waters' edge. The tide was coming back in now, but the sea was so flat that the breaking waves barely registered, each one just a tiny wrinkle leading out to a glass-flat expanse. It was deceptively peaceful. This same bay will, of course, have been lashed by storm and spray, the whole force of the Atlantic thrown against it. But for the moment it was a model of tranquillity and solitude.

You could, I suppose, look at a place like Swordle Bay and think that it is about death. But that wasn't how it seemed to me. Yes, there was a history of burial here that went back millennia. But that Viking in his boat, those ancient cairns – they were also all symbols of life, of a connection to this land and to the sea beyond. Certainly, as final resting places go, this one is surely hard to beat. That view across the sands, out past Eigg and Rum, to where the sun sets on the open water. Whether in death – or in life – you are always gazing towards that horizon. And wondering where it will take you.

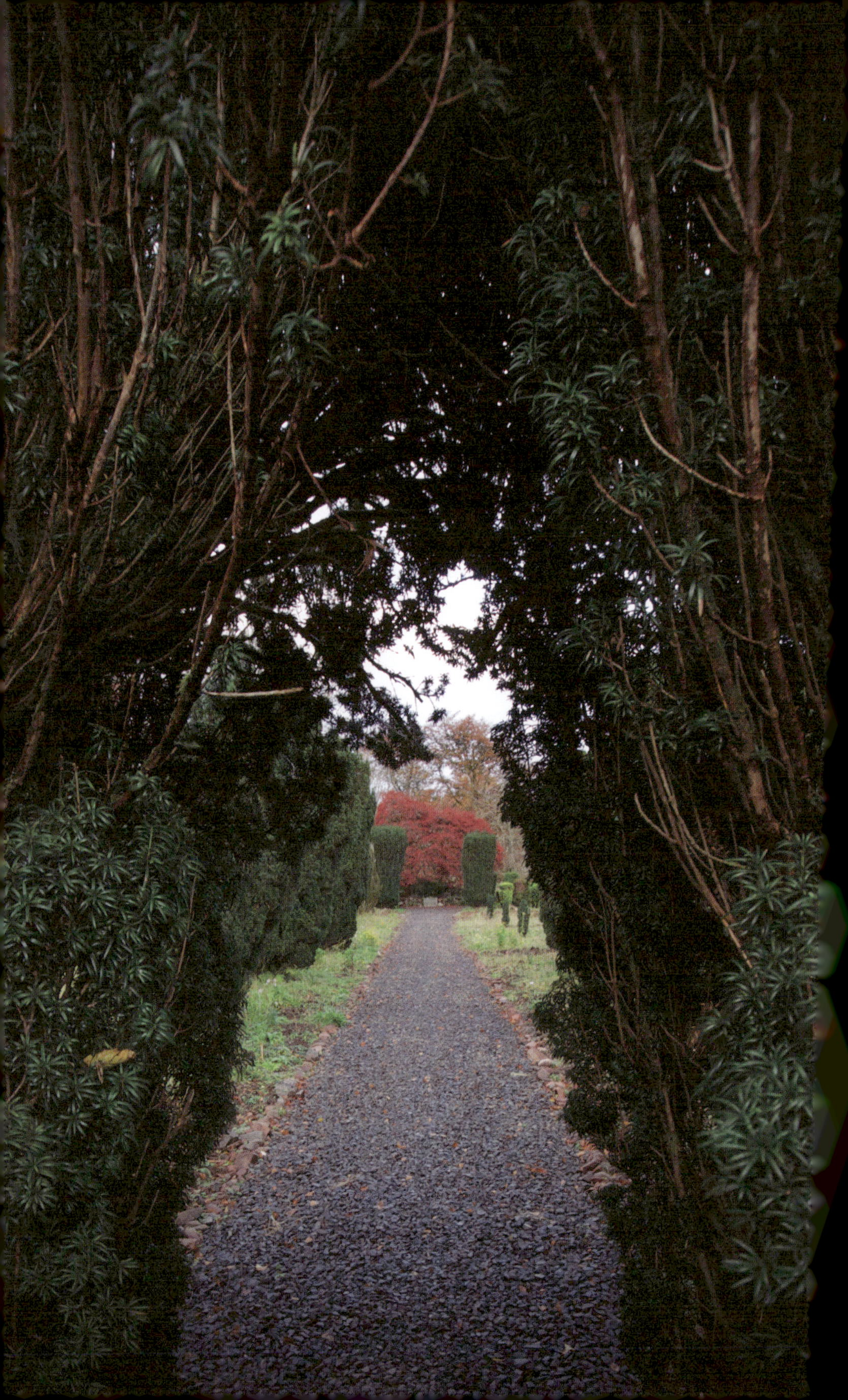

Glencruitten 'Cathedral of Trees', Oban

NM 8813 2928

I had made the detour on my way to catch a ferry to the Isle of Mull, turning south at Connel to follow a narrow, single-track road into the low, rolling hills that rise above Loch Etive. This route traced the course of the Lusragan Burn into a quiet valley. Farmers' fields ran down to the river, while clumps of birch, elm, beech and Scots pine ranged over the higher slopes, surrounded by expanses of bracken that had tipped from burnt orange into a kind of lurid red. It was the last days of autumn, and the landscape was in that final state of bright decay before the dulling onset of winter.

After a few miles, the road turned west and crested the Black Mount, the last rise before the land dips back down towards Oban and the sea. Near the summit, a stony track led past a white gatehouse into a dense bank of trees: the entrance to seventy hectares of woodland surrounding the late-nineteenth-century baronial mansion of Glencruitten House. Much of it was given over to plantations of Sitka spruce. I parked and followed a forestry track through an avenue of trees. The trees soon gave way to swathes of recent harvesting: neat piles of logs sitting alongside long, torn-up stretches of hillside. The track dipped down between two steep knolls to reach a little flat plateau. There, amid all the stumps and broken branches and shattered soil, was a tiny, scrappy oasis.

A beech hedge had been laid out in a clear rectangular shape, its leaves a mix of gold and ochre. There was a narrow break in the hedge at one end, revealing a neat path of grey pebbles that ran in a straight line through two yews that overlapped to from an archway. A makeshift postbox had been formed out of wooden planks and two slabs of slate. It held a flowerpot with a sign asking me to drop a pebble in the pot to record my visit. I scooped up a stone from the ground and added it to the four that were already there. Above the pot there was another message, this one welcoming me to the 'Cathedral of Trees'.

The foundations of this cathedral – its literal roots – are now a century old. Its architect was Alexander Mackay, the founder of a Dundee accountancy firm who went on to develop trans-Atlantic business interests in everything from Texas cattle ranching to Arizona copper mining. Mackay bought the Glencruitten estate in 1917, and straight away – in response to the dire timber shortage at the end of the First World War – dedicated most of its land to afforestation. The scale of the planting drew a large local workforce, particularly the many veterans returning from the trenches of the Western Front.

As time passed, however, Mackay noticed that there was one area – a little flat patch of valley at the bottom of two slopes – where the trees just would not take. Beginning in 1921, he began to focus intently on this stretch of boggy ground, determined to 'redeem' the land, as he put it. More workers were brought in to dig out extensive drainage channels and, once complete, Mackay himself drew up very specific instructions for what to do with the space.

Instead of tightly packed rows of Sitka spruce, lime trees were planted in the outline of a large, boxy cross. A second outline, just inside the first, was made of beech and chestnut trees. These were to act as the external walls of what Mackay envisaged as a 'living' building: a tree cathedral that modelled its size and layout on the great medieval cathedral of St Andrews. Inside, Irish yew trees were laid out and closely clipped as rows of 'pillars' running along an eighty-metre-long central 'aisle'; three golden yews were the 'choir stalls' – complete with 'book rests' – while the 'altar cross' was a mix of another golden yew and a bank of dwarf junipers. Behind the altar was a 'stained glass window', facing to the east. The impression of sunlight pouring through this window was formed by the bright crimson leaves of a red Japanese maple.

Mackay intended the tree cathedral as a memorial to the fallen of the Great War – all those men who never returned from the fields of Belgium and France. For years it grew taller and stronger. In 1936 Mackay died and was himself buried beneath the maple tree. Ten years later, his wife Edith was buried on the same plot of ground. And so, subsequently, were other members of his family.

In the early 1960s, the cathedral, which had always been open to public visits, was closed. The trees remained, of course, but largely untended and so the 'structure', such as it was, soon fell into disrepair. The rapid growth of the surrounding commercial spruce increasingly cut out the light, and the ground grew wet and boggy once again.

In 2016 the site came under the management of a charity established to carry out a 'restoration' of the cathedral. Ever so slowly, the old building was reclaiming its shape after decades of abandonment. 'Walls' were being repaired, the 'floors' cleared and swept, ready to be replanted in a 'mosaic' of grass and flowers. I had come, of course, at a time of natural deterioration. A living building cannot help but turn threadbare as winter approaches: its walls had collapsed all around it, its flowers withered, only its yew pillars remaining solid and strong. Maple leaves lay in a red carpet all around the graves of Mackay and his family.

I left the cathedral, passing back through its yew archway, to climb up the slope directly opposite, scrambling over the mass of now-smashed spruce that had cut out its light for so many years. High banks of grey cloud were being split by tendrils of blue sky. To the east, I could see patches of sunlight drifting across the orange slopes of Beinn Mheadhonach. The panorama continued to include the great bulky head of Ben Cruachan, snow-capped and partly obscured by mist. The cathedral stretched out below me, pointing towards those distant mountains, its outline still bare and haphazard. It remained a ruin – but a ruin that was different, I suppose, to any other I had ever seen. A ruin that was able, with a little help and attention, to renew itself. To rise up from its crumbling remains according to a blueprint written into the earth a hundred years earlier: a blueprint still preserved in the composition, the nutrients – even the 'seed memory' – of the soil.

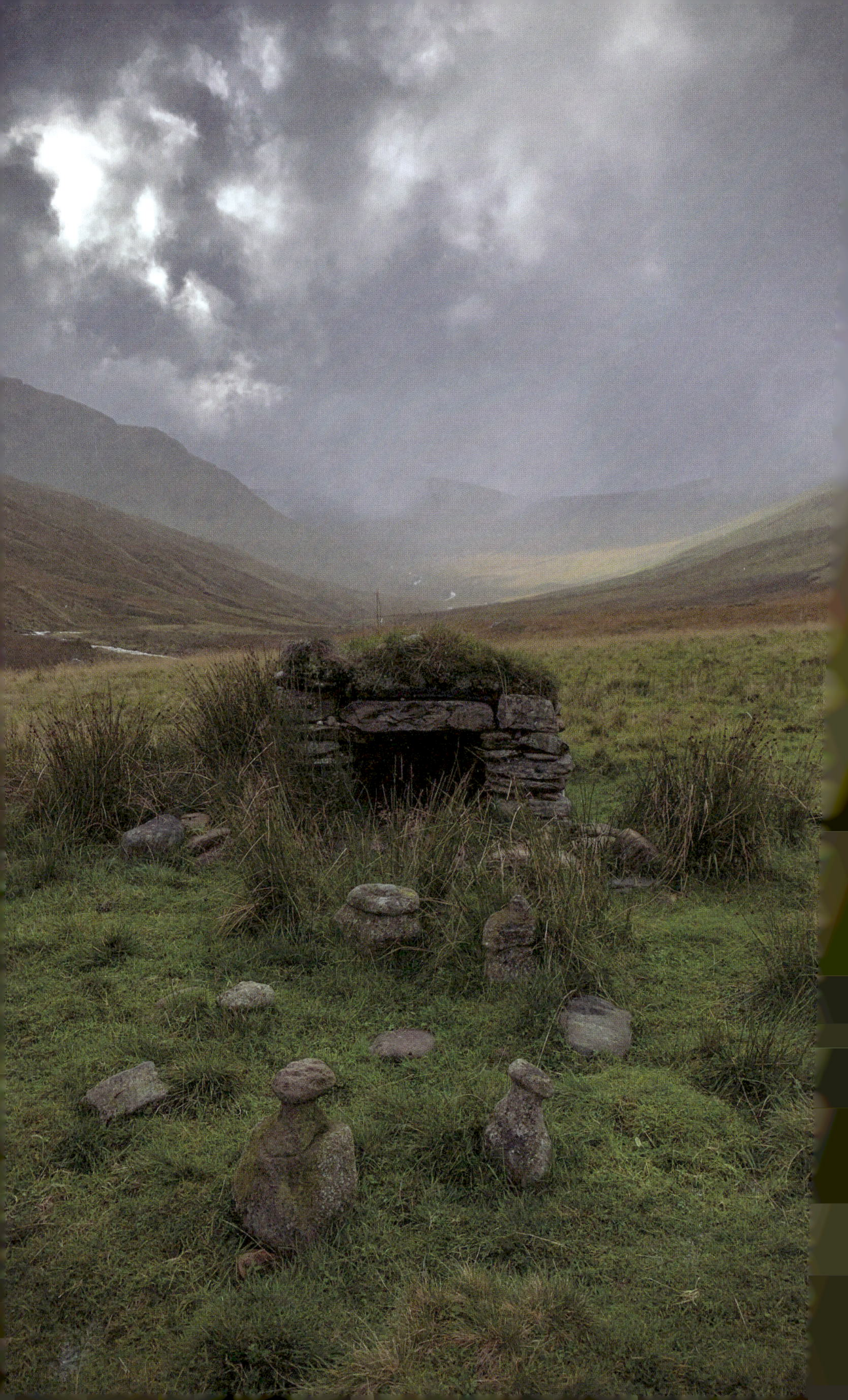

Tigh na Cailleach, Glen Lyon

NN 3805 4271

The weather came in over the mountains at the head of the glen. Tall clouds, white-tipped but dark-bodied, were flowing down the slopes of Meall Buidhe, Beinn Achaladair and Beinn a' Chuirn. The sun was enveloped and, within seconds, the first intermittent spots of rain, racing ahead like a raiding party, arrived on the wind. I was standing in front of Tigh na Cailleach, the 'house, or shrine, of the Cailleach'. And now, it seemed, the Cailleach herself had arrived.

In Gaelic mythology, the Cailleach could be many things. Meaning literally 'old woman' or 'hag' – and derived from the Old Irish for 'veiled one' – she began as a divine giantess, responsible for the creation of the whole landscape of Scotland. According to one legend, she fashioned the country out of rocks she had carried across the sea from Norway. The outlying islands of the Hebrides were pebbles that had fallen from her creel, while the great lump of Ailsa Craig was a stone that had dropped through a hole in her apron.

The Cailleach was also the harbinger of winter – a storm-raising elemental, who carried a hammer to shape the hills and a staff to freeze the ground. She was said to travel each autumn to the tidal whirlpool of Corryvreckan between the islands of Jura and Scarba. There she would wash her great plaid (in Gaelic, Corryvreckan means 'cauldron of the plaid'), a process that would create a huge tempest that raged for days. Once finished, her plaid would emerge a pure, pristine white and the first snows of winter would cover the land.

Over time, the Cailleach became less a titanic, godlike figure and more akin to a nature spirit. Wanderers in the hills or the forests would tell of seeing an old woman clad in grey, her hair – 'white as an aspen covered in hoar frost', as the folklorist Donald Mackenzie put it – and her skin a dull, icy blue. She was said to be the mistress of the deer herds, leading them safely through the harsh extremes of winter. For a hunter to see the Cailleach was a bad omen – they were sure to return home empty-handed. Even worse if the Cailleach transformed herself into a hind, which was a trick intended to lead anyone foolish enough to follow her down into the underworld.

As the centuries passed, however, these sightings waned. Writing in 1900, in *Superstitions of the Highlands and Islands of Scotland*, John Gregorson Campbell claimed that the Cailleach hadn't been seen since around 1880, when there was an account of her appearing in Lochaber. By this point, the former giantess was so diminished – shrunken, perhaps, by a lack of belief – that she was said to be 'no bigger than a teapot'. In 1917 a gamekeeper reported seeing her in the hills near Corrour, just north of Rannoch Moor. And then nothing. The Cailleach had disappeared from the very land that she had created. Or, perhaps, she had retreated to its heart.

I had come to look for her in a place that is set almost exactly in the centre of Scotland. Glen Lyon is the country's longest enclosed glen, running for thirty-four miles from the village of Fortingall in the east, to the tip of Loch Lyon in the west. And it is very much enclosed. Mountains press in on the narrow course of the River Lyon as it runs downstream to join up with the River Tay. It is not a 'lost' valley – there is another village, Bridge of Balgie, halfway along it; and a smattering of farms and houses – but even today, getting there is a commitment.

I had driven on the narrow single track that rises steeply from Loch Tay to wind along the slopes flanking the great bulk of Ben Lawers. Topping out at around 1,800 feet, it then begins to drop down again into the tight 'V' of the glen at Bridge of Balgie. It takes another ten miles along a road of near endless undulations to reach Lubreoch Dam. Constructed in the 1950s to create the vast, five-mile-long stretch of Loch Lyon, it was a piece of monumental landscape manipulation of which the Cailleach herself might have been proud.

From the dam head, I followed another four miles of track on foot. The clouds hung dark and heavy on the mountains, but the sky above the loch was clear, and its waters shimmered in blue and silver. Halfway along the

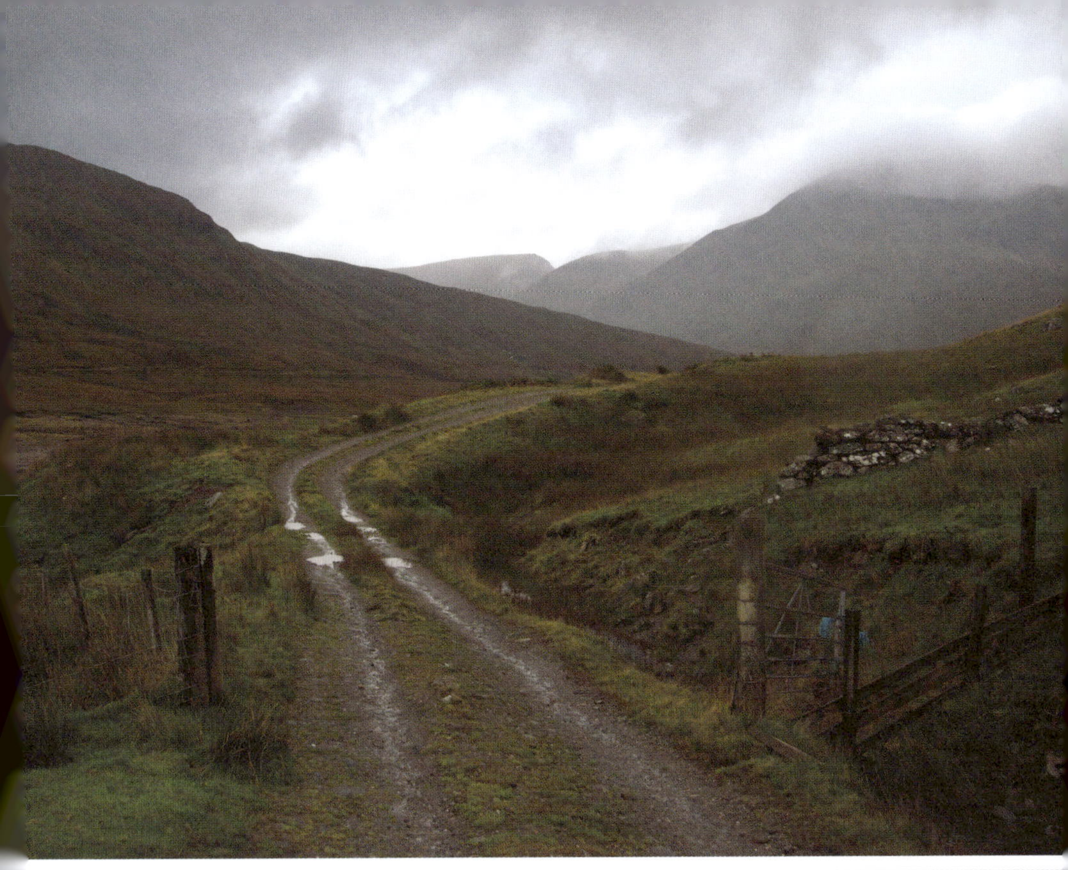

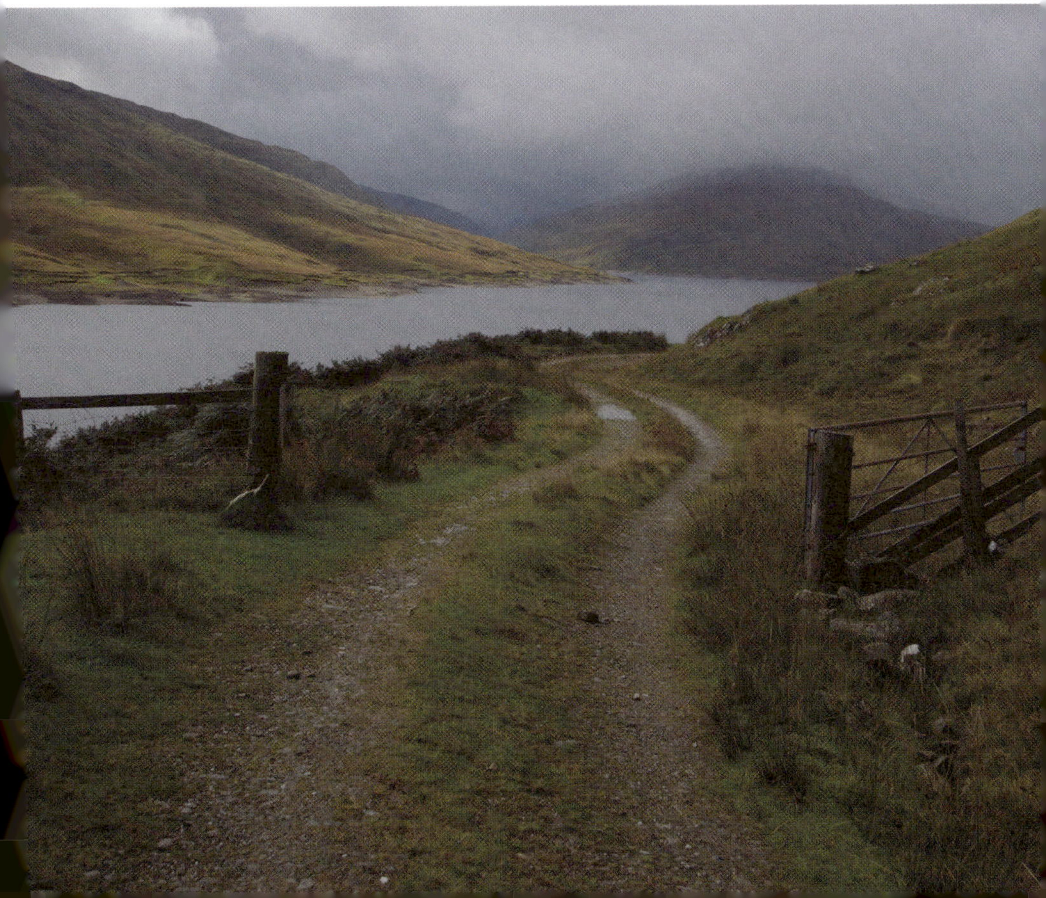

loch, the track turned to the north to reach a ford crossing the Allt Meurain river. Days of autumn rain had swollen and widened it, and I had to wade across in bare feet – the water, in places, rising up to my knees. Thankfully, the current was not strong. Traces of ruined houses, abandoned shielings and sheep enclosures were all around. An eagle appeared in the distance, its huge wings flapping lazily as it crossed my path and then curved around a hillside, disappearing from view. On the other side of the river, the track began to rise steadily into a narrow valley leading away from the loch. It is known as Gleann Cailliche, 'the glen of the Cailleach'.

According to another folklorist, Dr Anne Ross, this was where the Cailleach had come. Researching this region in the 1970s, she uncovered a story passed down by the people who had once lived in a farming community near the head of the glen. During a fierce snowstorm, it was said, a man and a woman – with grey hair and eerie blue skin – had walked down from the high mountainside. The two strangers asked for shelter and, grateful for the hospitality they received, decided to stay for good, living in a thatched house that was built for them. Immediately, the weather in the glen improved, bringing mild winters and warm, dry summers. Crops and animals thrived. The couple remained there for years, and the woman even gave birth to a daughter.

But one day they announced that it was time for them to move on. Before leaving, they told the crofters that, if their house was kept in good order and not allowed to fall into ruin, then the climate which the glen had enjoyed since their arrival would hold and 'peace and prosperity would always be with the people who had been so generous to them'.

It was there, between the path and a fast-flowing river – the Allt Cailliche – that I found the house. Or at least a version of it: a tiny representation of a dwelling place, a couple of metres wide and half a metre high. It was made up of three walls of dressed stone with a solid lintel doorway facing to the east, roofed by a thick clump of turf and moss. Four river-worn stones stood in front of the entrance, taking the abstract shape of human figures. These were the statues of the Cailleach and her family.

Every May Day – according to that old tradition – the statues are taken out of the house and placed facing down the glen. And every Halloween, they are returned inside, to wait out the winter. Some accounts suggest that

Tigh na Cailleach, Glen Lyon

this ritual has been going on since at least the end of the eighteenth century. In the twentieth century, it was kept up by the glen's gamekeeper, Bob Bissett, and, after he retired, the task was taken on by his successors.

The sun had been shining when I arrived at the house but, almost as soon as I had dropped my backpack and begun taking photographs, the clouds seemed to build to the west. This end of the glen was a steep funnel – mountains on either side like sheer walls, with the three peaks at the head a steep delivery chute for approaching weather. Within minutes, rain was falling hard and steady, wet spots blowing straight onto my camera lens. The glen felt tight and close all around me, and I had the overwhelming feeling of being watched (by the Cailleach? Or, rather more likely, by the current gamekeeper, from somewhere up on the hills above). This place was secluded – or isolated, depending on how you wanted to see it. An intimate space: and I was an outsider. The notion was fanciful – that the Cailleach had sent down one of her storms because she did not want her shrine disturbed. But after hours of driving and walking in solitude to one of the most far-removed places in the country, it was still hard to shake. I crouched down to stare at the figures, their sandstone bodies smoothed by water, and they stared back at me. It was the middle of October. In a couple of weeks, they would be inside their home again, sheltered from the winter for another season.

I still had four miles to hike back to my car, and the sky over the glen to the west was looking heavy and threatening. I left the shrine, turned to the east and retraced my steps down the track towards the loch. Within minutes, the rain moved on and the sun was breaking the clouds.

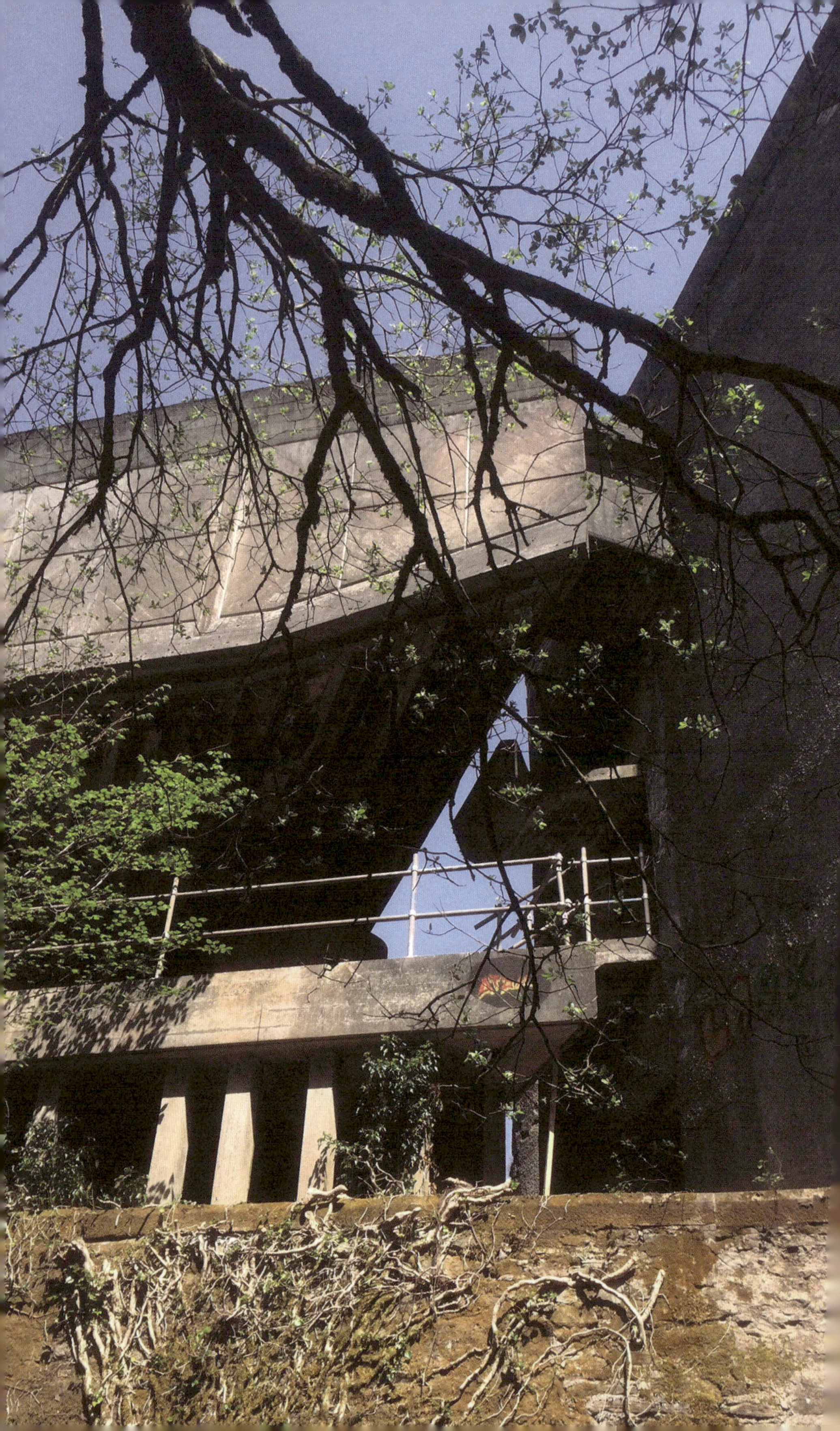

St Peter's Seminary, Cardross

NS 3530 7840

I entered the woods beneath a sky more Mediterranean than Scottish – a high, liquid blue, unblemished by any hint of cloud. It was a late morning in the middle of May, the air hot and still. Light slanted through the thick tree canopy in shards. A dusty road wound up the hill ahead of me, crossed the narrow gorge of the Kilmahew Burn by a latticed, wrought-iron bridge, then climbed an ever-steepening slope.

The concrete, when I first saw it, was shining grey-gold in the sun. A great slab of curving wall emerged from the treetops. The road curved alongside this wall – which bent back in on itself in a tight spiral – then passed through the gate of a high steel fence to reveal five large concrete knuckles, like a series of grain silos pressed together. Rising above them was a hulking structure, taking the form of four long, harled steps rising to a flat, and mostly missing, roof. There were no windows, no doors, nothing at all beyond the bare frame of the building itself. That perfect blue sky poured through the gaps.

This strange edifice, nestled and concealed by dense woodland, owed its existence to fire. In 1946 a college for trainee priests in Bearsden in the northwest of Glasgow burned to the ground. Two years later, the college – which was known as St Peter's – moved to occupy a Victorian-era, Baronial-style mansion, originally built on this hilltop for the son of the founder of the trans-Atlantic Cunard Line. Another five years on and the decision was taken to commission an extension, to be designed in a late-Modernist style by the Glasgow architects Gillespie, Kidd & Coia.

For decades, Gillespie, Kidd & Coia had been the firm of choice for Scotland's Catholic Church, and in particular the archdiocese of Glasgow. The postwar period had seen radical changes to the social fabric of the city, with mass demolitions of the old, decaying tenements, and the relocation of large sections of the population to new homes or, indeed, entirely new towns. These communities – often built from scratch – needed purpose-built places for religious education and worship. And so, increasingly, modern architecture began to reimagine what spaces for faith and spiritualism could look like. Churches were being built to stark and striking geometric designs – all hard lines and unadorned exteriors, fashioned in great slabs, or huge boxes. Everything from roofs and walls, even down to crosses and altars, was being cast in bare concrete.

All of these ideas and innovations were poured into the designs for the new St Peter's College, a vast extension which would surround – and in size, dwarf – the old mansion house. There was a huge central sanctuary space, above which ran three floors of student accommodation 'cells', linked by internal and external walkways. There were kitchens, libraries and reading rooms, a wide-open refectory area, a series of small 'side chapels' created out of 'semi-domes' of brick and concrete – those 'grain silos' I had seen when I arrived – a basement crypt and a great central altar formed by a slab of solid granite. An additional, wedge-shaped classroom block was set at right angles to the main sanctuary, on the very edge of the steep drop down into the valley below, appearing to defy gravity as it cantilevered out into empty space. Viewed in crude terms, the whole thing had the appearance of a UFO crash-landed from outer space, or at least from the West Coast of California, which, in the context of a hillside above the little town of Cardross on the Firth of Clyde in the 1960s, amounted to pretty much the same thing.

The new seminary was finally opened in November 1966. And, almost instantly, it was an anachronism. The previous year had seen a fundamental shift in Catholic Church policy – most specifically a desire that priests be trained not in isolated seclusion, but in the heart of the communities that they would come to serve. As one of the lecturers at St Peter's, Father James Foley, said of the college, 'There was a false monasticism in the design, a modernisation of the monastic concept. But the diocesan clergy were not meant to be monks!'

There was also the rather more basic matter of the fabric of the building itself. Doors and windows constantly broke and jammed. The central heating

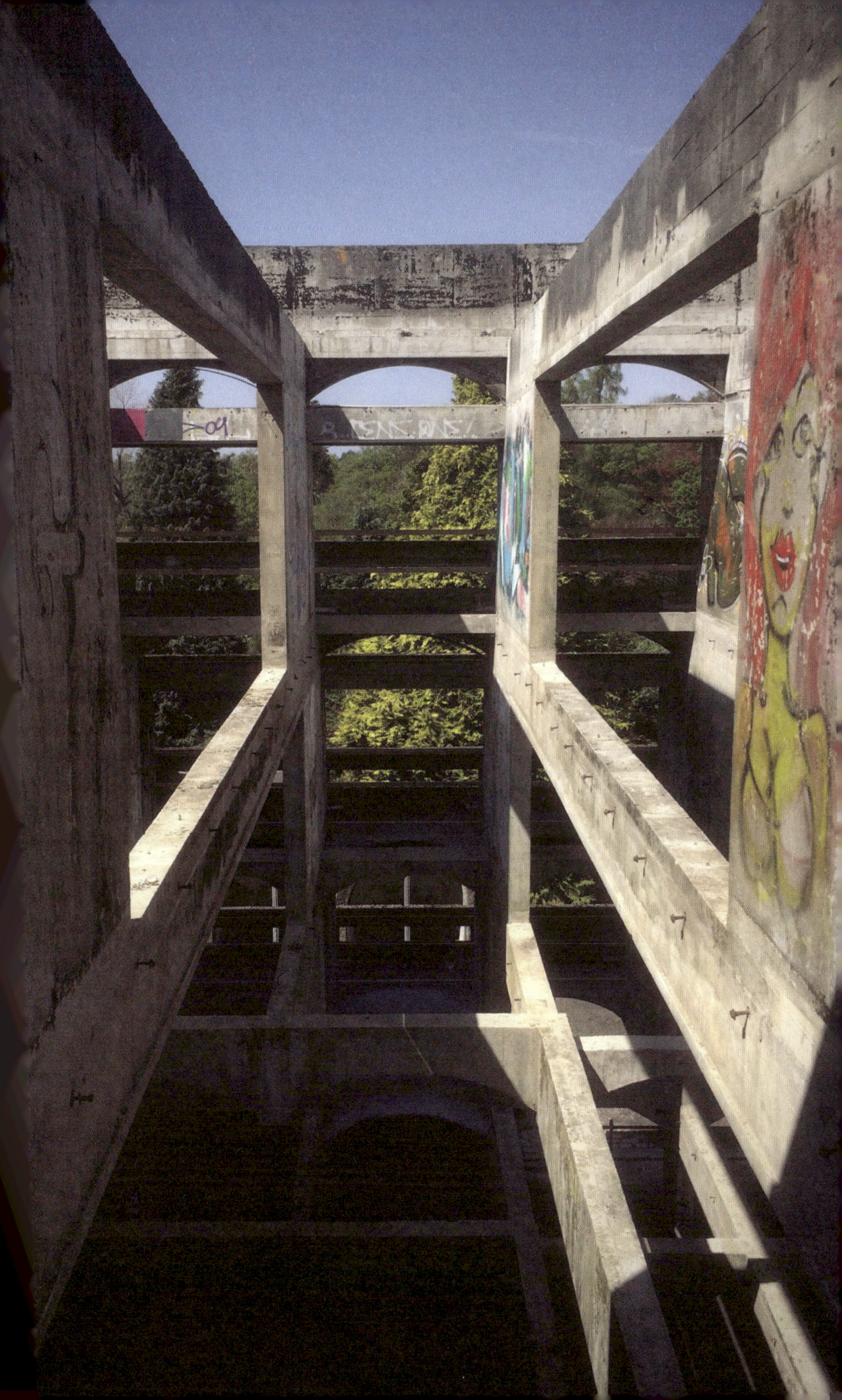

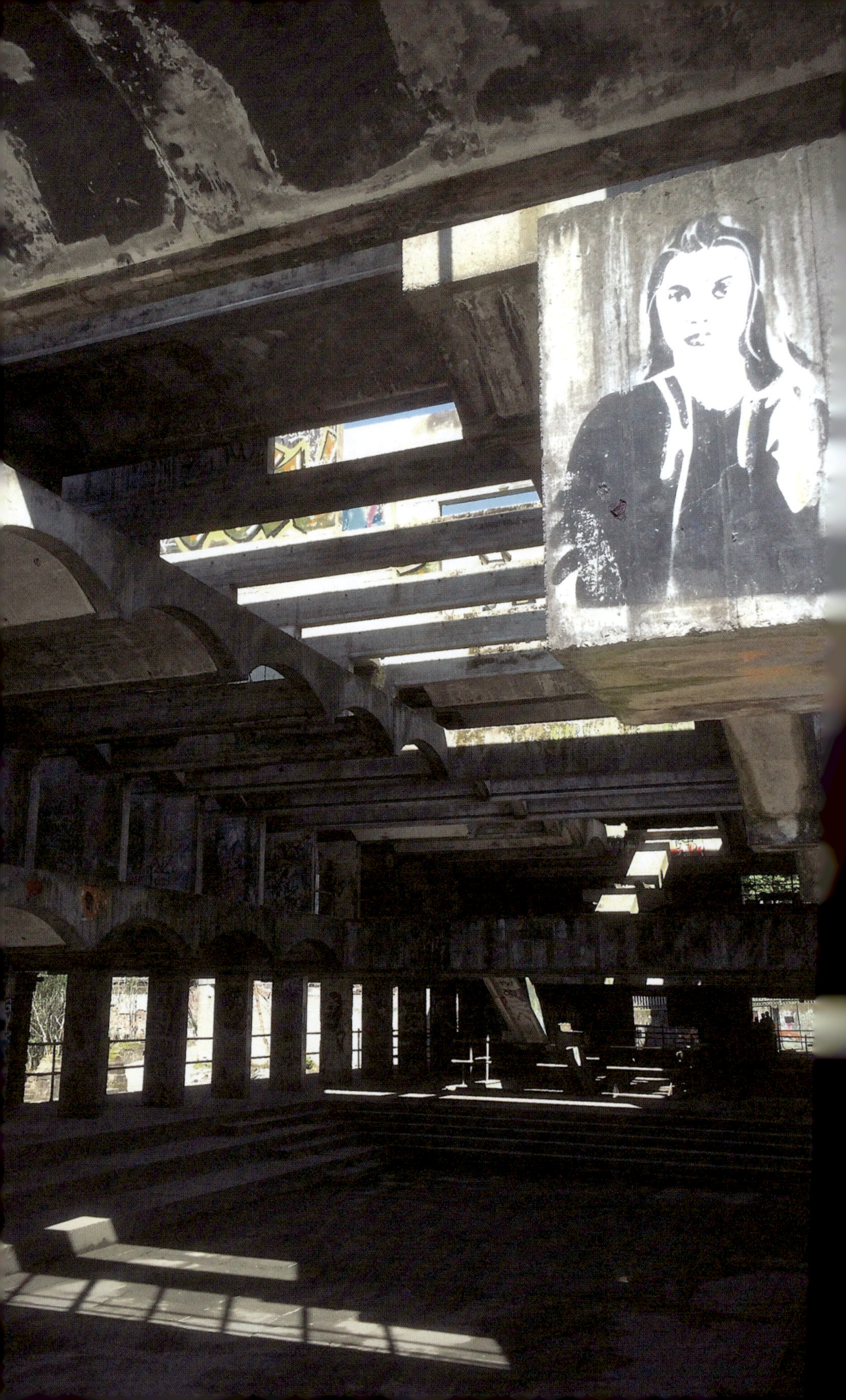

struggled to warm the space sufficiently. Most problematic of all was the impact of the wind and rain. The building was continually springing leaks – one resident trainee counted fifty-three separate holes in the sanctuary roof one morning. Creeping damp was colonising the stone and the woodwork. When one priest, Father Fitzsimmons, raised the issues with the architects, he was simply told by the head of the firm, Jack Coia, that 'God did not create a perfect world'.

In 1979, just thirteen years after it was opened, the decision was taken to abandon St Peter's. It closed for good in February 1980 and – apart from a brief repurposing as a drug rehabilitation centre – was never used again. What followed were four decades of decay, vandalism and destruction. The old mansion house was gutted by fire and, in 1994, the decision was taken to demolish it. This left just the ruin of the Modernist extension: left without the building that it was originally designed to extend. Increasingly a site of illicit partying and urban exploration, it had become a kind of post-apocalyptic shell, its walls covered in graffiti, its structure ravaged by the weather. It had also, at the same time, received Category A listing – the highest level of heritage 'protection' – as one of Scotland's most important examples of twentieth-century architecture. And so began a – still unending – cycle of proposals and projects aimed at preserving or repurposing St Peter's. All of which have failed.

I had made my visit in a moment of optimism. The site had been acquired by an independent arts organisation called NVA, whose aim was to turn it into a curated ruin-cum-arts venue, and home of what they called the 'Invisible College' – a network of writers, thinkers, researchers, architects and local people who would use the building as a 'centre for informal leaning and a locus for debate and new thinking'. A full-scale industrial clean-up of the site had been carried out, and I had arrived the day after it was finished, in the late spring of 2016. Decades' worth of detritus had been removed – huge accumulations of shattered wood and glass and metal, great piles of mud and muck and moss, little forests of weeds and bracken sprouting from every floor and flat surface.

This was the most pristine the site had been since the time of its abandonment – indeed, given the issues with damp and flooding, perhaps since its initial construction. There was something both bizarre and affecting about it all. Walking the polished shell of a building that had first failed, then been abandoned, then been left to rot; and yet, all at the same time, had acquired a cult-like status as the perfect, tragic, 'iconic' modern ruin – a place of pilgrimage for generations of architectural devotees. As the architectural historian and long-term 'biographer' of the fate of St Peter's, Diane Watters, has described it: with the building's emergence as a 'legendary' and almost 'mythical' space, it had long ago been set adrift from any connection to its original purpose as a college for priests. 'It might be more accurate,' she wrote, 'to talk of today's complex as an essentially new artistic project, constructed around a postwar architectural skeleton.'

I climbed all around this skeleton, up and down its floors, along the rim of its broken roof, across the bare walkway to the open shell of its impressively projecting classroom block. It was a place that demanded to be seen in bright sunlight, the concrete awash with dark shadows, its hard lines sharp and clear against that flawless sky. With only the gentlest breeze whispering through the superstructure, and with a drowsy heat filling the air, it felt like stepping into a painting by Giorgio de Chirico. It held the quiet aura of a monolithic temple: although a temple to what, or to whom, remained entirely unclear. Not to the original building, that was for sure. It was dead and gone.

In the end, NVA's ambitious project foundered. The money ran out and St Peter's time in limbo, now approaching half a century in duration, goes on. Before he died, one of the building's architects, Isi Metzstein, expressed his desire that 'everything be stripped away apart from the concrete itself – a purely romantic conception of the building as a beautiful ruin'. This stripped-back skeleton persists, even if no one knows what to do with it. In 2019, the government declined an appeal to take it into state care, instead describing its long-term fate as one of 'curated decay' – whatever that means. Slowly, the weeds and the rubbish and the suffocating rhododendrons are returning. The woodlands are swallowing the bones once again.

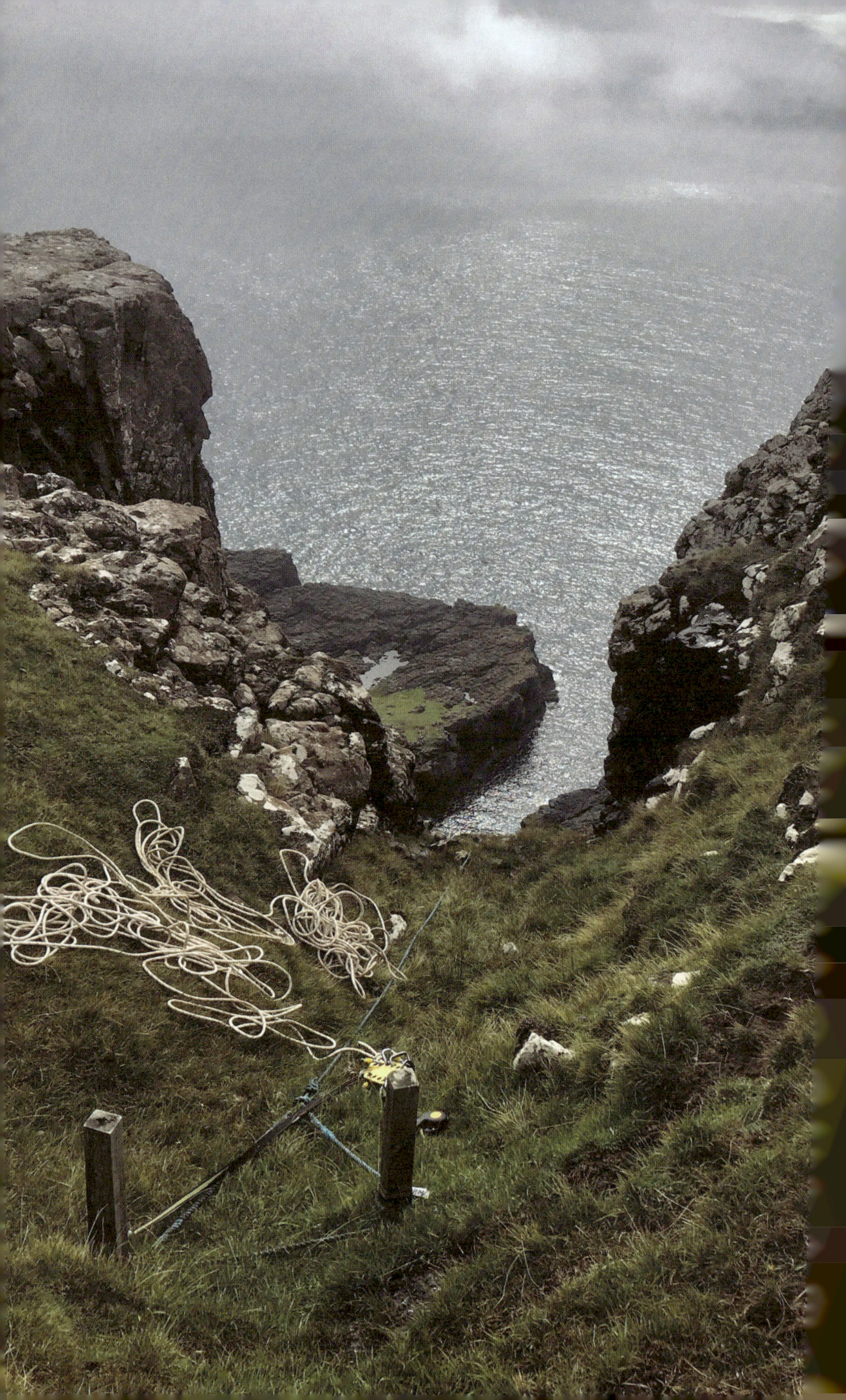

Sgorr nam Ban-Naomha, 'The Cliffs of the Holy Women', Isle of Canna

NG 2299 0439

Two wooden posts were sunk into the earth, about a metre apart. Thick, turquoise-blue ropes were tied off around each post and then knotted together into a single strand. From there, the rope ran down a small depression in the cliffside before disappearing over a precipice. Through that gap, a hundred metres below, I could glimpse a rocky headland jutting out from the base of the cliffs. Beyond that was a slate-grey sea, shimmering here and there with white sunspots.

We had left Mallaig at dawn, our boat pulling out into fog and smirr. The wind was light and, as we crossed over to Skye, the fog began to lift – only to reveal a high canopy of mottled-grey clouds. Waiting at the harbour at Armadale was Jonah, a mountain guide who would help with the cliff descent on Canna. For the next two hours we rounded the rocky, abrasive northern flank of Rum. In one of many seemingly inaccessible bays, a shipwreck was wedged between a pink sandstone cliff and a giant sea stack. It has been there for years now, a French fishing trawler run aground en route to Ireland after it lost its bearings in a squall. It was called the *Jack Arby II*, and it has joined a long list of wrecks on this same stretch of island coastline. Other losses include the *Bounteous*, a steam trawler that was driven ashore in December 1917; the *Midas*, a wooden barque out of Kragero in Norway that foundered at Kilmory Bay in December 1896; and a nameless American ship, which sank just off Guirdil Bay in 1819, but reputedly left a single box of ribbons behind, bobbing on the surface.

A millennium and a half ago, another boat journeyed through these waters. It was made of wicker and stretched animal skins, most probably cowhide, the joins between hides sealed together with tar. A small group travelled in the boat, not more than a dozen perhaps. Most, if not all, would have been manning the oars. You assume they picked their day. Waited until the skies were clear, the seas calm, the wind favourable. Did they talk or sing as they rowed? Or pray? How many hours would it have taken? They passed the dark, jagged shadow of Rum and, stroke by stroke, reeled in the island beyond.

Perhaps they knew it by its ancient name, An t'Eilean Tarsainn: 'the island lying across'. Canna came later, a Norse intrusion in the language. Was there anyone there on the island to watch them arrive, to see them, exhausted, pull their boat – their currach – up onto the beach? They were emissaries from the abbey at Iona, from the flock of Colm Cille: Saint Columba. Just like him, they had 'crossed the wave-strewn wild region' of the Western Isles, as Saint Beccan of Rum described it in the seventh century, 'foam-flecked, seal-filled, savage, bounding, seething, white-tipped, pleasing, doleful'. And they had brought with them stories of a man who had died hundreds of years ago and thousands of miles away. Stories of a new god.

They built a church, perhaps even a monastery, on the hill at A' Chill, looking down over the bay and back towards Rum. But then they ventured further along Canna's coast and, at the base of the island's towering southern cliffs, built something else – a refuge, a hermitage. A place to withdraw from the world. Once, a narrow path led down the cliffs to the site. Natural erosion and landslides have long since taken it away. Rope is the only way down now.

Jonah had rigged a static line for a controlled descent. I climbed into my harness, clipped in the rope, and made my way to the edge. The route down was a cleft in the basalt rock, a partial stream bed that cut, sometimes near vertically, down to the base of the cliffs. Several times, loose rocks gave way under my feet and at one point I slipped, twisting briefly in thin air on the end of the line before swinging back to grasp the face.

About fifty metres down, the cliffs gave way to a grassy, boulder-strewn slope. I unclipped the rope and made my way to a narrow, flat terrace, sitting just over the sea. There, right on the edge, was a huge, circular drystone enclosure, nearly forty metres in diameter, its wall reaching up to two metres in height. I passed through a break in the circle – possibly the original entrance. This wall was once the boundary between the secular and the spiritual world. But nature is no observer of such things and the bracken had overrun this site, in places growing over my head. At the centre was another, much smaller, circular stone structure. Beyond that, at the northern edge, where the enclosure meets the base of the cliffs, I could still make out the traces of a series of stone beds – known as *leaba crabnach*, 'scared couches'. Places to rest in contemplation of the divine.

Decades ago, crosses were found here, carved into the heaped stones of what may once have been an altar: the distinctive markings of early Christianity. Did those pilgrims who first came to this island sometime in the seventh century believe that their ideas would sweep across all of Scotland in the years to come? Or did they have their doubts, was their faith tested, out here at the edge of everything?

The day had remained calm, the cliffs offering shelter from what little wind there was, the sea washing gently against the rocks below me. What does it mean to 'withdraw' from the world? Some extreme hermits, known as anchorites, would enter a stone cell for the rest of their lives. People came from far and wide to seek their spiritual guidance: wisdom proffered through one small window. Just like the prophets or oracles of the ancient world. Could the structure at the centre of this site have been one of those cells? And could its occupant have been a woman?

The name of this place – 'the cliffs of the holy women' – offers an enigmatic hint at a single-sex religious community. There is a letter from the Abbot of Iona to the Pope, written centuries later, in 1428, that tells of a convent on Canna. Yet the evidence of anchorites in Scotland is so faint as to be almost non-existent – although they were commonplace in the early Christian world of Ireland and England. And, beyond that one letter, there is no other mention of a convent here. We will never know exactly who lived here or what this place was for.

I climbed inside that central stone structure – that hermit's hut, or chapel, or cell – and looked out. Birds wheeled through a brightening sky. The sea shone blue and silver. If you could have only one window onto the world, there are worse places you could put it.

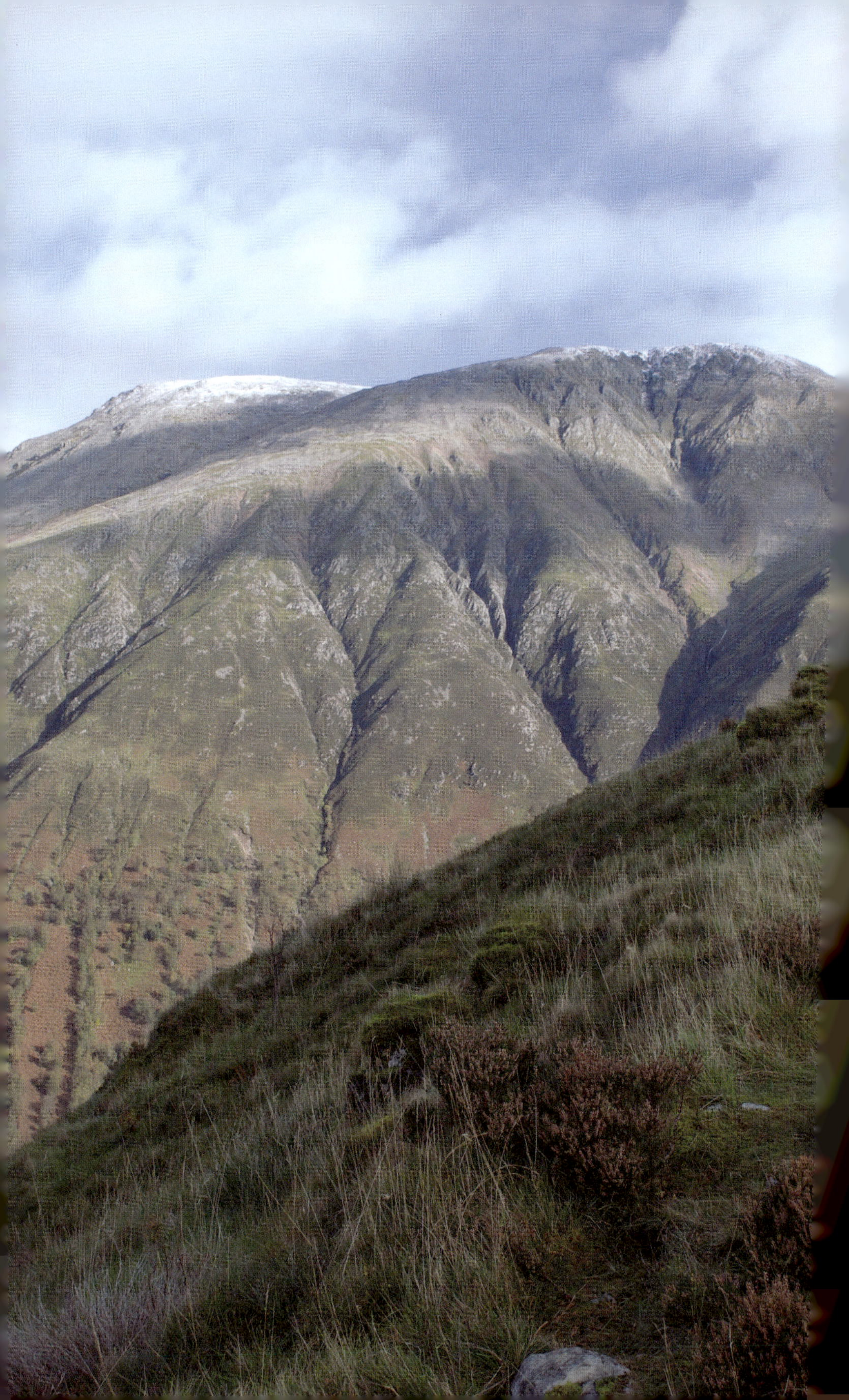

Dun Deardail, Glen Nevis

NN 1270 7012

Imagine a whole hilltop on fire. A huge ring of timber is burning – maybe a hundred metres or more in circumference. Trees, which have been cut into logs, then bound together and raised up several metres high to make a wall, are being consumed by the flames. A vast column of smoke and superheated air is rising upwards, black with ash and charcoal and flickering with millions of red embers. The heat is so strong that the stone and timber foundations of the wall are beginning to melt. Temperatures in the heart of the fire are rising above 1,000°C. The water contained within the rocks boils, making gas bubbles bloom. The stones become molten, start to soften and flow, their mineral composition changing. The fire rages for many days, even weeks. Eventually, it burns itself out, its fuel used up. But in the process, the melted rocks have merged and, as they cool, they are fused together – a process known as vitrification. The hollow spheres of the gas bubbles are still preserved inside them, fossilising forever the moment of the fire's incredible heat. The whole hilltop is a blackened stump. Desolate and unusable.

This was exactly what had happened to the summit where I was standing. Known as Dun Deardail, it sits high on the western side of Glen Nevis, facing directly across the valley to Scotland's highest mountain. We even know, to within a few decades, when the fire happened here. The great quantities of charcoal and ash expelled into the atmosphere eventually fell back down to earth, lodging in the surrounding peat bog – the ideal environment for preserving organic material. In 2017, when researchers took a core sample of the peat, the evidence of the burning was so clear it was visible to the naked eye. A line of dark, charcoal-rich sediment had been deposited around 310 BC. Deeper layers showed other less distinct 'fire events' – caused by tree clearing, perhaps, along with the continuous low-level particles likely generated by hearth smoke. But after 300 BC, the charcoal traces disappeared from the peat almost completely. A literal line was drawn under the life of the community here.

Dun Deardail was originally built some 2,500 years ago: a hillfort that boasted one of the most extreme – and spectacular – vantage points in the whole country. I had hiked to it on the very well-trodden path of the West Highland Way, which climbs in a long diagonal line up the slopes of Glen Nevis before curving off to the south-west to drop down into the valley of the River Kiachnish. But at a height of a thousand feet, a tiny path runs away from the main track to pass around the edge of a spruce plantation. Beyond the trees, the fort appears as an almost comically obvious silhouette – two steep lines on either side rising to a horizontal top. Like a giant's thumb has pushed against the summit of a triangular hill, squashing it down to leave behind a perfect, flat fingerprint.

It was a mild, late-October day, and I had taken a seat at the far western point of this fingerprint. Here, the land dropped very sharply down to the valley floor of the River Nevis. The result was to make the edge of the fort feel like a precipice. I was confronted by a great vault of space, bound a few kilometres away to the east by the huge rock wall of Ben Nevis. Its facing slopes were like a colossal knucklebone, cut into segments by waterfalls tumbling down a series of sheer gulleys. A blanket of red bracken rose up to a thin band of greenery, before bare, grey rock took over. The top was dusted with the first snowfall of the season. Ben Nevis is around four times the height of Dun Deardail, yet the view across the glen offered the optical illusion of a kind of parity. I could imagine that those who lived here felt an acute sense of dominion. Of course, as is the familiar refrain of archaeology, we still know precious little about the people who built this place. *How* they built it has emerged from the earth and the rock and the soil. But *why* remains a matter of – unresolvable – speculation.

We think, for instance, that they were farmers and herdsmen, keeping sheep and cattle and cultivating the surrounding land to grow wheat and barley. Research has identified that, some 3,000 years ago, Scotland experienced a sharp downturn in its climate, which continued until the country was at its coldest and wettest around 650 BC. Inevitably, this would have put

Dun Deardail, Glen Nevis

a premium on good farmland, potentially leading to competition and conflict. As a response, were hillforts intended as bristling statements of power and ownership? And was the fire here the result of an attack, a tribal war over territory that burnt the residents of Dun Deardail out of their home?

There is, however, another theory. Around sixty of Scotland's near 1,600 known hillforts show traces of the same vitrification process that took place at Dun Deardail, all occurring around a similar time period. This has led some to speculate that the settlements were set alight by their own people. That the fires were great rituals of departure: a ceremonial burning of the past as a tribe prepared to move on, a celebration that the protection afforded by the hillfort was no longer needed. Build a bonfire so big that it can melt the very rock beneath your feet.

It is hard to overexaggerate the spectacle, and the innate power, of such an event. The heat, the noise, the ferocity of the destruction. Whether prompted by violence or catharsis, it must have been an awe-inspiring sight. By contrast, Dun Deardail today is a lonely, peaceful place. Those vitrified rocks still surround its perimeter, but now they lie mostly covered by grass and soil. I walked around this two-millennia-old ring of fire and tried to imagine putting a torch to my home and watching it burn.

Cathkin Park, Glasgow

NS 5896 6193

It was summer in the city. A hot, dry wind blew down the Cathcart Road and raised a cloud of fine dust out of the gutters. I crossed the road and entered a bank of tall trees. After walking a short distance, a gap emerged in the trees and the land fell away. A curved wedge of concrete sloped downwards to a wide, flat oval of grass. Two flights of stairs were cut into the wedge, running between a series of wider, shallower steps studded with groups of rectangular metal frames. Everywhere the tall shoots of weeds and nettles sprouted up through the cracked concrete to sway in the breeze. What I was standing above was a ruined football stadium – a crumbling relic of a ground that was abandoned over half a century ago now. Not just any ground either. Once, this place had been Hampden Park: the home of Scotland's national football team.

That anything survives at all now is part accident, and part by-product of the often-furious pace of the development of Glasgow. Beginning around the middle of the nineteenth century, it became a city propelled outwards by the incredible scale of industrial expansion. In the 1850s, when the OS prepared their first maps of this area to the south of the River Clyde, it was all farmland, with the exception of a colliery near Govanhill and a handful of brickworks. Yet, by the beginning of the twentieth century, it was filled entirely with housing, and overrun by factories and steelworks, all linked up by a network of roads and railways.

This inexorable push outwards continued up until the period after the Second World War. And, as a result, the decline that followed – taking hold in the 1960s and becoming terminal by the 1980s – left Glasgow littered with the ruins of old industry: empty dockyards, derelict canals, mothballed factories. With the boom of production replaced by the bust of high unemployment and social deprivation, there was little money to redevelop or build on many of these sites. Rather, they were left, often quite literally, to rot.

I made my way down the terracing, over its crumbling stairs and fragments of broken glass, to the curved perimeter wall leading to what was once the pitch – now a recreation ground carpeted with daisies and dandelions. Three sides of the old stadium still remain, a horseshoe of terracing, large parts of it entirely overgrown by trees.

Just as much as a graving dock, say, or a broken-down steelworks, this football ground was also a fragment of industry. The incredible rise in the popularity of the game at the end of the nineteenth century was linked inextricably to the emergence of the industrial working class. Rapid urbanisation, increased spending power and the development of Saturday afternoon leisure time fed an insatiable desire for mass spectator entertainments. These ranged from cricket, rugby and horse-racing to boxing and the theatre – but football dominated above all others. Most particularly, through the emergence of stadiums, it introduced an entirely new type of building to the Victorian city. (Industry even shaped what these stadiums looked like: the Glasgow-born architect Archibald Leitch, who became the pre-eminent builder of early-twentieth-century British football grounds, adapted his designs for grandstands from factory buildings.) Increasingly, nowhere else outside of the workplace could compete as a site of mass congregation.

This was, in part, the very reason for locating Hampden Park here, in 1883, on the east side of the Cathcart Road. By this time, it was already the second home of the national stadium. The original had sat just 200 yards away, on the other side of the road. The club that owned it was Queen's Park FC – Scotland's first-ever football club (formed in 1868 by a group of 'gentlemen' who held regular kickabouts on the nearby Queen's Park recreation grounds). In those early days of international football, it was also the club that provided all the players that made up the squad of the Scotland team.

That first Hampden was built in 1873, but the Cathcart and District Railway Company wanted to run a new line right over the top of it. And so Queen's Park moved to this second site, leasing the land from an iron manufacturers. Over time, it was developed into a 25,000-capacity ground, including a two-storey brick pavilion with changing rooms, baths and a

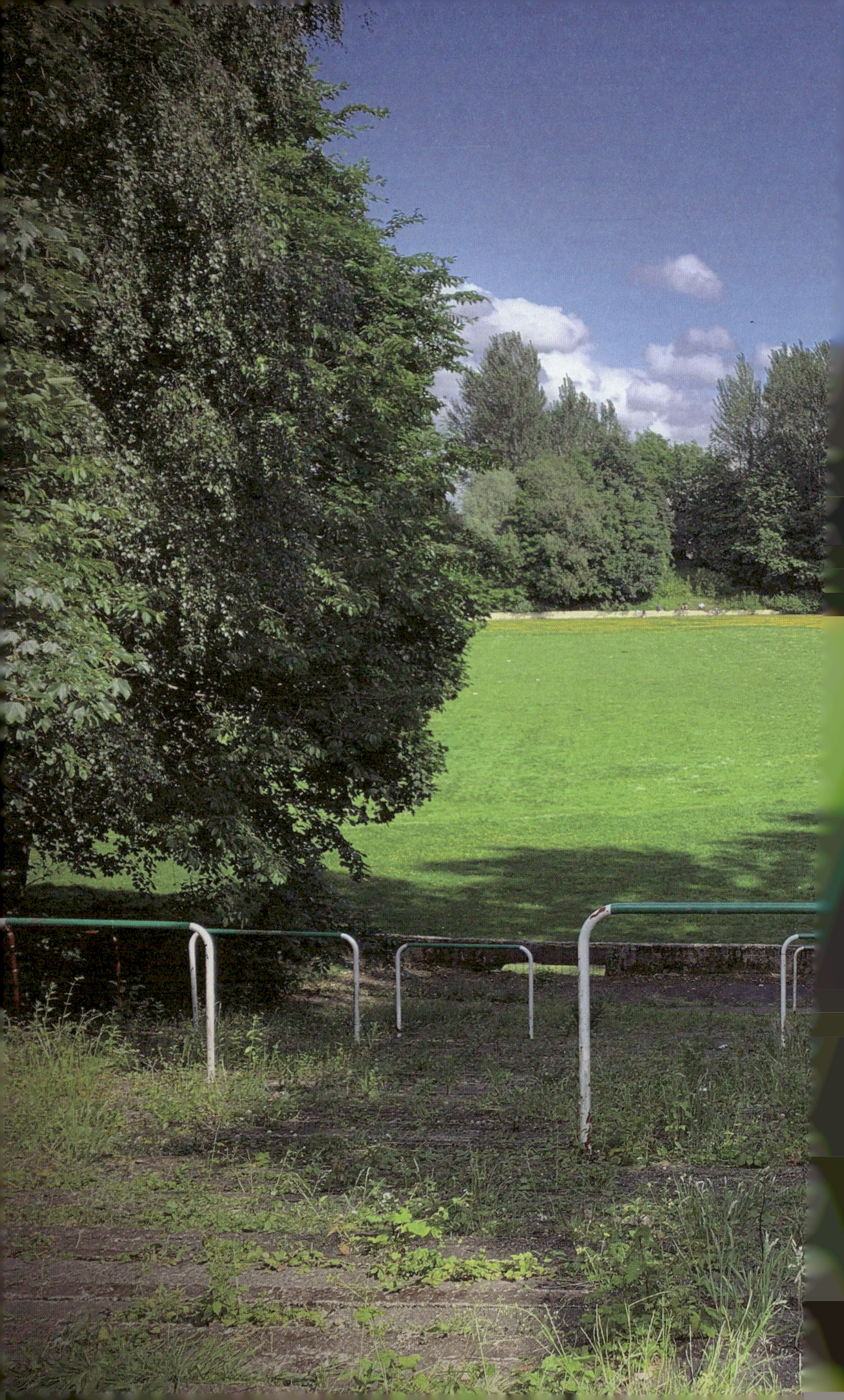

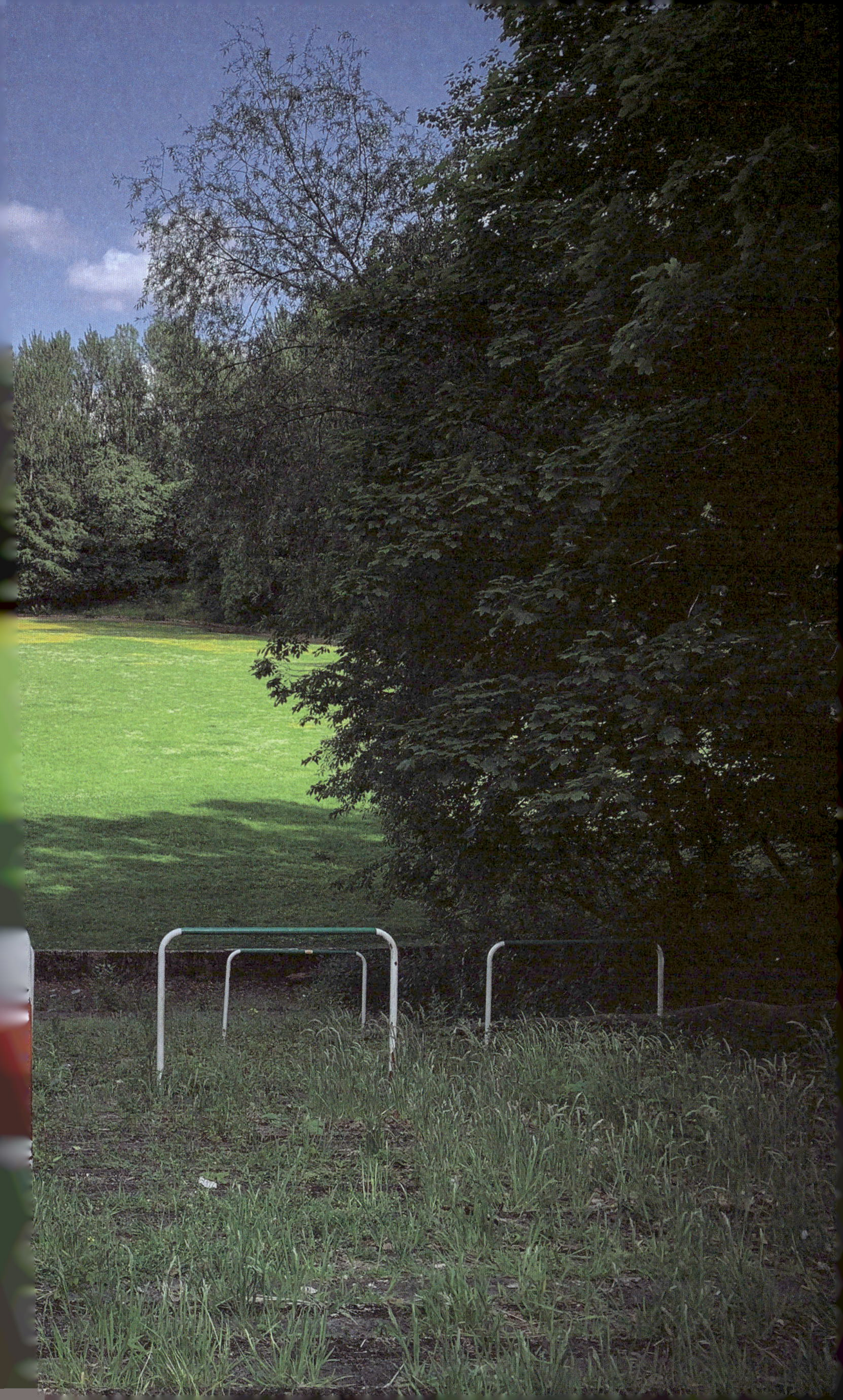

gymnasium. Even this, however, proved too small to meet the demand. At the turn of the century, Queen's Park bought their own piece of land, which was just another few hundred yards away to the south. There, in 1903, they completed construction of the third Hampden Park. Capable of holding up to 150,000 fans, it was at the time – and would remain for the next half century – the largest football stadium in the world.

With Queen's Park having moved on, the second Hampden was taken over by another club, Third Lanark, who renamed it New Cathkin Park – although, eventually, it became just Cathkin Park. They played here for over six decades, until 1967. Financial mismanagement of the club – which, just a few years earlier, had finished third in the Scottish Football League – saw it go into liquidation and then disappear entirely. With Third Lanark gone, the stadium simply fell out of use. One side of its terracing and its main pavilion were demolished, and the rest was left behind.

I walked back up through the weed-choked terracing, and then across the road and the railway towards the site of the original Hampden Park. Today, it's occupied by a rose garden, a bowling green, a neat terrace of red sandstone houses and the same trainline that first forced it to move. An archaeological dig was underway in the garden, part of an attempt to find the exact spot once occupied by the pitch and the vanished stadium. A series of excavation trenches had been opened up, and in one of them, lying perfectly flat, was the brickwork of a collapsed wall. It was, the dig's lead archaeologist Paul Murtagh told me, quite possibly the remains, or the foundations, of the exterior wall that once surrounded the pitch. What had been created here, he said, was the very first enclosed international football ground in the world.

'So, the feeling you get when you go to a football ground,' he said, 'the sense of place, the smells and the sound, the singing and the thrill of the game – it all started here. Every single football stadium that has ever been built since based their architecture on *this* stadium. It was the first to have turnstiles, it had a ticket book for season tickets. So, all those things can be traced back to Queen's Park.'

I looked down into that small trench, and at the blackened lattice of bricks that had emerged out of the ground. For Paul, this was a beginning – as he put it, not just one of the most important archaeological sites in Glasgow or Scotland, but in the whole world, especially for those interested in its modern social history.

The archaeology of football. It might seem strange, but there is no denying the impact of the game on not just the cultural, but also the physical fabric of the twentieth century. Glasgow's emergence as an industrial heartland shaped the very evolution of football, and then football shaped the structure of the city in return. Cathkin Park had been deserted when I walked its terraces, with an almost eerie quiet to the place. It was a sensation not unlike exploring the remains of some ancient amphitheatre. If Paul was right, a template had been born here – and then its concept refined over three incarnations of the *same* stadium, rebuilt in the space of less than one square mile. The origins of a global game now watched by billions of people, buried beneath a rose garden and bowling green on the west side of the Cathcart Road.

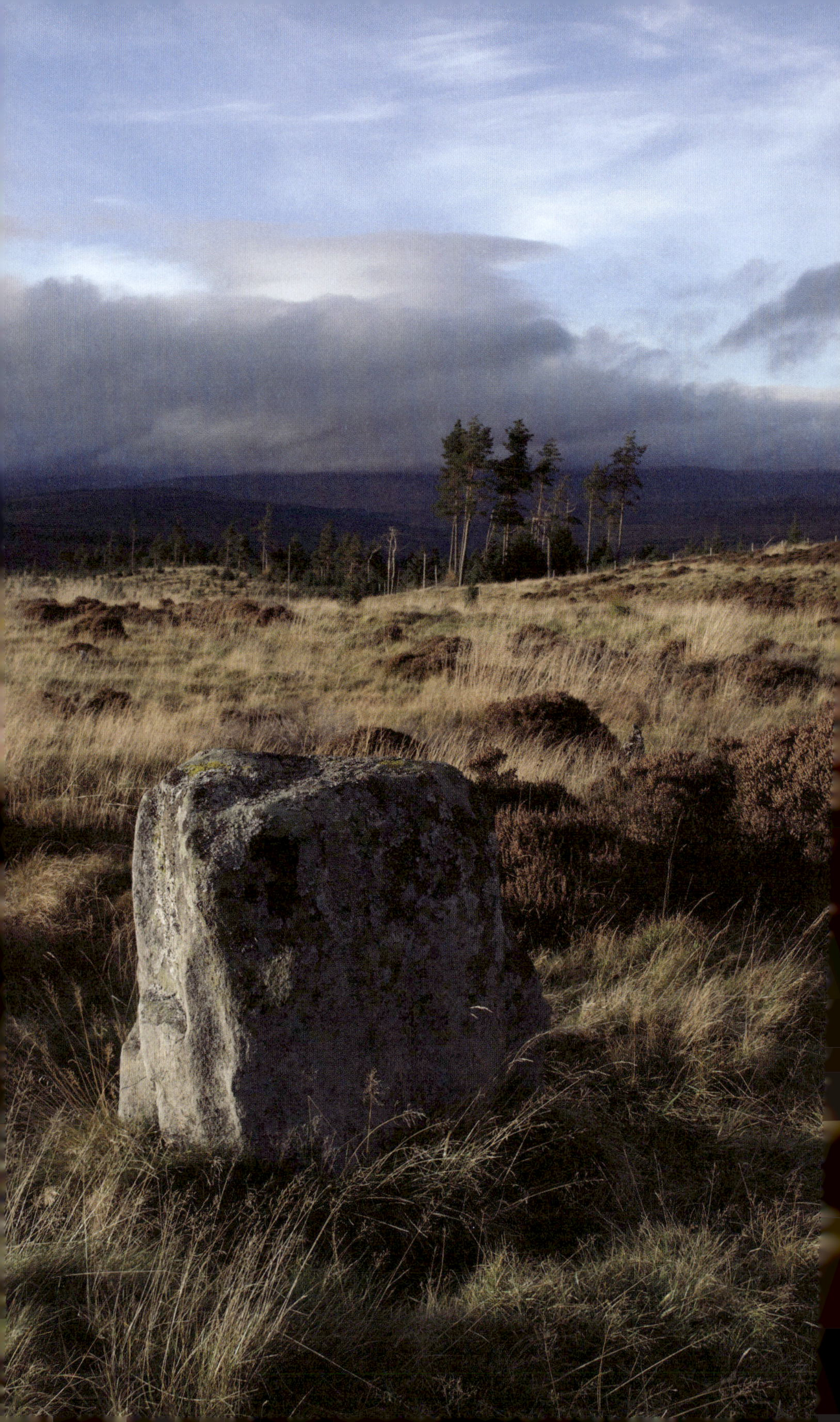

Na Clachan Aoraidh, Loch Tummel

NN 8386 6200

Some seven miles to the west of Pitlochry, the land rises steeply up from the north shoreline of Loch Tummel to a high plateau of grassland. This grassland forms a thin layer above the hard bone of a flat-topped ridge of dark limestone known as Cnoc na Craoibhe. Climbing up here in 1907, Fred Coles, the archaeologist and Assistant Keeper of Scotland's National Museum of Antiquities, wrote with wonder of how, on this 'level crest of wide-rolling moorland' it was possible to see 'no fewer than sixty separate and distinct hill summits, peaks, knobs, knocks . . . extending from Ben Vrackie on the east to the rugged heights of Farragon in the south (with the whole great mass of Ben Lawers beyond), Schiehallion, the wide-spreading Rannoch moorlands in the west, the Glen Tilt hills and Ben-y-ghloe ranges to the north-east, with innumerable smaller eminences intervening'.

To reach Cnoc na Craoibhe, you must first pass through Allean Forest. On a mild, almost windless November day, I followed the track that meanders steadily upwards from the lochside. On the lower slopes, the forest was a jostling mix of tree species – towering Scots pine, Douglas fir, larch and red cedar. Pine needles lay so thick on the ground it was like walking on a deep-pile orange carpet. Everywhere leaves had turned the colour of sunlight. Higher up came dense plantation blocks of Sitka spruce, interrupted here and there by open stretches of harvested woodland – flattened prairies of overturned ground and denuded, bleached stumps. Even higher, just a little above the spruce treeline, I reached the plateau.

A narrow path led off the main track to a wooden gate. Beyond the gate, the way onwards was little more than a furrow, a flattening down of the grass that ran in a straight line, and very gently upwards, for a hundred metres or so through isolated clumps of heather. At the end of the line, silhouetted against the sky, was the squat shape of an upright stone. Closer, and that one stone was joined by three more. Four large boulders – one standing, the others leaning on their sides – arranged in a circle some four and half metres wide.

It was these boulders that had brought Coles to the plateau a century earlier. Known as a 'four poster' stone circle, it was a style of monument that appeared to have proliferated around 3,000 years ago, in Scotland's middle and late Bronze Age. And while its setting had impressed Coles greatly, the basic elements of its construction had not. 'Surely, if ever the prehistoric circle builder (supposed to be a Star-and-Hill worshipper) sought for a noble panorama within which to rear some rude image of Stonehenge, this were the very spot!' he wrote. 'And yet, what he did erect are only four great unshapely, somewhat squat, and very rough boulders in the centre of a slight mound, circular, and marked off from the wild moorland by a rim of small boulders.'

Coles appeared to consider these stones a missed opportunity. As if significance must be weighted in parallel with monumentality. *If only it were bigger, then it would be really special.* Certainly, I found it a deceptive site – that the one still-upright stone was visible from so far away, yet almost seemed to diminish in size the nearer I got. Arrive at the centre of the circle and you tower over the stones, rather than the opposite. What it lacked in scale, though, it more than compensated for in intimacy. Which made it seem not so much mysterious as self-evident. As if some form of human marking or intervention on this very spot was predestined.

In 2016 people came here and lit an illegal bonfire in the centre of the circle. To assess the damage, the Forestry Commission excavated the site – and in the process discovered traces of a far, far older fire. Down below the recent scorched surface, the diggers found a central pit, filled with a dense grey silt loam, alder charcoal and burnt human bone. Analysis of the bone fragments showed that they belonged to an adult woman, while carbon dating determined that she had been cremated around 900 BC. The fire that reduced her to ashes had not been lit on the site of the stone circle, however. The surrounding soil bore no traces of ancient burning. Instead, the remains had been brought here and placed carefully in the ground. What I was standing on, was a grave.

Na Clachan Aoraidh, Loch Tummel

The stone circle, it seems, came after. First, the remains were buried in that loam. Then the earth here was raised up into a circular platform of sandstone cobbles, and finally the four large boulders of quartz-seamed schist were set in place. Maybe this happened years, maybe decades, later. In the centre was a natural hollow. The excavation revealed that this was the depression left behind by an uprooted tree. The name of this upland ridge, Cnoc na Craoibhe, translates as the 'hill of the tree'. Perhaps this woman's burnt body was set deliberately into the absence left behind by a sacred tree? Or maybe that tree was the fuel for her cremation, the two living things brought together in death?

The view from here was – and is – startling in its immensity: the huge extent of the sky with the panorama of mountains below like the rim of some colossal amphitheatre. It was mid-afternoon, and the low November sun was hovering above the summit of Schiehallion to the south-west. Tendrils of low cloud kissed its upper slopes and, backlit by the light, they gave the impression of a beacon burning on its summit. In old Gaelic folklore, the caves below Schiehallion were said to lead to the Otherworld. Stone circles, too, are often thought to have been built as portals, 'thin places', where the borders between the earth and the sky, the living and the dead, meet and become permeable. Such ideas and myths can, perhaps, take the circles and their creators away from us, make 3,000 years seem like a chasm between then and now. But the hills have not changed. The sky has not changed. The earth beneath my feet, where the woman was buried, has not changed. There is no mystery in commemorating those who pass on, in honouring a connection to the land that you live – and die – on. In that respect at least, it is likely that we haven't changed much either.

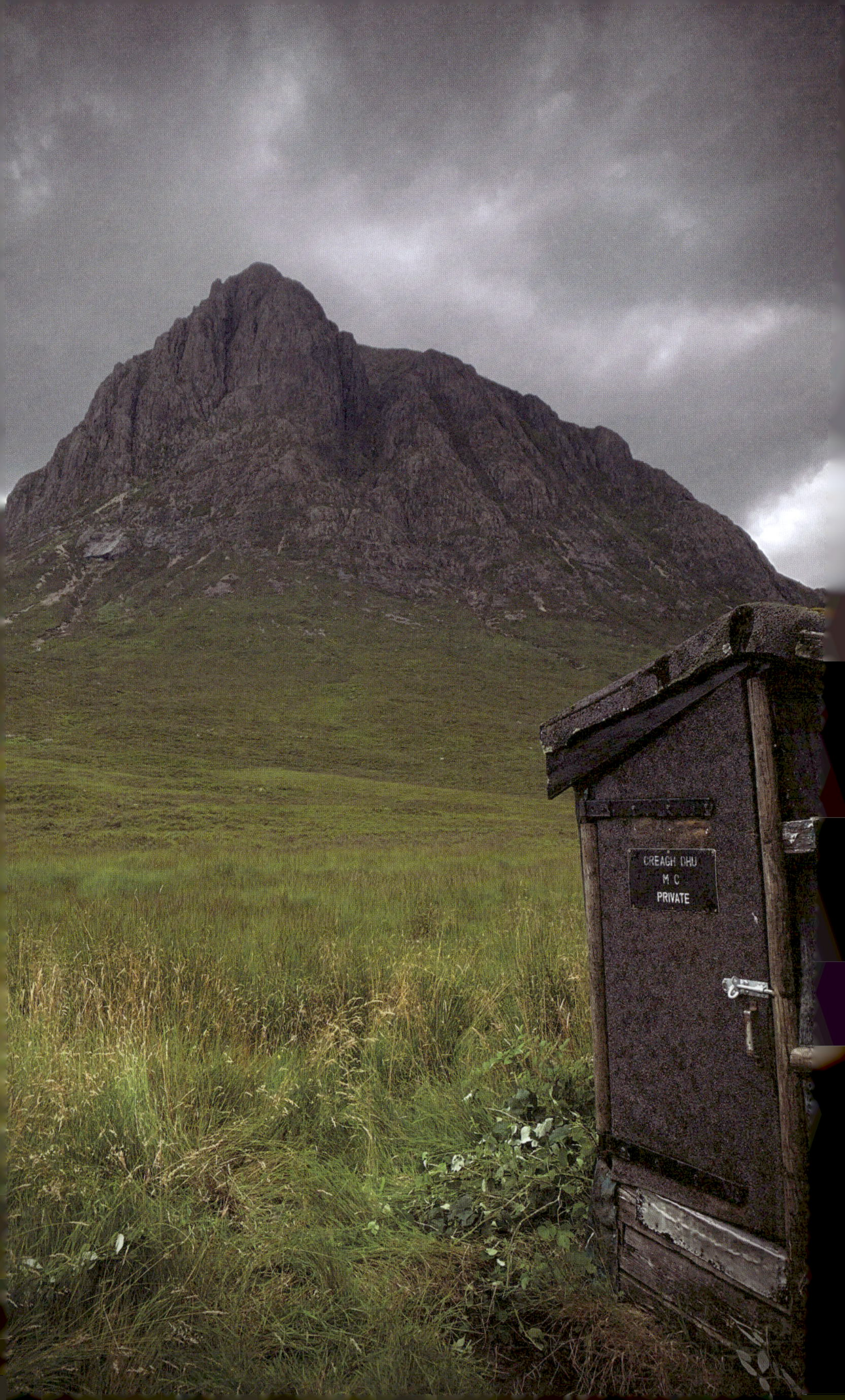
CREAGH DHU
M C
PRIVATE

Jacksonville Hut, Rannoch Moor

NN 2347 5527

'I think it's natural,' Willie Gorman said to me, 'to look at blank walls and say to yourself, I wonder if there is a way up there?'

We were standing on the north bank of the River Coupall, staring up at one of the most imposing walls you can find anywhere in Scotland: the mountain ridge of Buachaille Etive Mor, its granite rock, seamed in pink and grey, pushing up like a clenched fist to mark the end of Rannoch Moor and the descent into the valley of Glencoe. Dark clouds were gathering beyond it. A summer storm was approaching, the wind rushing in strong from the west, carrying a hot smell of rain on the air.

On the far side of the river, just a few metres above its southern bank, was a squat black rectangle. It was cradled in part by an L-shape of large, rough boulders, covered in moss and lichen. Walls, formed of tarp and canvas, were stretched around a basic wooden frame, with a triangular roof, sagging in the middle, covered in layered sheets of bare bitumen. At one end, poking through the roof, was the little metal spout of a chimney. It was this black hut – at once somewhat dilapidated and stubbornly robust – that Willie had brought me to see.

The hut can trace its origins back to a small clearing some fifty miles to the south-west, just a little off the route of the West Highland Way, in a woodland ridge between the Campsie Fells and the Kilpatrick Hills. In the late 1920s, as the Great Depression forced upwards of a third of Glasgow's workers into unemployment, groups of idle men began to strike out into the countryside, to walk and explore the landscapes that rose up beyond their city. At a place called Craigallian, a fire was lit, and – so the story goes – for the next decade or more, it never went out.

Since 2012 a modest commemorative monument – a granite boulder, set in a cast-iron pit – has marked its location. Before that, a simple wood and paper sign, leaning against a rock, explained the history of the fire. 'Within its glow,' it read, 'philosophy, socialism and hill-lore were discussed at length, and the fire-flickered woods echoed with songs which were sung well into the night.' Many men would stay up in the hills for days, returning to the city only to collect their dole money, before instantly leaving again. The Craigallian fire was a site for congregation, conversation and the sharing of ideas. But it was also a first stop and staging post for those wanting to go onwards, to follow the old roads beyond the hills and into the Highlands. 'The fire was the cradle for all the other fires which warmed wanderers in howffs, dosses, bothies and caves as they explored further north.'

One group of men – all of them Clyde shipyard workers – was particularly drawn towards the mountains. In 1929, while gathered around the fire at Craigallian, they founded what they called the Creag Dhu Mountaineering Club. Focusing their attention first on ascending and summiting the peaks of the Arrochar Alps, they roamed gradually further northwards, following the route of the West Highland Way beyond the Trossachs and across Rannoch Moor to the foot of Buachaille Etive Mor. It was there, just beside the river, that they found the line of old boulders – the ruins of a sheep enclosure built over a century before – and converted it into a makeshift shelter. In 1950 one of the members of the Creag Dhu, Jimmy Jackson, built it up into the hut that still stands here today. And it's from Jimmy that it takes its name: Jacksonville.

We crossed the river, Willie in wellingtons, me taking off my hiking boots and wading barefoot. The wind rippled hard across the surface of the water, and the first spots of rain began to flicker in the air. Willie led me on to the hut, unfastened its padlock and held the wedge-shaped door open for me.

'It's harder to get in here than it is to get into the House of Lords,' he said, laughing.

Jacksonville soon became the spiritual home of the Creag Dhu. And entry to the club – and to the hut – was strictly by invitation only.

'Quite elitist, I suppose,' Willie said. 'Its numbers were always limited to a group who all knew each other.'

Willie first came to Glencoe in the 1950s, when he was in his early teens.

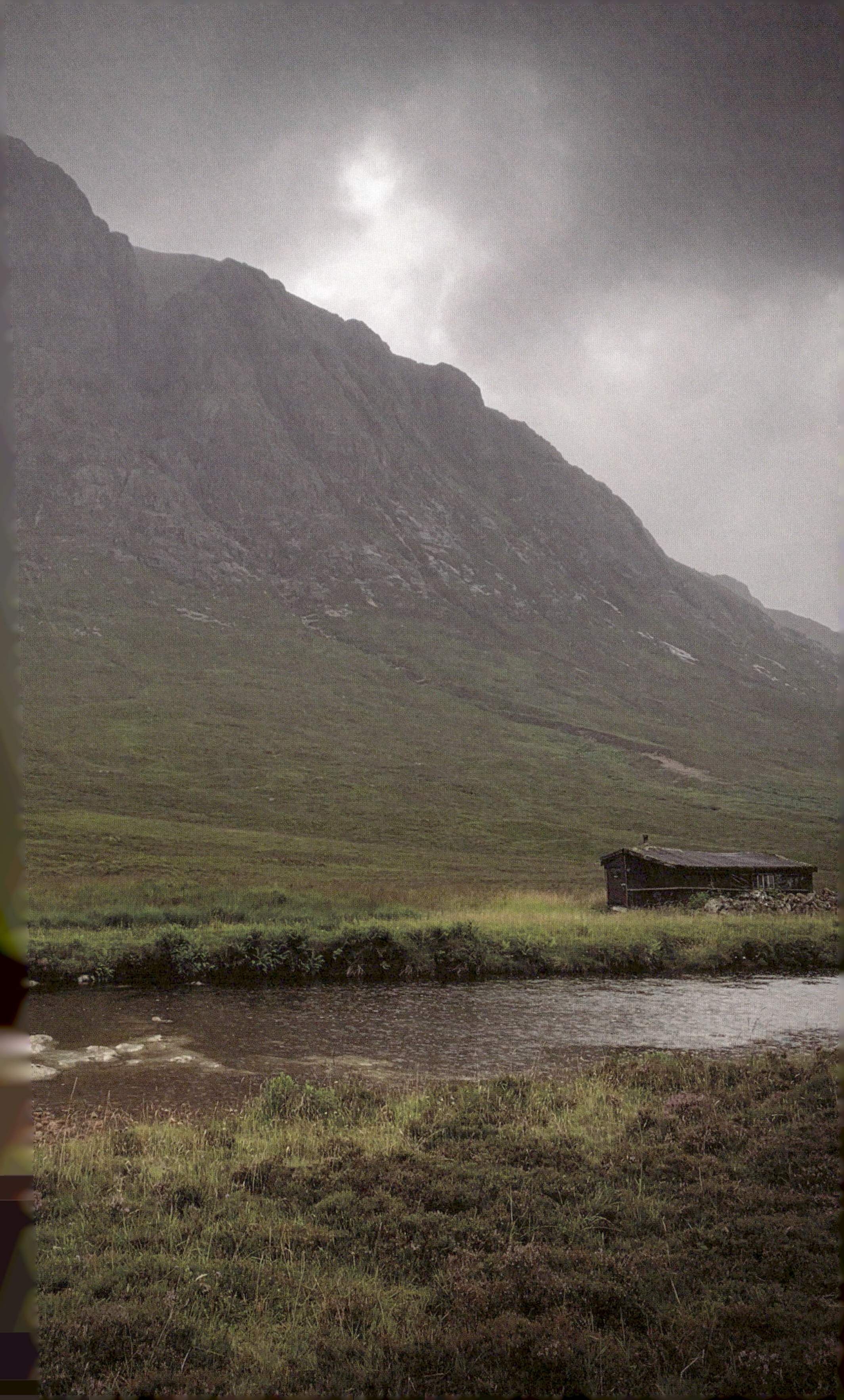

His father worked for the railways, which gave family members free travel passes. From the age of twelve Willie had started venturing out on his own, taking the train to distant Highland stations then walking off into the hills and the mountains. He went to school in the north side of Glasgow, had a classroom several storeys up, with views over the Campsie Fells towards the Arrochars and Ben Lomond. During lessons, he couldn't stop looking off towards that horizon. He started climbing with a school friend, or often just by himself, moving from scrambling to roped ascents – except, in place of ropes, he used the closest substitute he could get: washing lines scavenged from tenement back-courts. Whenever he came to climb the Buachaille, he and a friend would set up their tent on the south bank of the river, near Jacksonville.

'We saw people using this hut,' he told me. 'We didn't realise it was the Creag Dhu. We just got chatting, and we were telling them what climbs we'd done. We were shy at the time, and they were obviously very respected climbers. Eventually, we wore them down and they invited us in.'

By this time, it was the beginning of the 1960s. Inside the hut, stories of ascents and pitches were told to a soundtrack of the Beatles and the Rolling Stones. After a while, the members of the Creag Dhu said to Willie that he could use Jacksonville whenever he wanted. Within a year, they asked him if he wanted join the club.

'And these guys were so good, climbing at a very high standard,' he said. 'Probably the highest standard in Britain at the time. One guy in particular, John Cunningham, was a fantastic climber, doing climbs that nobody had ever done before.'

Cunningham was born in 1927 in the East End of Glasgow. Apprenticed as a shipwright at John Brown's in Clydebank, he joined the Creag Dhu at the age of seventeen. In 1953, along with another Scottish climber, Hamish MacInnes, he embarked on an expedition to Nepal with the aim of being the first to reach the summit of Mount Everest – only to discover that Edmund Hillary and Tenzing Norgay had just beaten them to it.

'Because of John,' Willie said, 'there was a flowering. The rest of the group all made fantastic progress as well. It was a revolution in climbing standards, a golden age of climbing. And it was the working class that had done it. The only climbers before them were middle-class climbers, who stayed in hotels and lived totally different lifestyles. Because the guys in the Creag Dhu came from a tradition of really hard work in the shipyards, because they were out in all sorts of weather, they were hard men. They were sleeping rough but enjoying the countryside and the freedom that gave them. And there was a tremendous dignity in that.'

We were inside the hut, Willie sitting on an old stool, me on a raised wooden platform used for sleeping. There was a solid cast-iron burner up against the back wall and the air was thick with the smell of woodsmoke, built up over more than seven decades. Above us, the sturdy roof beams were carved and inked with names and phrases. The rain had come on hard and was rattling against the hut's south-facing window, which was filled with the huge silhouette of the Buachaille.

'If you look up at it now,' Willie said, pointing towards the mountain, 'and then you look at a guidebook, dozens and dozens of climbs up there were done first by the Creag Dhu. They made the Buachaille their own.'

For Willie, Jacksonville – set on the footprint of that old sheep fank – is living history, an almost sacred site for Scottish climbing heritage. This hut, like the fire at Craigallian that preceded it, was a focal point: a place of pilgrimage for a certain type of person, for those drawn to the extremes of the landscape.

'If Jacksonville wasn't here,' he said, 'would the Creag Dhu have withered away?'

Outside, the wind had bent the long summer grass flat. Rain pelted against the walls and windows. Inside, it was hushed and warm. We sat and watched the storm arrive. The mountain blurred, then grew faint, then finally its summit – the summit that the people who built this hut had found so many new and different ways to reach – was swallowed by the clouds.

Square Cairn Cemetery, Bay of Laig, Isle of Eigg

NM 4669 8790

I walked down to the cairn cemetery at sunset. There was no wind, but the gentle warmth of the day had dulled to the cool, sharp bite of approaching evening. I was following the single road that runs through Cleadale – a scattering of crofts and houses that occupies the north-western corner of the Isle of Eigg. Somewhere, off in the distance, was the metallic hum of a piece of machinery – a generator, or a tractor engine. Small birds flitted back and forth on the overhead electricity wires, while a small group of brown-feathered hens tiptoed through the field alongside.

A path led off the road towards the great, wide, C-curve beach of Traigh Chlithe. The tide was retreating out into the Bay of Laig, leaving an expanse of slick wet sand with the perfect, polished sheen of a mirror. Reflected in that mirror was the paling, blue-yellow sky, and the black, serrated silhouette of the Isle of Rum.

'The wildest and most repulsive of all the islands,' as the Scottish geologist John MacCulloch called it in 1824, Rum has the look of a line of mountain peaks cut out of some towering alpine range and simply dropped into the sea. The names of those peaks mix Norse and Gaelic – Askival, 'the mountain of the ash trees', Trolvall, 'the mountain of the trolls', Sgurr nan Gillean 'the peak of the young men' – as does the name of the island itself. Rum may come from *rom øe* in Old Norse, meaning 'wide island'; or, even more apt, the Gaelic *i-dhruim*, the 'isle of the ridge'.

A local story, very possibly apocryphal, has it that J.R.R. Tolkien came to stay in a house on Eigg in the 1930s and '40s. It was after looking out on Rum, behind which the sun sets in a fiery, volcanic red, that he first conceived of the lands of Mordor, home of Sauron, the evil protagonist of *The Lord of the Rings*. True or not, there was certainly no escaping the sight of Rum from the beach. Everything was orientated towards it, its ridgeline so close – just a couple of miles away across the sound – that it almost felt within touching distance.

Reaching the beach's southern end, I climbed across a burn washing out to sea, then up through the dunes to a grassy field. The shoreline rose in terraces. Heaps of sand and soil had, over many centuries, been blown into steps, now overgrown, that lifted the earth higher every few metres inland, like a series of petrified waves. It was here that I found the cairn cemetery. Or, at least, what was left of it.

The bodies had been buried close together, in three rows. Each grave had been lined with dressed stones, then sealed above with a large slab of rock. On top of the slab, and laid out in a near perfect square, came cobbles that built up, layer after layer, into the heaped mass of a cairn. Eight of the graves were on the lowest terrace, five on the next level, and a further two – which were the largest, at nearly five metres square – were positioned above them.

Now, in place of the cairns, were hollows. The fifteen graves were still visible – clumps of stone, set in obvious geometric shapes – but they all had depressions at their centres: a clear sign that, at some point in the past, they had been dismantled and opened up. The reasons are lost to us. Robbery? Removal of the bodies to take them to some other site, or removal of the stones for building work? There is no evidence beyond the mere fact of their emptiness. Even their age is something of a mystery. Similar square-cairn graves are thought to date from Pictish times, around a millennium and a half ago – although almost all have been found in northern and eastern Scotland. Apart from a single similar grave that was discovered in South Uist in 1998, containing the body of a forty-year-old woman, these were the only examples of their kind on the west coast and the islands. A sign, perhaps, of a Pictish presence far beyond what has normally been considered as the limits of their kingdom? Or the evidence of a small community who came here in exile, or who fled from the east – yet still buried their number according to the old ways, following the only traditions that they knew?

Death – or, rather, the commemoration of the life that preceded it – is, inevitably, one of the most common things that our ancestors have left behind. The ritual of burial is an exceptionally old one, with evidence showing that it began at least 130,000 years ago. It may, quite conceivably, be the first-ever form of religion practised by humans. Go back just a fraction of that time, to a field near Forteviot in Perthshire around 3000 BC, and you can find the earliest example in Scotland of what is now a near-universal modern ritual – leaving flowers with the dead. Meadowsweet was laid across the body of a man, along with a bronze dagger, and the tooth of a sperm whale.

The emptying of Eigg's graves was not an uncommon phenomenon. Several circular burial cairns, dating from the Bronze Age, have been found across the island – and all had been robbed of their stones and their contents. One survived until 1861, when it was dismantled by a party of roadbuilders, who described a stone 'cist' – from the Greek for 'box' or 'chest' – covered by a 'fine earthy matter, containing some small pieces of charred bones'. On the south-east of the island, in an underground chamber in a large mound in a farmer's field near the ruined early-Christian church and graveyard at Kildonnan, the discovery was made of an ornate silver sword-hilt, an iron axehead, a whorl fashioned from amber, and fragments of bone. All of these dated to the Viking period – except for the burial mound itself. It was far older. Likely constructed in Neolithic times, it had been robbed and reused by its far more recent occupant. Bury something, even a body, and there is no guarantee that it will remain forever below ground. Certainly, the evidence from archaeology suggests that just as strong as the human need to venerate the dead is the desire to find out what they may be hiding.

I stood over the hollowed-out cairns, and their grass-grown ruins. Their missing stones could easily have made their way into a nearby dyke or the walls of a sheep enclosure. It was surprising, perhaps, that there was anything to see at all: that those ghostly imprints of the square cairns remained, lined up in rows just as they had fifteen or more centuries ago, looking out across the sea to Rum.

I walked back along the beach, then sat in the dunes for a while above the bay. There was an old sofa placed down near the tideline, and a figure was slumped on it smoking a cigarette and looking out to sea. A teenage boy appeared on a bicycle and began to ride in wide parabolas across the wet sands, silently circling the sofa. With the sun dropping below the horizon and the sky flaring crimson behind Rum, it was a bizarre, strangely beautiful, almost filmic sight. That view out to the west was hypnotic, transfixing.

As dusk set in, I made my way back through Cleadale. Near the end of the road, there was another cairn – a thumb-like uprising of dressed stone, fixed with a bronze plaque. This cairn, however, was little more than a decade old, built in 2006 to commemorate those islanders who had served, and died, in the First and Second World Wars. It was another kind of memorial, to bodies that would never return to the soils of Eigg.

I was staying for a few days in a tiny artists' bothy, set just below the cliffs that tower above Cleadale. Back inside, I lit the wood burner and cooked some dinner. The end wall of the bothy was a floor-to-ceiling window which looked out across the sea. A desk and an old armchair were set in front of it. I sat in the armchair and watched as the darkening sky merged with Rum's mountainous outline. The light dimmed, and dwindled, and then sank finally into total blackness.

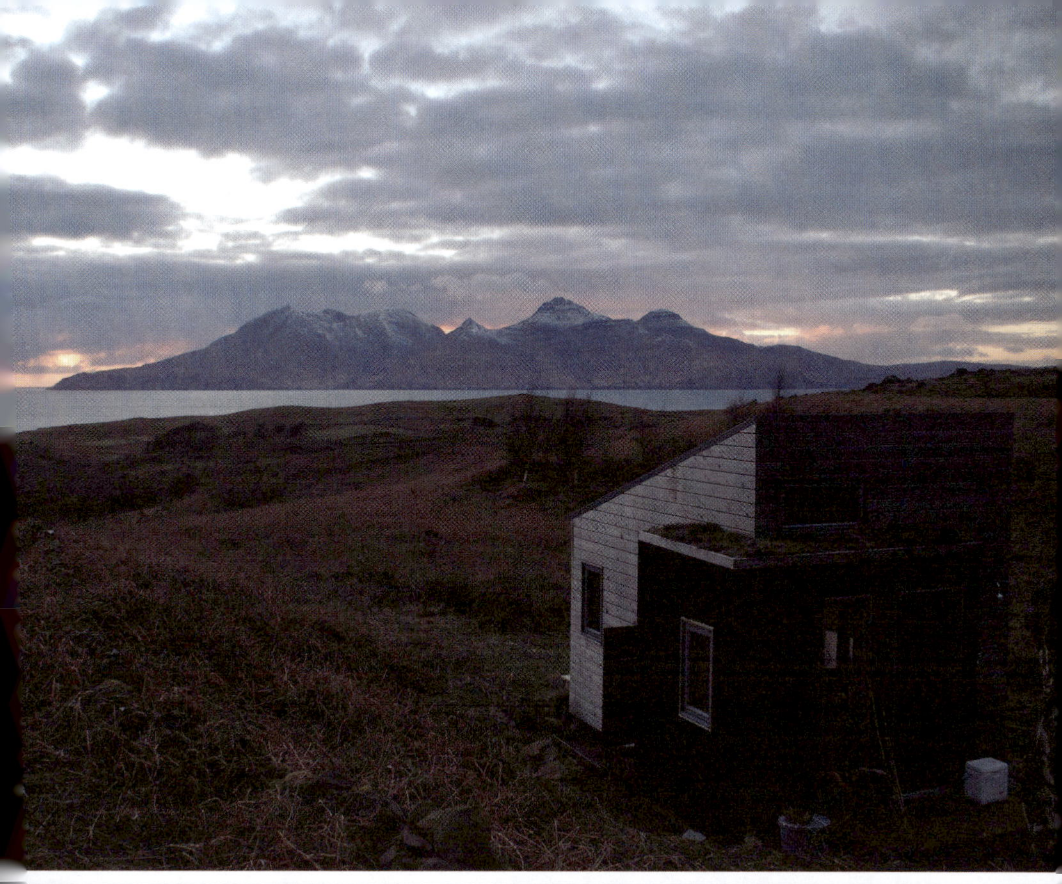

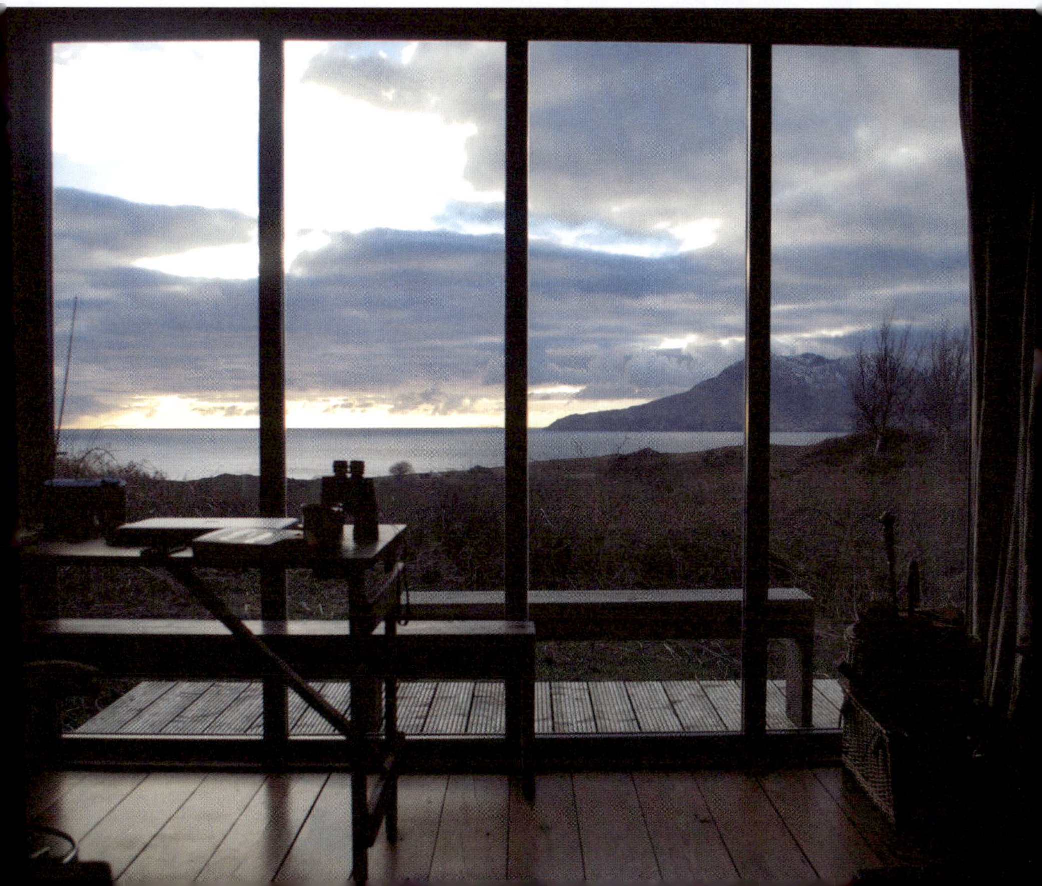

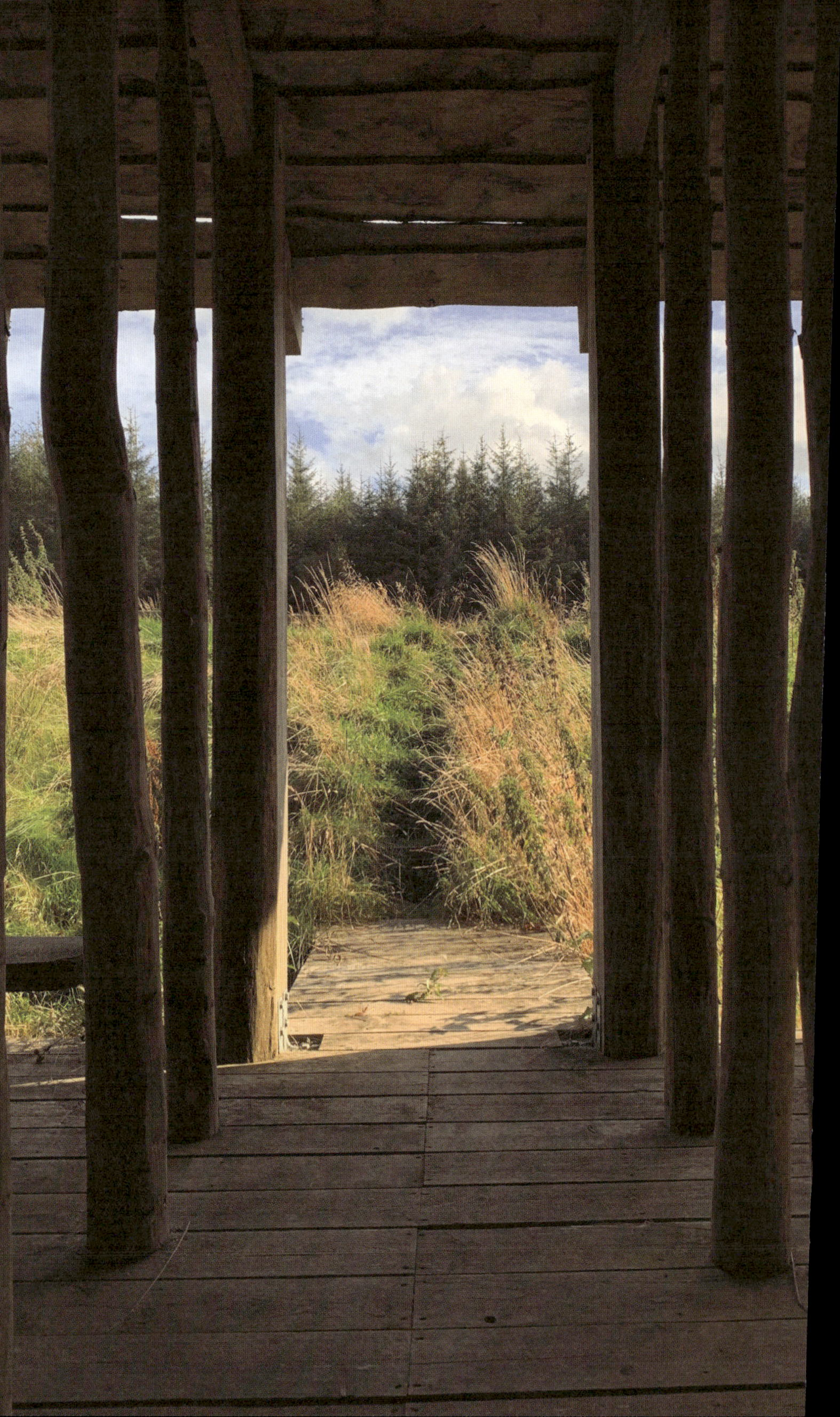

The Forest Pitch, Selkirk

NT 5086 2817

One day in August 2012, some 500 people made their way over fields from the town of Selkirk to arrive, three miles later, at the Clarilawmuir Plantation. There, they walked along paths cut through blocks of Sitka spruce and, drawn onwards by the sound of a brass band, came to the centre of a forest.

Almost exactly seven years on, I was following one of those paths – a rutted, stony breach in the solid wall of plantation trees. There were no signs, nothing to point the way to what I was trying to find. The lines of tall spruce on either side were bunched shoulder to shoulder; seeing through them was impossible. I came to a crossroads, took a guess at a left turn, then continued on. After a few minutes, I reached another path, winding off to the right this time. It was slick with mud, speckled with puddles. But a few steps down it and I could finally see something – a building in silhouette, rows of pillars holding up a roof, beyond it clear sky. A break in the trees.

I reached the building and stepped up into it. The whole thing was fashioned from wood. There were planks for the floors and the roof, whittled trunks for the pillars, tree bases holding up a long bench on one side. There were no walls, but a double line of the pillars ran through the centre of the building to form a sort of corridor, leading out to a platform and a flight of ten wooden steps set into a grass banking. I climbed the steps – now almost entirely overgrown – and came up onto a wide rectangular clearing. It was surrounded on all four sides by a simple wooden fence. And at each end, just visible through clumps of young trees, were goalposts. The Forest Pitch.

This pitch was the work of artist Craig Coulthard, a contribution to the 2012 Cultural Olympiad. Craig's idea was to create a full-size football pitch right in the heart of a spruce plantation in the Scottish Borders, use it for just one day and then abandon it to nature. One substantial section of the forest was felled, the ground was cleared, raised up for drainage, levelled out and then turfed. On 25 August 2012 it hosted two matches, watched by those 500 spectators. Teams were named in honour of the original Olympics. In the women's match, Delphi beat Corinth 5–1. In the men's game, it was Nemea who came out on top over Olympia, 4–3. At the end, ceremonial olive wreaths were placed on the heads of every player, the winners took home trophies fashioned from the spruce trees that had once stood on the pitch, and everyone walked back out through the woods, to leave the whole thing behind.

There was one brief return, however. Schoolchildren came to plant trees all along the white lines that marked out the playing surface – hawthorn, Scots pine, aspen, birch, wych elm. The aim was for these native species to grow up in the middle of the non-native spruce, creating, as Craig put it, 'a symbolically diverse eco-system' and a 'huge three-dimensional sculptural representation of the pitch'.

I stepped through great clumps of tussocky grass to get to the centre of the pitch, then walked back and forward to each of the goalposts. The crossbars were bowed downwards, but the frames were still standing. Greeny-blue lichen had spread all along the wood. One stanchion was filled entirely with a huge spider's web. Some of the young trees were already three or four metres in height. They crowded in a line around the goals, like a defensive wall awaiting a free kick. The silence and stillness was startling. The dark presence of the spruce beyond the clearing's perimeter seemed to act as both wind-break and sound-break. The sun was still just high enough to catch the whole pitch and, looking west, it backlit the trees and grass with hazy, bronze halos. I wished I'd brought a ball with me.

The act of clearing a ceremonial space in a forest is a very old one. Go back to the Bronze Age, say. Considerable time was taken by our ancestors to make such spaces, to cut the trees – then to carry the wood away, to build with or to burn. Preparations would be made, building towards a specific day, a specific time. Many people would travel to the site, often from far away. A ritual would be performed, a place of insignificance turned into one of significance. The wilderness made sacred; a memory imprinted in the landscape. We think of such spaces, and the reasons for them, as thousands of years distant, arcane and unknowable. Not less than a decade old. And not about football.

I sat awhile on the simple wooden bench in the simple wooden building, the sun on my face, watching the clouds drift over the clearing, the sky turn from blue to orange. In the stillness, the hut with its ranks of pillars had the feeling of a temple. I sat there for a long time, longer than I realised. Then I walked away from the pitch, glancing over my shoulder until the trees took it. Back through the dark of the forest.

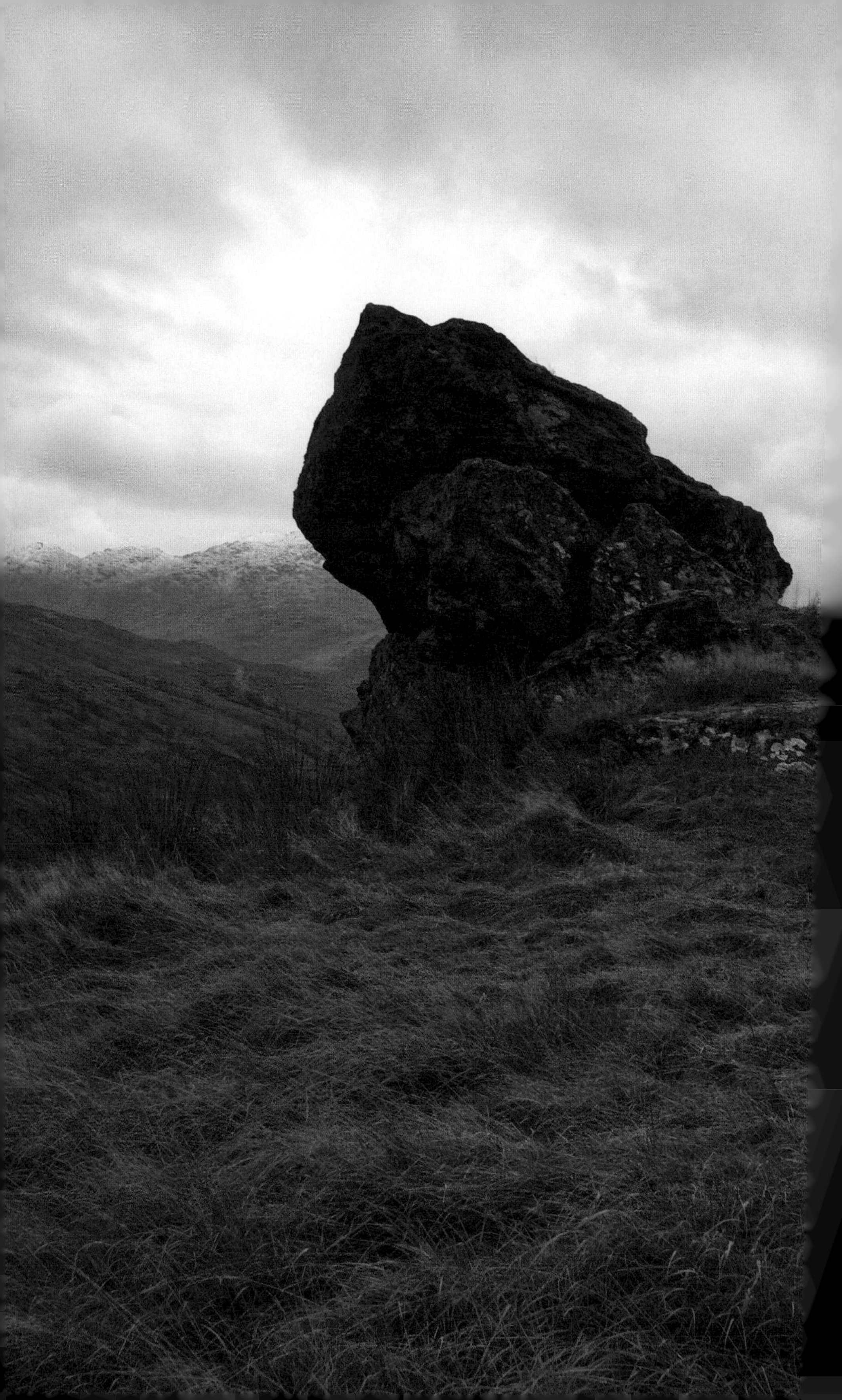

Contested

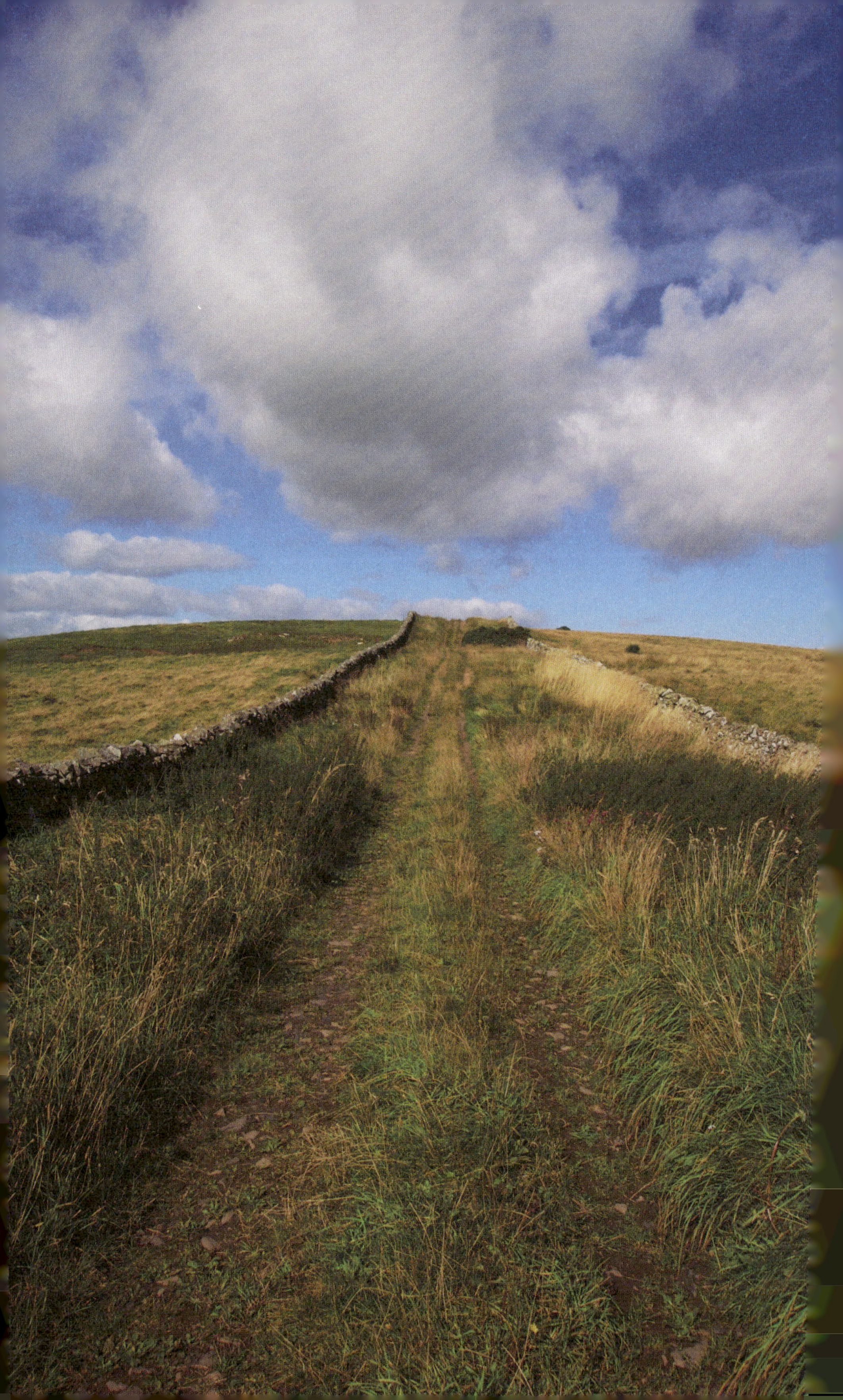

Dere Street Roman Road, The Borders

NT 7419 1868

The road ahead was a lonely stretch joining nowhere to nowhere. I was perhaps a couple of miles east of the town of Jedburgh, a little less than a mile north of the border with England. Surrounding me was open moorland: a rolling landscape, 1,000 feet above the Tweed Valley, looking onto the rising spine of the Cheviot Hills. The line of the road was etched into the landscape. It was bound by an old, crumbling drystone wall on one side, a line of wire-strung wooden fence posts on the other. Golden wild grass fringed the wall and the fence, while the road itself was a verdant green, a few metres wide, dipping down and curving slightly west, to run out of sight over a low hilltop about half a mile in the distance.

This road is near enough 2,000 years old. Long overgrown, but still persisting. When it was built, it would have looked not entirely unlike the roads we know today (it was, for instance, quite easy to imagine it unrolling across the moor in tarmac, a grey ribbon dotted with white lines). Layers of compacted stones – large cobbles or boulders driven into the earth – had been spread with a fine dusting of gravel and pebbles, creating a metalled road, from the Latin *metallum*, meaning 'quarry'. It was also, as far as we know, Scotland's first-ever road. Built to carry the boots, hoofs and wheels of the advancing army of imperial Rome.

It wasn't as if there weren't footpaths already traversing the country. Well-trodden ways that had come, over centuries, even millennia, to thread between the hills and valleys. But this was different. This was the process of deliberately cutting and imbedding a route into the earth – raising it up and shaping it and finishing it with a solid surface of quarried rock. It is hard for us today to understand just how significant an intervention this must have seemed in the landscape. Those old, local paths had emerged out of practice and custom and – ultimately – culture. They spoke of intimate knowledge of the terrain, flowed almost like water, drawn by gravity to find the quickest, most natural course onwards.

What the Romans brought was, by contrast, almost entirely unnatural. While it is a hoary old myth that they only built straight roads, it emerged out of a more general truth. Their engineers were always seeking the most efficient way to join one point to another. Straightness was an aspiration mediated by the realities of topography – rivers, mountains, bogs, ravines. Yet all the same, there was a kind of implacable tyranny in this will to attain linear perfection. A constant push towards the unswerving that carried within it the essence of an aggressive, alien sensibility.

The road into Caledonia was constructed between AD 78 and 84 under the orders of the then Roman Governor of Britannia, Julius Agricola. We know it began in York, crossed the border into present-day Scotland at Carter Fell, and then continued through the Tweed Valley and over the Lammermuirs to Edinburgh and the military outpost of Inchtuthil, near Perth. Although the Roman name for the road is lost (over time it has come to be called Dere Street – derived, perhaps, from Deira, the sixth-century Anglo-Saxon kingdom of Northumbria, through which the longest proportion of it runs), there is no doubt that it was conceived, quite specifically, as a conduit for invasion and conquest. Every inch or foot or mile completed brought conflict closer. There was nothing benign about a road back then.

In recent years, archaeologists have dug down below its current surface in search of trace elements of its original, 2,000-year-old materials. At Dun Law, a boggy stretch of hill on the northern side of the Lammermuirs – now a sprawling wind-farm site – they opened an eighteen-metre-square trench, removing the upper layers of vegetation and peat to expose the true road.

First came the cobbles. There was even obvious evidence of repairs to the original surface (the filling-in of Scotland's first potholes . . .). Then came a sub-base of pinkish-red clay, which had been laid out in advance to level the road in preparation for the cobbles. Below that were preserved fragments of ancient logs. These, it seemed, had been combined with twigs and small branches to create a lattice of brushwood matting that aided drainage and allowed the road to cross areas of wet marshland. Wood, soil and pollen sampling revealed the species used in the lattice – birch, hazel, alder and ash. There were even sections showing the burrow holes of death-watch beetles – evidence that old wood had been used in construction, most probably brought all the way north from England.

Just these few metres of road contained within them both the sophistication and terrifying determination of the Roman advance. Yet they also symbolised the everyday reality of invasion – that the vast majority of military energy was expended not in battle but in the mundane task of developing infrastructure. In digging drainage ditches on lonely, windswept moors. Boots deep in the muck and the mud and the glaur.

It is no surprise, then, that contemporary Roman accounts of the Caledonian campaigns dwell on the weather and the often-saturated terrain. 'The climate is foul with frequent rains and mists,' wrote the historian Tacitus at the beginning of the second century AD. He bemoaned Britannia's 'abundant moisture of land and sky' in general. But when it came to Caledonia, the landscape was even more extreme, he said – seeming as much comprised of water as it was of earth. 'Nowhere does the sea hold wider sway. It carries to and fro a mass of currents and its ebb and flow is not restricted to the coast, but passes deep inland and winds about, pushing in even among highlands and mountains as if in its own domain.'

Dere Street Roman Road, Borders

Writing a century later, Cassius Dio recounted how the armies of Emperor Septimius Severus 'experienced countless hardships in cutting down the forests, levelling the heights, filling up the swamps, and bridging the rivers; but he fought no battle and beheld no enemy in battle array'. The Caledonians, Cassius Dio said, simply drew the Romans on further and further, using the terrain to wear them out. 'The water caused great suffering,' he wrote. Legions were 'lured into the swamps, whose waters their bodies could not endure as the Britons could'.

At the intersection of written history and archaeological reality, you can find that lattice brushwood matting which formed the base of much of Dere Street. *The water caused great suffering*. You can only imagine the hours, days, months of construction. Transporting and arranging your logs and branches. Digging endless small quarry pits to extract rock from the roadside to lay on top. Years spent extending your line over bog and marsh and moor.

I had been walking for several hours now. With the English border in sight, I finally turned back to the north. The moorland glowed in the early autumn light, a faint haze across the blue sky offering a golden filter for the sun. The wind was soft, but persistent. I thought about the last Roman to have walked this road. Did they leave in relief or disappointment? Their boots striking those cobbles, one foot in front of the other, to cover the miles. Were they wondering if it was all worth it; or did they simply follow the man in front, who in turn followed the man in front of him, on and on, in a departing column that stretched off into the southern distance? Separated by nearly 2,000 years, we passed each other on the road, this last phantom Roman and I. Heading in opposite directions, we exchanged a nod of greeting, as walkers do. And then continued on our separate ways.

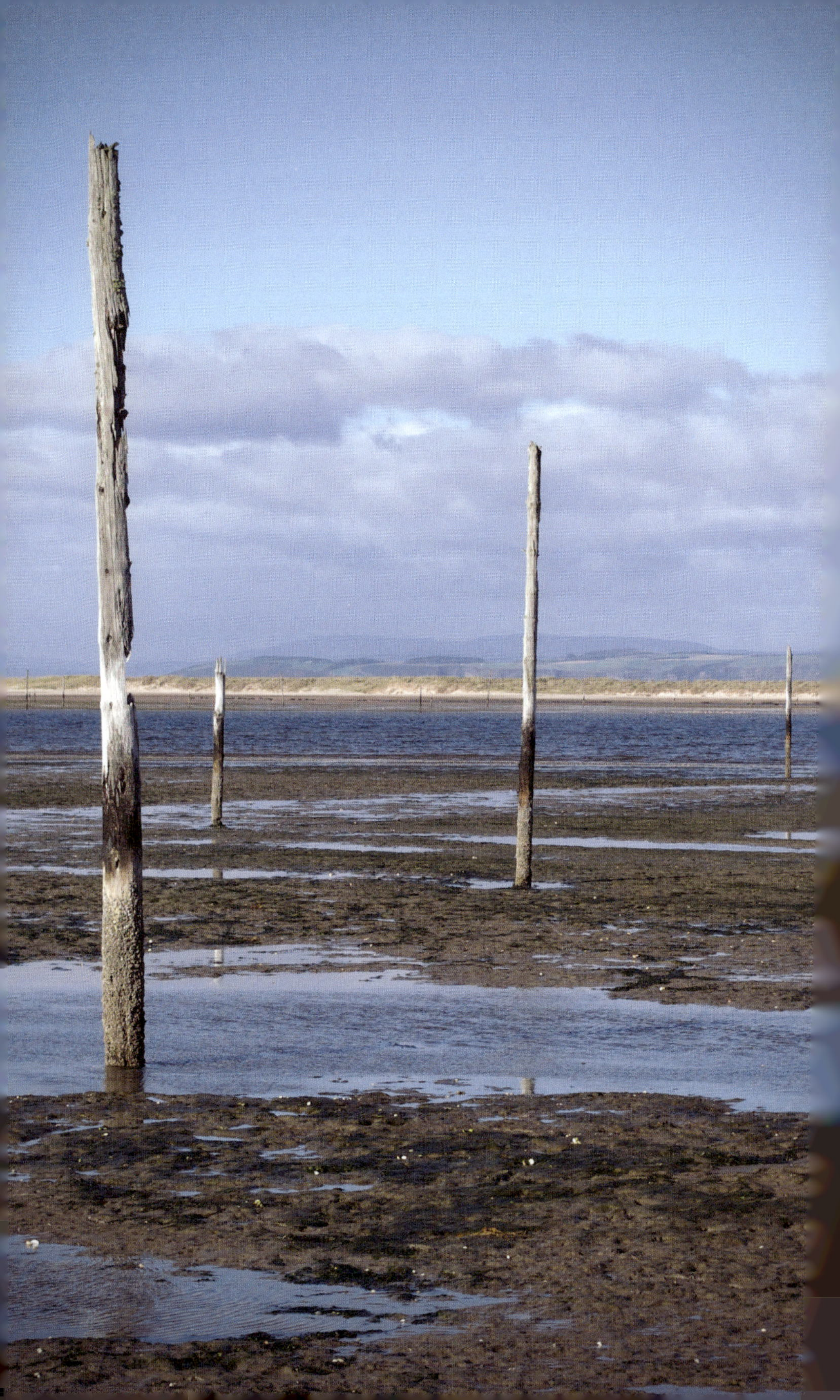

Culbin Sands Poles, Moray

NH 9754 6317

The poles run for some nine kilometres along and across the beach. There are more than 2,000 of them – although no one has ever actually counted every single one – and they are spaced out in irregular rows, each set fifteen to twenty metres apart. The poles themselves are made from the thin trunks of Scots pine, their branches whittled away to leave slender totems, some still standing four metres tall, others broken down to stumps that only reached up to my waist. They are all bleached a pale, brittle white, apart from a single band of dark tide-marking, showing where the sea rises around them, day in, day out. Below the mark, they are encrusted with layers of tiny grey barnacles so thick they look like poured concrete.

It was mid-morning and the tide was receding fast, leaving hard ripples in the mudflats, and long, shallow rivulets of water which caught and reflected the unbroken blue of the sky. I had cycled here through Culbin Forest, past miles of Scots and Corsican pine, until I reached an overgrown track that ran gently uphill through a narrow avenue of trees before sloping back down again. It was only on this very last stretch of forest that I was able to catch a glimpse of the sea.

A little more than a century ago, there had been almost no trees here at all. As a 1950s Forestry Commission report put it, Culbin's coastline had been reduced to 'a virtual desert of quick moving sand'. This was the site of what was known as the Great Sand Drift. In one night in 1694, sixteen farms – along with the house of the laird, Alexander Kinnaird – were swallowed up by a colossal sandstorm. As John Martin of Elgin wrote at the time, the wind had come 'rushing down through the openings between the hills, carrying with it immense torrents of sand with a force and violence almost overpowering'. Nothing could be seen, he said, 'but sand above, sand below, sand everywhere'.

Some locals blamed the laird himself, saying that the catastrophe was God's retribution, because he had been seen in his house playing cards with the Devil on a Sunday. Kinnaird, for his part, claimed that he and his lands had been cursed by a witch. It wasn't long before a local woman, Isobel Gowdie, was arrested. She confessed – under torture – to making a pact with the Devil to raise the storm and, after a six-week trial, she was burnt at the stake.

The real reason for the sandstorm was far simpler. Drifts had been on the increase for centuries along this coast: the result of the local people uprooting the marram grass that bound the dunes together. As more and more marram was taken – mainly for thatching the roofs of houses – the dunes became unmoored completely. When the big storm hit, there had been nothing left to keep them in place.

Culbin was abandoned almost entirely until the beginning of the twentieth century, when the Forestry Commission undertook a programme of planting which was intended to knit this landscape back together. It was, their report said, 'a formidable undertaking', including tackling a 'vast stretch of dunes, reaching to about 100ft above sea level' where 'sand was constantly on the move'. While progress was at first 'tedious and costly', with many seedlings torn out by the wind, over time the replanted marram grass stabilised the ground, and the pines grew and spread to cover the hundreds of acres of the drifting dune systems. As a result, the traces of the community that had once farmed this land were now *twice* buried.

By the time this process of afforestation was completed, however, the sands at Culbin presented a new threat. In the early years of the Second World War, the great extent of the beach itself, beyond the now tree-covered dunes, was deemed strategically vulnerable. By the summer of 1940, German forces controlled almost the entire western coastline of continental Europe. The invasion of Britain was thought to be only months away. According to one plan – codenamed Autumn Journey – German troops were set to launch a major offensive from Norway, targeting the beaches of north-eastern Scotland. Culbin – miles long and, at low tide, miles wide – offered the perfect landing point.

Culbin Sands Poles, Moray

The response of General Edmund Ironside, Commander-in-Chief of Britain's Home Forces, was to 'create an extended crust of defence along the probable invasion beaches'. Long stretches of the whole country's eastern shore, 'from the Shetlands to Swanage', became studded with the concrete husks of anti-tank blocks and pillboxes, and bristled with tight rolls of barbed wire. At Culbin, the network of wooden poles was a crucial part of this 'crust'. Rather than an obstacle for tanks or ground troops, however, its specific purpose was to prevent an aerial invasion. The poles were spaced out according to the anticipated wingspans of enemy gliders. They may even have been joined together by long strings of steel wire, creating a giant labyrinth of wood and metal. In the end, of course, this invasion never came. And, ironically, by 1944, Culbin was being used as a practice site for the Allied landing plans for D-Day.

As for the poles, dug deep into the ground more than eighty years ago: they were just left where they stood (although, if wires had once linked them, now they were long gone). I walked further out across the wet, open sands, between pole after pole; my own movement within them creating a profusion of lines and angles, as viewpoints through and along the rows of the wooden uprights collapsed and unfolded all around me. The low morning sun was causing the poles to cast long shadows; at the same time, their reflections shimmered in the pools of retreating tidal water. It seemed to me, in those moments, that the poles had become far less a relic of strategic military infrastructure, and far more a giant piece of land art. As if they had been designed, quite deliberately, to impose a strange and beautiful geometry on a wide and empty stretch of coastline.

I was the only person out on the beach that morning, but I was not alone. Oystercatchers hopped busily across the mudflats, poking their long beaks into puddles. Scoters and eider ducks bobbed among the poles still part submerged by the shallow sea. Birdcall filled the air. An onshore wind had come on strong, riffling the surfaces of the seawater pools. The poles did not move, but the light, the sea, the sands, the birds, the weather, the seasons – they all shifted endlessly around them.

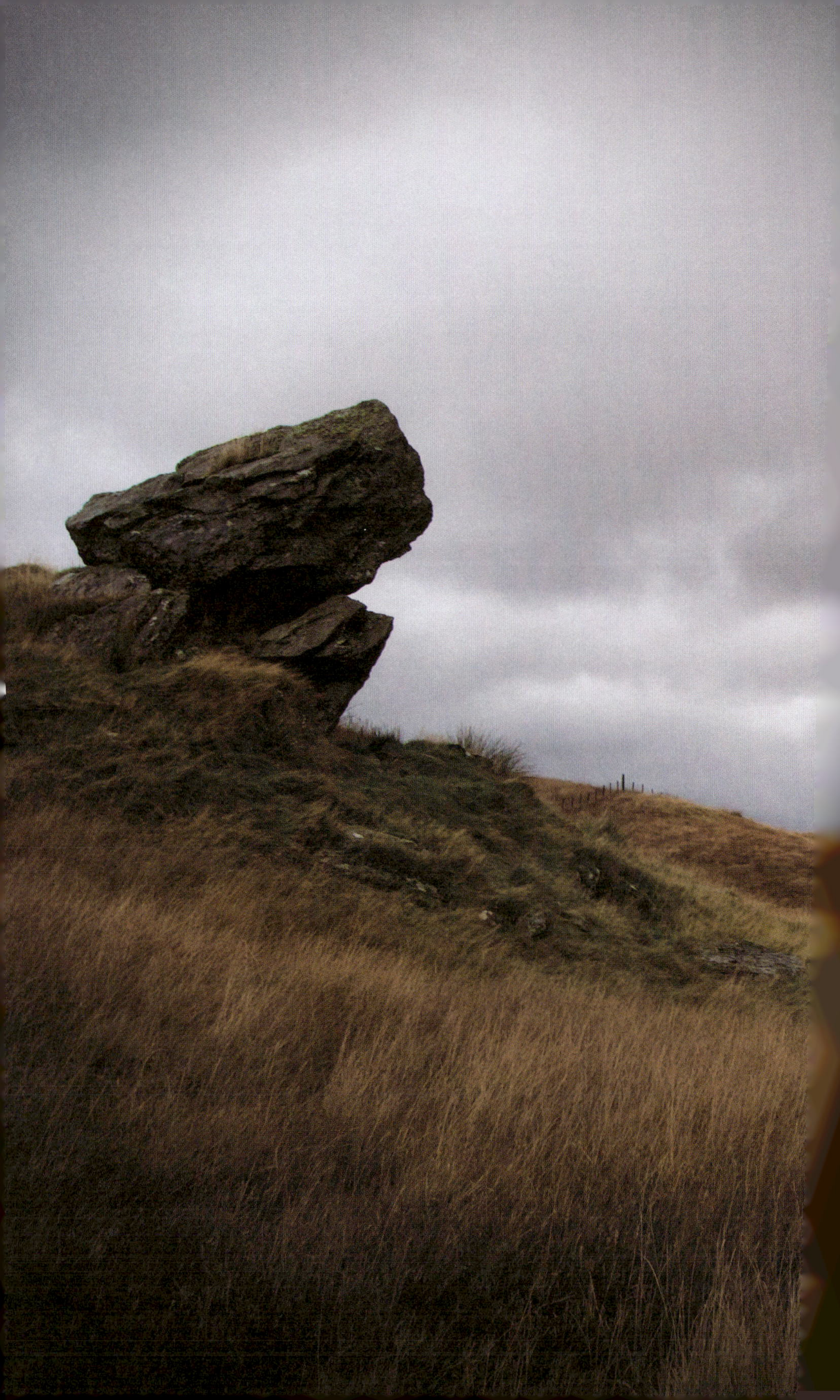

Clach na Briton, Glen Falloch

NN 3371 2161

Rust-red, overgrown bracken fringed the narrow path as it led beneath the tracks of the West Highland Line. A sheep gate barred the far end of the short tunnel. Water was pouring beneath the gate and running in thick rivulets down the stone walls on either side. Underfoot, it was slick and slippery, and I had to brace myself against one wall to get the gate open without falling. Out the other side, the track was little more than a rocky, fast-flowing stream bed. I splashed through it uphill for another thirty yards or so, and then it just disappeared completely.

It had been raining through the night. Not far above me was the margin where the rain had turned to snow. The surrounding mountains shifted abruptly from wide stretches of burnished copper to tips of pale white. I was making my way up the steep slope on the northern side of Glen Falloch, just above the point where the deep cut of Allt Fionn Ghleann rushes down to meet the River Falloch on its way south to Loch Lomond. The burble of water mingled with the rumble of cars passing along the A82 on the valley floor below. Climbing higher, the sound dimmed to a faint buzz and was soon lost on the wind.

It was hard going, the whole hillside thread-veined with streams. Every other step, firm ground gave way to puddles of bog. Here and there, stones protruded from the slopes. I followed these faint, rocky seams upwards. One steep hillock would level out for a few yards and then lead straight into another. I wasn't worried about missing my destination, though. I just needed to get higher. Sure enough, after about half an hour of walking, I reached the top of yet another rise, and there it was.

From a distance, it seemed to defy gravity. One giant boulder, pointing up to the sky at a near forty-five-degree angle, balanced on top of a cluster of smaller boulders. These stones, in turn, surged outwards from a large grassy knoll, a halo of green surrounded by orange-red deer grass. From the base of this mound to the top of the boulder was a height of at least thirty feet. The closer you got, the more it loomed.

I scrambled up around the back of the knoll. From this angle, it was clear it wasn't just one massive stone, but two: one great flat block – the capstone – lying on top of a second massive slab, which disappeared down into the earth. Their grey surfaces were mottled with patches of white lichen and thick, lush moss. The view took in the whole landscape. To the east was the high ridgeline of peaks on the other side of Glen Falloch – Ben Ghlas, Beinn Chabhair, An Caisteal. To the south, the valley opened out towards the head of Loch Lomond. To the west was Fionn Ghleann and the snow-capped summit of Ben Oss. North, the forested slopes of Breadalbane.

Drops of rain began to spatter on my jacket. I looked off to the southwest. A huge grey cloudbank was travelling at speed towards me. The mountains blurred, then disappeared completely. I climbed down underneath the slab and pulled myself up into the space between the lower boulder and the huge, overhanging capstone. The rain came on hard, but I was sheltered.

Around 1,500 years ago, people heaved these colossal schistose slabs into place. Indeed, this whole knoll itself may have been built beneath them: a super-sized cairn, now covered over with grass so that it is only the stones at the very tip that appear to burst out of the land. What I was sitting inside was a sort of ancient triangulation point. More than that, it was a border.

This heap of stones was erected as the place where three realms met. It marked the northernmost frontier of the kingdom of the Britons of Strathclyde. It was, at the same time, the westernmost limit of Pictland. And it was also the southern and eastern fringe of the lands of Dalriada. Glen Falloch would have been a natural borderland, hemmed in on every side by steep, towering mountains. The valley floor offered a route north or south and, for travellers, this distinctive boulder landmark, set high up on the western hillside, would have been impossible to miss. Pass in any direction in its shadow and you would know the risks. You were leaving one domain. Entering another.

The shower soon moved on. I watched the clouds shift northwards carry-

Clach na Briton, Glen Falloch

ing their sheets of rain beneath them. The eleventh-century Irish abbot Tighernach wrote of a border battle fought here in AD 717 between the Britons and the Dalriads, right alongside this very stone boundary marker. He called the stone 'Minvircc'. Today, it is known as Clach na Briton: 'the stone of the Britons'.

Few people come here. No feet have worn a path. No one debates or fights over this land, this lonely, boggy hillside. Once these boulders held a great, symbolic power. The very sight of them would have been charged with significance: a nexus point, a triple frontier. But then kingdoms come and go. Boundaries shift or disappear. Clach na Briton has lost its purpose and its potency. Its great capstone still points up to the heavens. It knows when it was made, and what it was made for. But this border has been open for centuries now. All it stands sentry over is a memory.

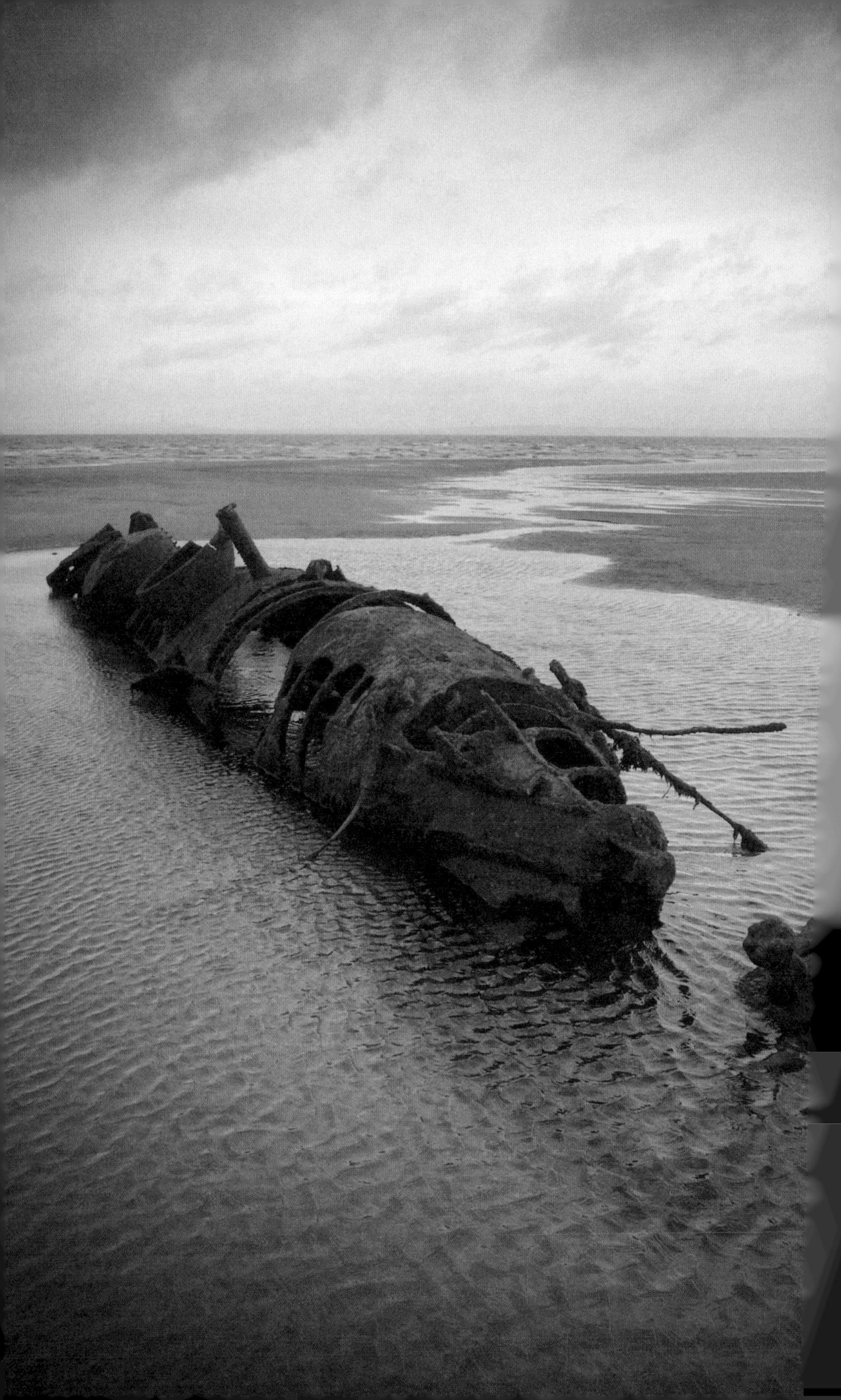

X-Craft Midget Submarines, Aberlady Bay

NT 4518 8144

At low tide, the sands of Aberlady Bay stretch out for near enough a kilometre before they reach the sea. I had come on a grey day in early autumn, the clouds high and distinct, backlit by a sun that made them glow but could not push through their massed canopy. There was a strong onshore wind, which sent skeins of sand running in erratic patterns all across the flat expanse of the bay. To the west, the hills of Edinburgh were dark silhouettes. To the north, the Fife coastline was not visible at all. With no other person in sight, the sense, clear and palpable, was of walking out across some lonely desert shore.

I saw the black shapes sitting at the far extent of the low-tide line, just short of the breaking point of a procession of white-tipped waves. There were two of them, set perhaps a hundred metres apart, with a large cube block halfway between. From a distance, they looked like the skeletons of unfortunate sea creatures, long-since run aground and stranded on the sandbank: a couple of basking sharks, or a pair of minke whales perhaps.

On approach, this impression only intensified. The closest lay in a shallow tidal pool, and its body seemed to stretch out from the empty, interconnecting arches of a broken ribcage into a long tail tipped with a ridge of small fins. The whole thing was coated in seaweed and a kind of mossy dark green fur. Less a shark now than the saurian carcass of a sea dragon. The second was more intact than the first. It had that same profile of exposed ribs, but this one had a head too. There were sockets for eyeholes leading to three thin shafts with the unnerving appearance of insect antennae. Viewed front-on, it was like a giant, wingless wasp, crushed and drowned in the watery sand.

These skeletons have lain on the tidal flats now for nearing eight decades, exposed and drowned tens of thousands of times by the retreating and advancing sea. At first, they were moored to that huge concrete cube; but presumably any tethering rope had long since rotted away. Remarkably, men once lived and worked inside them. Two, maybe even three, in each. They were known as X-Craft, or midget submarines: tiny vessels designed and built during the Second World War to undertake sabotage missions on ships docked in enemy harbours. Conditions inside were, unsurprisingly, extreme – cramped, cold and damp, with almost no space to move. Operations could run for as much as two weeks at sea, with food cooked in a tiny glue pot. Each X-Craft had what was called a 'wet and dry' compartment – an air lock that would allow a crew member to don a diving suit and open an external hatch so they could work outside the ship, cutting holes in submarine netting, or planting depth charges.

Training began in June 1942 in a secret naval base on the shores of Loch Erisort, just south of Stornoway on the Isle of Lewis. Some sixty men were transferred from their operational base at Port Bannatyne on the Isle of Bute, undertaking test runs along the loch bed in the X-Craft and even smaller 'human torpedoes' – nicknamed 'chariots'. Days were split into three eight-hour periods, one for submarine operations, one for exercising, one for sleeping. From orientation and basic controls, they moved on to navigation and endurance, and then finally full dummy runs, cutting nets and attaching bombs to a ship's hull. Pilots suffered everything from burst eardrums to unconsciousness. In their spare time, they swam in the loch and fished from its banks, late into the long summer evenings.

A year later, a group of those same men were moving beneath the waters of a Norwegian fjord, some 100 miles north of the Arctic Circle. Six X-Craft with sixteen crew were part of an attack codenamed Operation Source. On the evening of 22 September 1943, they breached the submarine nets strung across the harbour mouth of the village of Kåfjord and succeeded in planting two charges on the hull of the *Tirpitz*, a German warship. Although ten of the crew died, and the other six were captured, the operation was judged a success. The explosions from the charges ruptured the battleship's fuel tanks and tore holes in its bulkheads. The *Tirpitz* did not sink, but it was effectively crippled.

The X-Craft were later co-opted by Operation Overlord in the spring of

X-Craft Midget Submarines, Aberlady Bay

1945, tasked with surveying the beaches of Normandy in preparation for the D-Day landings. Over the course of several nights, one of the submarines approached what would become Omaha Beach. In the darkness, two divers swam to land to examine the terrain and the defences – even going so far as using condoms to collect soil samples.

It is, perhaps, a strange legacy that these two training prototypes of the midget submarine – craft that once chased fish and crab along the floor of Loch Erisort – have ended up scuttled here on the sands of Aberlady Bay. There was little sentimentality in how they were treated as the war ended. Towed all the way from the west coast in 1946, they were tied to that heavy concrete block and, for a time, used as targets for RAF fighter planes. Yet still they persist.

I watched as the strong wind ruffled the surfaces of the tidal pools around them, and the flow of the water began to turn. The tide was coming back in. Out on the very edge of the sand flats, this change was not subtle. With every passing second, the waves ran closer and closer, gulping down large stretches of the beach. Soon the submarines would be back beneath the waves once again. Back where they belonged? This is their unintentionally poetic fate. Submerging and surfacing, submerging and surfacing, over and over again. Until – and it may take decades, may even take centuries – the waves finally prise their bones apart, scatter them out to sea or bury them in the silt. As the foamy water rolled in, I turned away, walked towards the distant dunes on the shoreline, rivers of sand blowing all around my ankles.

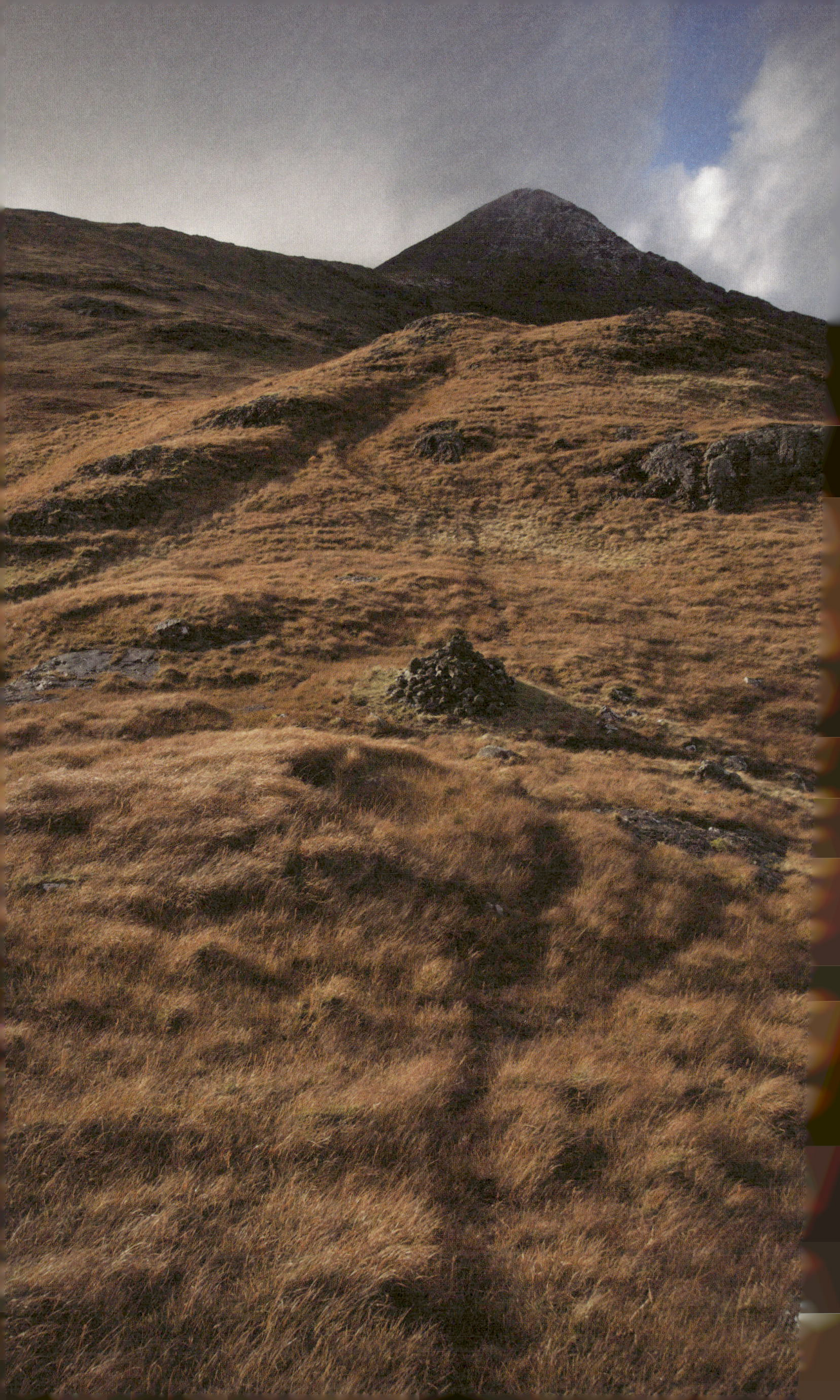

Cairn Cul Ri Albainn, Isle of Mull

NM 5535 3324

I took my time picking the stones, fishing around in the limpid stream bed. Behind me, water smashed and slapped. Here the mountain stream met a hard seam of rock that it could not cut, and so it tumbled several metres straight down to form a wide plunge pool. I was crouched at the far end of the pool.

I spotted one stone, bright red, and plucked it out. It had been smoothed into a dented sphere, about the size of a squash ball. I picked out a second: jagged-edged, a shark's tooth, covered in blue-green seams. I shook them dry and zipped them into my jacket pocket.

I was following an old path that began at the remains of a disused humpback bridge on the valley floor at the western end of Glen More. It was late October. The bracken and deer grass were at their most vivid. They had turned the hills and mountainsides of Mull into an expanse of near-unbroken orange. Only the highest peak, Ben More, remained untouched. A stubbornly monochrome presence: its conical head of black rock etched with fine wrinkles of snow.

The route cut directly across the watershed. My map told me the path would bisect no less than twelve streams, each running straight down through tight contours to rush out to sea at Loch Scridain. Crossing those streams required varying degrees of creativity and invention. Nearly every ford was submerged or in torrent.

The first glimpse of the cairn came from several hundred metres away. The path curved around the hillside and a pyramid of stones appeared in the distance, set on the flat ground of a high saddle of land – known as Mam Clachaig – that links the pinnacles of Ben More and Cruachan Dearg. As recently as the 1960s, this cairn marked the summit pass of a drove road, taking cattle northwards to the pier at Salen for shipping to the mainland.

Before that, in the nineteenth century, drovers travelled in the opposite direction, bringing their herds south over the saddle to descend to Glen More and on to Grass Point on the far eastern corner of the island. There the cattle would be ferried to the island of Kerrera to swim the final stretch across the sound to Oban. Post-runners followed this route too, one travelling south from Salen over Mam Clachaig to meet his counterpart from Bunessan at Kinloch, where he'd exchange letters and then turn around, repeating the climb in reverse. But the story of this cairn goes back far further than that.

In 1645 the Dutch cartographer Joan Blaeu published the first-ever 'atlas' of Scotland. In his map of 'Mula Insula' – the Isle of Mull – he recorded this cairn, calling it Karn Culri Allabyn. He also noted a second cairn, Karn Culri Erin, located just to the south, as if on the valley floor of Glen More. Allabyn and Erin: Scotland and Ireland. Blaeu's map was, it seemed, referencing a division, a boundary, filtered through a prism of half-truths and folklore going back another thousand years.

The nineteenth-century Scottish historian William Forbes Skene thought the relevance was obvious. He traced the origin of the cairn back to Saint Columba's religious community, established on nearby Iona in the sixth century. Skene noted how Columba's biographer, Adomnán, continually referenced missionary journeys eastwards into the lands of the Picts. These expeditions always required crossing what Adomnán called a 'dorsal ridge' running through Scotland, a great spine of mountains known as Drumalban: the watershed between east and west. On one side were the Picts, and on the other the Scots of Dalriada – the kingdom that controlled most of what is now Argyll, along with the lands at the northern fringe of Ireland.

Historians have long argued over the precise location of Adomnán's Drumalban – and still continue to search for it today. Skene's view, however, was that the northern boundary of this ridge could be represented by 'a line drawn from the mouth of Loch Leven through the district of Morvern . . . then through the island of Mull by the great ridge of Ben More'. Right where

Wild History

I was standing. Alba and Erin. Pictland and Dalriada. Mull cut in two, divided between kingdoms by its own towering mountain range. Many have since disputed Skene's theory, and the evidence remains, at best, confused and fragmentary. Others believe, for instance, that the cairn was not a border between kingdoms, but rather marked the far boundary of the lands gifted to the Iona mission: lands which reached beyond their island refuge and along the Ross of Mull to this very spot.

I looked at the cairn. Could any part of it really date from the days of Columba? Deep inside, perhaps at the very bottom of the pile, were there stones placed by the hands of pilgrims. By Adomnán? Or even Columba himself? It seemed fanciful. But then, why not? There is no miracle in carrying a stone, placing it and continuing on your journey. Travellers pass back and forth, the cairn grows, collapses a little, is reformed, is touched by hundreds of hands, then thousands. Centuries pass. Layer is placed upon layer, stone upon stone. Lichen coats the surfaces, moss grows. The cairn becomes, quite literally, a touchstone (or, rather, touchstones). It marks the way onwards. And the way homewards.

North, past the cairn, was Glen Clachaig and, in the distance, Loch Ba. The other side of Mull's watershed. And a very different landscape. The valley I'd walked up was narrow, a steep 'V' cut through by a fast-flowing river. Beyond, however, the land was like a giant bathtub, scoured out by glaciation. Countless streams and rivulets poured down its sides to a wide, flat bottom, feeding a river that flowed to the loch. The way north was bigger somehow, offered a vastness that dwarfed individual scale in a way that the view behind me did not. Another country? It was easy to imagine how you could see it that way.

I took the stones out of my pocket, added one to the very tip of the cairn, and wedged the other down into the stonework. Then I touched the cairn one last time, turned and headed back down the path to Glen More. The sun was dropping below a mass of dark rainclouds off to the west, yellow light glinting on the waters of Loch Scridain and the sea beyond. I could almost, but not quite, glimpse Iona in the distance, somewhere out past the hazy silhouette of the peninsula. The cairn was behind me. And I was on my way home.

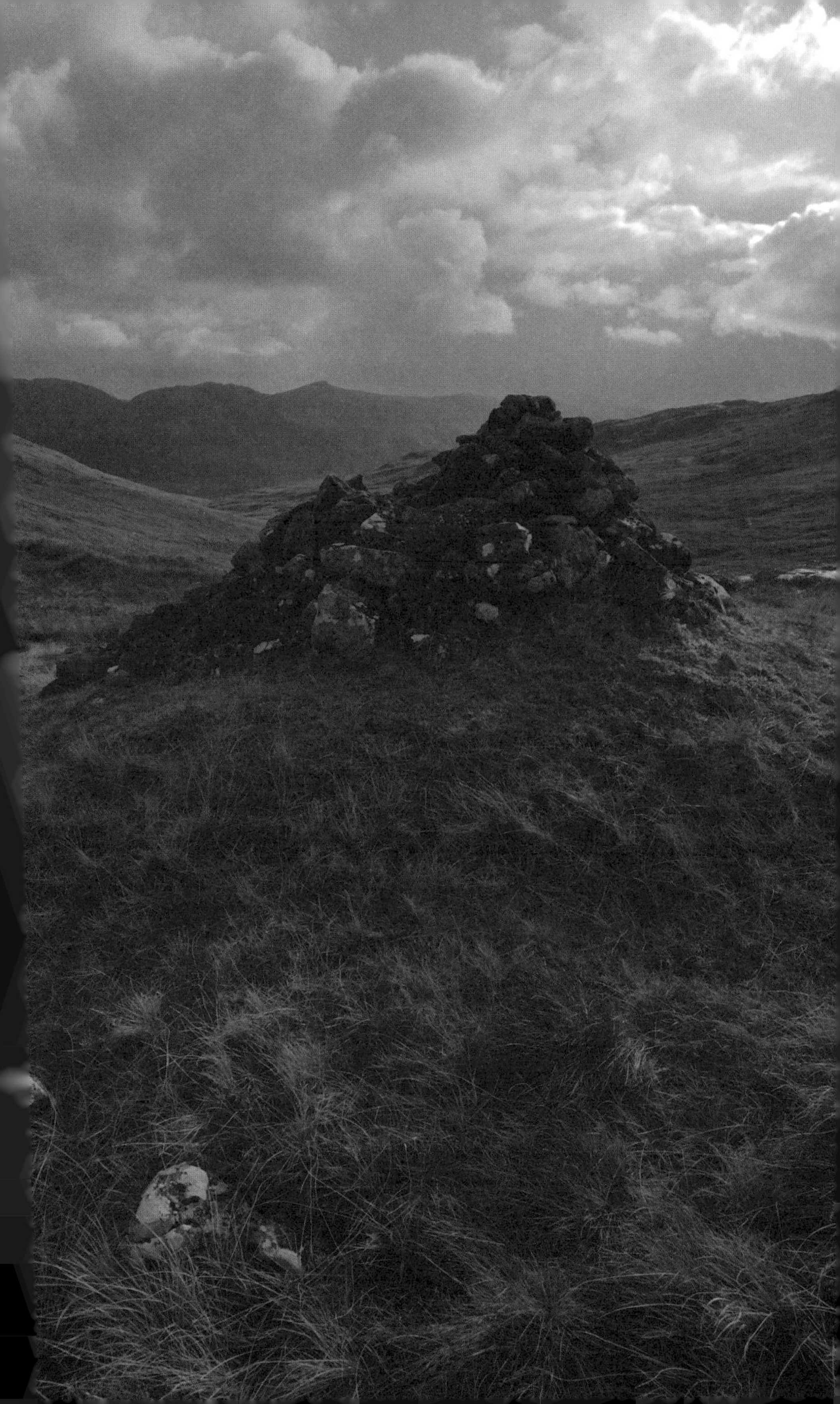

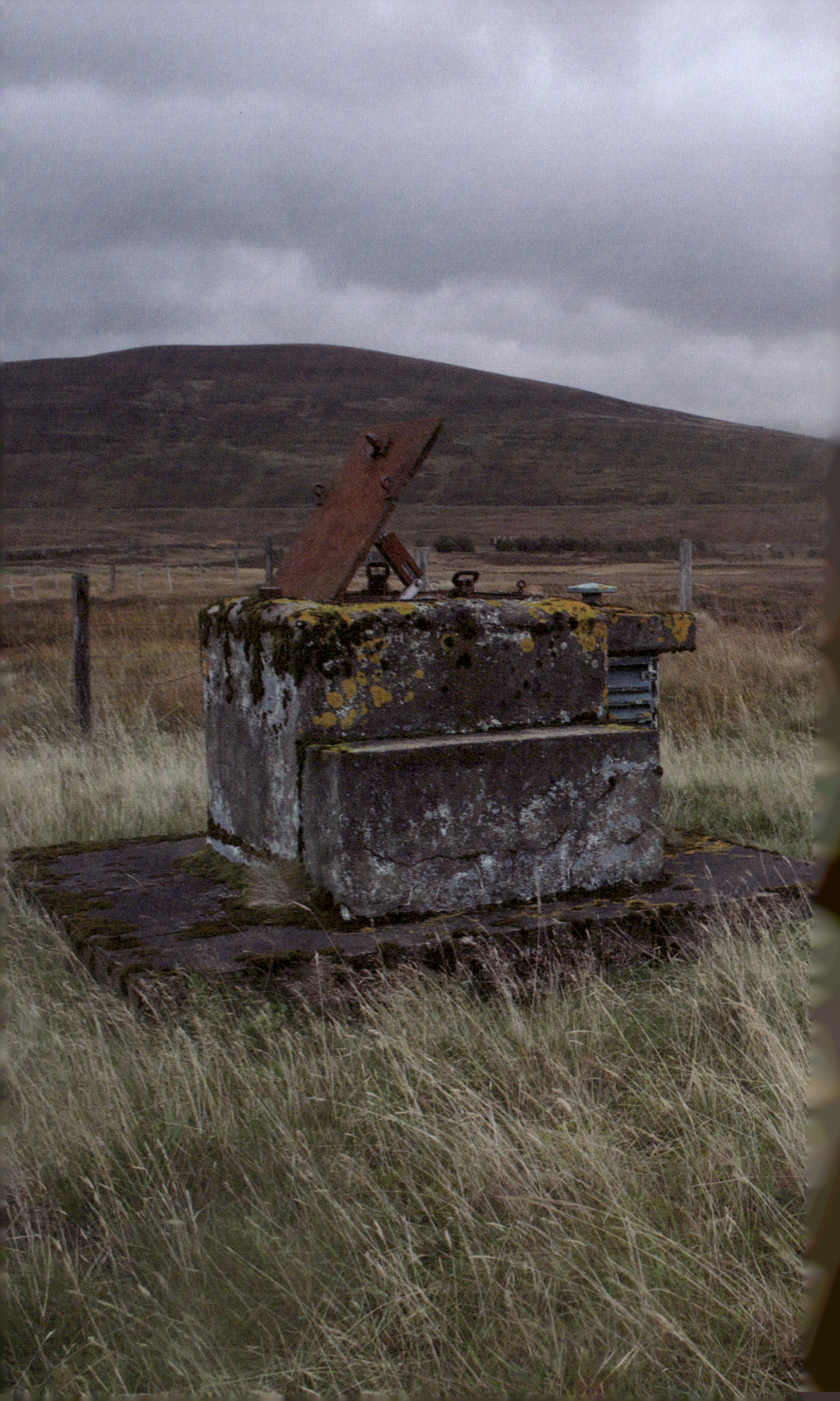

Royal Observer Corps Monitoring Post, Kinbrace

NC 8558 3118

To approach the tiny village of Kinbrace from the west, you cross a stretch of lonely, wide-open country on the eastern edge of Sutherland. The single-track road follows the contours of shores of Loch nan Clar and Loch Badanloch as they feed out in the River Helmsdale. To the south, many miles away on the far horizon, are the looming shapes of the three peaks of Creag na h-Iolaire, Ben Armine and Creag Mhor. But mostly the landscape is a great expanse of flat moor and bogland, a patchwork of peat and moss, thread-veined with dark pools of water.

It was mid-October, and the grasses were such a bright, uniform red that it felt like driving across the surface of Mars. A dense blue cloudbank, which had lingered to the south-west all morning, was now advancing at speed. The wind rushed in to push the grass to horizontal, and sheets of rain were being thrown visibly across the moor.

Just as Kinbrace appeared in the near distance, a huge stag trotted up onto a hump of ground overlooking the road. He had the bunched, muscular shoulders of a prize-fighter, and his stance was almost comically proud. He seemed to look down at my passing car as if it were a provocation and he kept pace in parallel as I drove on. A hundred yards ahead, and right next to the road, was a small concrete box. I parked alongside it and climbed out of the car, the stag watching me all the time. We locked eyes for maybe half a minute and then, with a dismissive toss of his antlers, he turned and strode off.

The box in front of me was covered in green moss and vivid yellow lichen but retained a few flaking patches of what must have been its original turquoise paintwork. A few yards away, two pipes emerged out of the ground, the larger one fixed with a louvred grate. On top of the box was a rust-red metal hatch. I heaved it open, and it caught on a latch with a counterweight holding it in place. Underneath was a silver ladder fixed to a wall. The ladder descended deep below the ground, into darkness.

There were once 1,563 sites exactly like this, spaced roughly eight to fifteen miles apart, across the whole of Britain. They were built between 1956 and 1965 to a standard design: a concrete shell sunk fifteen feet down and made up of two rooms – one with a desk, telephone, radio set and two bunk beds; the other containing a small chemical toilet. The people chosen to occupy these underground chambers faced the prospect of an unspeakably grim task: identifying the epicentre and magnitude of nuclear blast waves and tracking the extent and movement of the ensuing radioactive fallout. At the height of the Cold War, with nuclear attack a very real prospect, they studded the landscape as symbols of a bleak, apocalyptic future.

Manning them were the uniformed civilians of the Royal Observer Corps (ROC). Originally established to monitor German Zeppelin raids during the First World War, the ROC's role had evolved in tandem with the technology of warfare. In the aftermath of the mass aerial bombardments of the Second World War, the nuclear age had taken the possibilities of destruction to horrifying new levels. Now observers were tasked not with warning of imminent attack, but of tracking its inevitable devastation.

Their equipment included a bomb power indicator, a 'ground zero' indicator, and a Geiger counter. Interlinked Teletalk units – blue briefcase-sized boxes with bright-yellow interiors – would allow monitoring posts to communicate with each other and their area headquarters to collate all readings and measurements. The goal was to build as complete a picture as possible of the real-time impact of a nuclear blast.

Inside the monitoring posts – 'bunkers', by any other name – there was no running water and a limited connection to mains electricity. The interiors were lit only by a single six-watt bulb, and there was no heating. Those vents rising up to the surface did not filter the air. There was every chance that the radioactive fallout that the observers were tracking would seep underground and kill them. To descend that ladder in an emergency, pulling the metal hatch down behind you, was, in all likelihood, to seal yourself inside your own tomb.

Royal Observer Corps Monitoring Post, Kinbrace

Less than a kilometre away, just south of Kinbrace on the slopes of the hills that overlook the track of the Far North Line, are a series of large, chambered cairns – underground burial sites from the Neolithic era that are several thousand years old. It is tempting – albeit macabre – to think of how some far-future archaeologist, in a world recovering from nuclear holocaust, could have one day uncovered the thousands of ROC monitoring posts around the country and wondered at the rituals that led to the burials of two or three men together with their strange artifacts, their bunk beds, and their pink government-issue toilet roll.

I lingered over the hatch and the ladder and contemplated climbing down. The weather was harsh and wild – the clouds massed and heavy and black above me. The empty landscape, clad in its autumn colours of scorched red, looked quietly apocalyptic, in its own way. But I was alone and had visions of the hatch falling closed behind me, or the old ladder breaking away from the wall under my weight: of being trapped in a subterranean concrete box with no way of calling for help.

On 30 September 1991, all the monitoring posts were ordered to stand down. As the threat of the Cold War dwindled, they were no longer needed. Many were filled in, flooded, demolished. A few, like this lonely outpost in Kinbrace, remain. I was staring down into an empty tomb, built for a future that, thankfully, has not come. I lifted the hatch further, let the counterweight release, and then guided it slowly and heavily shut again.

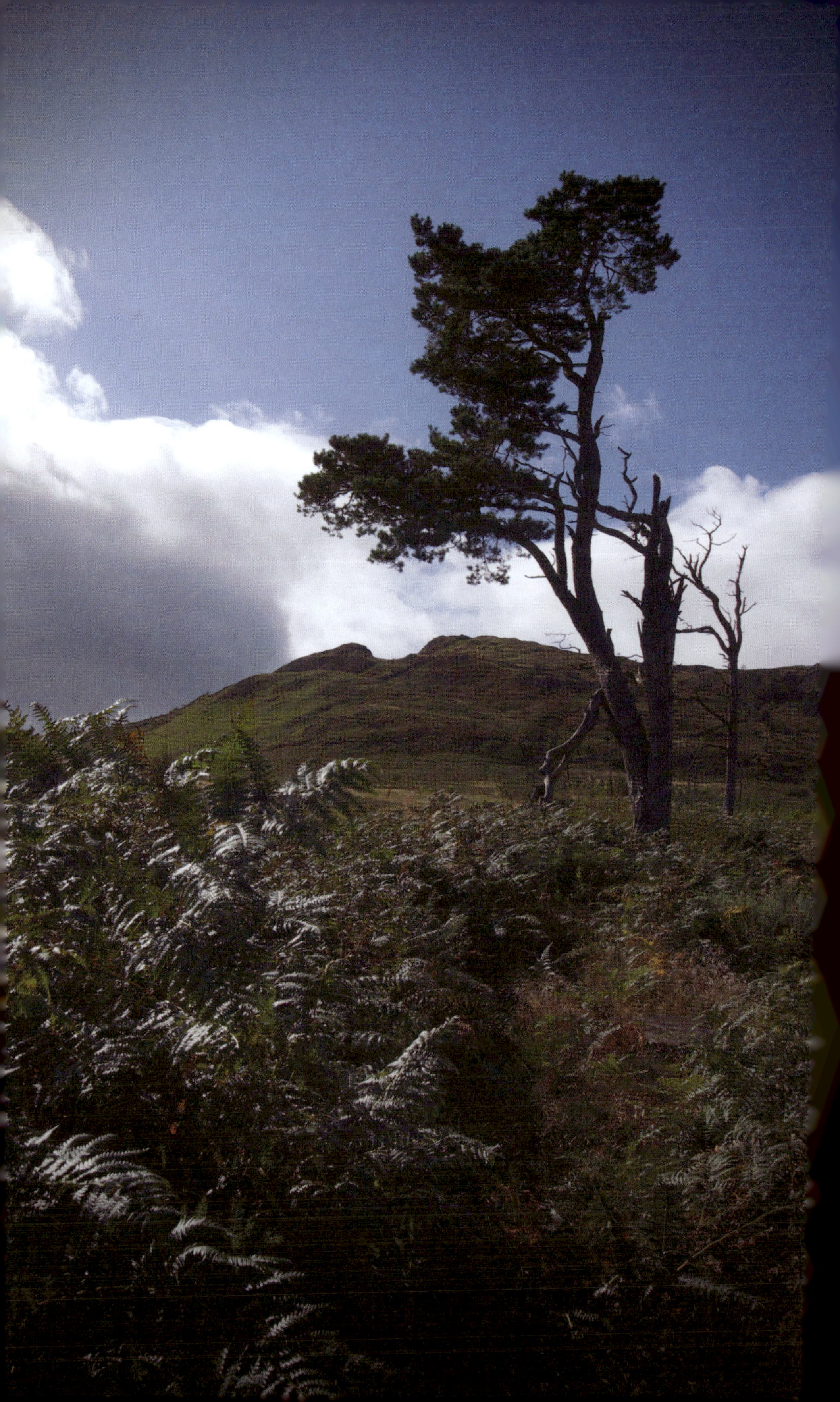

Roman Signal Station, Rubers Law

NT 5803 1557

Looked at on an OS map, Rubers Law has a perfect, pleasing simplicity. Its contour lines are drawn as a series of near-unbroken concentric circles: ripples in a pond, drawing the eye to the tiny dot – the summit – at its centre. There is nothing to break the perfection of the pattern. The comparative flatness of the surrounding terrain – the flood plain between the Rule Water and the Teviot and Tweed rivers – allows the hill to stand almost in isolation above the rest of the landscape.

The result is that Rubers Law is steep on all sides. In the space of less than half a kilometre, it rises up from its lower slopes, around 200 metres in height, to a peak of 424 metres. It is like a hill spun on a potter's wheel: even down to the slight depression at its centre, as if an errant thumb had pushed against the still wet clay. When viewed from either east or west, it offers a distinctive silhouette: a hill with two humps.

I made my approach through a forestry plantation that extends like a wedge across the north-eastern flank of Rubers Law. After a few hundred metres, the trees opened up and gave way to a path that disappeared into a long field of tall bracken, laced with tendrils of thornbushes. The path ran parallel to a drystone wall, enclosing a green meadow filled with the slightly bizarre sight of many grazing red deer. This was no wild herd, but domesticated animals, bred for their venison. They barely looked at me as I passed.

Up ahead, standing like a warped totem pole against the blue sky, was a lone, dead Scots pine. Its remaining branches were black and twisted, but the bark had peeled off the rest of the tree, revealing a stark, grey-white bone of trunk. Beyond the tree, the path climbed out from the overgrown bracken and onto an open stretch of heather and grass. The gradient here steepened markedly, and the hill's U-shaped summit loomed above.

In 1905 Alexander Curle began investigating, and digging, on the top of Rubers Law (at this time, three years before he took up his post at the Royal Commission, Curle was co-secretary of the Society of Antiquaries of Scotland). There was a considerable rocky scatter on the higher slopes, along with seemingly man-made trenches and a rampart. Curle wrote of 'rickles of stones many feet deep, either the wreck of a wall which crowned, or faced, the earthen rampart, or perhaps placed in their present position to impede the rush of an enemy'. Clearly, at some time in its history, Rubers Law had been fortified. As Curle explored the site further he kept finding, among the rough debris, blocks of unusual – and carefully worked – stone. Red and white sandstones, some cut with diamond patterns, others with herringbone or feather-shaped carvings. 'There can, I think, be little doubt to anyone examining these stones,' he wrote, 'that the work on them is Roman.'

It was not a small number of stones either. There were over 200 of them, of which at least seventy had been dressed skilfully in the typical Roman style. Their haphazard incorporation in the wall around the hilltop seemed to Curle a clear case of opportunism. The worked stones were surely too numerous to have been brought from elsewhere by subsequent builders. Some he discovered 'protruding through the turf on the summit itself', while on the slopes immediately below 'they occur in greatest numbers; in the ruins of the wall around the plateau they are occasionally visible and as you descend the hill they rapidly cease to appear'. Their source, and epicentre, appeared to be the summit itself: a Roman building erected there and later abandoned and allowed to fall into ruin. Curle's conclusion was that the 'most extensive prospect' offered by Rubers Law made it the ideal location 'for a post of observation, or for a signalling station'.

Sitting among the heather and rock of the hilltop, I found it hard to argue with this theory. Certainly, the sheer extent of the view was astonishing. Looking in any direction, there was nothing to break my line of sight. The landscape simply rolled away for miles and miles into the distance. To the east and south, I could see clear to the spine of the Cheviots. To the north, the Eildon Hills rose like two black whale backs; beyond them, shimmering blue in the distance, was the long line of the Lammermuirs. In the west, a patchwork of fields led away to the high slopes of the Ettrick Forest and the

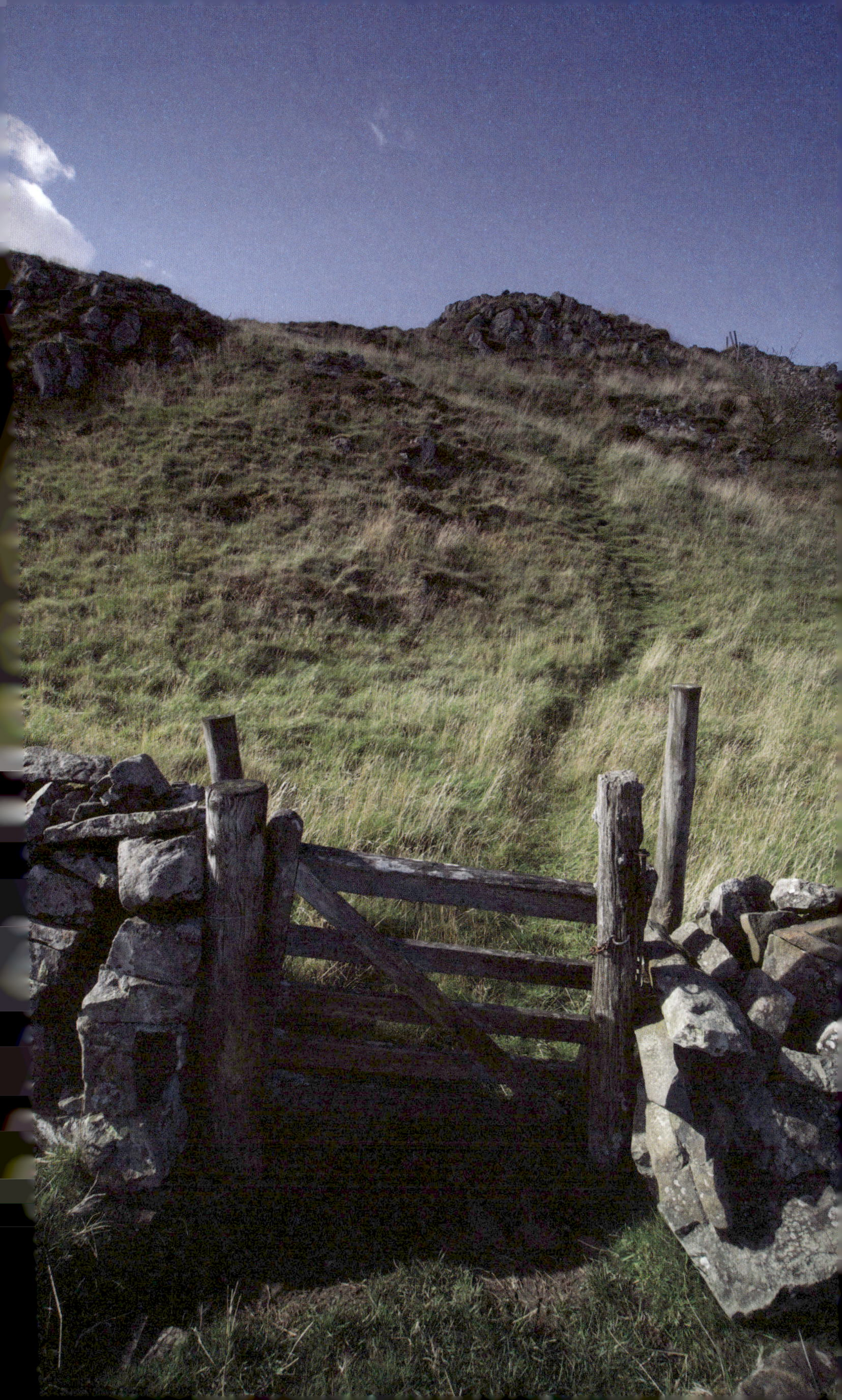

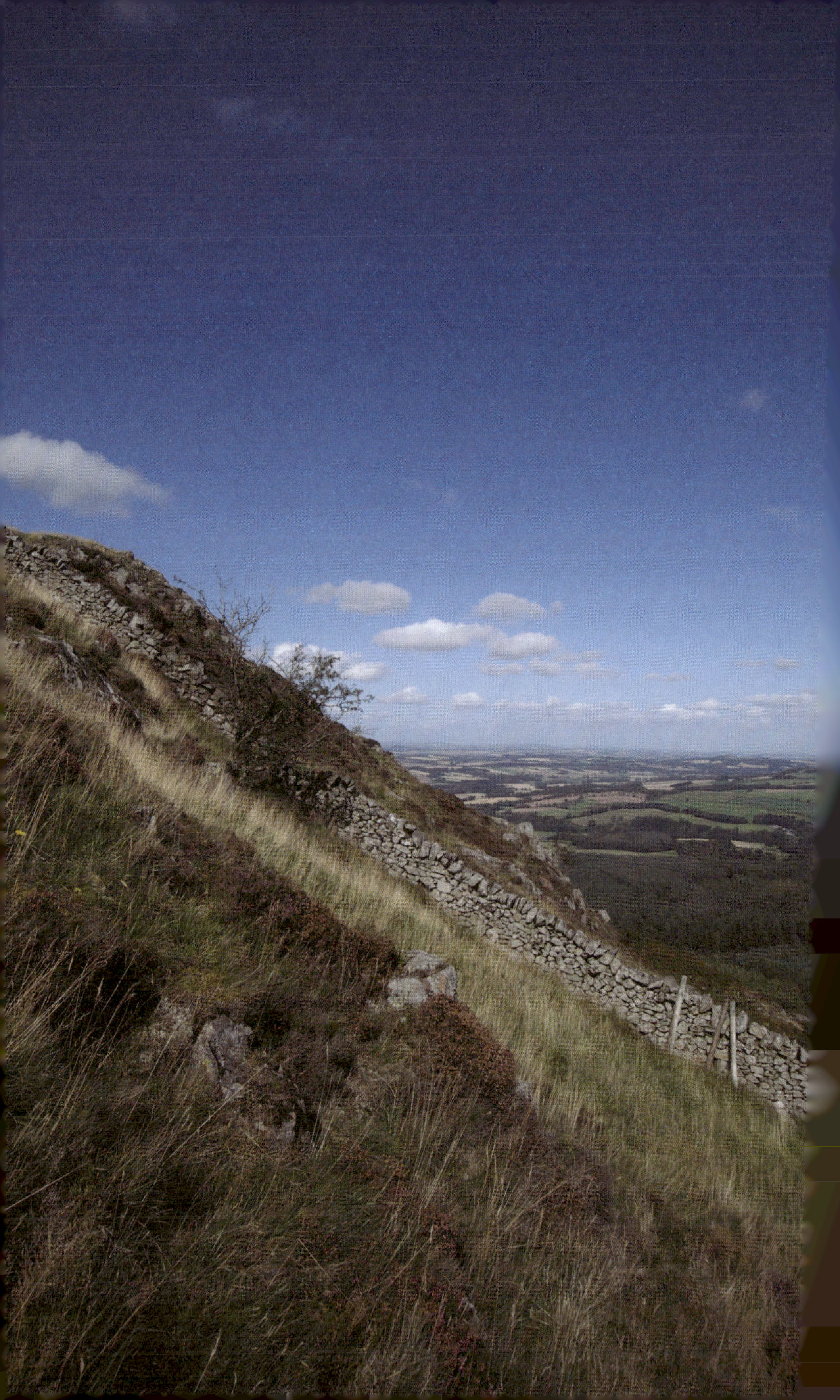

Roman Signal Station, Rubers Law

distant outline of the hills of Dumfries. Perhaps it was just an illusion brought on by the bright, Kodachrome clarity of the day, but it felt almost as if the view's only limit was the subtle curve of the Earth itself.

More than a century on from Curle's discovery, we still don't know with any certainty if the remains on Rubers Law came from a signal station or watch tower. Signal stations *were* common throughout the Roman Empire – and the traces of a number have been identified in Scotland – but they were almost always constructed from wood. Rubers Law certainly fits, almost as a nexus point, into the network of Roman military roads and camps that extended into southern Scotland. But the presence of the dressed stones is an enigma.

All the same, I couldn't help but be drawn to the idea of a watchtower. As I rested on the summit on that hot, clear September day, it was easy to imagine a solider manning his post, overlooking a panorama of alien terrain. I thought of the procession of sunrises and sunsets. The loneliness and the tedium. The indifferent beauty and the endless waiting.

Watchtowers have long been the subject of drama and literature, going from Homer and Aeschylus – sentries manning mountain beacons to be lit to announce the fall of Troy – all the way to Jack Kerouac working as a 'fire lookout' on the top of Desolation Peak in Washington state. Kerouac wrote at first of feeling happier than he had in years, of looking out on 'seas of marshmallow clouds', sunsets like 'mad orange fools raging in the gloom'. But soon the solitude swallowed up everything else. 'I was alone on Desolation Peak for all I knew for eternity. I was sure I wasn't going to come out of there alive anyway.' Many was the time he thought he'd 'die of boredom or jump off the mountain'. He longed, constantly, to go back down to the world below.

This was, admittedly, an idle, amused daydream on my part – a Roman legionnaire as a frustrated, ancient beat poet in a far-flung land. Maybe the truth was that the stones had really been part of some temple built to honour the gods. A place to make offerings and to bless the Caledonian invasion; a shrine erected on high. We will likely never know. And in that gap in our knowledge, I preferred to imagine the tower, the solitary, watching soldier, and the ever-changing, uncaring view.

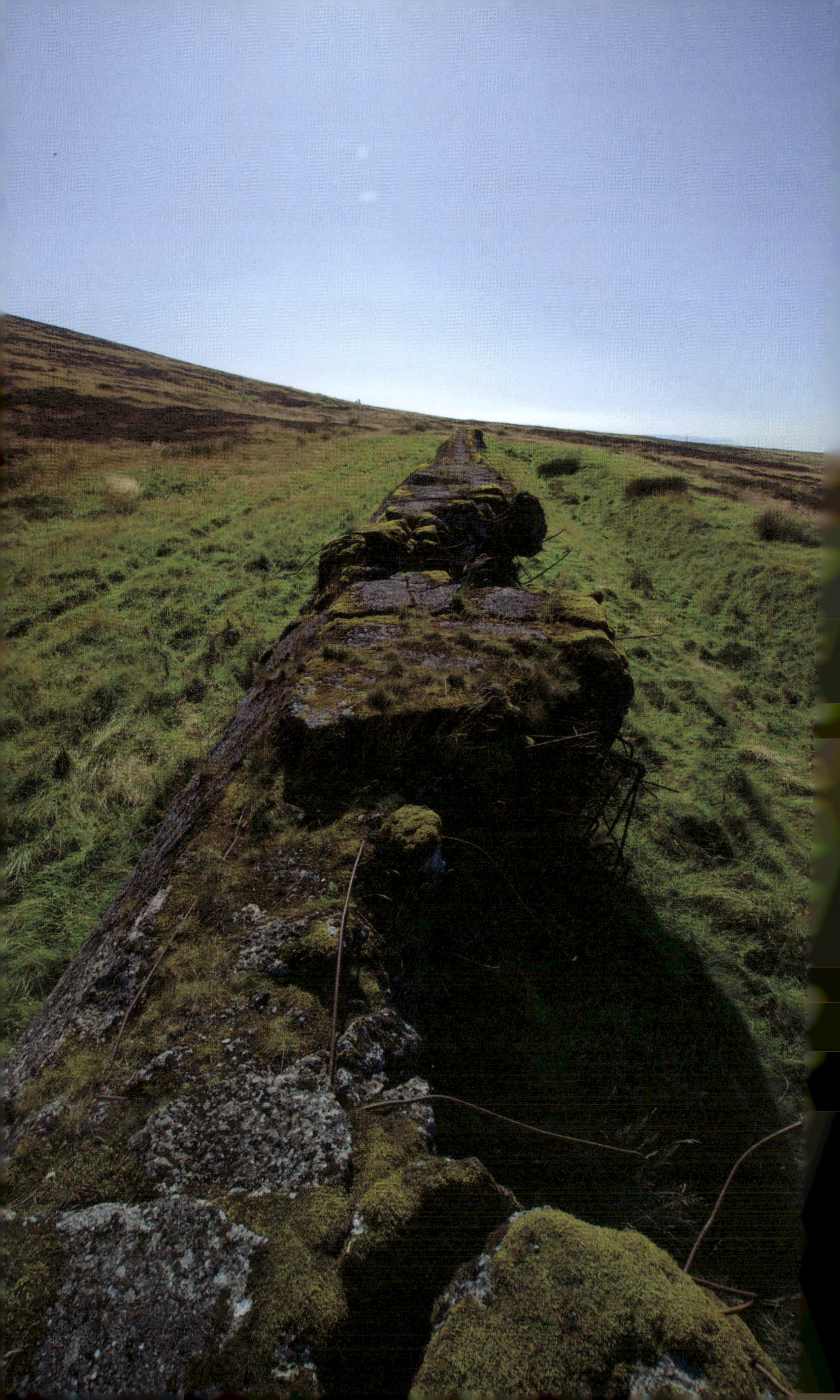

The Atlantic Wall, Sheriffmuir

NN 8378 0366

The wall ran for some eighty metres across the otherwise empty moor. It was not a boundary wall. It had not been erected to divide the land in any way. Rather, it sat right in the middle of it, on a gently sloping hillside, surrounded by wide open reaches of tall, yellowing grass and archipelagos of thick brown heather. It was a big wall too. Three metres in height and just about the same in thickness. Backlit by the sun, it became a line of solid black, appearing like a lost locomotive, stranded with its carriages at the remote halfway mark of some long-overgrown railway; abandoned and turned to stone.

It was an unseasonably hot day in late September. At dawn, a thick white mist had coated the land, but it soon disappeared under the glare of the sun. I had followed the tiny road that runs south from the village of Greenloaning, rising above the route of the A9 on the valley floor to track the winding course of the Millstone Burn through a smattering of quiet farmlands. The road climbed steadily and at times steeply, and soon the farms gave way to the western flank of the Ochil Hills. I parked in a little space beside a cattle-grid and walked the rest of the way to the wall through a mass of tall nettles and high wild grass.

For over a century now, this landscape – bare, nondescript, largely featureless – has been a surrogate for other, more distant landscapes. Four decades before the wall was built, it was a stand-in for a sparse, rocky peninsula jutting out into the Aegean Sea. Soldiers from the 52nd Lowland Infantry Division of the British Army came here in 1914 and dug down into the earth to make lines of trenches. A Scottish moorland – set 300 metres above sea level on the cusp of the Highlands – was recast as the coast and plains of Gallipoli. Next it became the fields of France and Belgium. Young men trained here and then died hundreds or thousands of miles away, under another sky.

The wall did not appear until 1943. It had its origins in, of all things, a biscuit tin. At that time a truly colossal wall was being built along the entire western coastline of mainland Europe. Known as the Atlantic Wall, it was intended as a vast line of military fortifications running from the Spanish/French border to the northern tip of Norway. When a French painter and decorator gained access to the offices of the German engineering firm charged with constructing the wall, he took the chance to steal the blueprints, hid them in that biscuit tin, and then smuggled them across the English Channel.

This replica Atlantic Wall, high up on the moor, was built to be destroyed. Shot at. Blown up. Knocked down. As per the stolen plans, it was fabricated in reinforced concrete, laced throughout with iron rods, and shaped to create a protruding, overhanging lip on one side. I was approaching the wall from the north-west, directly up the hill, just as the soldiers would have done. The specific angle of the slope here was also crucial. As preparations and rehearsals began for the Allied D-Day landings, the intention was to recreate the same topography as the coastlines of France. The wall was the beachhead and the ground falling away below it was an imaginary stretch of Normandy sand, shelving gently into the sea. Down at the cattle grid, where I had parked my car, was effectively underwater.

Over and over again, the troops stormed this facsimile shoreline. 'Dryshod-exercises', they were called. They assaulted the wall from different angles and with different artillery. Its entire 'seaward' face was pitted and cracked by the impacts of bullets and shellfire. Holes of various depths were drilled into its surface to place explosive charges. An entire British Army unit, known as the Anti-Concrete Committee, was formed to devise the best methods for breaching the wall.

The success of these trial-and-error experiments was demonstrated by a clear absence near one end of the line: a glaring gap in the wall around four metres wide. The missing section lay scattered in a fan of rubbled debris that ran up the hill for almost forty metres. Now-rusting iron rebar jutted out of the break – the wall's exoskeleton shorn of its concrete flesh. The power of the detonation must have been terrific. But there was no echo of it remaining

The Atlantic Wall, Sheriffmuir

up here on the moor. At least not for me anyway. The sounds, the explosions, the gunfire – they had left this place long ago. It was silence that dominated above all else. Under the high sun, with a heat haze crackling the heather and blurring the distance, the wall had taken on a strange, monolithic, sculptural quality. Its shadowy blackness exuded a dense gravity when set against the pale-yellow hillsides, as if it was sucking in the surrounding light and noise and movement. This was most pronounced in that yawning breach in the wall. It was a frozen moment, an inaudible scream.

    I climbed up on top of the wall and walked along it as far as I could, from one end to the other and back again. Thick moss grew on the edges, covering holes and pickets that once held rolls of barbed wire. I sat on the overhanging lip and looked off to the north-west, down a slope that had once doubled for Turkey and Flanders and Normandy. The light wind, sighing in the grass, was the only sound.

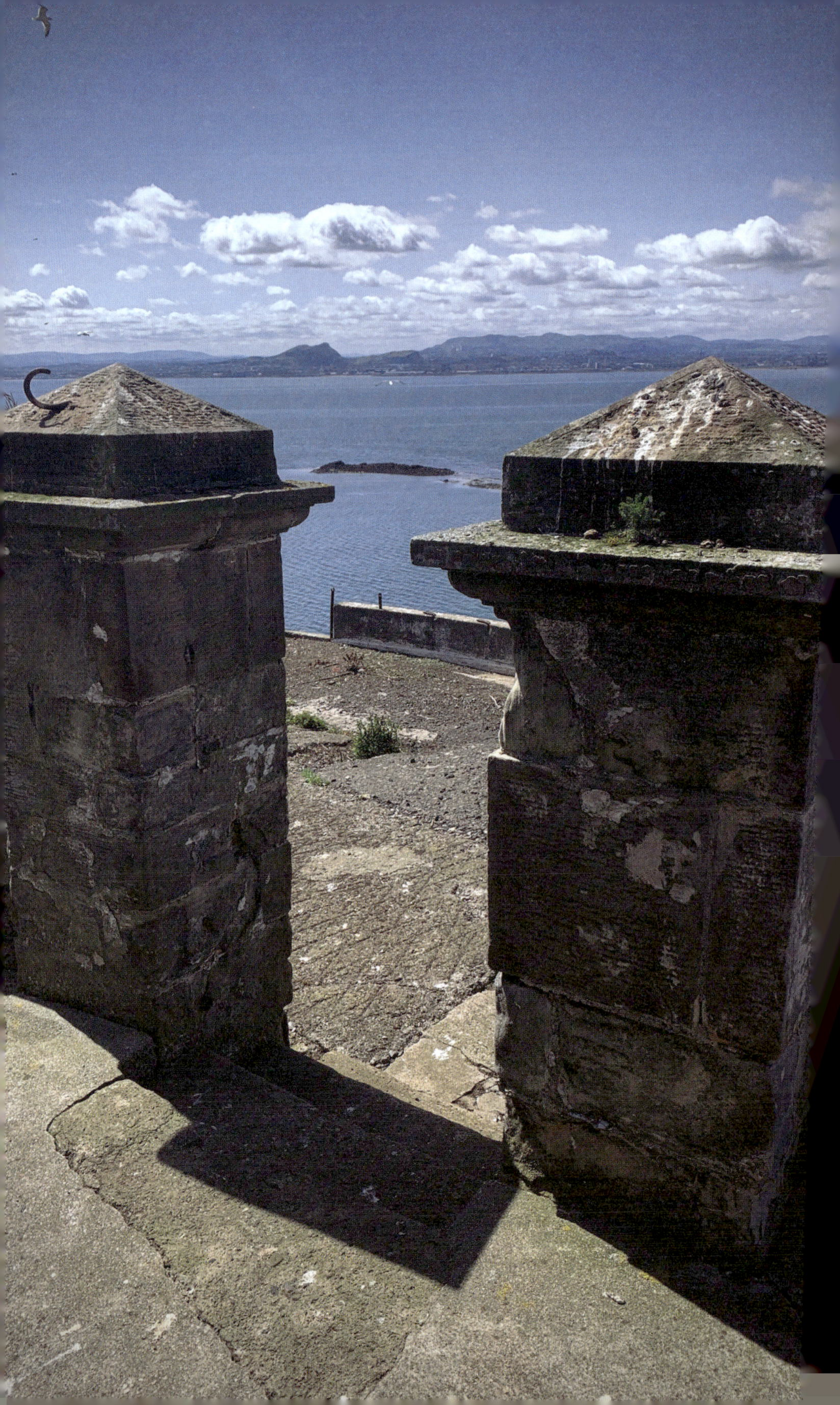

Inchkeith Island, Firth of Forth

NT 2933 8280

The cries of the gulls were incessant. A cacophony that had only increased in pitch since I landed on the island: angry shouts, protesting the intrusion of a stranger. The ammonia-smell of droppings was, at times, overpowering. And it mingled, again and again, with the thick, dusty odour of death. Carcasses lay strewn all over the ground – of birds, or rabbits, or creatures so diminished by dismemberment or decay as to be all but unidentifiable.

It was the height of summer, a hot, near-cloudless day. Plants and weeds and grasses sprouted up tall and dense – pink-tipped thistles, foxgloves, buttercups, dandelions, daisies, nettles. They swamped the island's many concrete pathways and squat brick buildings – climbing their walls or covering their roofs, leaping from cracks in their stonework. Shed seed-heads drifted in the breeze in clouds as thick as smoke. Nature was in control here now. Or rather nature was *un*-controlled. It had taken this place as a raw, brutal, visceral outpost. As much as anywhere I've ever been, this felt wild.

Perhaps this was so pronounced because of the sheer scale of human intervention on the island. Sitting just four miles across the waters of the Firth of Forth from Edinburgh, Inchkeith's history was, until the last half-century, one of constant use. Go back to the Second World War and there were over a thousand men living here – an incredible number for a narrow hump of rock that is barely a mile long. The island's surviving ruins are, almost entirely, a legacy of conflicts: haphazard architectural strata, taking you from the 1940s, through the First World War and the Napoleonic Wars, all the way back to the Anglo-Scottish Wars of the mid sixteenth century. Inchkeith was fortified and re-fortified, fought over and captured and re-captured – changing hands between the English, the French and the Scots –

for more than 400 years. The very atmosphere of this place bristles. Any wonder, then, that the gulls were so belligerent? It was, it seemed, in Inchkeith's nature to be claimed and to be held by force, against all-comers.

I made my way inside one of the old battery buildings. Constructed from dressed stone and part carved into a rocky hillside, its arched entrance was inscribed with the date '1880'. Corridors led off to the left and right, with a long flight of stairs ahead of me. It was cool and dark, and the acrid smell grew even stronger, catching the back of the throat. Halos of abandoned nests littered the floors, and every wall and surface was coated in a mix of fluff and downy feathers. Walking up the staircase, I felt my shoes crunching down on old, discarded bones. On the first landing was the decaying husk of a dead gull, lying on its back, but with its wings spread wide as if in flight. There was something unsettlingly sepulchral about the building, like stumbling into a vampire's tomb. I did not linger long before returning outside to the light and the relentless noise.

This wasn't always a gulls' island. Go back to the 1960s, just a decade or so after Inchkeith was first abandoned, and their numbers were in the hundreds. It was in the years that followed that their colonies exploded – herring gulls and lesser black-backed gulls now dominate, nesting here in their many thousands. They are joined, albeit in far fewer numbers, by fulmars, cormorants, shags, kittiwakes and guillemots. Around the eastern tip of the island, perhaps as many as 1,600 puffins have burrowed into the earth. Hundreds of grey seals now call the beaches and rocky reefs around Inchkeith home.

More than 500 years ago, before there was much of anything on the island, King James IV was said to have used it as a training ground for his hunting hawks. Inspired, perhaps, by Inchkeith's emptiness and solitude, he went on to choose it as the ideal site for a bizarre experiment. According to a – very likely apocryphal – account by the sixteenth-century chronicler Robert Lindsay, in 1493 the king had a mute nursemaid and two infants transported to Inchkeith, to live alone until the children reached an age where they could speak. Deprived of all outside influences, the experiment was intended to see if they would revert to an 'original' uncorrupted language – which would, in essence, be the language of God. 'Some sayis,' Lindsay reported, 'that they spake goode Hebrew.' Others reported that they

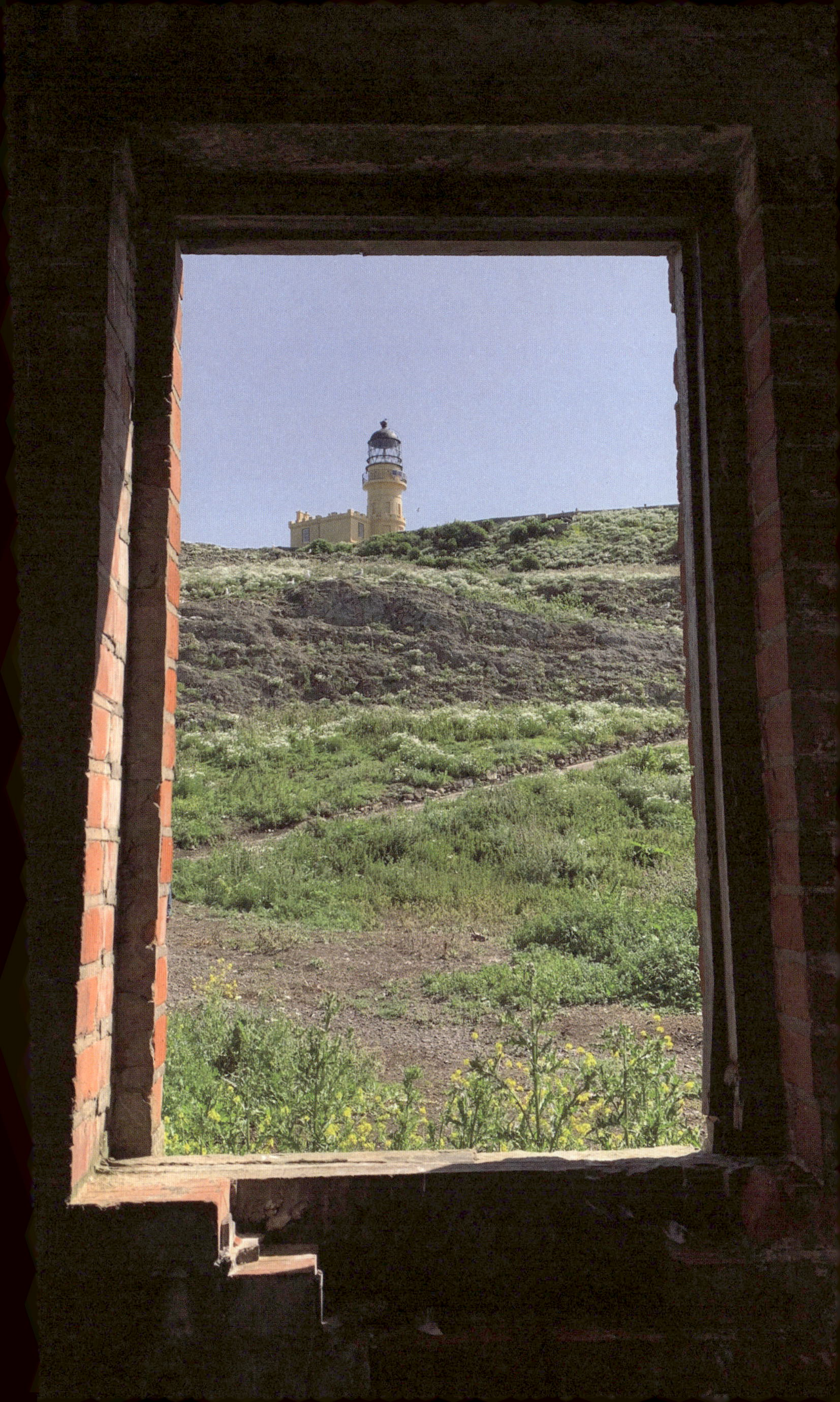

bleated incomprehensibly, mimicking the sounds of their only other companions, the island's goats and sheep. Whether true or not, what is clear is that it offered up a model for a very specific way of using Inchkeith – as somewhere to put people to separate them from others. Just four years after the experiment was said to have taken place, it became the epicentre of enforced self-isolation in Scotland. A quarantine island.

At the end of the fifteenth century, a new and deadly disease was ripping through Europe, seeming to move at incredible speed from country to country. The French called it the Neapolitan disease or the Spanish disease. The

Italians and the Spanish called it the French disease. The Russians called it the Polish disease, and the Polish called it the Turkish disease. The Turkish, in turn, called it the Christian disease. In Scotland, it was known as the Grandgore. Syphilis. Most likely travelling through the movement of troops – with the first major outbreak recorded in 1495 after a French army invaded Naples – it reached Scotland two years later, arriving first in the ports of Edinburgh and Aberdeen. Symptoms in the early stages were particularly virulent, and it could lead quickly to blindness, dementia and ultimately death. And there was no known cure.

Wild History

The authorities in Edinburgh reacted quickly and decisively. Passed in September 1497, the Grandgore Act ruled that anyone suffering from syphilis – and anyone caring for a sufferer – was to assemble on the beach at Leith, where boats were waiting to transport them to Inchkeith. There they were to remain 'until God restored them to health'. (Anyone who refused, or anyone who professed to offer a cure, was to be branded on the cheek by a hot iron and exiled from the burgh.) Strictly speaking, this removal to Inchkeith wasn't a quarantine. The practice of quarantine had emerged out of the horrors of the Black Death, where boats entering Italian ports were required to remain at anchor for forty days before anyone could come ashore. Forty days in Italian was *quaranta giorni*, giving us the word 'quarantine'. If passengers survived that long, then they were assumed to be disease-free. Syphilis, however, could take years to kill – and an effective treatment was still four centuries away. All of the sick who travelled to Inchkeith must have died here. They left no trace. There is no graveyard, no physical record of their existence among the crumbling shells that litter this landscape. Their isolation was also their abandonment.

I climbed up to the highest point of the island, some ninety metres above the sea. Three cottages stood together here, their slate roof tiles almost entirely gone, but their wooden A-frames still in place, like ribs on a rotting skeleton. Edinburgh was right there, just across the water. I had a perfect view of the volcanic uprisings of Arthur's Seat and Salisbury Crags, with the matchstick spires of buildings running in silhouette up the long tail of the High Street to the summit of Castle Hill.

Boswell and Johnson came here in the late eighteenth century, with Johnson musing on the great potential of Inchkeith as a home. 'I'd have this island: I'd build a house,' he wrote. 'A rich man of hospitable turn here, would have many visitors from Edinburgh.' His idle thought offered a glimpse of an alternative history for this place: luxurious isolation – an isolation of choice – on a pleasure island set apart from the everyday world. I looked around at the broken concrete, the rotting timbers of the cottages; watched the gulls shriek and wheel all around me, so many filling the sky, riding and floating on the wind. Inchkeith was their house now. And they will not give it up easily.

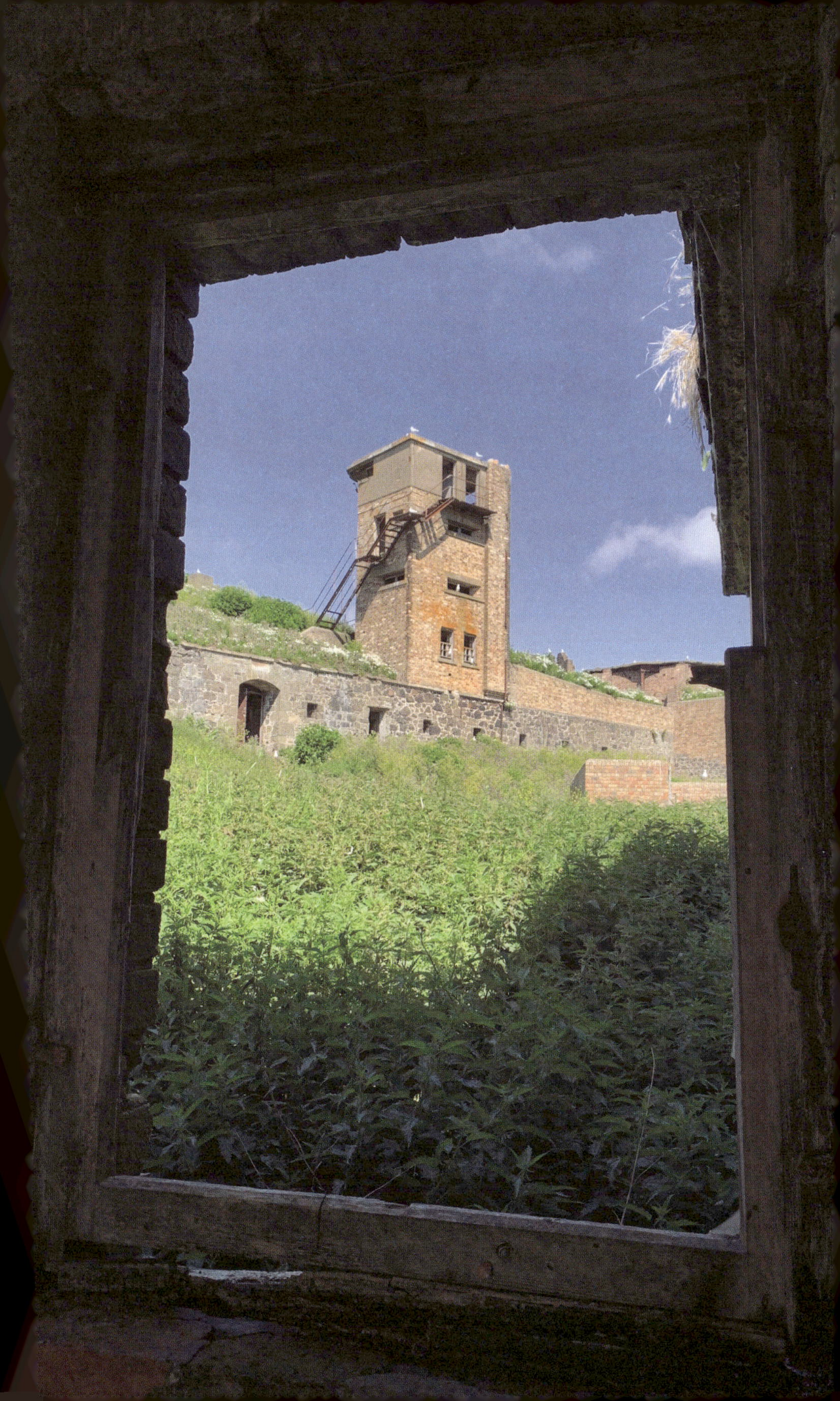

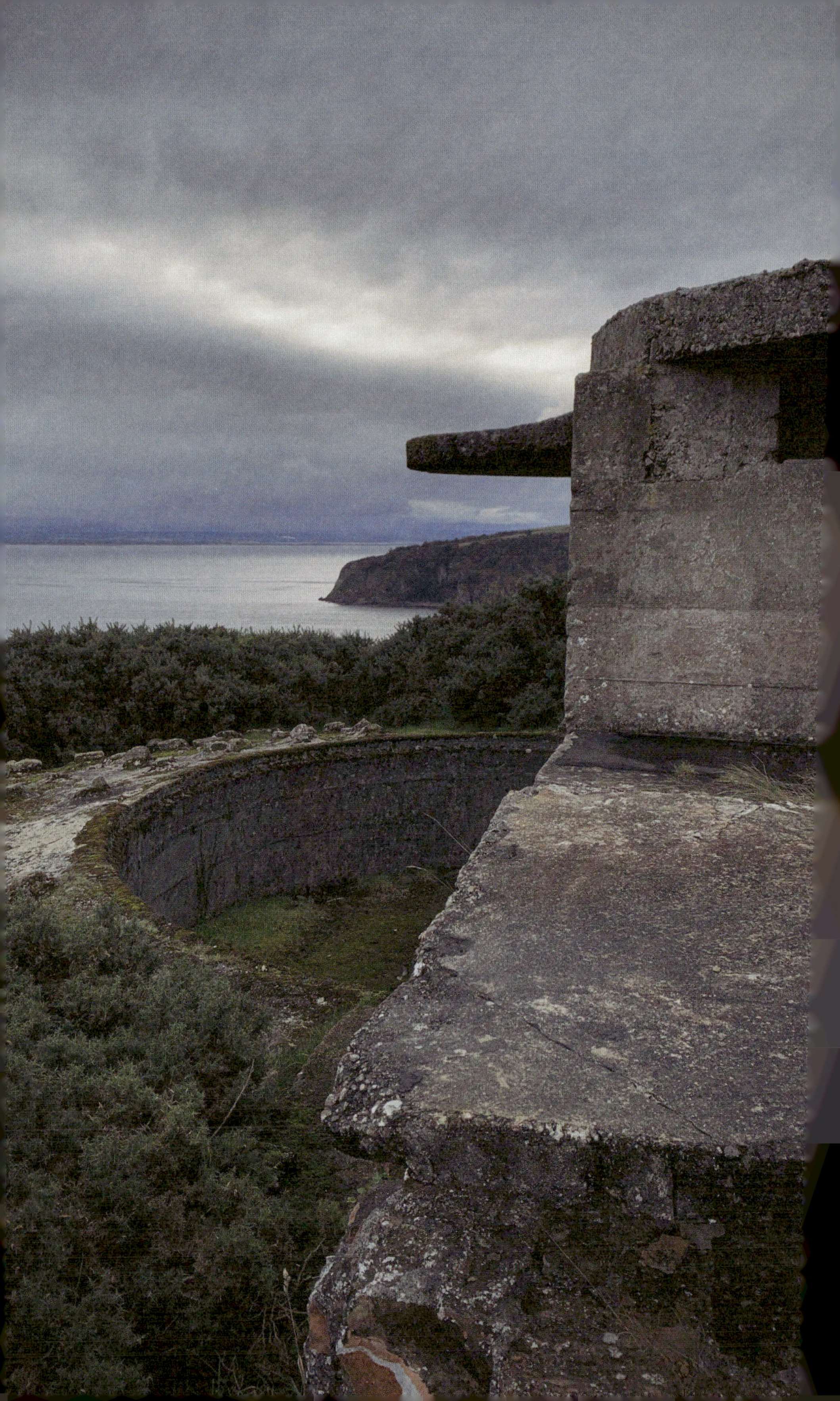

North Sutor Battery, Cromarty Firth

NH 8184 6887

The hill rose upwards in a steep wedge to meet the high cliffside. Behind me was the long, deep inlet of the Cromarty Firth and the industrial sprawl of the Nigg Oil Terminal. From the summit of the hillside, now almost 100 metres up, I could see all the way back down the length of the firth, a panorama that took in the port towns of Cromarty, Invergordon and Alness and stretched off towards the distant mountains of Easter Ross. Rigs and platforms ran in a line through the water, all in various stages of decommissioning: a procession of giants picked apart and recycled, their steel being cut down into processed lengths, their engines, generators and pumps removed to be resold.

This landscape has always – according to local legend, at least – been a refuge for giants. The mouth of the firth is formed by two massive pincers of rocky cliffs that stretch towards each other to create a narrow entrance. They are known as the 'sutors' – from the Latin, and then later the Scots, for 'shoemaker'. The old story goes that there were two giants – possibly brothers – who lived right on the headlands, one on the north side, the other on the south, so tall that if they stood upright their heads touched the clouds. They were both cobblers, but they only had one set of tools, so they had to share, throwing their equipment back and forth across the mile of water that separated them.

A strong wind was blowing as I made my way along the northern headland – the North Sutor – the sky filled with a high canopy of dark clouds, rippling like ocean waves. As I approached the cliff edge, a faint path emerged, leading on into thickets of tall gorse. After following it for a few hundred metres, the land opened out again, and the buildings began to appear. Most were simple, rectangular blocks of brick and concrete, and many were now roofless. Once they had been guardhouses, command posts, pillboxes, engine houses, mess halls, barrack blocks; even the remains of a foghorn. A little further down the slope – hanging over the precipice of a steepening drop – was an oblong concrete shell, angled to face south-west across the mouth of the firth. It contained a wide circular pit, with a ring of rusted, moss-grown metal at its centre: the base for a huge, 9.2-inch gun.

In 1913 both North and South Sutor, those one-time giants' workbenches, were turned into two substantial coastal batteries by the Royal Navy. The cliffsides were fortified with an extensive series of gun and searchlight emplacements and surrounded by trenches and barbed wire. A year later, after the onset of the First World War, a massive submarine net was strung between the Sutors, supplemented with tethered, remote-controlled mines. The Cromarty Firth offered a natural safe anchorage and was even, for a time, chosen by Winston Churchill, then First Lord of the Admiralty, as the home for the Grand Fleet (a decision later reversed in favour of using Scapa Flow in Orkney). The port of Invergordon took on the role as a major refuelling station and, in the latter part of the war, became a base for the US Navy.

It was from the mouth of the Sutors that the US Mine Squadron helped to lay what was known as the North Sea Mine Barrage – a field of some 70,000 mines spreading over 230 miles in length across the neck of the North Sea, from Scotland to Norway, in a line that was twenty-five miles wide and which extended downwards below the water to depths of up to 240 feet. The commander of the Mine Squadron, Reginald Belknap, wrote of the very first evening of the operation, recalling how he watched from the deck of his ship, the USS *San Francisco*, as the mine and escort ships emerged from the mouth of the firth in the gloaming, their 'long low forms slinking against the dark background of North Sutor'. Soon, he said, they were arranged in formation and ready to move out to sea. 'The whole squadron stands on, without pause, together, 10 ships in two parallel columns, 500 yards apart. Ahead and on either side are four destroyers, 12 in all. No signals, no lights, no sound but quiet tones on the bridge and the swash of the water overside.' Up on the Sutors, men would have watched as the ships slipped out into the night – knowing that there was every chance that some might not return.

North Sutor Battery, Cromarty Firth

Inevitably, almost as soon as the First World War was over, the batteries were abandoned – only to be refortified and extended some twenty years later, when a new conflict began. Once again, Invergordon was called into action as a major refuelling base. In 1938, just above the port in the forest of Kinrive, workers began constructing six colossal underground, bomb-proof fuel tanks, 237 metres long, 9 metres wide and 13.5 metres tall. These were vast, cathedral-like spaces that could contain up to 32 million gallons of oil and pump them down to the port – ensuring that Britain would have enough reserves in place in the event of a German blockade.

In the aftermath of the Second World War, the posts on the Sutors were not vacated immediately. For a time, they were kept in readiness – on what was described by the military as a 'care and maintenance' basis – until they were finally closed in the late 1950s.

These coastal batteries were, of course, built for function. Brick and concrete thrown up at speed, cemented onto and dug into the cliffside. I had taken shelter from the wind inside the echoey shell of the large gun emplacement. A short flight of concrete steps led to a platform set above the circular pit where the gun had once stood. The far end of the pit and the overhanging lip of the roof framed a long thin rectangle of sea and sky. How many days, or months, or years, I wondered, had someone spent watching this same vista? Seen it shift with the seasons. Always waiting. If the architecture here speaks of anything, it is, perhaps, a mixture of acute tension and anxious tedium. When this battery was manned, that view couldn't be looked at without, in some sense, looking into the future. What might be coming? Was anything approaching over that horizon? What would the war bring? When – and how – would it end?

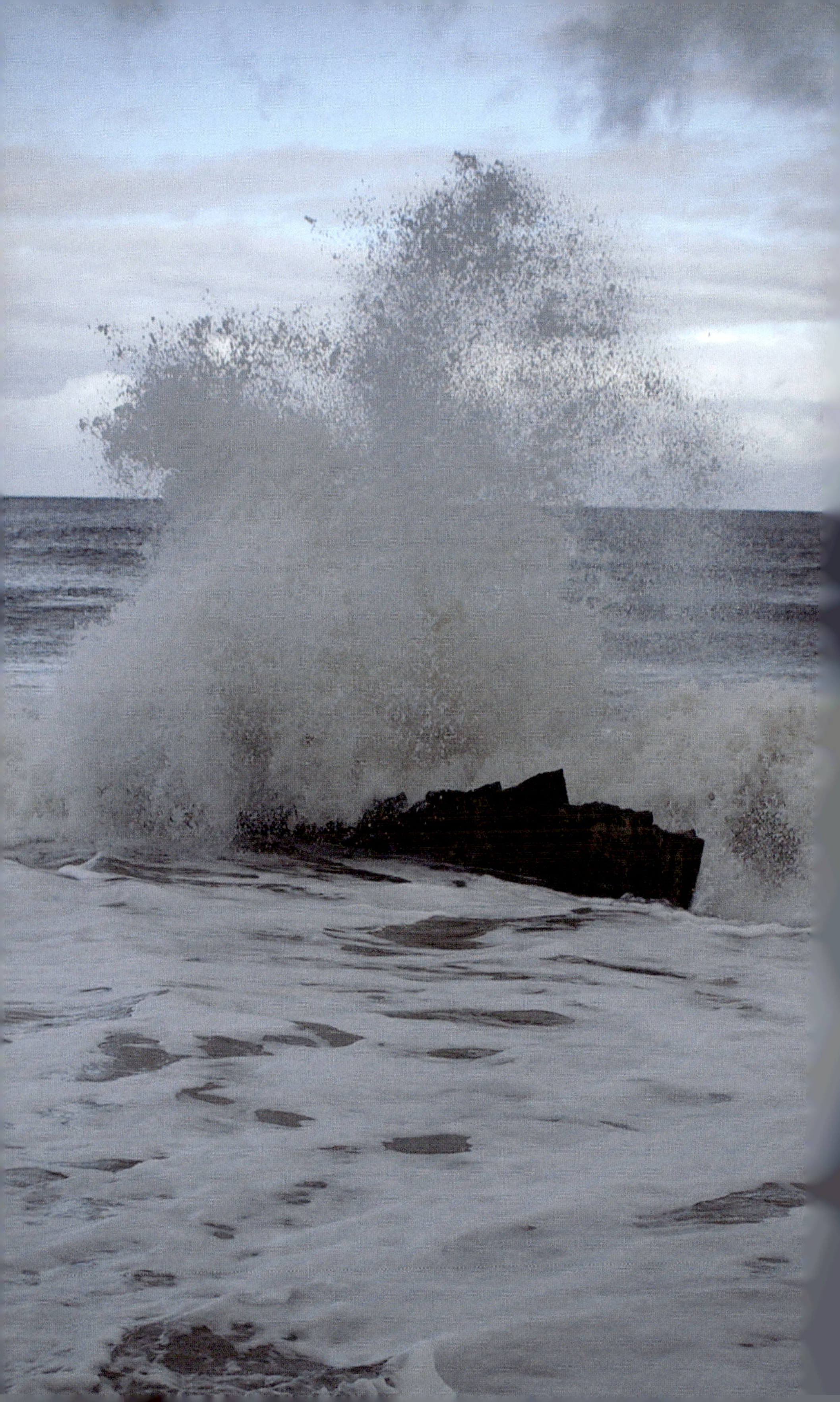

John Randolph, Torrisdale Bay, Sutherland

NC 6836 6214

Work began to lay down her hull on 15 July 1941 at the Bethlehem-Fairfield Shipyard in Baltimore, Maryland. She was a Liberty-class cargo vessel, an emergency ship, built to a newly devised and standardised design that replaced riveting with welding to allow for fast, low-cost, mass production. Over the next five months, she rapidly took shape, the exoskeleton of her keel filled up with bulkheads and girders, which were soon segmented into five large cargo holds and three deep storage tanks. The upper deck was laid – with its three mast houses with booms for cargo loading – and then the external hull was welded tight around it all.

The completed ship was 441 feet long and weighed over 7,000 tons. Powered by a single triple-expansion steam engine built by the Worthington Pump & Machinery Corporation of New Jersey, she had a top speed of eleven knots and a carrying capacity of up to 560,000 cubic feet of grain. The name – *John Randolph* – came from a Virginian politician, tobacco planter and slave-owner who had served under President Andrew Jackson in the 1830s as the US ambassador to Russia.

She was launched on 30 December 1941, the nineteenth out of 2,710 Liberty-class vessels built between 1941 and 1945. This was the largest number of ships ever constructed to a single design, with eighteen separate American yards working on the orders all at once – which averaged out at the production of a brand-new ship every three days. After the United States entered the Second World War, many of the jobs in the shipyards were taken on by women, with much of the Liberty fleet welded together by female workers.

The reason for all this furious production was to win a war within the war

– what was known as the 'tonnage war'. In simple terms, the aim was for one side to sink more ships than the other was capable of building. In 1940, for every 2,000 tons of Allied ships built, 9,000 tons were sunk by the German fleet. When a vessel is lost, it doesn't just go down with the cargo it is carrying, but with all the cargos it might carry in the future. The Liberty programme played a major role in turning the tide. By 1942 the ratio of new construction to losses was almost even, and by 1943 it was nearing two to one, where it would stay for the rest of the war.

John Randolph began her work with the military shipping of sulphur and oil supplied by the Union Sulphur and Oil Company of Louisiana. By the summer of 1942, however, she was part of Convoy QP 13, one of thirty-five merchant ships travelling westbound from the Russian Arctic ports of Arkhangelsk and Murmansk back towards Britain, Iceland and North America. Having just delivered food and supplies to the Soviet Union, most of the vessels were empty of cargo. Although shadowed for a time by enemy air reconnaissance and U-boats, the convoy was passed over by the German fleet, who moved instead to target another – fully laden – group of Allied ships heading eastwards.

On 5 July, the convoy sailed into heavy fog lying over the seas to the north-west of Iceland. Visibility was down to less than a mile, and so the commander of one of the escort ships, HMS *Niger*, ordered the six vessels that she was leading – including *John Randolph* – to form up in two columns. To starboard was the vast, ocean minefield known as the Northern Barrage, and to port was the North Cape of Iceland. At ten o'clock that evening, the *Niger* spotted land and ordered a course correction. Forty minutes later, a massive explosion breached her hull. She sank within minutes, with the loss of all but eight of her crew of 127. Unwittingly, in the dense fog, *Niger* had mistaken an iceberg for the Icelandic coast. She had turned away from it to lead the ships right into the middle of the minefield. One by one, the others were also hit. Four went down soon after – SS *Heffron*, SS *Massmar*, SS *Hybert* and SS *Rodina*. A fifth, SS *Exterminator*, was damaged, but could still sail. *John Randolph* exploded and broke in two. The aft sank beneath the waves, but the forepart stayed afloat and came to be beached on Iceland's far north coast.

The US Navy came to salvage what remained, towing *John Randolph* into

John Randolph, *Torrisdale Bay*

port at Reykjavik, where her still operational mast house and crane were used for cargo handling. She stayed there for a whole decade, until the summer of 1952, when the decision was taken to tow her remains to a shipbreaking yard at Bo'ness, in the Firth of Forth, for scrapping. On 1 September, the Dutch tugboat *Oceanis* began to pull her south through the Atlantic. Four days later, however, caught in high winds and rough seas off the north coast of Scotland, she broke free of her tow. The forepart was seen drifting steadily inland. Later that night, she became imbedded in the sands of Torrisdale Bay in Sutherland, overlooked by the little crofting community of Bettyhill.

This was the life of *John Randolph*. She has never moved again. Seventy years later, I had come to stand in front of her, on the mile-wide stretch of Torrisdale's beach. Her wreck sits a little below the tideline, and so it appears and disappears twice every day.

I had walked in from the tiny hamlet of Borgie, first along a narrow road, then following a path down to the bay that ran parallel to the River Borgie. It was an October afternoon. The morning's wind and heavy rain had given way to a quiet stillness. By the time I reached *John Randolph*, crunching towards her over the crust of pinkish sands, the waves were returning, and she was already part submerged. Her prow pointed almost directly inland, a broken triangle, deceptively small for a 400-foot-long ship. The metal was blackened and broken, its shape and jagged edges looking like the lower part of some giant jaw. A heavy swell sent waves crashing against her hull in a spray of white foam. Apart from her, the beach was empty.

Cramond Island, Firth of Forth

NT 1965 7856

From the balcony of the gun emplacement, I could look almost straight down the line of elongated, flat-topped pyramids that ran for near enough a kilometre from the island to the shore. It was mid-morning in January. The sun sat low in the south-eastern sky, just above an advancing cloudbank, and its light hit the faces of the pyramids just a little off-centre. All stood three metres tall (except for a handful, whose bodies had part-broken and toppled down) and they cast long, thin shadows across the sands behind them – like an assembly line of giant sundials, extending off towards a distant vanishing point.

The gun emplacement was built of red brick and concrete, set on a rocky outcrop at the very southern tip of the island, known as the Knoll. Its flat roof, cast into a kind of irregular star-shape, once held a large searchlight, while below, on the balcony, would have been a heavy, seventy-five-millimetre artillery gun. In its place now was a little rectangular depression on the floor, filled with rainwater. The walls of the emplacement were covered entirely in graffiti, layers and layers of it, giant tags that had been sprayed and resprayed for decades now. Similar buildings lay in various states of ruin and abandonment across the rest of the island. More gun emplacements and searchlight platforms; ammunition stores and barrack blocks and engine rooms.

Cramond Island is not much more than seven hectares in area. A teardrop of land rising to a height of twenty-four metres above sea level, it sits a kilometre and a half off the southern shore of the Firth of Forth, opposite the outflow of the River Almond. Twice a day, at low tides, the waters around it recede to reveal the wide expanse of the Drum Sands, offering the chance to walk across from the mainland. For over a century now, the island's purpose has been defined by war. Or rather, for two short, intensive periods during the last 100 years, it was co-opted by war: just one small part of a landscape-sized fortification system, a defensive 'crust' that came to line large stretches of the entire east coast of Britain.

The construction of this crust was fast and functional, favouring concrete, cement, bare brick and barbed wire. The First World War brought twelve-pound guns, trenches and a mooring post for a giant submarine net, which stretched out into the Forth to connect to the islands of Inchmickery and Inchcolm, and then continued all the way across to the coast of Fife. At the end of the conflict, the military left Cramond Island behind, only to return twenty years later. They repaired and rebuilt the existing defences, then added more guns and searchlights and troop accommodation. To the north, they reattached the great submarine net, but to the south, where the Drum Sands could be inundated enough by the sea to be navigated by boat at high tide, they decided to create something rather more permanent.

Around 1940, work began on laying a narrow-gauge track across the tidal flats towards the island. In the short windows when the sea retreated, a steam-powered crane and a pile-driving rig would set out down the track: the rig hammering in foundations, the crane lifting the giant pyramid blocks into place in two sections, joining them together with iron rebar. Iron rings were also driven into the top of the blocks, used for attaching steel wire and netting. Hour by hour and day by day, the track and the line extended onwards, with a new pyramid put in place every metre and a half.

When first completed, this procession of concrete obelisks must have looked startlingly pristine – a long row of off-white teeth rising and falling in the waves. Today, the teeth are rather more blackened and rotted. Everywhere, chunks have been chipped or crumbled away. Barnacles cling to the surfaces of the lower halves, while rust and seaweed stain the tops. The result is a kind of unintentional brutalist sculpture, less makeshift defensive structure, and more abstract land art.

A cobble and concrete causeway runs directly parallel to the barrier, allowing walkers to access the island. When I had crossed it that morning, moving beside the pyramids along the wet surface, the bright winter sun lit everything in sharp contrast, and reflections and shadows flickered on the

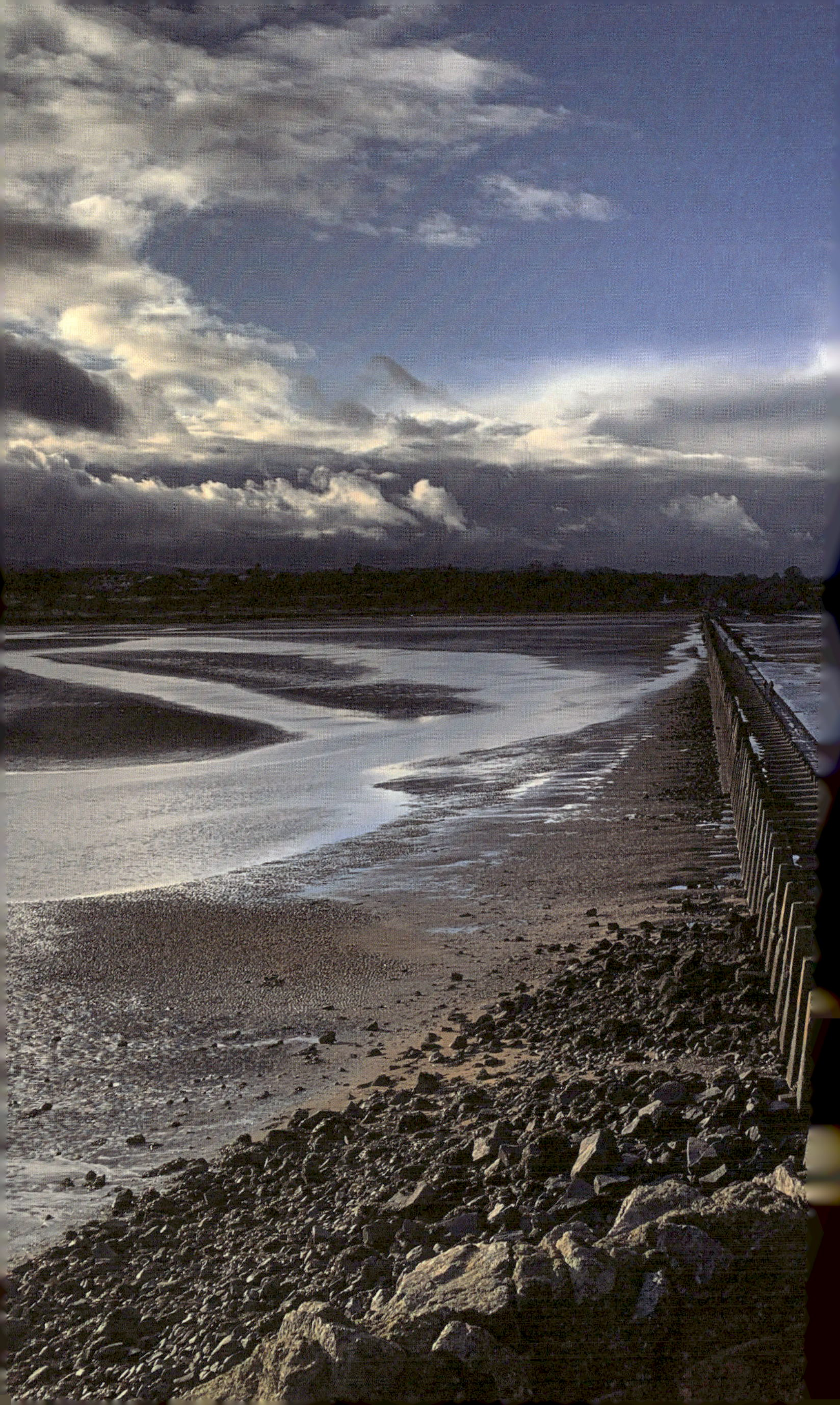

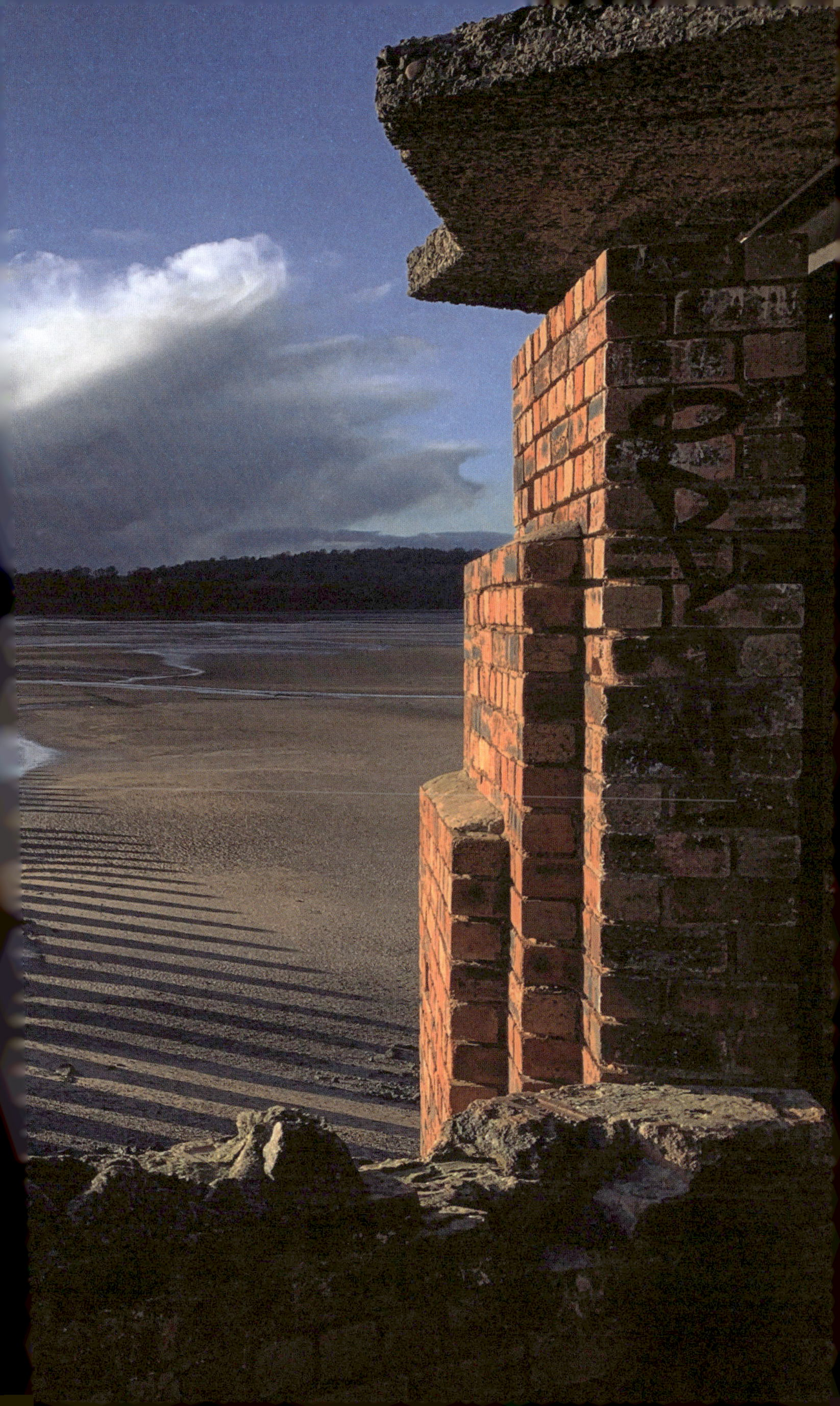

sands and in shallow tidal pools. It gave the whole structure a distinctly uncanny feel, as if you were encountering some futuristic ruin, or a piece of alien archaeology. We know today exactly what the barrier is and why it was built. But over time that memory and that knowledge may blur and fade. Give it long enough, and all you might be left with is a line of curious, crumbling pyramids.

There is a distinct irony to Cramond's twentieth-century role as a bulwark against invasion. Two thousand years ago, this whole area of Scotland had already been overrun by a foreign army. The Romans controlled this landscape. Just above the shore on the mainland, they constructed a fort, which was connected to a series of other forts by a network of newly built roads. The area around the mouth of the River Almond offered a natural harbour and was likely used as a berthing point for ships delivering troops and supplies.

The Romans who came here left behind their own monuments to war. Buried in the earth around the fort were centurial and legionary stones, and large altars to Jupiter and the goddesses of the Earth and the parade ground. Just a few hundred yards east of the river mouth, in a rocky outcrop, was a relief carving – now much weathered away – of what may once have been the imperial eagle, or the figure of Mercury. But most potent of all was the discovery made right alongside the very place where the modern concrete barrier meets the shoreline.

In 1997 a local ferryman running short trips from one side of the River Almond to the other noticed an unusual shape emerging from the eroding silt. When archaeologists came to investigate, the object they raised out of the mudflats offered a visceral depiction of the brutal psychology of conquest. Carved out of a huge slab of – not local – sandstone was the great, muscular figure of a lioness. Beneath her front paws, she held a naked and bearded man, bound with his hands behind his back. The sculpture was capturing the very moment that the lioness's jaws clamped around the man's head and her teeth began to sink into his skull. The symbolism was stark – the regal beast devouring the barbarian; the ferocious might of Rome, and the inevitable fate of all those who tried to stand in its way.

The tide was returning, slipping silently across the sands. I walked back over the causeway to the shore, sunlight strobing between the pyramids with

Cramond Island, Firth of Forth

every other step. I lingered at the very end, at the place where the barrier stopped and the lioness and her victim had been sunk beneath the mud. What a strange nexus point it was. Two sides of a historical coin of invasion and resistance, separated by two millennia. If it hadn't been that ferryman who had found the lioness, but rather those workers back in 1940 – sinking their foundations and raising up their concrete blocks against an impending attack – you wonder if, just on seeing the statue, they would have understood exactly what it meant.

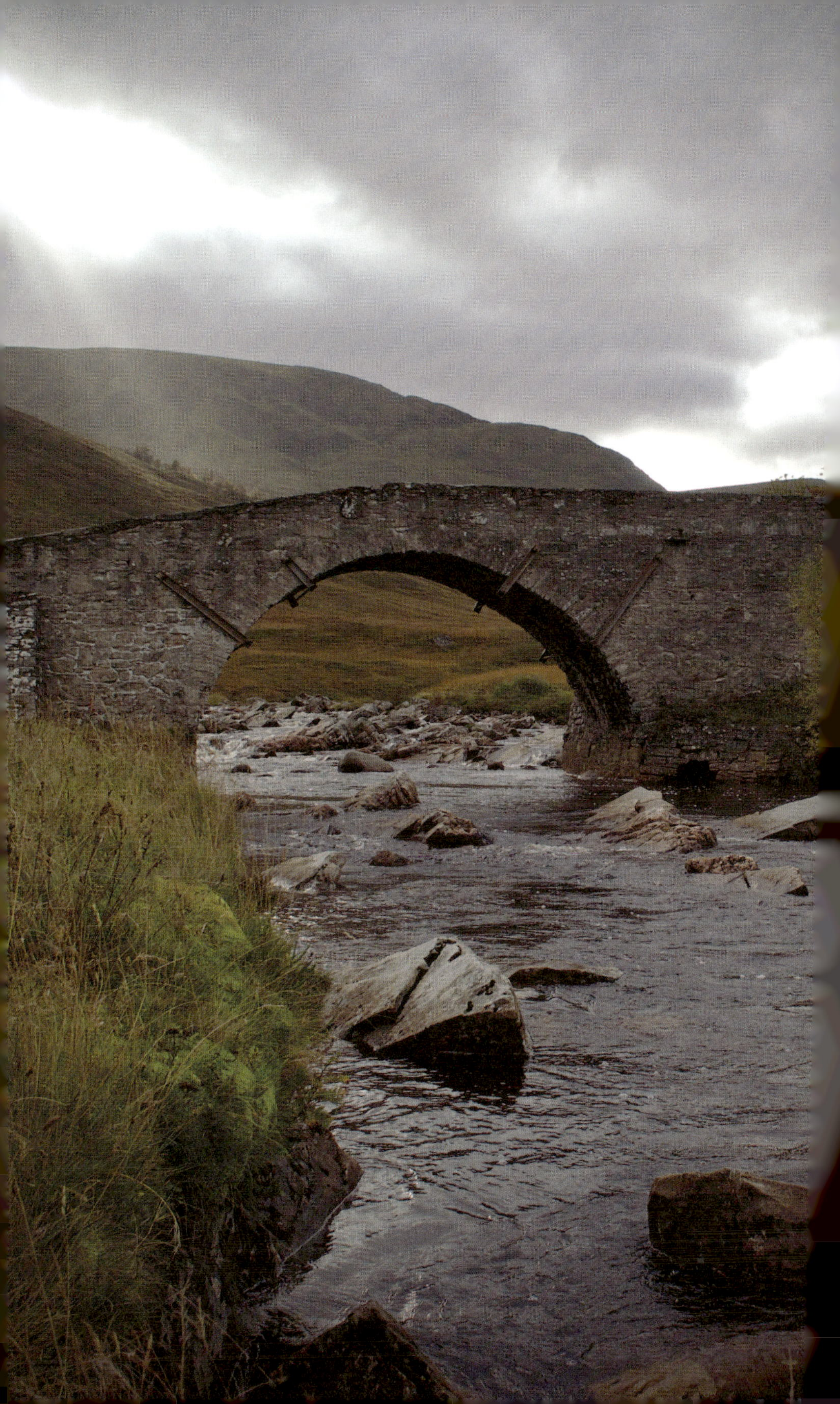

Garva Bridge, General Wade's Military Road

NN 5217 9475

There is a difference between paths and roads. Paths are a product of habit. They exist because movement has made them – the passage of feet, or hooves – and they mark the ground as a line of purpose and of memory. People know them as 'the way', even if they are no longer sure at what point they became 'the way'. Paths need traffic or they will disappear. They are *worn* into the landscape, and the landscape will take them back if they fall out of use: erasing their presence, and memory's impression in the earth.

Roads, on the other hand, do not need a history. While they might co-opt a path – convert it into something more solid and substantial – they will also strike out across places that have never known the habit of passage. Paths are a product of the terrain. But roads seek, ultimately, to overcome the terrain. They are an imposition of will, indifferent to tradition or memory.

I was cycling along one of those impositions, following it west from the tiny village of Laggan into the increasingly narrow valley that holds the headwaters of the River Spey. It was a bright, crisp, autumn day – high broken cloud, and visible shafts of sunlight drifting across the bright orange mountainsides. The road tracked the course of the Spey and, just beyond a small farm at a place called Garvamore, crossed it via a solid, two-arched stone bridge. This bridge was built almost 300 years ago, in 1732, as part of a major project of road construction led by General George Wade. Not just any roads either, but 'military roads': a network of routes linking army bases throughout the Highlands. The Jacobite Rebellion of 1715 had brought war to this landscape – a landscape about which the Hanoverian government forces soon discovered they knew almost nothing and had no way of navigating.

Roads were seen as the solution. Every summer between 1725 and 1733,

Wade travelled north with some 500 soldiers, splitting them into working parties and setting them digging. The roads were built to a standard width of sixteen feet, reduced to ten feet in more difficult terrain. Soil and peat were dug up and thrown into banks either side, then large stones were placed into the trenches and overlain with layers of gravel. Over the course of those nine summers, Wade oversaw the construction of some 250 miles of new roads and forty new bridges.

Direct parallels were drawn – certainly by its creators – between the scale and extent of this road network and the road-building efforts of another army, which had come to Scotland long ago: the Romans. An inscription was added in Latin on the largest of Wade's bridges, built in the town of Aberfeldy, that read, 'Marvel at this military road beyond the Roman borders extending this way and that . . . mocking moors and bogs, opened up through rocks and over mountains, and as you see crossing the indignant Tay.' The implication was that while the Romans had failed in the end to subjugate the Highlands, the Hanoverians had succeeded. Taming and 'mocking' the landscape, leaving rivers 'indignant' at being bridged.

Later writers would come to mock not the moors and the bogs, but what the geologist John MacCulloch described as Wade's 'inveterate rectilinearity': that the general's roads refused to budge 'one yard from the true line laid down by the canon law of the Praefectus viarum and rival of Hannibal'. When Thomas Telford embarked on his own commission to improve transport links throughout the Highlands, he bemoaned that Wade's roads had been built 'with other Views than promoting Commerce and Industry', with the result that they travelled 'in such Directions, and so inconveniently steep as to be nearly unfit for the Purposes of Civil Life'.

I had stopped to rest beside the bridge, down on the banks of the Spey. The river here was rocky, its dark waters coursing over large slabs of pinkish sandstone. Wade's work parties had set up camp here too, pitching tents and erecting huts as they prepared to begin the construction of one of the most ambitious sections of Wade's roads – carving a route north-west, up the steep slopes of the Corrieyairack Pass to cross the mountains and then descend again to the southern tip of Loch Ness and the government barracks of Fort Augustus. Topping out at 2,507 feet, the road was (and, indeed, remains today) the highest ever built in Britain.

Garva Bridge, Wade's Military Road

Beyond the bridge, the route began to climb steadily. For a few miles, it remained a tarmacked surface, then, just beside a farm at Melgarve, it reverted to the original road surface of stones and cobbles, running arrow-straight into the distance through a landscape of red deer grass and spongy moorland. Right alongside was a rather more modern intervention – the marching electricity pylons of the Beauly–Denny transmission line. Centuries after Wade chose this line, the engineers looking to connect wind farms and hydro schemes in the north of Scotland to the south of the country picked the exact same route.

The road was becoming increasingly hard-going by bicycle – bare stones jutting out at odd angles, wide culverts constantly breaking the road surface to aid with drainage. Behind me the sun still flooded the valley; but over the mountains the clouds were thick and grey, and the air was noticeably cooler. The road clung to the side of the hill, first turned to the north to pass under the electricity lines, then kinked east again. And then it had no option. At the Corrieyairack Pass, the land simply soared upwards for hundreds of feet. At this point, Wade's 'rectilinearity' disintegrated completely.

In the 1730s, a government rent-collector called Edmund Burt came to this pass and described – as part of a series of letters to an anonymous correspondent in London – how Wade had conquered the landscape with his roads. The chief obstacles he listed as bogs, mosses, fords, declivities, woods, precipices and steep ascents. Of the latter, he said, the Corrieyairack Pass was 'the worst of them all . . . this mountain is so near the perpendicular in some parts that it was doubtful whether the passenger, after great labour, should get upwards, or return much quicker than he advanced'. Wade's solution, Burt explained, was 'seventeen traverses, like the course of a ship when she is turning windward, by angles still advancing higher and higher'. I attempted this ascent by bicycle, but gave up three traverses in, the loose stones on the steep hairpins giving way beneath my wheels. It was like riding the route of a coiled spring. For Burt, however, thanks to Wade's ingenuity, 'that steep ascent, which was so difficult to be obtained' had been turned 'more easy for wheel carriages than Highgate Hill'.

All the same, Burt, who clearly shared a similar passion for the straight line as Wade, was confounded continually by the difficulties that the Highland environment offered to perspective. Of the Corrieyairack traverses, he lamented that 'little is seen of it below, by reason of flats, hollows, and windings that intercept the sight; and nothing could give you a general view of it, unless one could be supposed to be placed high above the mountain in the air'. This, he said was 'so unlike your hills in the south, that, in some convenient situation of the eye, are seen in one continued smooth slope from the bottom to the top'.

More generally, he expressed frustration to his correspondent that the great achievement of Wade's roads might 'appear to you in a kind of whimsical disorder', as even straight lines could be warped by a landscape that makes a road 'visible to you for a short space, and is then broken off to the sight by a hollow or winding among the hills; beyond that interruption, the eye catches a small part on the side of another hill, and some again on the ridge of it . . . in one place a short horizontal line shows itself below, in another, the marks of the road seem to be almost even with the clouds'. The roads remained elusive. Although at least, Burt said, they appeared 'a very different colour from the heath that chiefly clothes the country' and so could 'be traced out to a considerable distance'.

Unlike the paths that had long crisscrossed the country. These Burt described as 'the old ways (for roads I shall not call them)' and said they 'consisted chiefly of stony moors, bogs, rugged, rapid fords, declivities of hills, entangling woods and giddy precipices'. It was, he said, a 'dreadful catalogue', with not a straight line among them. *Paths* and *roads*. One of Burt's guides, a Highland man, had been utterly bemused by all of Wade's furious building activity. What were the English doing, he asked Burt, '*fooling* away their Money, in removing great Stones and blowing up of Rocks'?

I had reached the summit of the Corrieyairack Pass, its high, bare moorland suddenly swept by a chill wind. The pylons stood sentinel on the summit and continued in a line off towards Fort Augustus. I was heading in the other direction now, however, back down the traverses, back along the road to the bridge and to Garvamore.

In 1914 the Scottish journalist and critic Neil Munro wrote a novel called *The New Road*. Set in 1733, it followed the journey of Aeneas Macmaster, travelling through the central Highlands to Inverness to investigate the death of his father. Of Wade's road, Aeneas said, 'It means the end of many things . . . and yet, this New Road will some day be the Old Road, too, with ghosts on it and memories.' I freewheeled down the Old New Road, over its broken stones, put there to replace the 'Old Ways'. Just seventy years after it was built, it had largely fallen into disrepair and was used, most of all, as a drove road. Another century on, after the arrival of the railways, and it wasn't used at all.

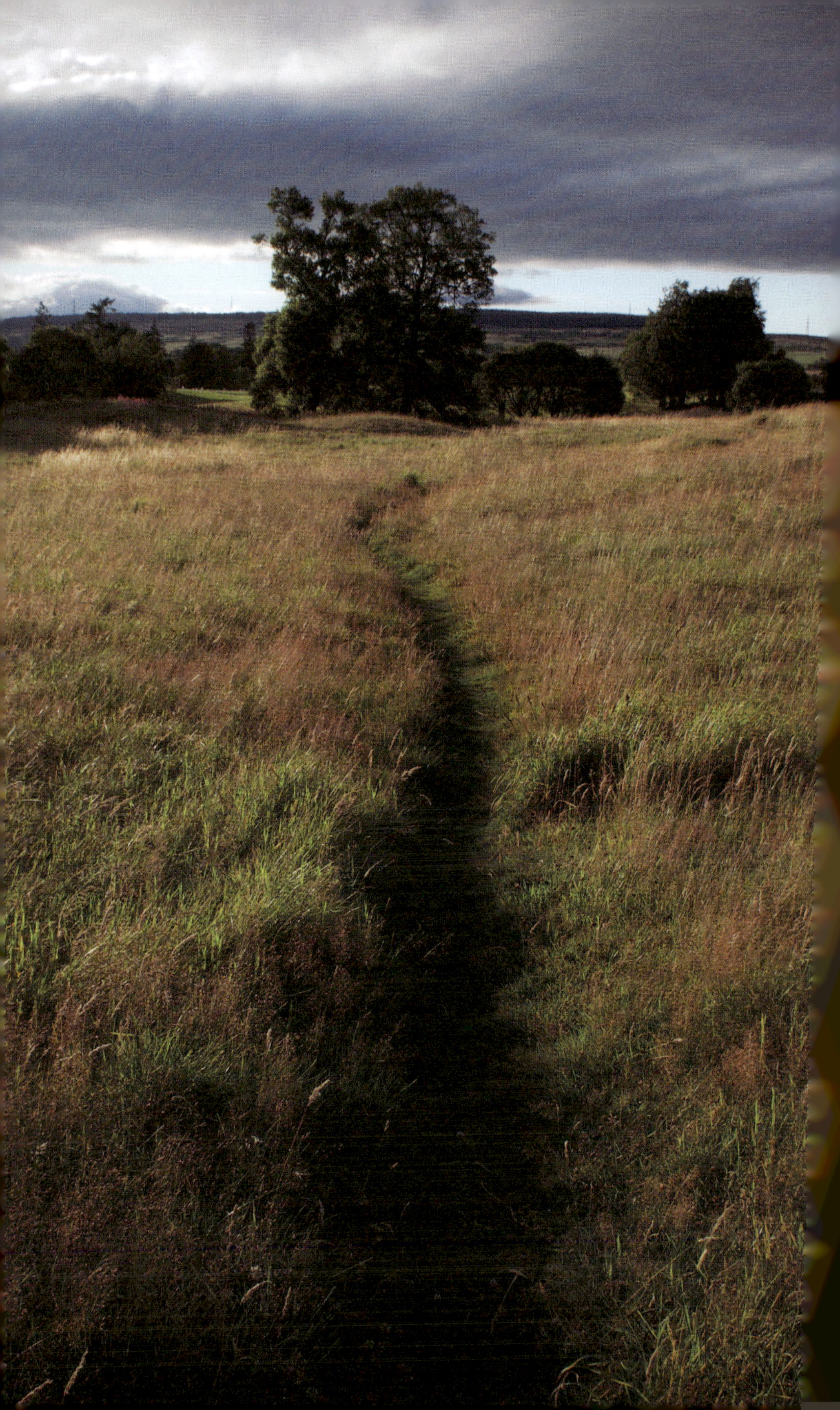

Ardoch Roman Fort, Braco

NN 8390 0990

On summer evenings when I was a teenager, I would set off on an old, reconditioned racing bike that had once belonged to my uncle, cycling the quiet, country backroads that led away from my house on the outskirts of the town of Auchterarder. One of those roads ran due west, across the undulating heather and grassland of the Muir of Orchil towards the small village of Braco. Just before the junction that led to the village, there was a break in a drystone wall that revealed a lightly trodden path.

    I would hop the wall with my bike and wheel it across a flat stretch of gorse and bracken towards a raised plateau. The land here contained a series of ridges and deep ditches surrounding a large, elevated patch of ground. I would sit on the summit of those ridges, stopping for a while to read a book or listen to music on the brick-like, cassette Walkman I used to clip to my shorts. It was a lonely spot. There might be the occasional dog-walker, but mostly I saw no one else. If I stayed for a while, into twilight, I would watch the sky to the west fade from orange to a soft purple, at which point I would finally return to the road and cycle the few short miles home. At the time, I was largely ignorant of – and certainly indifferent to – the history of the place. Yet I kept going back to it, all the same.

    A little over 1,900 years earlier, in around AD 80, a cohort of Spanish soldiers, conscripts to the Roman army, came here and started to dig. They began by carving rectangles into the landscape. The largest was around 800 feet long by 500 feet wide. Another was excavated inside the first, and possibly another one after that, to enclose a space of some eighteen acres. The trenches cut down as deep as eight or nine feet, with the distance from the lowest point to the top of the heaped bank of spoil reaching up to seventeen feet. It is likely that this moorland plain just above the banks of the River Knaik had never met a spade before.

After the earthworks came the construction. Trees felled and chopped to make tall timber walls and ramparts. Long lines of barrack blocks built on the flat interior – accommodation for hundreds, perhaps even thousands, of soldiers. A road led here from the south, cobbled and cambered to aid with drainage. Work continued to extend this road onwards: north for a few miles before it pivoted almost directly east at what is now the village of Muthill. There was digging and more digging. Building and more building.

Other large forts were erected, then smaller fortlets, all connected by the path of the road. Tall wooden watchtowers and signal stations were raised up between them, allowing rapid communication back and forth.

The road and its forts ran for some eighteen miles, mostly along a humpback of raised ground between the Pow Water to the north and the River Earn to the south, known as the Gask Ridge. Ardoch fort at Braco was the major base anchoring the south-western end while another, called Bertha, just to the north of the present-day city of Perth, marked the north-eastern terminus. An even larger site – the legionary headquarters – was under construction beyond this, at Inchtuthil, further up the course of the River Tay. In effect, this whole stretch of landscape was being turned into a military zone – a sort of hard border, or proto-frontier system.

Overseeing it all was the Roman General Julius Agricola. After years of campaigning in Britannia, the time had come, he said, to 'drive deeper and deeper into Caledonia and fight battle after battle till we have reached the end'. As Agricola's son-in-law and biographer Tacitus put it, the legions passed beyond the 'narrow neck of land' between the Forth and Clyde estuaries, 'into what was virtually another island'. The fortifications running along the Gask Ridge were effectively a bridgehead for invasion. They deliberately occupied the edge of the Lowland ground, facing on to the mountains and running directly parallel to them, but always at a distance. This was a geological borderline too: the Highland Boundary Fault, the place where sedimentary rock gives way to a hard igneous mass that rears up into an expanse of tall peaks and narrow glens.

The Romans had already circumnavigated Britain by boat and felt sure that they had reached the last extremity of the north-western Earth, the place where 'land and nature end'. As Tacitus said, come the summer, the night in Caledonia was so bright and so short that 'you can barely distinguish the evening from the morning twilight'. If the sky was clear, 'the sun's glow can be seen all night long: it does not set and rise, but simply passes along the horizon': a result of the 'flat ends of the earth' not being able to 'raise the darkness to any height'.

Agricola's campaign reached its climax in the summer of AD 83, in the shadow of a mountain called Mons Graupius. There, according to Tacitus, the outnumbered Romans overcame an army of tens of thousands of Caledonians. By the end, he said, the battlefield was a mass of 'weapons, bodies, mangled limbs and soil soaked with blood'. In the aftermath, 'an awful silence reigned' and the 'hills were deserted'. The edge had been reached and claimed, but it was a hollow victory – almost immediately Agricola and his men were recalled to fight an uprising in Germany. 'Britannia was thoroughly conquered' and then 'immediately abandoned'.

The location of Mons Graupius – if it ever existed at all – remains a mystery. But it did give a modern name to those mountains watched over by Ardoch fort and the frontier line of the Gask Ridge: the Grampians (the result of misspelling Graupius as 'Grampius' in an early, fifteenth century, printed edition of Tacitus's history). This failure to secure Scotland brought the Romans back on at least two more occasions over the next two centuries – first in the AD 140s, leading to the construction of the Antonine Wall between the Forth and Clyde estuaries, then again in AD 208 under the command of Emperor Septimius Severus.

This last invasion brought with it a huge army, over 30,000 strong. Severus travelled with them, carried, as the historian Cassius Dio put it, 'through practically the whole of the hostile country . . . in a covered litter most of the way, on account of his infirmity'. At Ardoch, they reconstructed the original camp from Agricola's time, digging out even more trenches, as well as setting up a temporary marching camp alongside – which was even larger in size than the fort. Its traces, though faint compared to the rippled earth of Ardoch, still remain as little humps in the soil, and lines of darker grass that reveal its geometric outline.

I had returned to Ardoch on another summer evening, cycling that same road to Braco and looking for the break in the wall that I used to climb through. I couldn't see it anymore. But I did find the old, worn path that approached the fort from the north. It was warm and quiet, the long grass backlit by the low sun; white specks of insects danced in the air. I took a seat as I always used to, high on the banking, on the remains left behind by an ancient war machine. The stillness and peace of this site today bears no relation to its former purpose. It would have been a place of constant noise, activity, movement, tension and harnessed aggression. Severus, a Roman emperor no less, would have come here, to this same patch of ground, to look out on this same sky. As he approached 'the extremity of the island', Cassius Dio said, Severus had 'observed most accurately the variation of the sun's motion and the length of the days and nights in summer'.

It was one of those same, clear evenings when the the 'sun's glow' would be seen all night long, passing along the horizon to the north of Braco. I sat on Ardoch's grass-grown ramparts and watched it dip, watched it trace the course of a Highland borderline – a frontier leading to the very 'flat ends of the earth'. Just as I had done when I was a teenager. Just as an emperor must have done here, once, long ago.

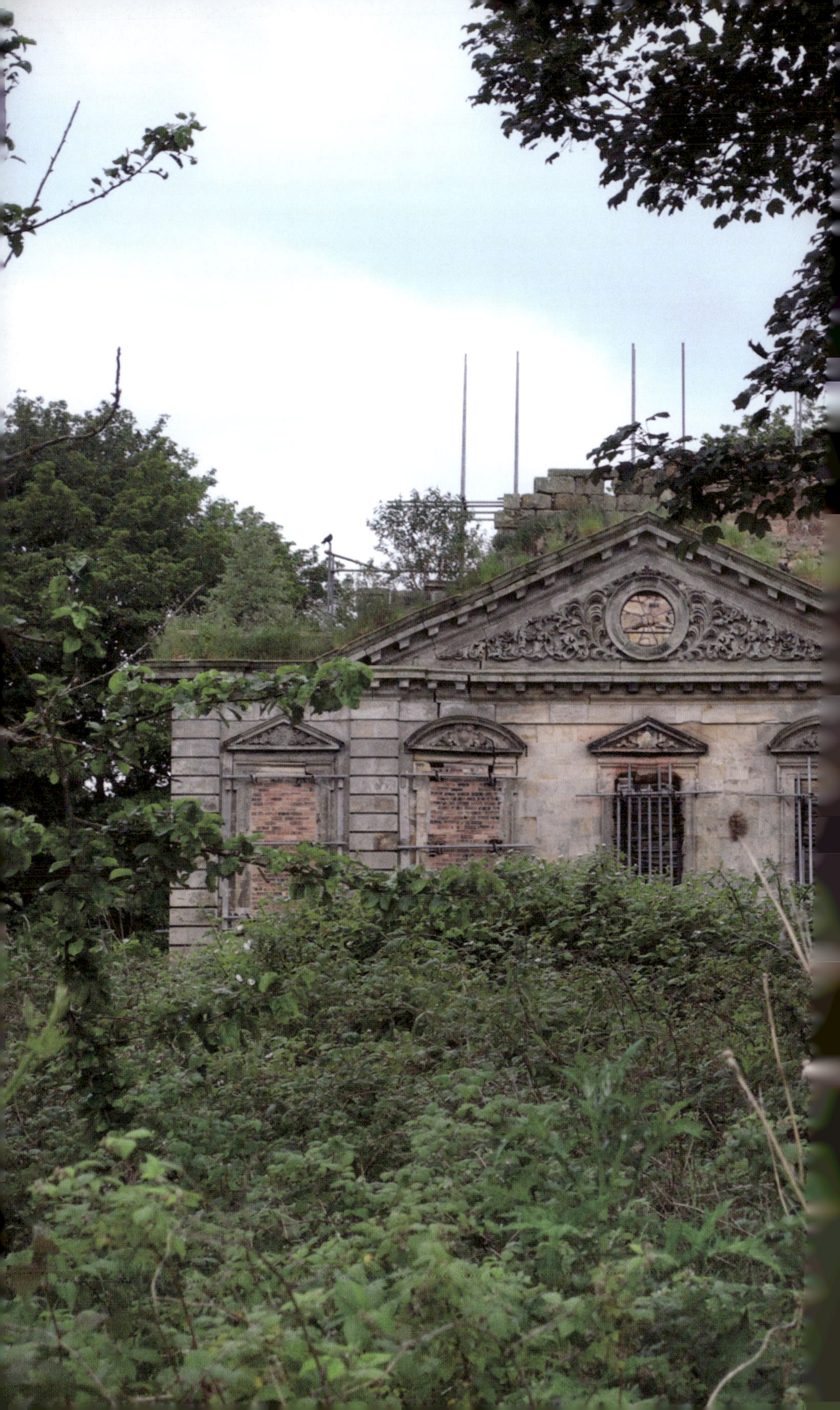

Sheltered

The Bone Caves, Inchnadamph

NC 2757 2060

It is easy to forget that Scotland was once entirely underground. Or, more accurately, it was subglacial. All of the country's rock and earth, all of its hills and mountains, were buried, often very deep, beneath a great, all-encompassing layer of ice. That ice, of course, was never static. It advanced and grew and retreated and shrank, shaping the earth below it over the course of millennia, to an extent that is hard for us, in our comparatively fleeting lives, to truly comprehend.

The most recent Ice Age in Scotland began around 33,000 years ago, and finally ended about 20,000 years later. As the climate warmed, the vast network of glaciers began to melt. Much of this melting was from the bottom up. Rivers formed and grew below the ice sheets. On the surface, moulins appeared (*moulin* is the French for 'mill'). These were patches of meltwater on the glacier surface which, once heated by the air and the sun, burrowed down through the colder ice, like water circling in a plughole, joining other moulins in a network of vein-like tributaries linking to the river flowing at the base. This was the colossal thawing of an entire landscape. And in the process, the departing ice began to drop whatever it had picked up. Mostly this was just rock and earth and sediment. But also, sometimes, there were other things too.

In the far north-west of the country, leading away from the tiny hamlet of Inchnadamph (from the Gaelic *Innis nan Damh*, meaning the 'meadow of the stags'), there is a steep-sided river valley. I followed this valley for a mile to the west and, just before reaching the head of the glen, came upon a sheer crag of light-grey, dolomitic limestone. There, where the green slope of the valley meets the base of the crag, I saw a series of black holes, spaced apart in a line, like doorways on a rocky tenement block. They were, in effect, absences. Weak spots in the limestone that had been probed and eroded and carved out a long, long time ago. Caves.

When the ice that encased this landscape began to disappear, some of its meltwater flowed into and filled up these caves. And in the process, it brought with it a huge cache of bones. In one cave was deposited a mass conglomeration of the antlers of reindeer. Nearly a thousand fragments – some even pre-dating the glaciers, at over 47,000 years old; others from the peak of the last Ice Age, 250 centuries ago. But the remains weren't just of reindeer. Into the holes of the caves swam the debris of nearly fifty different species: Arctic fox and lemming; lynx, wolf, badger, wild cat and brown bear; tundra vole, shrew, weasel and wood mouse; pig, ox, otter and puffin. Even the cranium of a polar bear, which had walked this landscape 18,000 years ago, came sloshing in. Here was an incredible accident of climate change and geology. The perfect combination of heat, gravity and chance; the caves positioned in just the right place to sieve the bones from the deluge of the melt and the flood.

It was early August, and the day was wet. It made the landscape an exuberant mix of sodden, bright-green bracken studded with long clumps of red-pink flowering heather – the limestone deposits have made the valley's soil composition rich and fertile. The sky, on the other hand, was a solemn grey. So low, in fact, was the cloud, I imagined that it couldn't be far off the height the ice once reached here. A ghost of the old glacial ceiling.

I picked my way into the cave mouths one by one, wary of the steep drop from the path down into the valley. They have names now, roughly according to the remains that they contained – first was Fox's Den, then Bone Cave, then Reindeer Cave, then Badger Cave. The bones were discovered in 1889 by two men, John Horne and Benjamin Peach, working for the Geological Survey. Horne and Peach dug into the sediments on the floor of what is now called Bone Cave and were soon bringing up chunks of lemming, lynx and reindeer. At the same time, they also found traces of people. There was, they wrote, clear evidence that, at some point, 'the cave was tenanted by man'. As they excavated down into the dirt and rock, they began to see 'in various layers, fireplaces and firestones, split and burnt bones'.

These hints of human occupation led to a far more extensive excavation

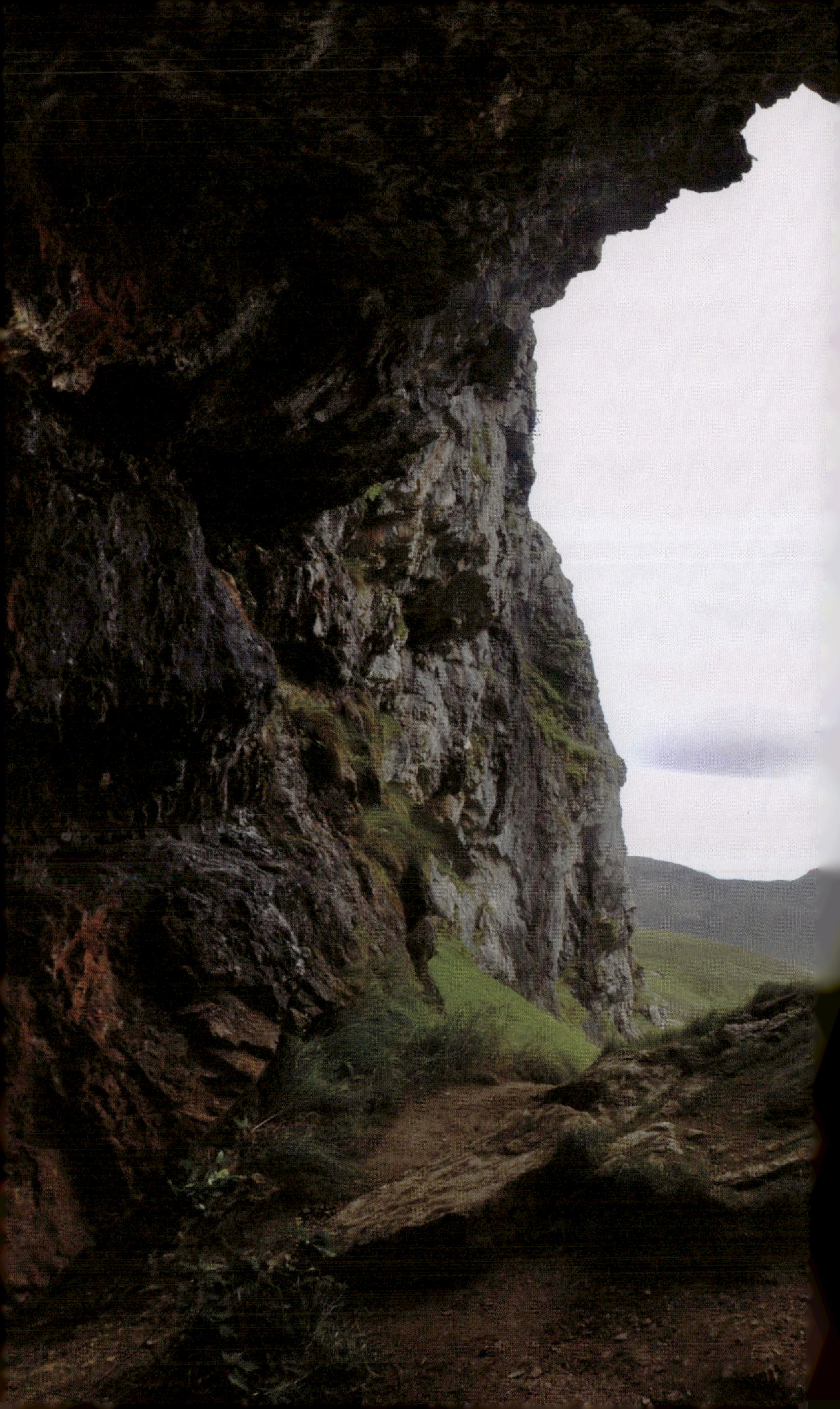

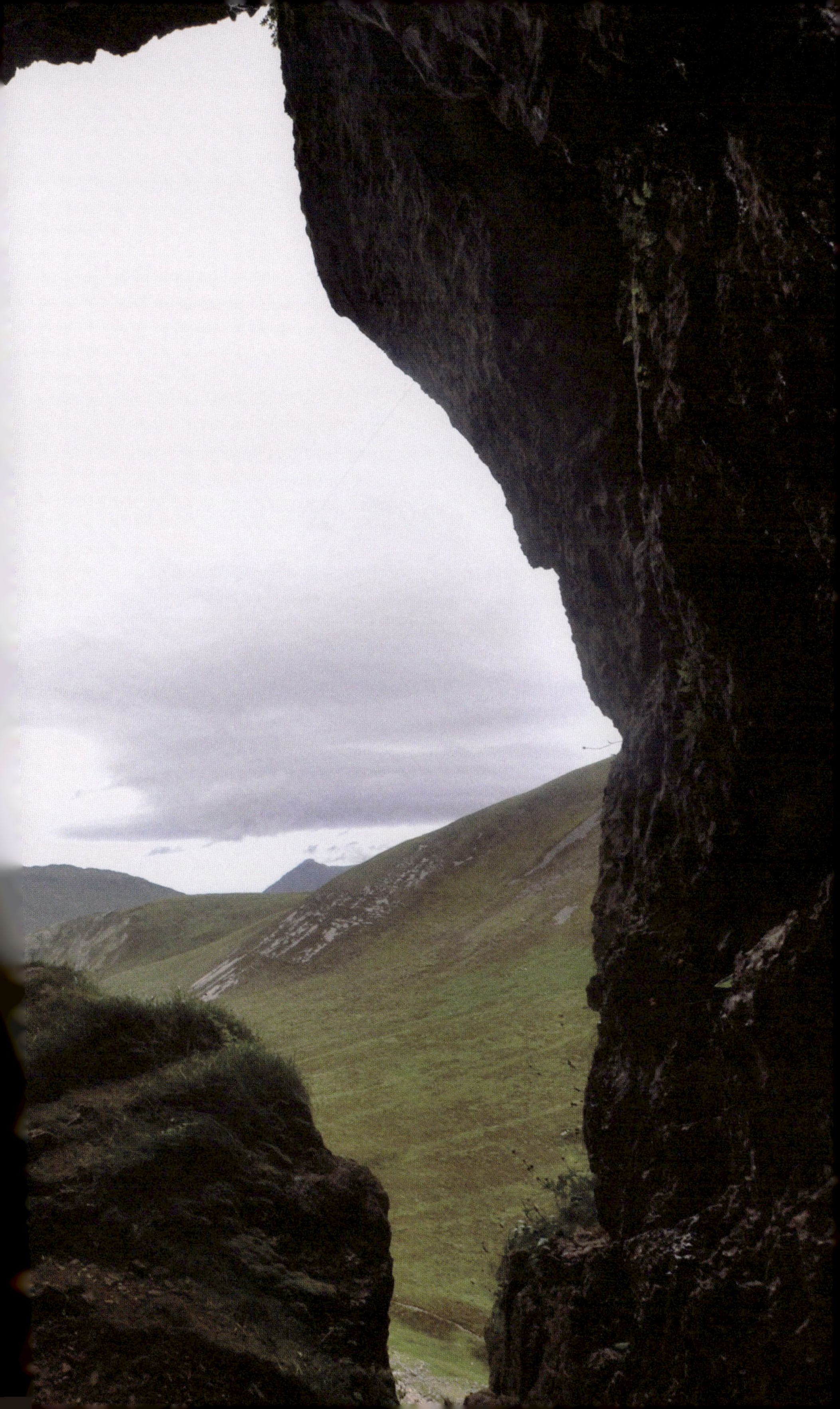

in 1926, undertaken by amateur archaeologist John Cree, and sponsored by the National Museum of Antiquities and the Royal Scottish Museum. Cree first brought up more and more animal remains – recording in his field notes 'vast numbers of shed antlers of young reindeer'; the giant canine tooth of a bear; and countless bird bones, from eider ducks, auks, ptarmigan, red grouse, barnacle goose and swan. And then, as he explored further in the earth at the back of Reindeer Cave, he found two human skulls, four vertebrae, a sacrum and a femur. Cree described the femur lying across the face of the skull and exclaimed, 'The whole thing savours of two bloody murders!' Then, in both Reindeer Cave and Badger Cave, came the objects. A ring-headed pin fashioned from walrus ivory. A smooth polished sliver of deer bone. A spear-point shaped from deer antler. Another shaft of antler, cut as if to form a socket and handle for a knife.

'Here we have evidence,' wrote Cree of the four objects, 'of man's existence in the north of Scotland at a time when ice, many feet in thickness, was covering the mountainous portion of the country and glaciers were slowly moving down the valleys.' This was, he concluded excitedly, 'proof for the first time of the existence of man in Scotland in the late Paleolithic period'.

In recent years, Cree's conclusions have been quietly and steadily debunked. The walrus ivory pin and the antler 'knife handle' have been dated to the eleventh century and are considered Viking in origin. The polished deer bone was too diminished to be carbon-dated, but it shares the same characteristic appearance of hair and clothing pins from the Viking period. The spear head, on the other hand, *is* some 13,000 years old. Yet further investigation failed to find any trace of it being worked or modified. It was, in the end, simply a broken antler tip.

And what of the human remains Cree discovered? They turned out to be just 4,000 years old. Neolithic people knew these caves and used them for shelter, or ritual, or burial. They lit fires, cooked and ate. Perhaps they, too, discovered some traces of animal bones in the dirt? And wondered what had brought the remains here in such density, so that they lined the very floor they sat on.

I rested for a while in the mouth of Reindeer Cave and thought about the people who had come here – how we would have shared that exact same view out across the valley. But really my mind was drifting much further

The Bone Caves, Inchnadamph

back, towards that frozen landscape which is so hard to conjure in our imaginations. These caves are a remarkable record of life – perhaps even an abundance of life – up on the surface of the vanished ice sheets. Countless generations of animals roamed a space that is now our sky – and roamed it for far longer than humans have called Scotland home. Most of all, I thought about the polar bear. About his life up on the white expanse, his territory an emptiness that no longer exists in any physical form. How he made his way, somehow, sometime, to the very place where I was sitting. To become just one more bone in the bone caves.

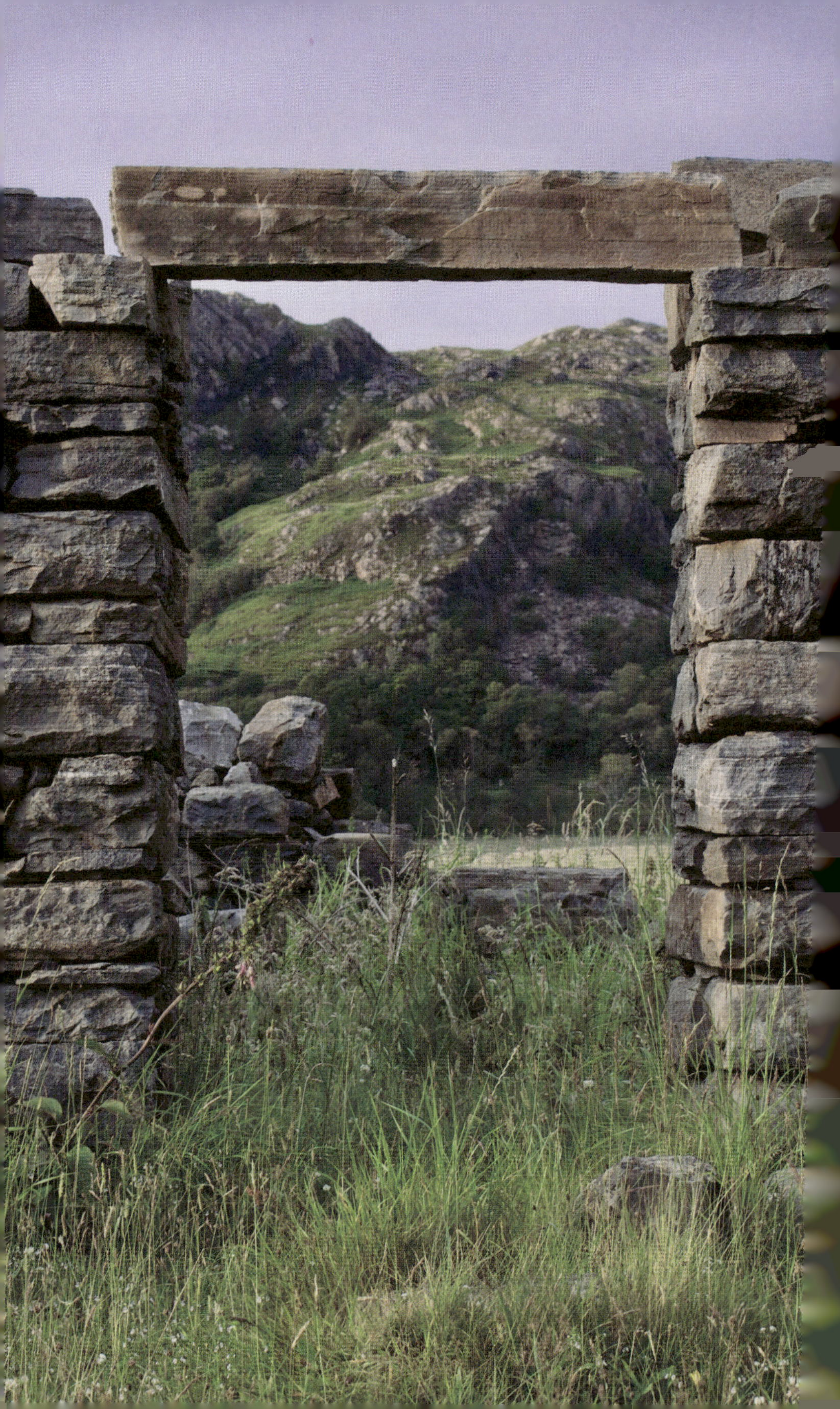

Peanmeanach, Ardnish Peninsula

NM 7123 8049

At the very beginning of the three-mile route that leads you to Peanmeanach, you cross the tracks of the West Highland Line via a squat concrete bridge. A bright-red sign offers a warning that the bridge is 'not suitable for vehicular traffic'. How you would even get a vehicle near to it, down a narrow gravel path, is unclear. The bridge itself is rudely constructed, its once solid hump reached by a now shattered, foot-high step overgrown with weeds and bushes.

From the apex of the bridge, you can look down on the railway tracks as they run away to the north, before curving out of sight to the west, where they go on to kiss the shores of Loch Beag. The railway marks, almost perfectly, a boundary line. Beyond it, you have entered the Ardnish Peninsula, a widening fan of rocky land, shaped like an oyster's shell, with the high, mountainous shimmer of Loch Doire a' Gherrain as the pearl at its centre. View it on a map and you can see quite clearly how the track slices the peninsula from the mainland at the root. This was an incision that had material consequences for the people who lived here. Completed in the first year of the twentieth century, the railway effectively cut Ardnish off from the modern world.

As a result, it has made the bridge across the line into a kind of portal. You can find many portals like this throughout Scotland – some more discernable and concrete (in this case, literally) than others. They are places that, as you move through them, offer an instant shift in your sense of your surroundings. It's nothing as basic or as clichéd as 'stepping back in time'. It's rather that time almost loosens and collapses around you. The past intrudes on the present, rises back to the surface. It's a feeling as much as anything else, a shimmer on the edge of your vision – that you are encountering the ghostly residue, not of a person, but of a place. While this is not necessarily an uncommon sensation, I've rarely experienced it as strongly as I did on the path into Ardnish.

Perhaps it was the timing, and the circumstances. It was an evening, just a few weeks after midsummer. Two days of torrential rain had given way to a clearing sky streaked with the torn fragments of clouds – the tail-end of the departing stormfront. The lowering sun had broken through, and the still-wet landscape appeared too bright and oversaturated.

Past the railway line was a fast-flowing burn, bridged by two large planks of now-rotting wood. The path then wound through a birch forest, before beginning a steep climb up the slopes of Cruach Doir'an Raoigh. Steps of rough-cut stone have been built into the hillside, first crossing and then ascending alongside a mountain stream. So heavy had the recent rainfall been, however, that stream and staircase often merged into a series of shallow but persistent waterfalls.

At almost 500 feet up, the route levelled out and turned west. I had reached the ridgeline of the peninsula. The waters of Loch nan Uamh stretched out below me, streaked bronze by the evening sunlight, with the dark silhouettes of the islands of Eigg and Rum marking the far horizon. The stone path, constructed by the people of Ardnish over a century earlier, continued into the distance. I followed it onwards as it dipped into puddles of accumulated rainwater or crossed huge rock slabs, sometimes ten or twenty metres long, seamed with lines of white quartz.

As Loch Doire a' Gherrain came into sight, nestled in a basin sunk between the ridgelines to the north and south, the route began a gentle descent downwards. For the first time I could see out to the peninsula's end. As I pressed on, the evening's stillness was filled with a soft rushing that grew steadily into a roar. The loch's outflow stream, normally crossable by a series of stepping-stones, was in torrent. Removing my boots and socks, I waded through the rushing water. Another portal.

The stone track reappeared on the far side, curving downwards to arrive at a slope shaded by birch and Atlantic oak. I emerged from the trees at the foot of the slope to be confronted by a quite remarkable sight. A completely flat expanse of land, covered by long grass and marshy reeds – looking almost exactly like stalks of corn or barley – that grew above my head. The path ran on for several hundred metres, perfectly straight through the middle of the field of reeds, towards a distant line of seven stone houses. All but one of those houses was in ruins. Out of the chimney of that single, still-surviving building came a soft wisp of white fire smoke. I had reached the village of Peanmeanach.

Occupied from at least as early as the Iron Age, this sheltered bay at the tip of the peninsula became a home to Norse settlers a millennium ago and, by the middle of the nineteenth century, was a busy fishing and crofting community of forty-eight people. A hundred years later, however, and there was only one person left. This last resident was Nellie MacQueen, the daughter of Peanmeanach's postmaster and schoolmistress, and she had lived in that last remaining building, which once served as both the post office and the schoolhouse.

One by one, the families around her packed up and left, seeking new work and new homes as the railway bypassed Ardnish to focus the fishing trade on the harbour at Mallaig, the terminus of the West Highland Line. Nellie clung on until the Second World War, when the rationing of paraffin to half a gallon per week, and candles to one per week, became too hard to bear. By 1943, Peanmeanach stood completely empty. For a time, Nellie's house was used intermittently as a byre until, in the late 1970s, the Mountain Bothies Association renovated the building – in particular, replacing its collapsing roof – to allow it to be run as an open-access bothy.

It was just after nine o'clock as I reached the village: the bay and the sea and the grass all glowing a warm, pinkish gold. The smoke from the bothy was a clear sign that it was in use. As I rounded the path to the front of the house, I came upon a family of four sitting drinking tea on the porch. They invited me to join them and as I rested my head against the sun-warmed stone of the bothy wall, they told me how they had canoed into the bay earlier that day, approaching Peanmeanach from the south up the course of Loch Morlich. As we talked, I watched as two men made their way towards us from the beach below: kayakers exploring the coastline who had decided to come ashore and rest for the night. After my silent, lonely walk in, it was jolting, slightly surreal – yet pleasant – to find these signs of life, albeit transitory, at the tip of the peninsula.

Nellie returned here once herself, in 1998, when she was in her eighties. She came with her daughter, and it's said that as she made her way along the line of houses, she used her walking stick to tap on the ruins of each of building, calling aloud the names of their former residents as she did so. A roll call, or an invocation. A litany of abandonment. Nellie, the last resident of this old community, died in 2011, aged ninety-six.

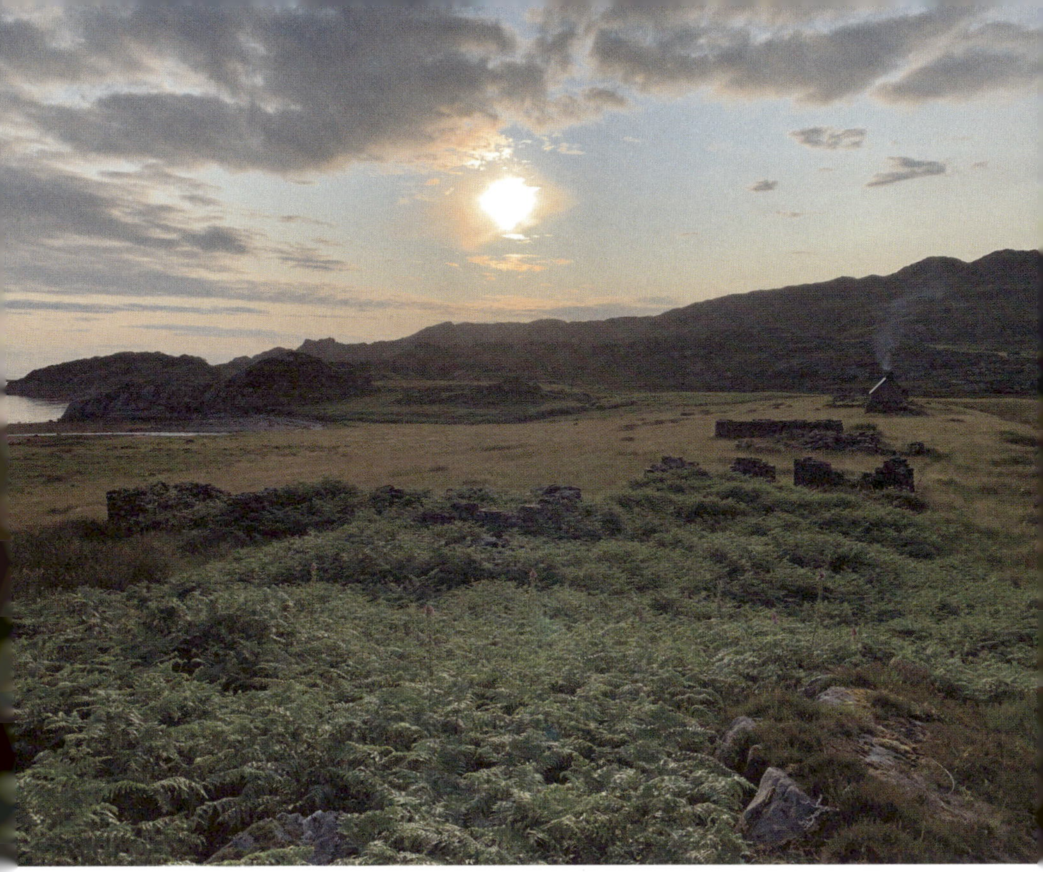

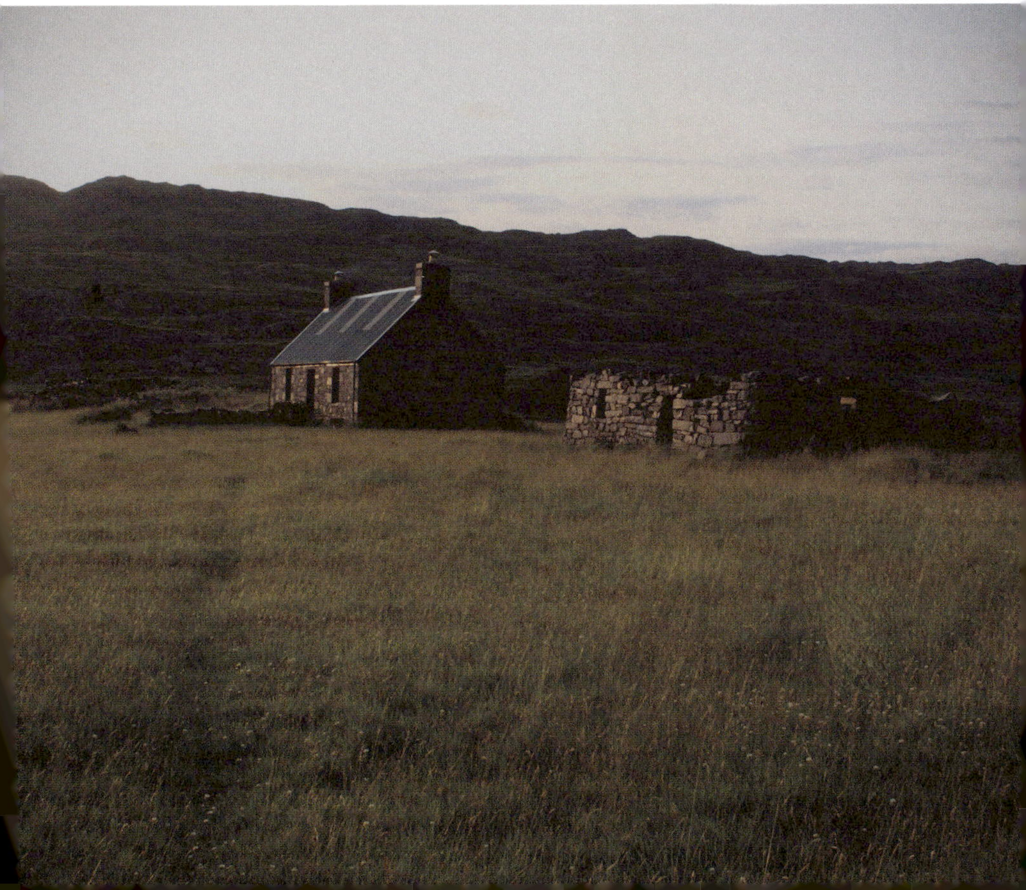

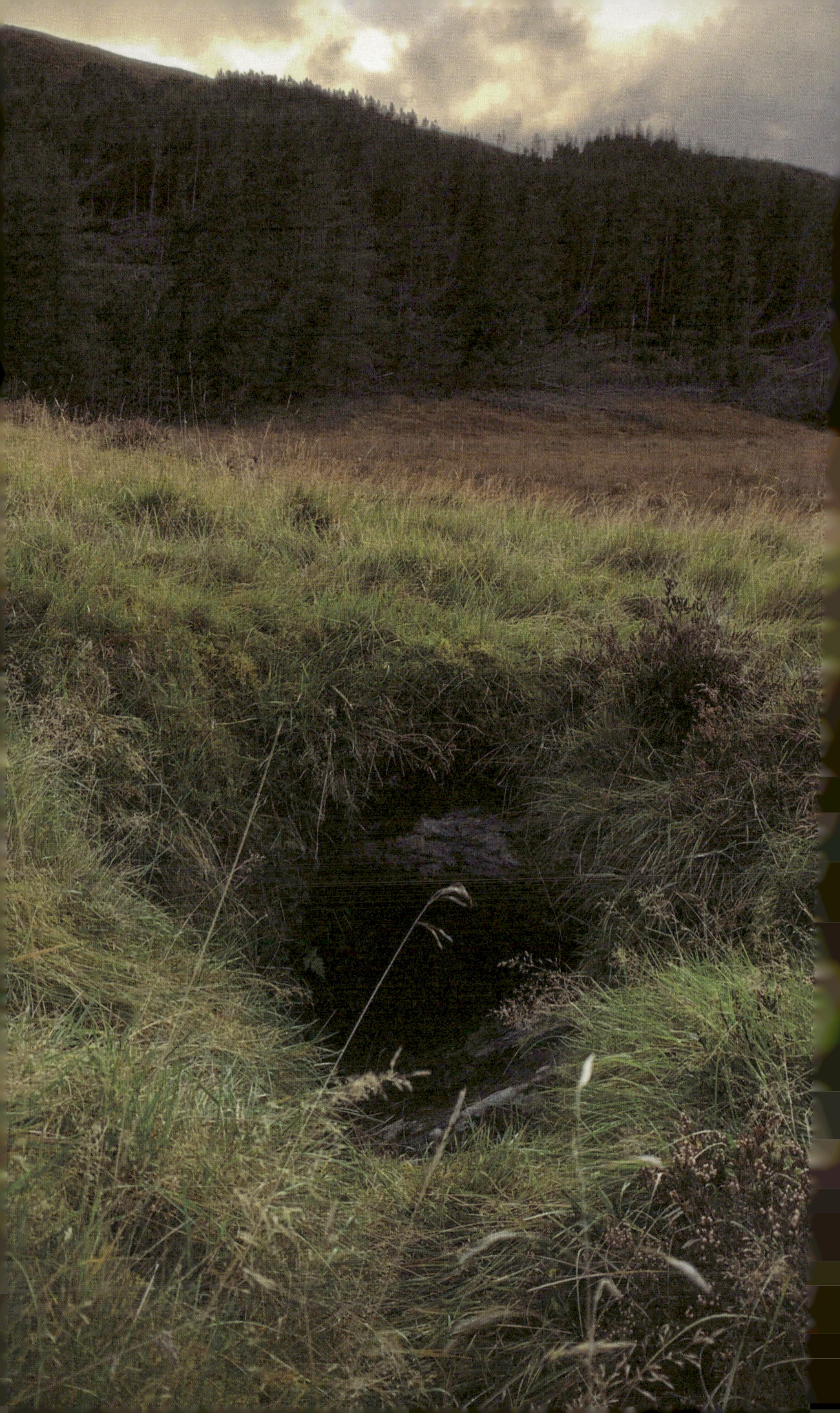

Cracknie Souterrain, Borgie Forest, Sutherland

NC 6655 5092

The hole was just two feet wide and a little under a foot high, set into a small hollow near the top of a tussocky knoll. It was framed by two large stones: a solid, moss-covered lintel at the top and a large, flat slab, lying squint, at the bottom. Little clumps of heather were growing above the lintel, and long stalks of grass sprouted all around, their seed-heads flickering in the wind. The hole was black. Beyond the two stones, daylight was simply swallowed up completely. It was a very old hole. Two and a half thousand years old – give or take a few centuries.

I had travelled much of the way to the hole by bicycle, riding for three and a half miles along a wide logging track that runs through the eastern flank of Borgie Forest. I say *through*, but huge tracts of Borgie's trees have been harvested in recent years. It was less a forest now than an open moorland. Swathes of grass, glowing a beautiful copper in the autumn sunlight, led off into the distance, towards the craggy slopes of Beinn Stumanadh and Ben Hiel. Behind them to the west, silhouetted a purple-blue in the distance, and partly swaddled by a long, horizontal bank of cloud, was the bell-curve slope of Ben Loyal.

For the last quarter of a mile, there had been no option but to leave my bicycle and make my way cross-country. The knoll was visible from the track, but to reach it meant crossing a stretch of new clear-fell. It had made for brutally slow progress: negotiating torn-up, muddy ground; clambering over the discarded detritus of hacked-up trees; dodging root-holes filled with murky peat-water; and venturing with tentative steps across spongy bog that pulled and sucked at – and often submerged – my boots.

Just over a century earlier, in the summer of 1909, the antiquarian

Alexander Curle made this same journey. Curle was also travelling by bicycle – his preferred mode of transport – and was one year into his new job as Secretary of the Royal Commission on the Ancient and Historical Monuments of Scotland.* Curle had begun his work in Berwickshire in August 1908, crisscrossing the county on bicycle, measuring rods strapped to his crossbar, stopping every so often to consult his six-inches-to-the-mile OS map (backed with linen to make it more durable) and asking locals for information on the locations of any unmarked ancient remains. A year later, he visited Sutherland, which was an altogether different proposition to gliding from village to village along undulating Borders backroads. 'Owing to the great extent of the county and the sparseness of its population,' he wrote, 'trustworthy information regarding its monuments was difficult to obtain.'

He came to Cracknie on 28 May 1909, cycling south from his lodgings in Bettyhill. A tip-off from a shepherd and a gamekeeper had led him towards Borgie Bridge, but here 'the road for bicyclists [was] absolutely impossible'. He left his bicycle behind a stone and was 'determined to push on over the further three miles of desolate moor'. It was 'a dreary afternoon', and the clouds gathering on Ben Loyal 'burst from time to time in heavy showers and made walking over swampy peat bogs anything but easy'. When he finally reached the knoll, the mark he had been given on his map was in the wrong place and it was only as he was leaving, after half an hour of searching, that he found the hole.

Curle wasted little time in going underground. 'I fixed the end of my tape line outside with a pin and lighting my candle made my first entry into an earth house. In that lonely spot, without a human being within miles and the cliffs of Beinn Stumanadh towering up above it was somewhat eerie.'

I knew exactly what he meant. Once I was up on the knoll, confronted by this strange little hole in the ground, the feeling of solitude and my own isolation was incredibly acute. The sun was flickering on and off, and the wind had dropped. Just as Curle wrote, it was an eerie place. And, at that moment, eerily quiet – there were no birdcalls, no buzz of insects, only the gentle hush of the breeze.

It took me a while to decide to enter the hole. The entrance was a tight

---

* See Introduction.

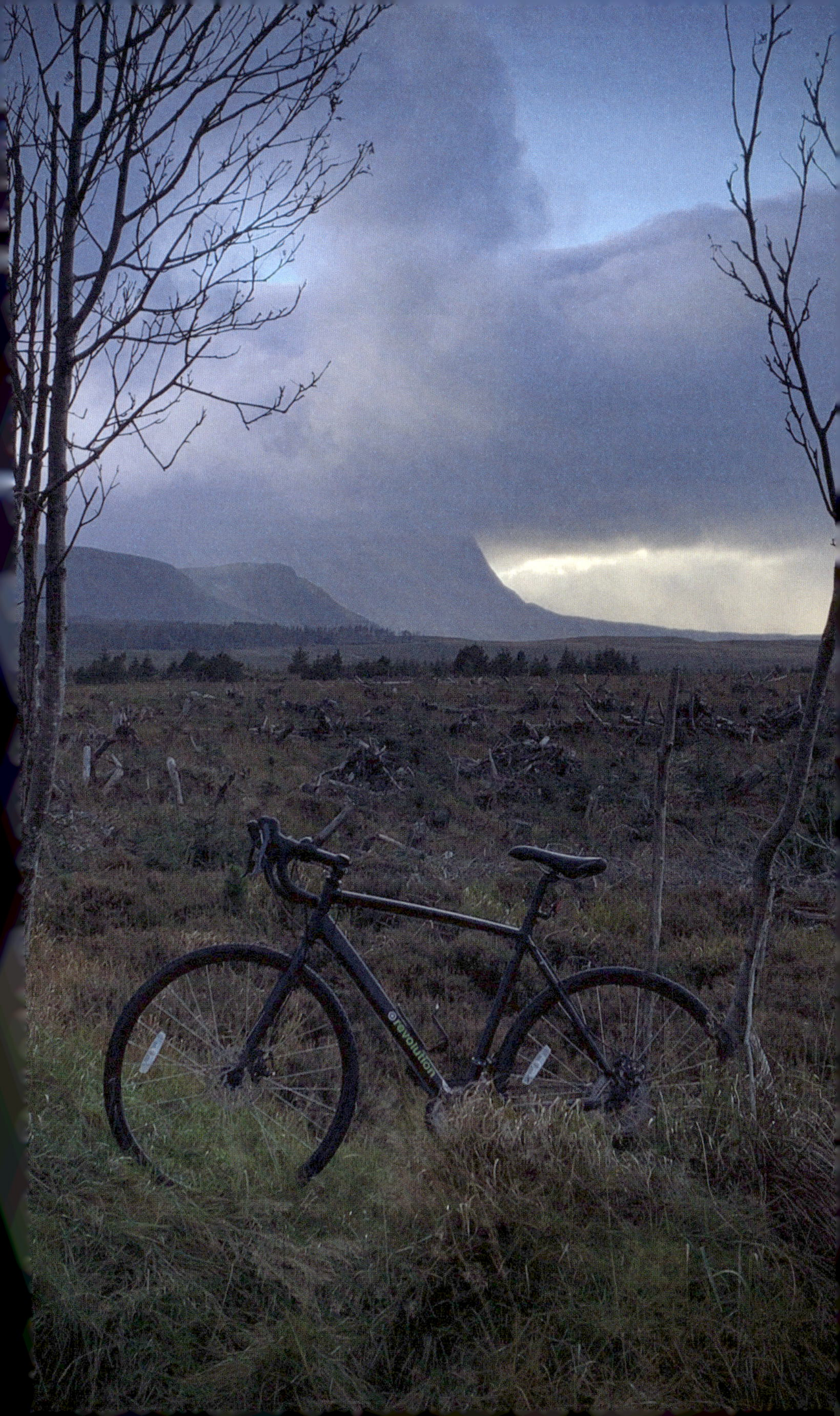
revolution

squeeze and I had to lie flat on my front and wriggle forward. My mobile phone torch took the place of Curle's candle. The stones on the floor were slick with mud which soon caused me to slide forward into the passage. It sloped downwards sharply and, in my shaking torch beam, I could see the walls curving round to the right and disappearing into further darkness. I kept on for a few more metres, pulling myself forward by the stone walls on either side. At one point, my phone slipped from my hand and I was enveloped in blackness, scrabbling frantically to pick it up. As soon as I lost sight of the entrance behind me, the urge to leave became overwhelming. It was like crawling into a giant, petrified throat. There was no space to turn around, so instead I had to just push myself slowly backwards. It took several minutes, but eventually my feet, and then my legs and body and head, re-emerged from the hole and into the daylight.

While inside, it was hard to shake the feeling that the passage wouldn't stop at all, would just keep descending. Curle was made of stronger stuff than me and continued on with his measuring tape for forty-two feet – just over thirteen metres – before reaching the end point of a small, semi-circular chamber. He called it an 'earth house': thinking that the passage was a primitive corridor leading to some collapsed ancient underground dwelling. The reality is a little more prosaic.

There *was* once a house here – but it had been built above ground, on top of the knoll. The passage was its cellar. Not just any cellar, however, but quite possibly the oldest surviving cellar in Scotland. It is what is known as a souterrain – from the French, *sous terrain*, meaning, literally, 'under ground'. A cool, dark place to store food, or possibly even to seek refuge in times of danger: a sort of Iron Age panic-room.

Souterrains are, in that sense, deeply domestic structures. Which also makes them peculiarly intimate. Cracknie's souterrain had barely changed since it was built over two and a half millennia ago. The hands of the people who lived here would have touched the very stones that my hands touched down inside the passageway. The descent beneath the ground would have looked and felt the same to them as it did to me. I was entering their private space, a space that was still surviving even though the house that it had once served was long gone. I was under their home. Or, in effect, still *inside* what was left of their home – the souterrain was hooked down into the earth like

Cracknie Souterrain, Borgie Forest

an anchor from the past. The sense of being an intruder was palpable.

Once I was out of the passage, I didn't linger. The darkness of the hole, its silent but insistent presence on this abandoned hillock on the edge of the plantation moor, was strangely unnerving. Curle himself admitted 'feeling very weary' after his long walk to Cracknie and stopped in on the shepherd's house at Dalness on his return to 'beg a glass of milk'. I clambered back to the forestry track, retrieved my bicycle from where it rested against the trunk of a pine tree, and rode away from the hole, across the open, broken landscape of Borgie Forest.

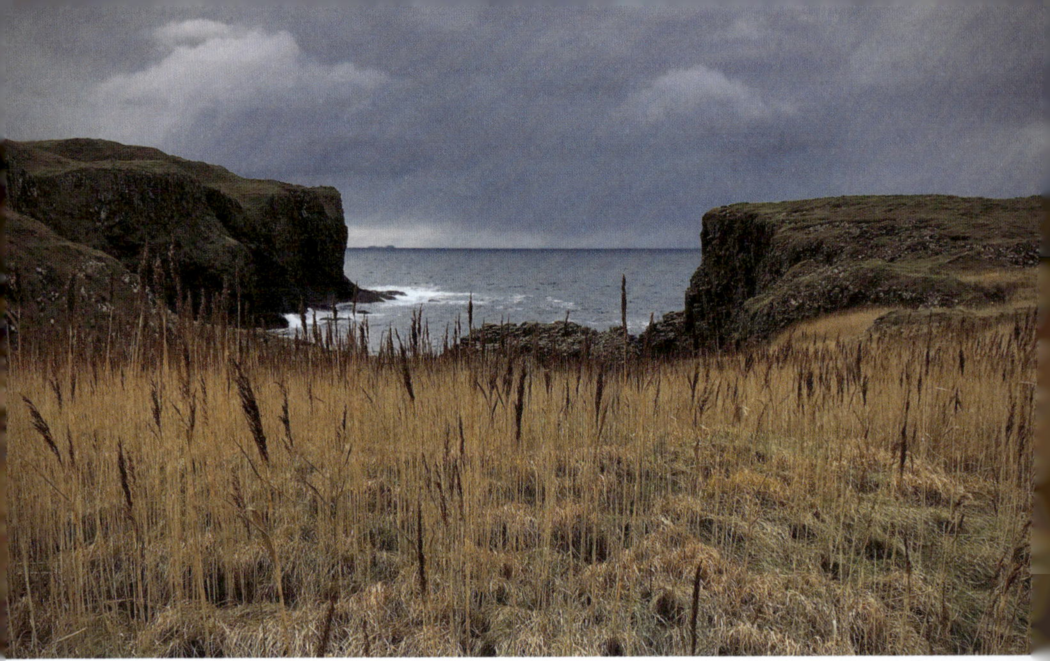

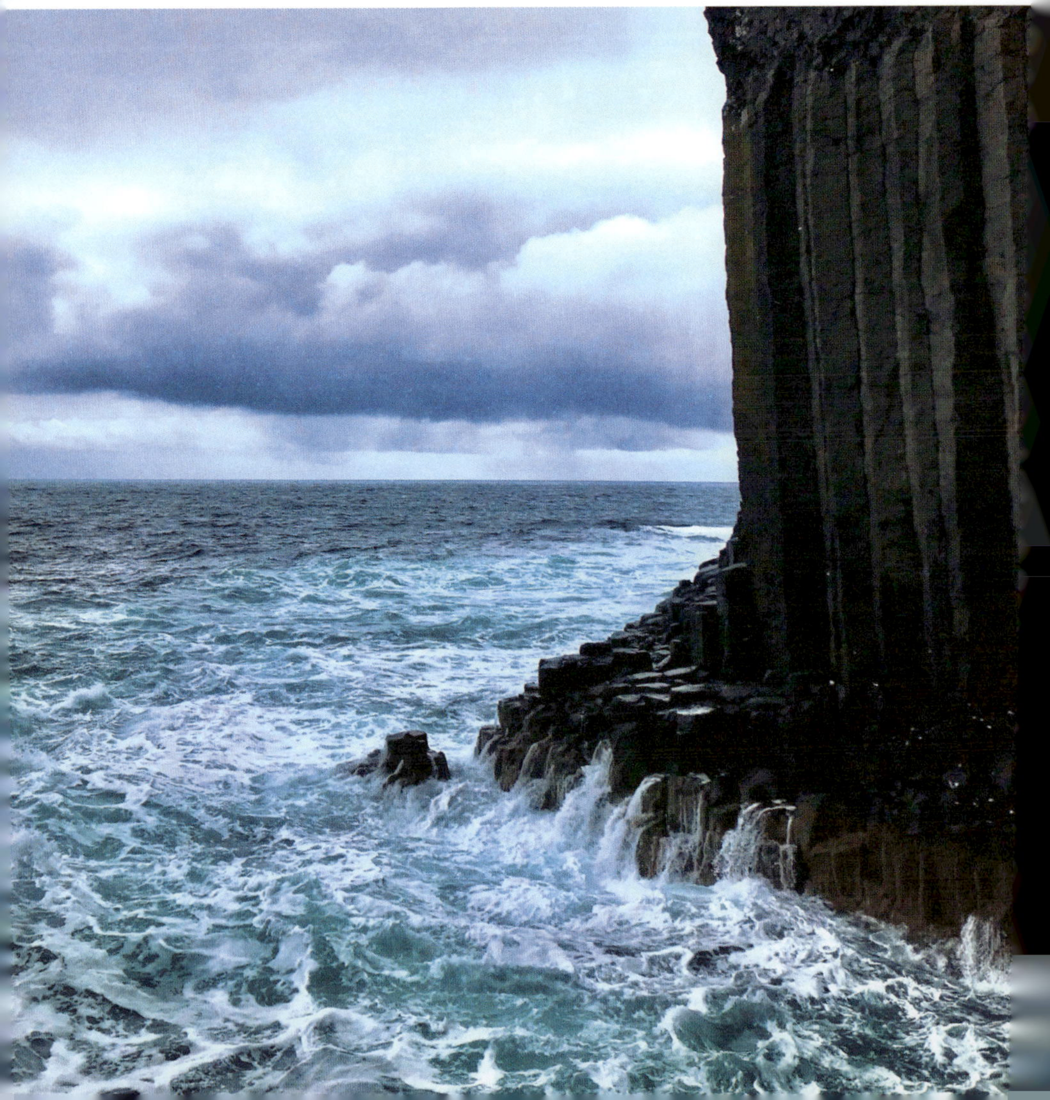

'The Bothy', Isle of Staffa

NM 3250 3558

The shell of the building backed onto a slope rising from the thin margin of soil and grass that sprouts, like an afterthought, from Staffa's towering basalt cliffs. Its roof had gone and its walls collapsed. But it is still known as 'the bothy'. The wind was up, carrying sheets of rain from the west in intermittent waves, like sea spray. The tumbledown walls provided some, admittedly meagre, protection from the elements.

The bothy was built in the early nineteenth century as a shelter for tourists. For some 200 years now, people have come to this island for just one thing – to gawp at its huge, vaulted caverns and cliffs, all those perfectly hexagonal rock columns, formed some 60 million years ago by the slow cooling of molten lava. In 1772 the naturalist Joseph Banks stopped here at the very beginning of a Royal Society expedition to Iceland and penned a description of the 'mouth of a cave, the most magnificent, I suppose, that has ever been described by travellers'. When he asked his Gaelic guide what the cave was called, the answer he was given was Fiuhn MacCoul. Fionn MacCool; Fingal – the hunter-warrior of Celtic myth. A cave of remarkable geological beauty. A cave that came with a story, and a name.

Banks did not discover Fingal's cave. But he did make it famous. Subsequent visitors were a 'who's who' of eighteenth- and nineteenth-century society: Keats, Turner, Tennyson, Walter Scott, Mendelssohn, Jules Verne, Wordsworth, Robert Louis Stevenson, Queen Victoria. Of course, Boswell and Johnson came here too, and expressed astonishment that the local people had not thought to mention the cave: 'When the islanders were reproached with their ignorance or insensitivity of the wonders of Staffa they had not much to reply. They had indeed considered it little, because they had always seen it.'

I wondered which of those famous visitors had sat where I was sitting now. Since the early 1800s, the bothy has collapsed, but the view it offers is no different. Look around and you can take in the whole plateau of the island: grass and low hillocks and edges. Edges everywhere. Directly below the bothy is a bay called the Port of Refuge, a narrow cleft framing a rocky beach which looks south-west, out over thousands of miles of uninterrupted ocean. Atlantic waves can travel huge distances before they break, right here, right in front of you.

I had crossed to Staffa that morning through a heavy swell. The day itself was relatively calm, but the sea still carried within it the memory of a hurricane that had recently torn across the Gulf of Mexico. Our boat had circled around the entrance to Fingal's Cave, and I watched as the wind and the prevailing current sent wave after wave directly towards its dark mouth. Every few minutes a particularly big breaker would roll in, disappear into the darkness, then a half second later explode back out again in a roiling cascade of spray and foam. Forget the fantasy and romance of Fionn MacCool – this is Staffa's reality. The sea and the waves never stopping. This squat island of volcanic rock hunkers down to meet the elements head on, again and again.

Not long after Joseph Banks's visit, the physician and philosopher Thomas Garnett travelled to Staffa. He came to this bothy too. In fact, he described a pair of buildings on the summit: 'Two wretched huts, built with fragments of the basaltic pillars and rude pieces of lava.' Before it was a bothy, the building I was sitting in was the home of a family. The other structure he saw, now just an overgrown circle in the grass, was a barn for the herd of cattle that roamed the island.

Garnett described how the family lived on a diet of potatoes, fish and milk, and, with no wood for fuel, had taken to drying and burning sods of turf. 'In winter their situation was frequently unpleasant,' he wrote. 'For during a storm, the waves beat so violently against the island that the very house was shaken, though situated in the middle of it: indeed the concussion was often so great, that the pot which hung over the fire partook of it, and was made to vibrate.' One winter storm was so severe that the family became convinced that the shaking of their pot could not be natural and had to be the work of an evil spirit. They lived there for three years, but after that incident they resolved to retreat to Mull and spend only their summers on Staffa. Soon, no one would live here at all. Perhaps it seems scarcely believable that they ever did.

Yet the earth on top of Staffa tells a different story. It is everywhere ridged and lined, the whole surface a mass of humps and depressions: a landscape in corrugation. This soil was clearly worked and farmed. But when and for how long? Right in front of me, at the entrance to the bothy, a large rectangle of turf had been removed and was now partially filled with rainwater: a trench from a recent archaeological dig. Just inches into the soil, shards of decorated pottery and a flint blade were discovered. Later, a burnt grain of hulled barley emerged from the yellowy clay subsoil. It has been dated to the Middle Bronze Age – around 1800 BC. Nearly 4,000 years ago. People, it seems, have lived on and farmed Staffa for a long time.

The rain passed and I left the bothy to walk to the beach. A seal and its bright-white cubs were nosing and flapping through the surf. Long cultivation ridges led in parallel lines straight towards the sea. The land here was now colonised by tall marsh grass: light-brown stalks topped with auburn seed-heads that swayed together in the breeze. I could almost picture it as a field of barley leading down to that expanse of blue-slate ocean. An edge, yes. But for those who had lived here, perhaps for thousands of years, the journey from the edge to the centre was just a short walk up a hill.

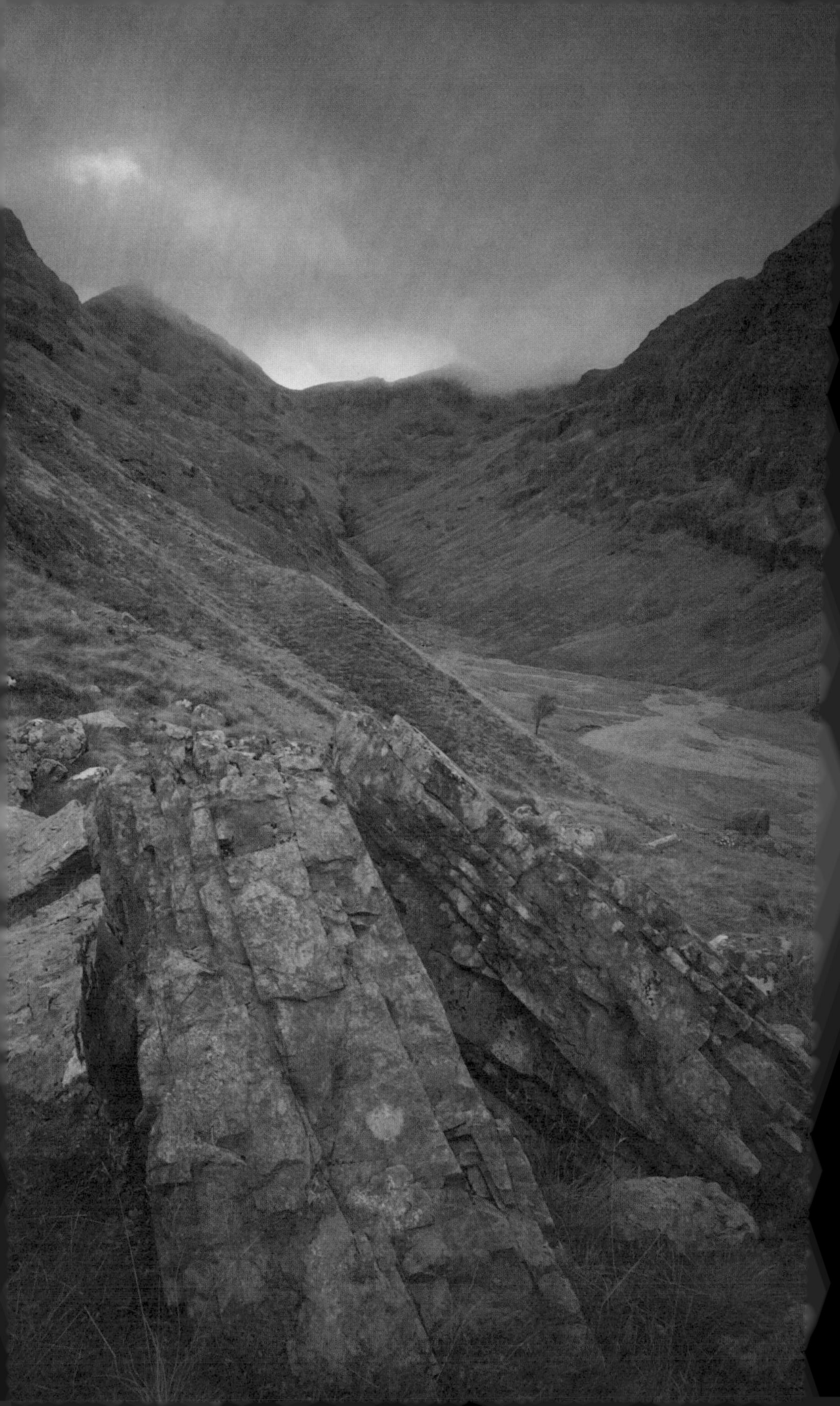

Coire Gabhail, 'The Lost Valley', Glencoe

NN 1660 5541

For a lost valley, it was remarkably easy to find.

In Gaelic, it is – or was – called Coire Gabhail, meaning 'the corrie of the bounty', or 'the hollow of the capture'. It was only later that it came to be known as the 'Lost Valley', or even the 'Hidden Valley': epithets that are at once evocative and, in many respects, nonsensical. How do you name something that is lost? How do you identify and locate what is hidden? Was there a time, between Coire Gabhail and Lost Valley, when this place was truly forgotten? Or has the memory of it always persisted, even after it was abandoned? Not so much a lost valley then, as a valley of loss.

There is a path now, beginning on the south side of the River Coe and reached by a footbridge built in the 1950s. The path is well worn, a mixture of bare, dusty ground and rock-cut steps, and it rises very steeply, climbing what appears, at first, to be an almost sheer slope. Glencoe itself is a colossal U-shaped valley, scoured out by a massive glacier that once flowed east to west and which, in melting, left behind a perfect funnel dropping down from the high plateau of Rannoch Moor to the sea. Mountains rise on either side with an immediacy which – particularly when you are at the low centre of that funnel – is often overwhelming: like standing on the flat base of an enormous rocky bathtub. Coire Gabhail, however, offers one of the few breaks in this valley wall. As the path ascends, and you pass through a sparse stretch of birch forest, it soon becomes clear that you are tracing a route up to and then along the precipice of one side of a very narrow, very deep gorge. A cleft within a cleft. A single, plunging knife-cut in Glencoe's solid quartzite side.

I had come very early on a September morning, the sun not long risen, grey clouds still hanging, lazy or heavy, over the mountaintops. The path rose to meet the waters that worked and worried the rock at the base of the gorge. The stream dropped down in steps, waterfall to deep pool to waterfall again. These two routes passed back and forth across each other, like intertwining strands of thread. The water was impossibly clear, tinged with the palest hint of blue. At around 400 metres up, the path met a giant boulder. The whole surface of the rock had been worn smooth by time and rain and river, but there was one groove, a seam or wrinkle that led diagonally upwards. And beyond it was the valley.

For generations, people had made their way up here. In the seventeenth century, Glencoe was home to a community of around 600, all members of the MacDonald clan, living in a series of farming townships strung out along the valley floor. In spring and summer, they fished the shoals of herring that massed at the head of nearby Loch Leven: but more than anything else, their lives revolved around their cattle. At peak, there were perhaps as many as a thousand of them corralled in the valley; short, black animals with large horns and shaggy hair. In winter, they did not stray far from the townships and were close-herded around Loch Achtriochtan at the foot of the glen. In summer, they were taken east and Glencoe all but emptied as the people relocated to their shieling huts on Rannoch Moor's open plain.

Some cattle were driven on to the markets in the south for sale and, as the summer wore on, the young men of the clan were given free rein to roam the landscape, hunting and fishing. Many returned with cattle lured away from whatever herds they encountered in their wanderings – often with the owners in pursuit. It was then that they would drop down into the floor of the glen before making their way up through that steep path alongside the gorge to reach Coire Gabhail. This was the origin of the valley's Gaelic name as a place of 'bounty' and 'capture': a secret corrie where the MacDonalds could stash their stolen cattle.

The sun was shining on the northern slopes of Glencoe behind me, but in the valley the sky was obscured by banks of low cloud. There was a smattering of birch trees and clumps of large boulders that had tumbled from the mountainsides. Ahead was an almost perfectly flat stretch of land, a diamond shape of grass and dried-up stream bed wedged in at the base of a steep-sided amphitheatre of rock. The whole place was grey and silent. Nothing moved apart from the almost imperceptible roll of the clouds above. I had arrived

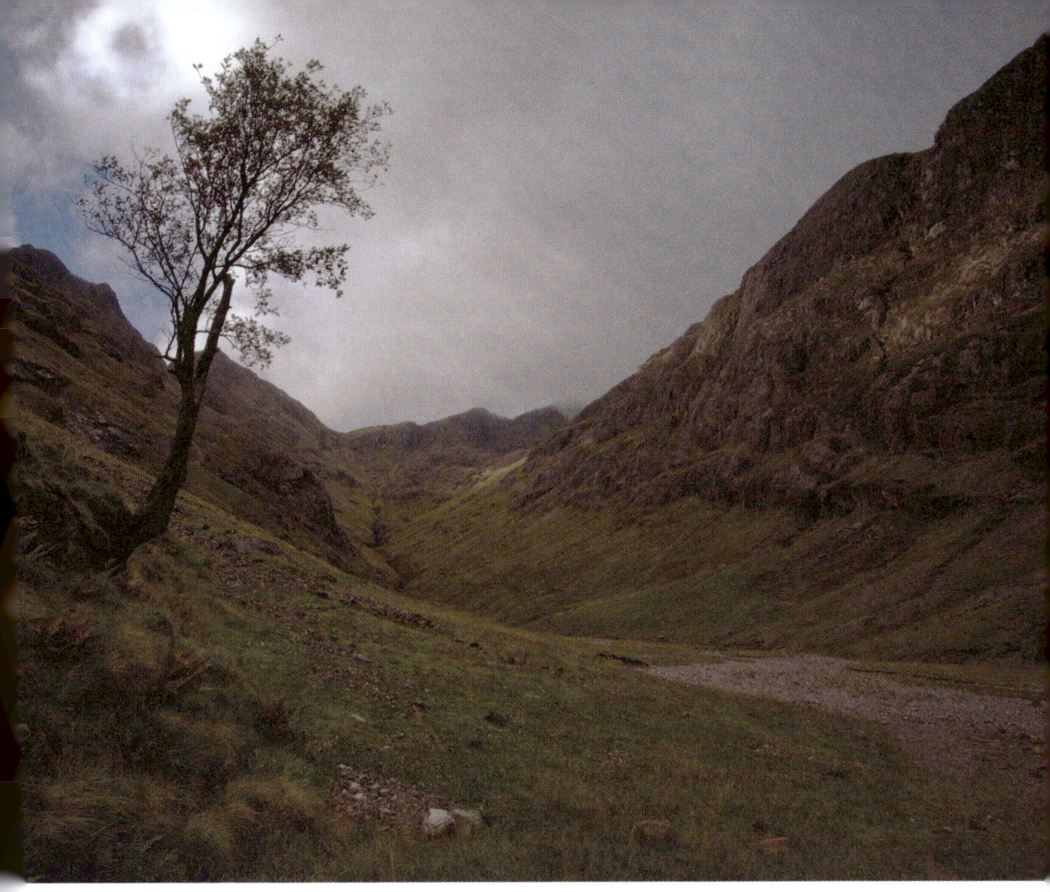

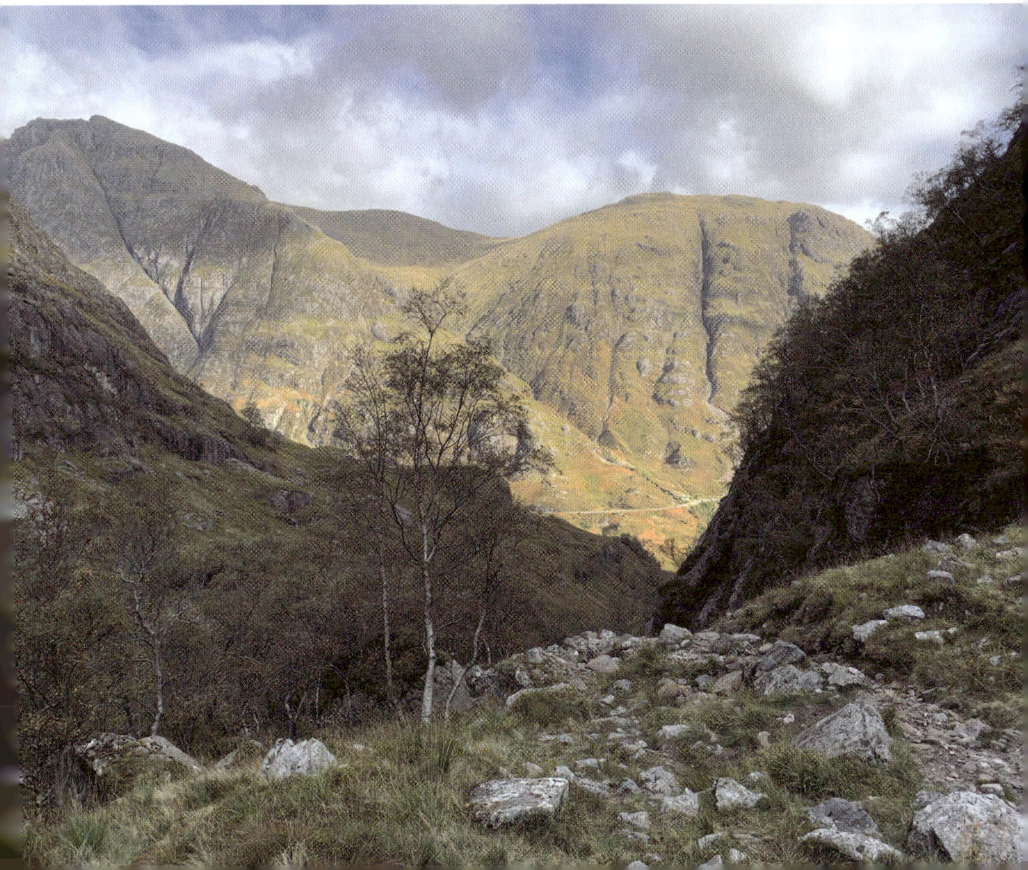

at a natural dead-end. A valley with only one way in, and one way out.

I could imagine the rustled cattle milling about on that flat floor. Groups of young men celebrating their audacity, singing songs about their exploits. Evenings spent here around a fire. Whisky and boasting and fighting. Shouts and laughter ringing off the rock-sides. A teenage hang-out, a site of joy and exuberance and illicit thrill. But this valley holds other echoes too. Glencoe today is most famous for two things: its sublime beauty, and a massacre, now over three centuries old. It makes for a strange combination.

The story of the killings is told now as much as myth as reality – a parable of betrayal against a cinematic backdrop. How government troops, under the charge of the Campbell clan, first took shelter with the people of Glencoe and then, on the evening of 12 February 1692, turned on their unsuspecting hosts and began to slaughter them indiscriminately. Their orders were that 'none be spared, nor the government troubled with prisoners'. Malcolm Laing's *History of Scotland*, written over a century later, described the events with visceral immediacy. He recounted how the clan chief was 'shot as he rose from his bed'. How his wife 'was stripped naked by the soldiers, who tore the rings with teeth from her fingers; and she expired next morning with horror and grief'. How 'nine men were bound and deliberately shot' and 'women perished with children in their arms; an old man of eighty was put to the sword; another, who escaped to a house for concealment, was burnt alive'.

Accounts estimate that perhaps as many as thirty-six were murdered. Amid the carnage, hundreds ran for the surrounding hills. More soldiers had been stationed at the head and foot of the glen, and so the people made their way to Glencoe's cracks and crevices. As their houses burned behind them, a large group walked the path to Coire Gabhail, knowing that, if they were followed, they would be trapped. Snow fell that night, and it is thought that many more died from exposure. When the people finally ventured back down to the glen, they found their houses in charred ruins and all their cattle gone.

Often this story is presented as the full stop in the human occupation of Glencoe. But the truth is that the people returned quickly – within a week, they were rebuilding and refashioning their community on the ashes of an atrocity. The massacre sparked a public and political outcry, in Britain and on the continent, and by August of that same year, the townships had been reconstructed and hundreds of MacDonalds once again filled the valley floor.

The true abandonment did not come for another century or more. The cattle that had filled Glencoe for hundreds, even thousands, of years were replaced by sheep. This shift in farming saw the villages thin out and the numbers of inhabitants dwindle. The sheep roamed all over the hillsides, stripping them of vegetation and precipitating constant rockfalls. As one traveller put it in 1818, 'The sheep farming system of Glencoe had done the work of extirpation of the inhabitants more effectively than the Massacre of 1692.'

As the clouds lifted from above Coire Gabhail, the morning sun hit the western side of the valley and drenched the rock in golden light. Against a backdrop of blue sky, the trees and bushes glowed in their early autumn colours. The grey pall lifted entirely, and the place seemed suddenly Edenic. I had been in the valley, by myself, for perhaps an hour or more, but now I heard voices behind me. A party of hikers, four of them, emerged from above the lip of that final, smoothed boulder. Within minutes, two more appeared. I left not long after, passing group after group on my way back down. Some French students. A couple of American retirees in golf clothes. An Australian man who told me he was a MacDonald and wanted to know how much further he had to go. The sun was warm. The procession of walkers bound for Coire Gabhail, for the Lost Valley, would continue all day.

Hermit's Castle, Achmelvich

NC 0520 2475

The young man arrived sometime in the spring of 1955. He walked past the small, sheltered beach, then continued up onto the headland – a clenched fist of rock that juts out directly west, to look across the waters of the North Minch towards the Isle of Lewis. At one of the fist's knucklebones, there is a narrow indentation that lets in a thin channel of sea. It was here that he began to erect a shelter – a turf hut, with a bedding floor fashioned from rushes picked from a nearby field.

This headland is just about as old a landscape as you can get. Grass grows in its hollows and depressions, but mostly it is formed out of thick slabs of Lewisian gneiss, a rock that has been heated and compressed into a distinctive mix of light and dark crystals over the course of some 3 billion years.

The young man met with a local crofter, explained to him that he wanted to build something on the headland – something more than just his temporary turf den. A bothy, of a kind. Part hut, part hermit's cell. He would craft it by hand, he said. Not with wood or stone, but with concrete. The crofter agreed to let him try.

The young man's name was David Scott. He was in his early twenties and had just qualified as an architect. His father was an architect too. It wasn't clear why he had come here – he had travelled all the way from the northeast of England to this spot on the Assynt peninsula in the far north-west of Scotland. The locals didn't ask too many questions.

For some six months, he worked day and night on his building. He borrowed a wheelbarrow and laid out planks so he could transfer sand and pebbles up to his tiny construction site from the small shingle beach below. He lugged heavy bags of cement across the headland from the end of the

Hermit's Castle, Achmelvich

nearest road, several hundred metres away. He mixed the sand, the pebbles and the cement to make his concrete, doing it by hand, most likely in a bucket. He then poured it into the makeshift moulds of packing crates given to him by a local fisherman. Week by week and month by month, the structure took shape. This was concrete – the building material of stark monumentalism and the impending brutalist movement – employed on the most delicate, intimate, artisanal scale.

Once the shell was complete, Scott added glass panes to a series of tiny square windows and fitted a door to the entrance. The interior had been shaped to offer a seat, shelves and a single berth for bedding down. There was a hearth and a chimney for a fire. The story goes that, after finishing the building, Scott spent just one weekend living inside it before leaving it behind and never returning. Over time, it became known as Hermit's Castle.

I made my own way there on a summer evening in early August. It was nearing eight o'clock as I crossed the beach at Achmelvich. The day had been unseasonably cold, and there was a sharp bite to the air. Rain clouds were shifting out to sea, but beneath them was a clear band of sky, lit a pale orange by the lowering sun. Just like Scott would have done, I clambered up above the shore towards those huge crystalline slabs of gneiss.

Achmelvich today is something of a tourist destination. Brightly coloured canoes and kayaks were pulled up beyond the tideline and into the dunes. A man on a jet ski was thumping noisily out across the water. The solitude and isolation that Scott once sought has largely gone from this stretch of coastline. But all the same, as I moved further out on the headland, the beach was soon obscured behind me. There were no other people and a stillness descended, broken only by the soft lapping of the waves. Half-walking, half-climbing across the hard, ancient rock, it was easy to imagine what it must have been like for Scott six decades earlier.

At the top of another rise, I was able to see the whole headland spread out below: narrowing to a thin waist of land, before expanding out again towards its craggy point. It took me a while to realise Hermit's Castle was already in sight. It was nestled in the rocks, both surrounded by them *and* built out of them. Because he had used the local stone and sand as aggregate, Scott's concrete was the exact same light grey colour. As I approached down the hill, the building's silhouette at last resolved itself against a backdrop of sea and sky. Two things struck me immediately – just how truly small it was and, at the same time, how complex.

Hermit's Castle emerged as a profusion of angles. Below its T-shaped chimney was a series of stepped roofs: four flat and one sloping at an angle, like two sections of an umbrella. There was a strange irregularity: a product, perhaps, of the tools Scott had available – those fish crates for concrete moulds – but also of a deliberate playfulness. As if the building was meant to be a puzzle, a conundrum, an Escher drawing given physical reality. The base was formed out of a series of platform steps erected in a fan shape and appearing, at one side, to fuse organically with the natural rock. This sense was only heightened by the many white shells which Scott had scooped up from the beach below and fixed hard into the concrete and cement.

The doorway was set directly over the inlet, above a steep drop down from the rocks to the sea. It was low and narrow, and I had to stoop to enter. Inside, the angles only continued, the walls clashing and closing in as a short, bending corridor led you to the building's single chamber. A soft breeze blew through the glassless square windows. The bed space below them was like a concrete coffin. It was cool and dark inside, although the hearth beneath the chimney flume bore the darkened shadows of old fires.

What was this – home, shelter, cell, castle? A piece of landscape sculpture? And why did Scott leave it behind after all that time creating it? Was he disappointed, in the end, by what he had made? Scott died over a decade ago and left no real answers. All we have now is the building. Some have suggested that he was working through some form of psychological trauma, that he had come to Assynt to escape the pressures of his studies, or of family expectations, or of society in general. Hermit's Castle, in that version of the story, was a vision of escape and isolation – a structure that, in its very design, represented a withdrawal from the world.

I was back outside, watching the sun hit the horizon, a glowing ember above the sea. Scott must have watched similar sunsets over and over in the months he spent here. Few buildings I have visited have felt so stark, so raw – so *emotional*. This was construction as therapy, architecture as salvation. A moment of personal crisis or catharsis from over half a century ago, preserved in stone and concrete.

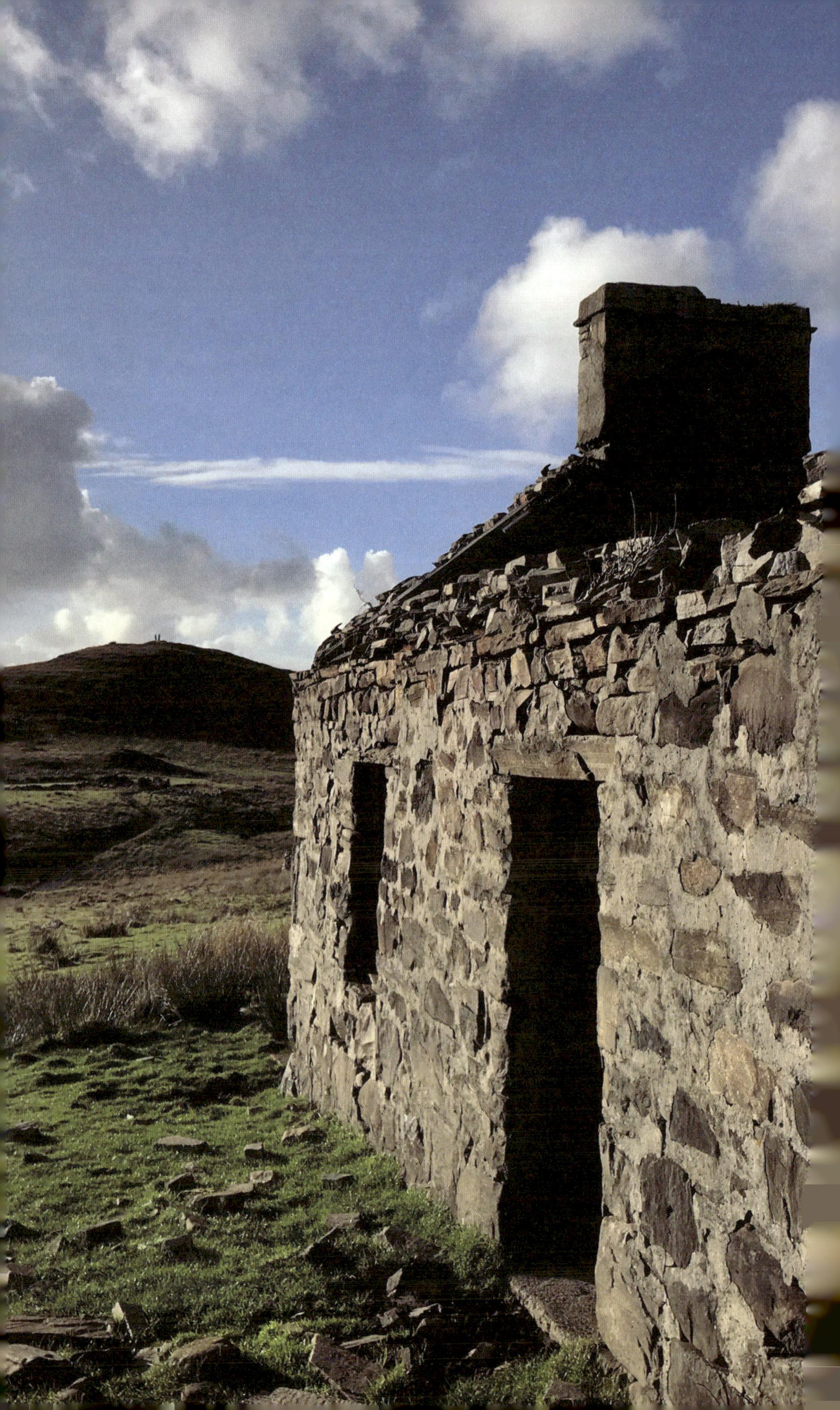

Shiaba, Isle of Mull

NM 4368 1916

I was sitting on a cliffside on the Ross of Mull, in what remained of Neil MacDonald's house, reading a letter which he had written over 170 years earlier. The sun was as low and bright as a spotlight. Below me was the hard blue surface of the Atlantic Ocean and in the far distance, to the south, were the hazy outlines of the islands of Colonsay and Jura.

The letter was dated 1 June 1847 and was addressed to the Duke of Argyll, the owner of the land on which MacDonald's house sat. At the time of his writing, MacDonald said, he was 'one of the oldest tenants' of his township of Shiaba and was 'verging on one hundred years of age'. Yet, despite having paid rent to the duke and 'your Grace's ancestors for upwards of sixty years', he had been ordered, along with the rest of his community of some 140 people, to leave his home and take away all of his possessions. He recounted how, just days earlier, the prospective new tenant – 'one individual who is not a native of the Ross' and who had never owned any land on the island before – had come with a group of men and shepherds to inspect Shiaba, and to offer a sum of money to take the people's sheep and other livestock off their hands.

The eviction notice had been served two years earlier, in 1845. The community received it with astonishment. Shiaba was the most prosperous township in the district. It had never missed a rental payment and had, as MacDonald put it, been occupied by the tenants and their forefathers 'since time immemorial'. This was a large settlement on rich, fertile land. Busy and bustling, it included kailyards, byres, a shop and a schoolhouse. They grew vegetables, potatoes, corn and barley – drying the grain in two purpose-built kilns and grinding it in two watermills. They kept horses, sheep and herds of cattle. The name Shiaba itself came from the cattle – from the Gaelic *nan sia ba*, meaning

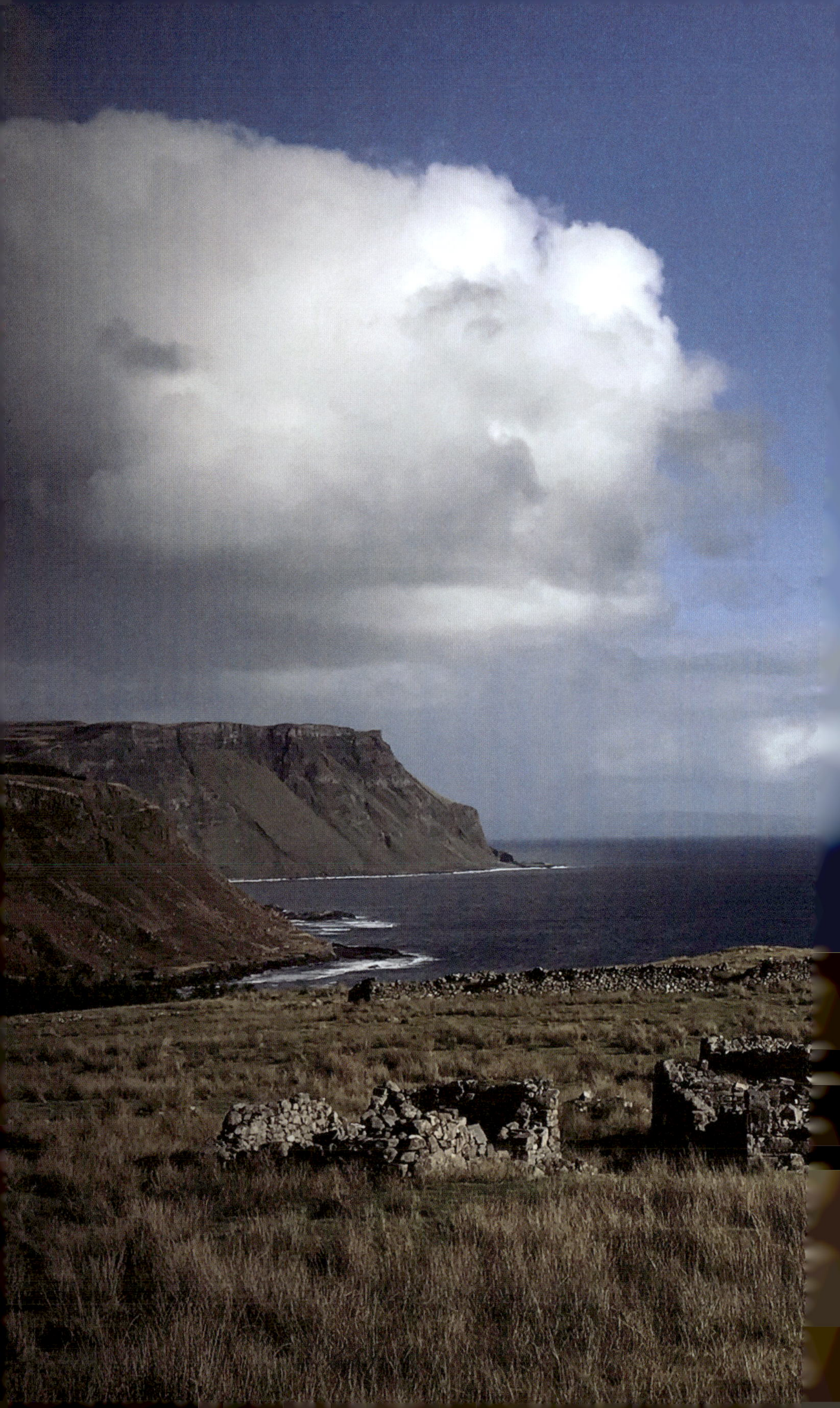

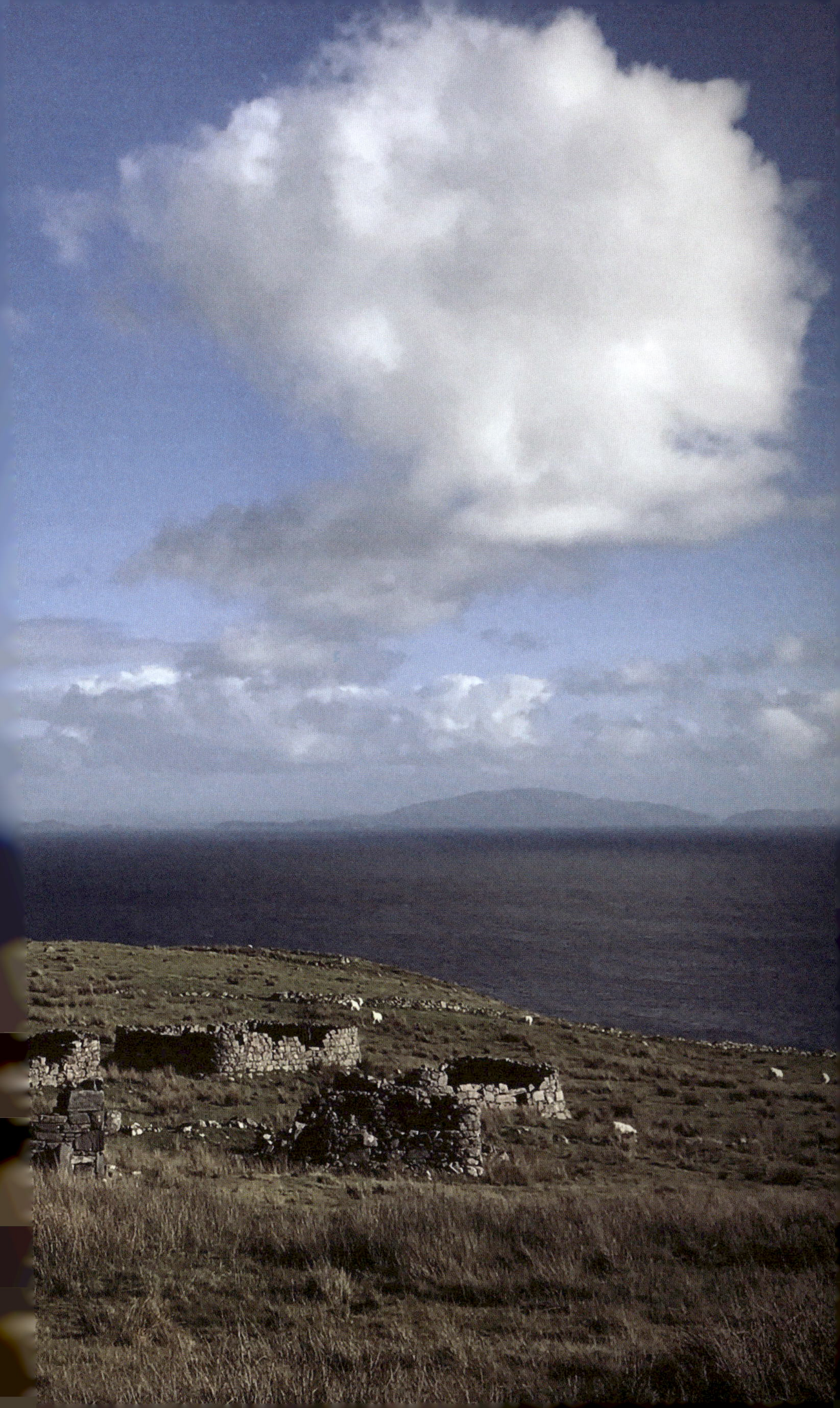

'of the six cows'. Down on the shoreline, above a beach that looked almost due west into the expansive ocean, were two fishermen's cottages.

It seemed inconceivable that the duke – through his son, the Marquess of Lorn, who managed his estates – was going to bring all of this to an end. As MacDonald concluded in his letter, which was sent with a petition undersigned by the rest of the tenants of Shiaba, 'It would be a great hardship and quite unprecedented to remove a man of my age, who, as is natural to suppose, is drawing close to the house appointed for all living.' In his final line, he wrote of 'trusting that your Grace will order an answer soon'.

As far as can be told from the surviving records, no answer ever came. The community had thought that the eviction notice was just a ploy to raise rents. But the reality was that the deal had already been done, the land sold out from under them. In the brutal financial calculus of the time, sheep had been deemed more profitable than people. Within weeks of MacDonald sending his letter, the clearance began. Some twenty-three households dwindled down to four and then, finally, just one. A few moved to other, poorer townships on Mull, or left to try their luck in the factories of Glasgow. Most travelled to Canada, boarding a boat that picked them up from the beach below the fishermen's cottages. The fate of Neil MacDonald, who had known this landscape for almost a century, is unclear. Certainly, a number died on the voyage across the Atlantic.

The one family that remained had been given the job of looking after the sheep of the new tenant, who was a livestock dealer from Islay. Their single occupied household sat among dozens of abandoned ones. Shiaba comprised some ninety acres, and a succession of shepherds remained here to look after the flock for almost another hundred years. The last family were the McKinlays, who finally left the township in 1937, when the entire roof of their cottage was torn off by a storm.

Today, Shiaba is reduced to a crumbling footprint. I had walked there across a boggy moor that stretches for a kilometre or so from the end of a farm track leading back to the little village of Bunessan. The township sat just the other side of a rocky uprising known in Gaelic as Cnoc na Feannaige, 'the hill of the crows', and was nestled in the shallow valley of the Allt Cnoc na Feannaige – 'the river of the hill of the crows'.

From the heights above Shiaba, the layouts of the old field systems were still clear – long lines left behind in the earth by centuries of cultivation and ploughing; the geometric patterns of boundary walls, some still standing, others reduced to overgrown humps. All of this continued right down to the Atlantic shore to the south and off across the land to the north, until the traces of drystone walls disappeared beneath the regimented mass of a modern forestry plantation. Most of the buildings sat above the river, on a sort of humped plateau, which framed the peninsula's towering, near-300-metre-tall cliffs away to the east.

I crossed to the houses via the tumbledown stones of the old ford, making my way in among them, until I found Neil MacDonald's home. Its walls barely came up to my waist now, and so I sat on a stone ledge above the grass-grown doorway to read a copy of his forlorn letter to the duke. Not surprisingly, the most intact building was the shepherd's cottage. The roof was gone, of course, whipped away on the wind near enough a century ago now. Part of the rear wall had collapsed too, but the rest remained as a solid shell – both gables and their chimneys, the portals that once contained the front door and windows. The interior had, however, been colonised by grass and tall foxgloves.

I moved to rest against the outside wall of the cottage, facing the warm October sun, which was dipping away to the south-west. The view was colossal, panoramic. Out to sea, a huge white cloud was dumping a column of rain. Beside it, light shimmered silver on the flat water. To stand here now was to look out from one ruin across the scattered remains of other ruins. But what about the people who had once stayed in this cottage, after the rest of the township had been cleared? To stand here then would have been to watch the process of ruination right before your eyes.

They would have witnessed, in real time, exactly what happens when you break a very long chain of occupation on a piece of land. What must it have been like to see the schoolhouse, or the homes of your former neighbours or relatives, slowly – or perhaps even rapidly – deteriorate? To wake one morning and discover that the first roof had gone or collapsed, with the disinterested sheep huddled among the debris. And then would come the next roof, and the one after that, and the one after that, until they were all gone. What would you think when it was only yours that remained? Would you feel a creeping inevitability? That it was only a matter of time before it – and you – would disappear too?

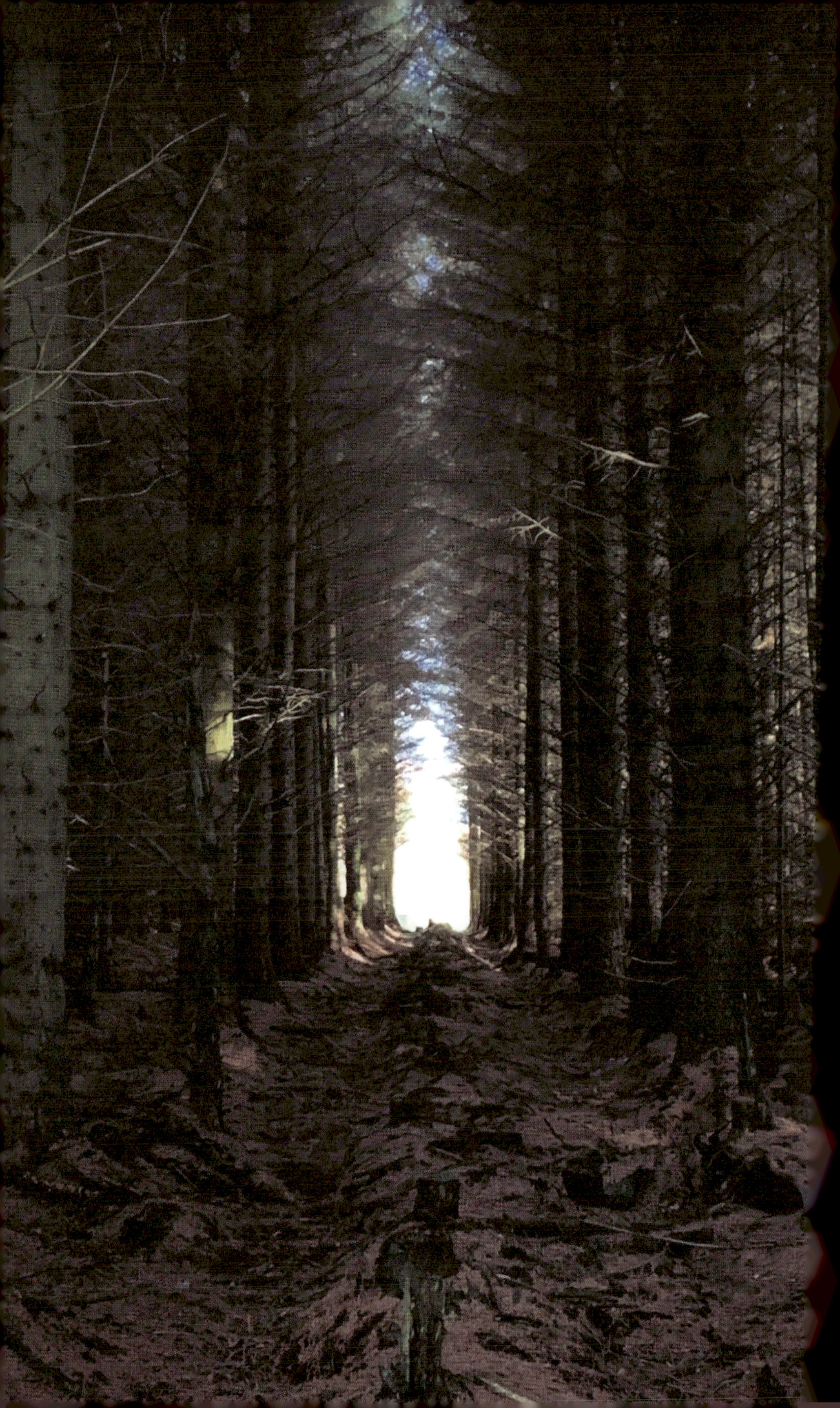

Northshield Rings, Eddleston

NT 2572 4934

Sometime around 2,000 or 3,000 years ago, a community came together to dig into the earth on a flat hilltop overlooking a loch. They worked for hundreds of metres to make two rough circles: two wide ditches with humps of hard-packed soil either side. On these raised banks, high wooden fencing was erected, using the timber from uprooted trees. Wooden houses were built inside. Later – hundreds of years later, perhaps – they were at it again, making a third circle inside the first two. Another ring of fencing was built. Perhaps watchtowers rose up, offering views for miles across the valley.

Centuries passed. Generations lived in or around this structure: farmers keeping cattle and sheep, growing wheat and barley in the tilled ground of the surrounding countryside, taking fish from the loch below them. And then, one day, they left. We can never know why or when. This place was never a home again. The wooden walls fell and rotted away. Houses collapsed, disappeared into the soil. Grass and heather swamped the site. All that remained were those ditches and ramparts – those rings – a memory of the hands that once scoured the earth, a giant, overgrown fingerprint in the landscape.

I came looking for that fingerprint. Just off the A703, north of the small village of Eddleston, a little road climbs up from the valley floor and curves towards the Moorfoot Hills. I found a little run-off beside a farm track, pulled in my car and began walking. The day was crisp, clear and windless; a morning in mid-autumn, the sun still warm, the air laced with the approach of winter. The track headed straight out through open fields to enter a dark corridor between two small spruce plantations. On the far side, it branched left and right: straight in front was a grass banking topped by a low stone wall. I made the short scramble up the banking and beyond the wall was the serene expanse of Portmore Reservoir. At the end of the nineteenth century, Portmore was repurposed as a source of fresh drinking water, but it was always a natural loch – and the home, according to some accounts, of a quite remarkable stock of fish.

When the Dutch cartographer Joan Blaeu mapped this region in the seventeenth century, his accompanying description said that the locals referred to Portmore as the 'west lake'. Every summer, he continued, 'about the first of August, such a great quantity of river fish, especially eels, abounds that, in a favourable wind (that is, one blowing from the head of the lake in the direction of its flow, where a little river breaks out), the local people, gathered there for the fishing and standing ready in the outflow of the lake for the opportune moment of taking them, are sometimes scattered by the force of the fish as they burst out'.

Blaeu's map showed the loch and its surrounding hills but made no mention of the ancient rings that crowned the summit above its southern banks. For that, you have to wait another century, for Mostyn Armstrong's 1775 map of the 'County of Peebles'. On a conical hill sketched in beneath the loch, Armstrong added two concentric circles, and a name – the Northshield Rings – taken from the nearby village of Northshield.

That village no longer exists. The whole settlement – a main street, rows of houses, plots of land – was removed completely at the end of the eighteenth century to make way for the country estate of the Earls of Portmore. They, in turn, sold the land to Alexander Mackenzie, an Edinburgh lawyer. It was Mackenzie's son, Colin – also a lawyer and a friend of Walter Scott – who transformed these hillsides into an extensive designed landscape. Colin kept detailed notebooks and accounts of the process, recording everything from the exhaustive lists of species and quantities of trees to be bought and planted, to personal reflections on the all-consuming process of estate creation. As he wrote in one letter, 'I am plunging up to my neck in farming and planting – pray for my good deliverance as both occupations have the effect of draining my purse.'

The planting and harvesting of trees still goes on here. Almost all of the slopes surrounding the reservoir have been given over to commercial forestry. I could see, on the opposite bank, that a huge swathe had just been removed, the whole hillside a mass of dark, overturned soil, leading down to row after row of neat piles of chopped logs.

The route soon curved away from the loch, taking me through a forest of golden-leafed birch, and then climbed up the far side of another spruce plantation. The trees here towered, easily thirty or forty metres high, primed for harvesting. Every so often the straight lines of planting aligned to offer a view back down to the sunlit loch; like looking towards a stained-glass window at the end of the vaulted ceiling of some gothic cathedral.

The steep path levelled out and emerged into a large, open area of heather, looking east to the peaks of Dundreich and Brown Dod. Pines and conifers were planted sporadically, their distinctive scent filling the air. Beyond one solitary conifer were the rings. They were just a ripple, a wrinkle in the landscape. Easy, perhaps, to miss. Closer, though, and you could grasp the scale of the earthworks. The ditches were huge. Deep grooves cut into the earth, lined with long shadows from the autumn sun. I climbed up one rampart, down into a ditch, up again, down again, and finally on to the raised plateau at the centre. When Colin Mackenzie planned out this land, he saw the rings and let them be. They offered a talking point for visitors to his grand mansion, which he built just a short distance down the hill, to the south-west. For no extra cost, he had an authentic site from antiquity nestled in his back garden.

Ironic, perhaps, that the Northshield Rings take their name from the very village which was erased and replaced by the Portmore estate. Two simple farming communities – separated by more than a thousand years – worked this land. The physical trace of the earlier one endures, but takes the name of the other, now vanished. Time merges two stories together.

Bird call filled the air. I could see the whole line of the Pentland Hills just across the valley. Looking north was the distinctive shape of Arthur's Seat, and beyond that the outline of Fife. Below me, on the loch, the white shimmer of a rowing boat. A figure stood and cast his line out across the water, once, twice and then a third time.

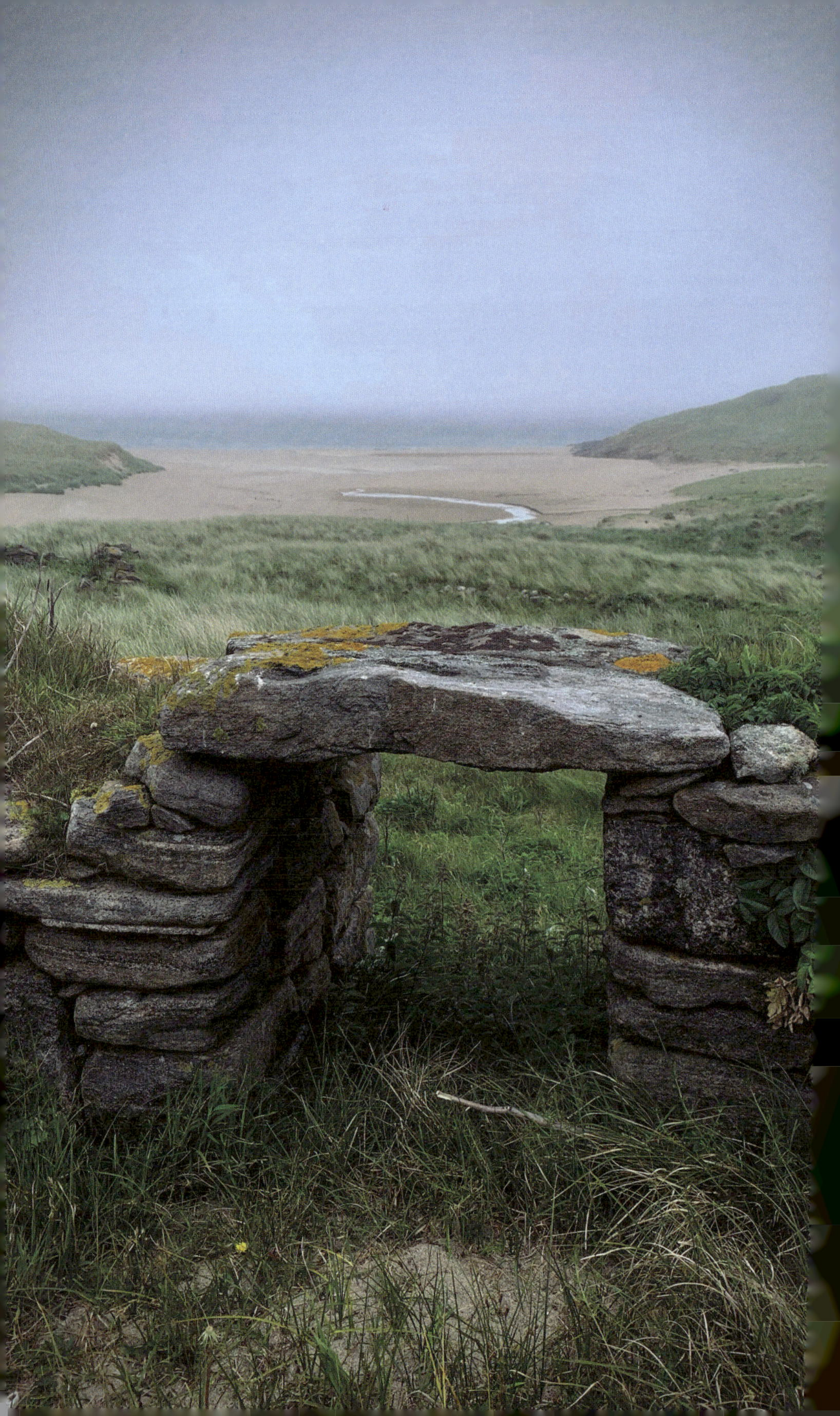

Mingulay Village, Outer Hebrides

NL 5650 8320

It was the day after midsummer. A storm had blown through the previous evening, with rain and high winds rushing in off the Atlantic. Now there was a relative calm, just the lightest breeze, but the sky remained low and heavy. I was standing out on the deck of the *Spirit of the Hebrides* as we crossed the Sound of Barra, skidding at speed over a grey-blue sea. Alongside, there was a smattering of tiny islands – dark, rocky outcrops, tipped white with bird droppings – which fringed the long green mound of the Isle of Barra itself, a barrier against the full swell of the Atlantic Ocean.

Writing in 1883, William Jolly, a school inspector for Inverness and the Western Isles, memorably described the Outer Hebrides as looking like the fossilised remains of some giant 'stranded ichthyosaurus': with Lewis as the skull, the Uists as the ribs, and the Barra Isles as the 'detached vertebrae' of its spine. At the very tip of this 'saurian tail', he said, 'rises the rocky islet' of Berneray. But immediately to the north 'there hides a larger island called Mingulay . . . an isolated colony in the Atlantic, in all respects a nearer St Kilda, as remarkable for sea scenery, solitariness, self-containedness, and the peculiarities thence arising, as the more popular place of pilgrimage'. This was my destination: the second-to-last bone in the 200-mile-long skeleton of the Outer Hebrides.

Beyond Barra, the widening gaps between the southernmost islands allowed the ocean tides to rush through. We passed Sandray, then began to close in on Pabbay. Away in the distance, still just an apparition in the mist, was Mingulay. Pinpricks of sunlight were piercing the grey ceiling, and the water around us was a rich, navy blue. Today these islands have become, in human terms at least, stepping-stones of abandonment: cleared and emptied by a modernising world. Sandray has been uninhabited since 1934. Pabbay since 1912 – a seeming inevitability after all of the island's adult men were killed a decade earlier, their fishing expedition caught by a brutal storm. Mingulay was the largest of the three – home to some 150 people in the late nineteenth century – but it too was left behind in 1912. No community has ever lived there again.

All the same, out on the water, there was no sense of desolation at all. As I watched from the deck, the one word that came to mind, more than any other, was 'abundance'. Life was all around us. Kittiwakes and guillemots skimmed across the sea. A flock of fulmars broke away ahead of us. For a while, a lone razorbill glided along beside our boat, dipping and rising and dipping again, before it dived down into the waves.

I moved into the cabin and took a seat alongside the captain, Angus MacNeil. He was calm and softly spoken, steering the boat one-handed while we talked. He had been sailing to these islands since he was seven years old, when he first started coming along with his father. Mingulay has special significance to his family, he told me, because it was where his grandmother was born and brought up. She had been part of the community that made the decision to leave the island for good.

'It's a magical place,' he said. 'A lovely place. Even on a day like this. You can see that the sun's actually shining in on the village, where everywhere else is surrounded by fog.'

This was, Angus told me, a strangely common phenomenon. While mist and low cloud will cling to the island's hills, often it lifts from the beach and the village nestled in its dunes.

Just as he had described, as we pulled in towards the shore the sun broke through, lit up the sea a vibrant aquamarine and turned the bay's wide bank of sands a bright golden-white. Sprawled across those sands, in a long black line, were more than a thousand seals. At our approach, hundreds of them splashed and wriggled into the sea. Very soon, curious heads were popping up all around our boat. It did not feel like we were intruders exactly – the seals had come out towards us, to watch our progress with that eager, uncanny gaze they have – but it was clear who the outsiders were now. Us. Humans.

In truth, this island, despite its long history of occupation, has always presented a challenging environment for people. In crude terms, when it comes to landing a boat, Mingulay's shape is just wrong. High cliffs on its western shore, and no natural shelter on the east. Despite its inviting appearance, the sands of Mingulay Bay shelf steeply into the sea and offer no protection from the swell or the wind if it blows from the south or east. The island's fishermen would launch and land their boats on the beach: wading out waist-deep into the water every time they left; and relying on those waiting on land to haul them in when they returned, riding their catch in on the waves. It was exhausting and treacherous. And, if the weather was extreme – as it often was – impossible. Weeks or months could pass when the seas were just too rough for anyone to come and go from the island. As the medical officer for Inverness-shire commented grimly in 1897, it was easier to get to America than to Mingulay.

Nowadays, if you want to go ashore, you avoid the beach entirely. Angus took us on past the bay to drop anchor in the lee of a shoreline of sloping cliffs. We transferred to a dinghy, which Angus aimed directly at a deep cleft in the rocks. It was just wide enough for our little boat, and we rode the – mercifully gentle – swell to wedge ourselves into the gap and loop a rope around a hump of stone which served as a makeshift cleat. This held us steady for the few seconds it took for me to shoulder my backpack and make the jump to land.

There was a sense of unreality about the walk to the village. The mist thickened as I climbed up from the rocks to join a grassy path. Salt was heavy in the air, and there was a quiet stillness which seemed almost unnatural. I passed the old schoolhouse, a handsome building surrounded by a tumble-down wall, now converted into a basic living quarters for a National Trust for Scotland ranger who stays there from time to time to monitor the island's wildlife. The path dipped down and then rose up again, crossing the brow of the hill that leads to Mingulay Bay. Flowering buttercups were everywhere around me, a bright-yellow carpet that covered the hillsides and led me on towards the ruins of the old village.

Now, at last, a noise broke the silence, a low keening that seemed to reverberate in the mist, like it was coming from all around me. It was, I realised, the seals on the beach – thousands of them calling over and over. It did not stop for the whole time I was on the island. A haunting, mournful cry, to my ears. But not, I'm sure, to the seals. This bay was theirs now, a refuge, a home.

Wild History

I picked my way through the roofless houses. Many of them had filled with thick deposits of sand, blown in off the beach below. One house was so inundated that the lintel of its doorway barely reached up to my knees. There was no particular plan to the village – rather, the houses clustered in tight bunches and at irregular angles, huddled together between the hills and the beach, as if embracing each other for warmth. More buttercups sprouted from their walls or covered their floors, while yellow-orange lichen coated their stones.

Towards the end of the nineteenth century, more and more people began travelling away from the island – many of the men to find work in Glasgow's shipyards – and they did not return. By the summer of 1908, only six families remained, totalling just over twenty people. And all of them were, one way or another, already planning to leave. By 1911, just five houses were occupied. And a year later there was no one. Mingulay, it was said, had become 'an impossible place'. When a photographer, Robert Adam, came to the island a decade later, in 1922, he found the roof of every house already gone.

Evening was setting in as I climbed the far slope, to the north of the village. From up high I could look back on the mass of seals rolling on the sands and skittering in the surf – their cries coming even louder now. Over 750 pairs of puffins were nesting on this hill. They had emerged from their burrows into the misty twilight and were careening erratically through the sky, tiny bodies flitting all around me.

Mingulay's story – its traditional story, anyway – is one of loss. Yet it was remarkable, coming here, to see how completely nature had filled the gaps that the people had left behind. Perhaps that's why abandonment plays so much on our imaginations. It offers a glimpse into our past, yes. But also, just possibly, a look into our future too. Could communities ever come here to resettle a deserted island? Deserted by humans, that is, but not by life. Because other populations now thrive among *our* ruins.

It was nearing eleven o'clock as I made my way back to Angus's boat. The wind had dropped entirely, and the sea was flat and still. The heads of twenty seals hovered above the water. If I looked too long in their direction, they would dive down out of sight – only to rise again seconds later. They kept watching, until we were far out to sea.

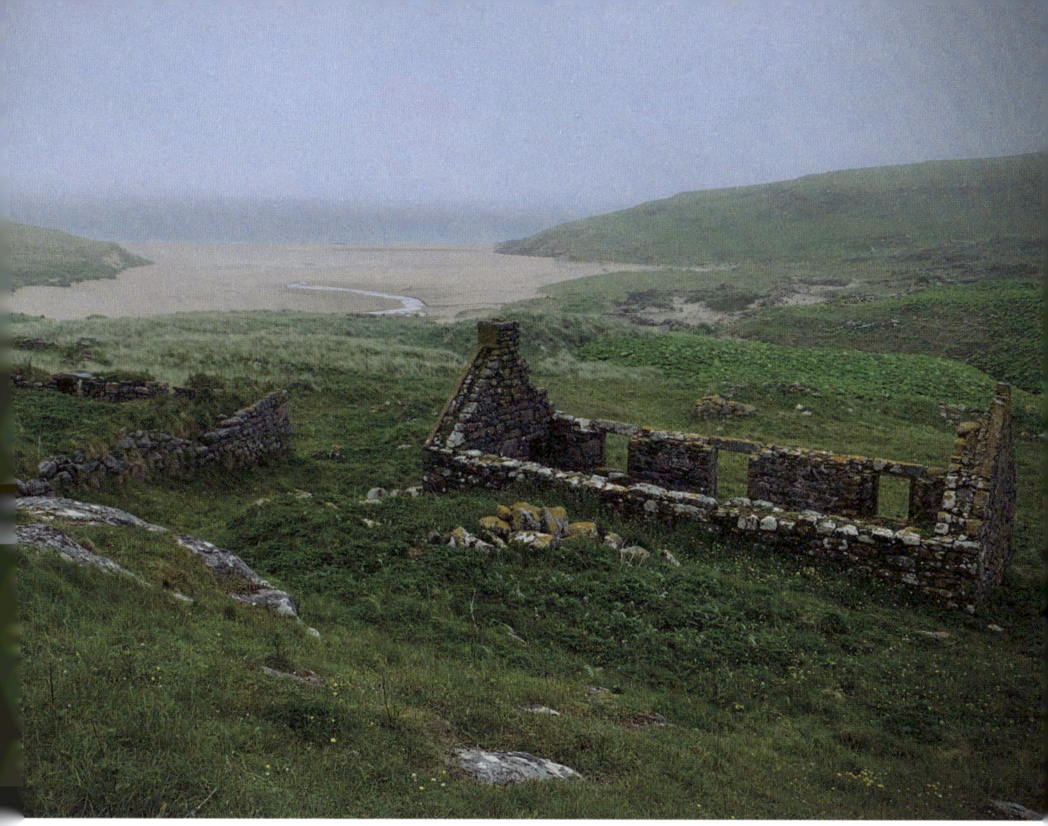

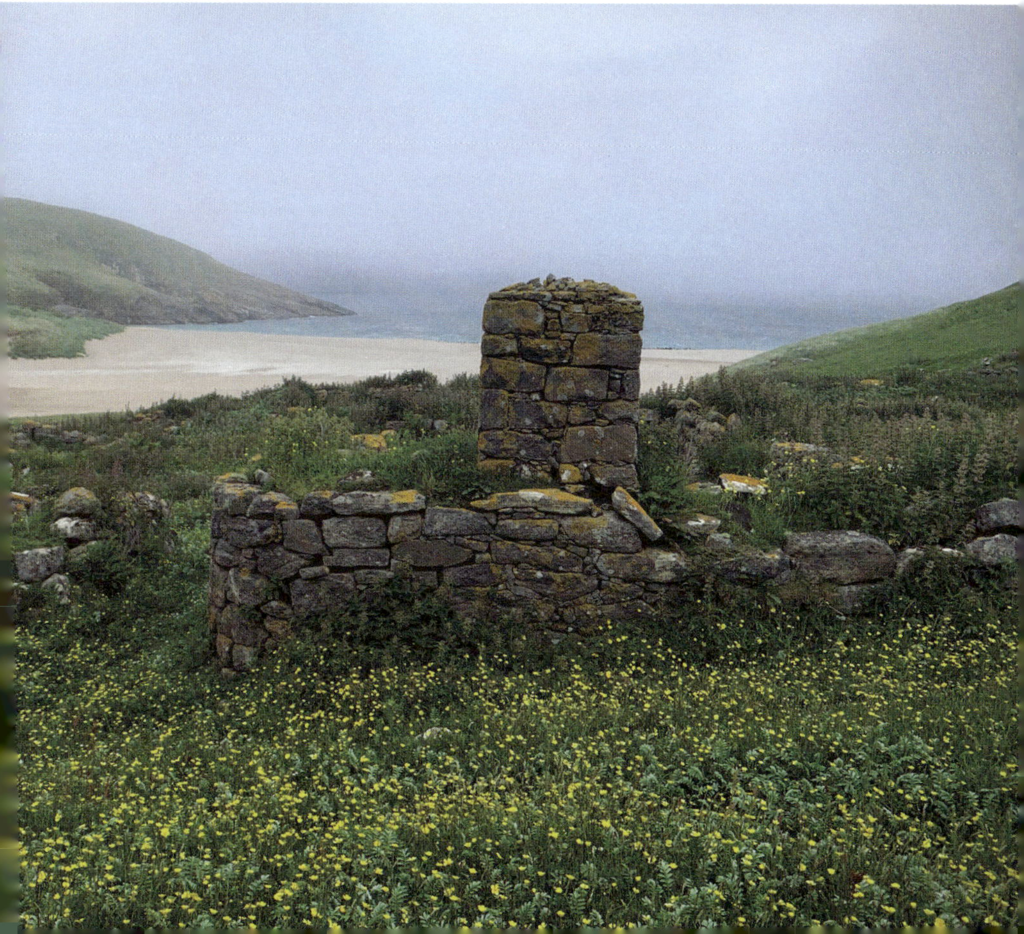

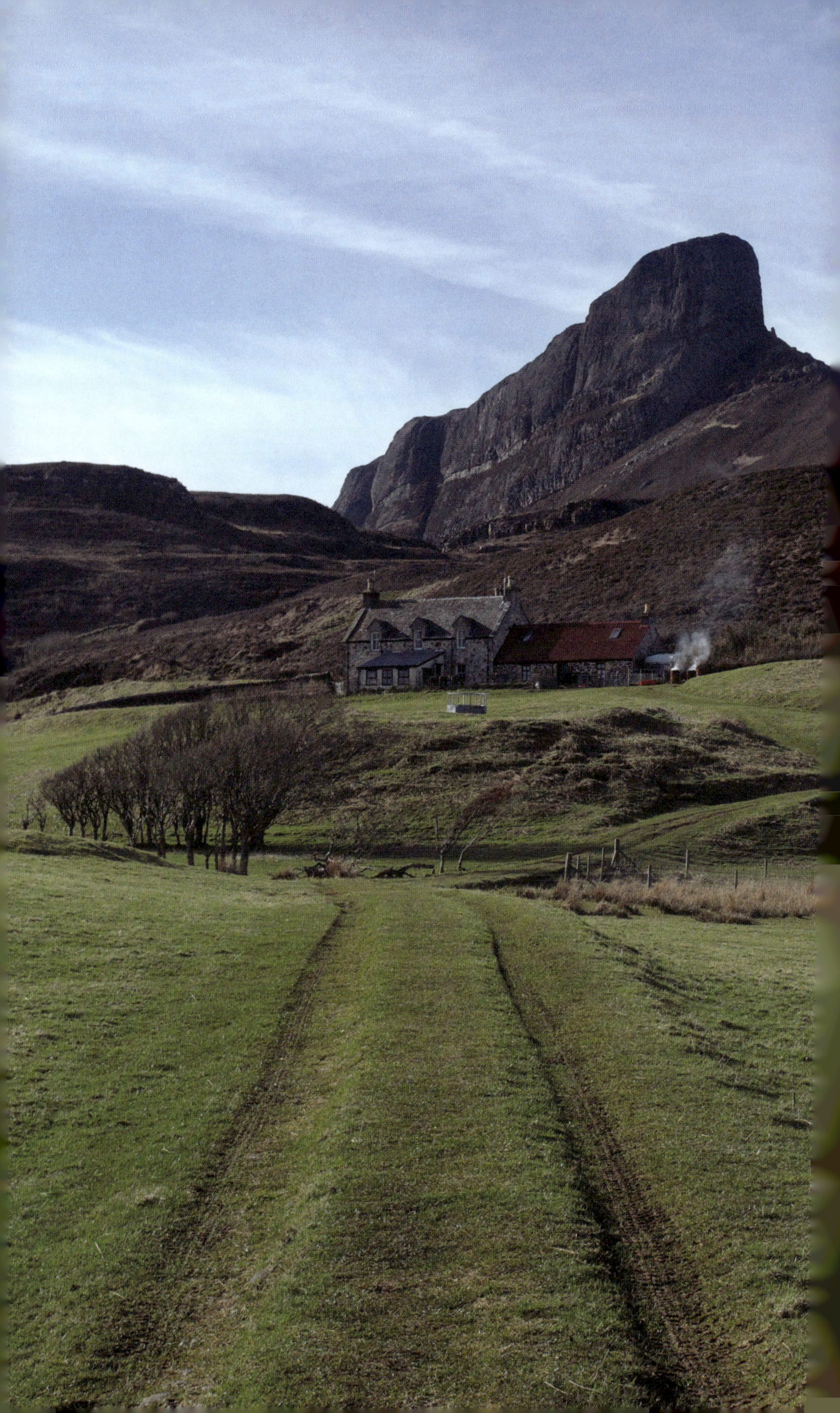

The Sgurr, Isle of Eigg

NM 4612 8474

In the summer of 1844, Hugh Miller – apprentice stonemason turned geologist and ethnographer – approached the Isle of Eigg in a sailboat called *Betsey*, owned and piloted by his childhood friend, the Reverend John Swanson. 'The slant light of evening was gleaming,' he wrote, as they rounded the Ardnamurchan peninsula, and then 'the sun set as we were bearing down in one long tack on the Small Isles'. They passed the Isle of Muck, saw the 'pyramidal mountains of Rum looming tall in the offing', and then continued onwards into the great shadow cast by Eigg's defining feature – a 400-metre-high protrusion of solid pitchstone known simply as the Sgurr. Miller considered its colossal shape, 'rising between us and the sky, as if it were a piece of Babylonian wall, or the great wall of China, only vastly larger, set down on the ridge of a mountain'.

This tendency to view the Sgurr as in some sense man-made was not uncommon. Its angular, near-geometric shape had invited many similar comparisons over the centuries. The geologist John MacCulloch, for instance, visited – and sketched – the Sgurr decades before Miller came to Eigg, and described how, from one direction, 'it presents a long, irregular wall, crowning the summit of the highest hill, while in the other it resembles a huge tower'. As a result, he continued, it 'forms no natural combination of outline with the surrounding land, and hence acquires that independence in the general landscape which increases its magnitude'. So tall is the Sgurr in comparison to the rest of the island that it often draws the weather in off the sea. At which point, MacCulloch said, it comes to resemble 'the castle of some Arabian enchanter, built on the clouds and suspended in the air'.

An even earlier visitor – and yet another geologist – Professor Robert

Jameson, similarly found it 'perfectly mural' and 'entirely columnar', with volcanic pillars reminiscent of those found in Fingal's Cave on the Isle of Staffa. For Jameson, however, the scale of the Sgurr was clearly far beyond anything that man could accomplish. Whereas on Staffa, 'the pillars are as distinct as if they had been reared by the hand of art', they had neither the extent nor the 'sublimity' to be found in the Sgurr. 'The one may be compared with the greatest exertions of human power', he wrote, 'the other characteristic of the wildest and most inimitable works of nature.'

To approach the Sgurr, you walk up a track from Eigg's only main road, passing through a smattering of trees to reach an open field of grass, sloping gently upwards to a sturdy farmhouse. Immediately behind the house, the landscape shifts abruptly to steeper slopes clad entirely in heather.

I had come in the middle of March, on a day of remarkable stillness and unbroken skies. Over the previous week, snow had blanketed much of the rest of the country, but here on Eigg there was only a hard frost, which gave way, as the morning passed, to the encouraging warmth of a spring sun. Its heat augured the thawing of the whole landscape, a definitive turn in the seasons. It also meant that, at times, the path ahead deteriorated into little more than a boggy river, carrying the steady trickle of winter run-off down from the island's heights.

Above me, the Sgurr grew larger and taller all the time. It was easy to see what Miller and MacCulloch had meant about the 'wall' and the 'tower'. There was something both recognisably structural and, at the same time, ludicrously oversized about its great slab of rock. For much of the year, the ground to the north of the Sgurr, which the path follows, never sees the light – it remains in permanent shadow. It was strangely disconcerting to step from the heat haze building above the russet heather on the moor into the lee of the rock; to suddenly find myself walking over snow patches and seams of ice set as hard and black as volcanic glass.

The route to the top was by a steep ravine, a great cleft in the Sgurr's wall. Here, the resemblance to architecture was even more pronounced – the columns of pitchstone ascending upwards like a rude, half-melted stairway. Miller felt this same sense of wonder and confusion, describing the rock formations here like 'the ribs of some wrecked vessel from which the planking has been torn away', or 'a range of stakes placed in front of a sea-dyke to

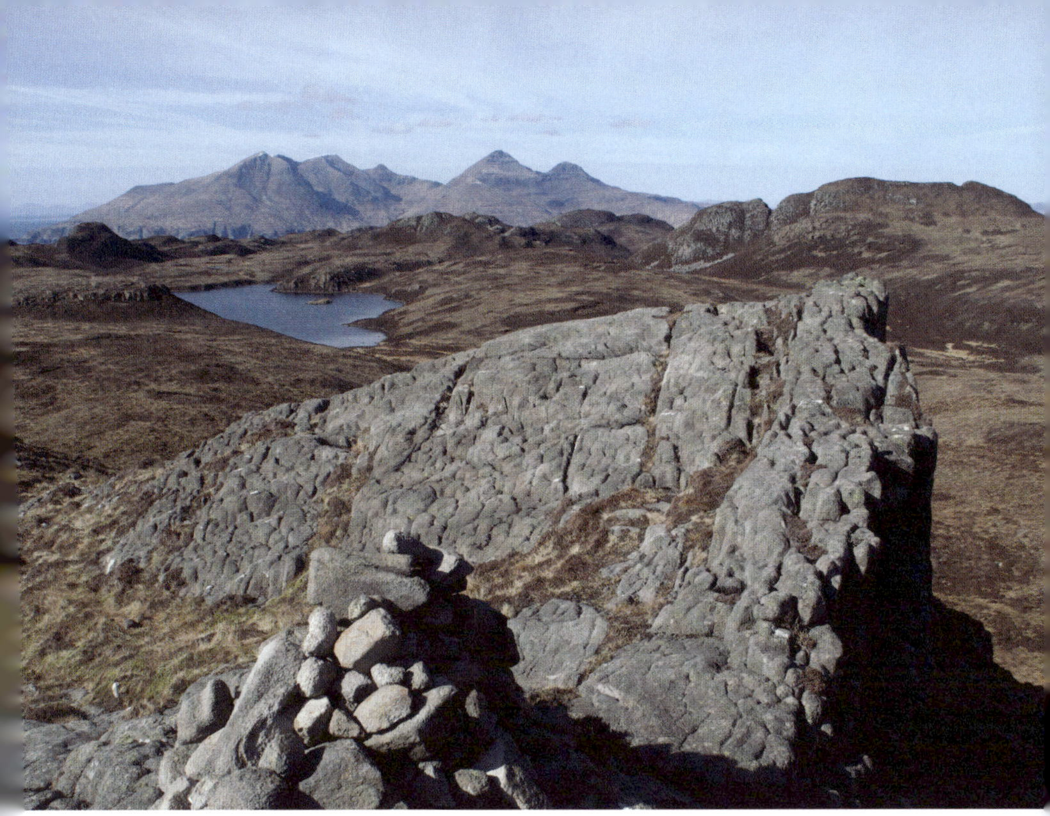

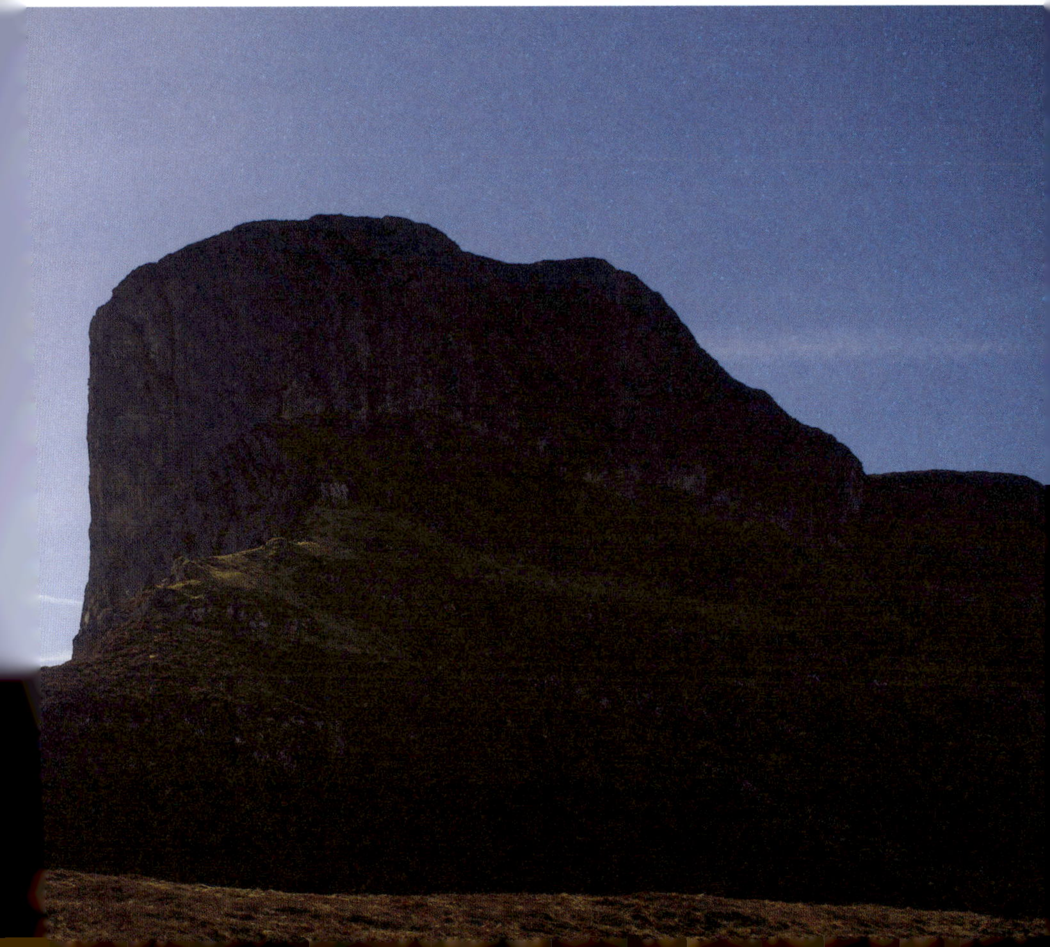

break the violence of the waves'. The regularity of the columns was unnerving. 'The feeling experienced,' Miller continued, 'seems more akin to that which it is the tendency of some magnificent ruin to excite, than that which awakens amid the sublime of nature. We feel as if the pillared rocks around us were like the Cyclopean walls of Southern Italy – the erections of some old gigantic race passed from the earth forever.'

MacCulloch said the same thing, noting the Sgurr's 'artificial regularity' when seen close at hand, how the very appearance of 'power exerted' in its creation conferred the impression of architecture and the 'efforts of art'. Faced by all of this, it would be easy to miss something truly man-made. But cutting north to south across the approach to the summit are the remains of a drystone wall. It is a single line drawn across the Sgurr from cliff edge to cliff edge, about eighty metres long and in places still nearly three metres wide and two metres high, with one gap of just a few metres forming the only entrance. It is, archaeologists believe, evidence that the Sgurr was once used as a hillfort – though no other signs of occupation have been found on the summit beyond the wall: an area that amounts to some five hectares.

I passed through and continued on to the very edge of the Sgurr. The summit was almost completely flat, a mixture of those volcanic columns – like a too-large, cobbled pavement – and patches of moss, grass and heather. Water still gathered in small hollows in the hard pitchstone, creating shimmering rock pools. I watched an eagle ride the thermals below me. It felt like you could see all of Scotland. To the north were the peaks of Rum and Skye. East was the mainland, its mountains still encased in snow. South was Muck, Ardnamurchan, then, faint in the distance, Coll and Tiree. West was the long tail of the Outer Hebrides. If there had been an 'ancient hill-fort' here, Miller said, it 'must have formed the most inaccessible in the kingdom'. Hard to get into, yes, but looking out from it – and certainly on a day as clear as this one – was to experience a jolting connection to the whole surrounding landscape. A sense I'd rarely felt anywhere else of seeing and being seen.

Just like Miller, I descended as evening set in, so that the shadow of the Sgurr was cast out far across Eigg. 'All the rest of the island, spread out at our feet as in a map, was basking in yellow sunshine; and with its one dark shadow thrown from its one mountain-elevated wall of rock, it seemed some immense fantastical dial.' Far below, he said, 'perched on the apex of the

The Sgurr, Eigg

shadow . . . we could see two indistinct specks of black'. Specks that 'elongated as we rose, and contracted as we sat, and went gliding along the line as we walked'. I too could see my tiny shadow, flickering miles away on the other side of the island as I moved back along the line of the Sgurr. Until I dropped down into the ravine, and the sun fell further, and the shadows lengthened, and then I disappeared completely.

Moine House, Sutherland

NC 5183 6004

The house came into view just as I crested the long hill that rises up steadily from the north-east bank of Loch Hope. It was shaped as simply as a child's drawing: a rectangle for the walls, two triangles for the gables either end, each topped by a solid chimney. All that was missing was the roof. With the land beyond levelling out into a wide plateau, it was the only thing breaking the flatness of the horizon. Although still just a wrinkle in the distance – I was around half a mile away on the road – it was an irresistible eye-catcher. In the panoramic vastness of the surroundings, the presence of one small, solitary building was striking, almost comical even: like a joke told to an empty theatre.

This house was sitting in the heart of a peninsula covered in heather, bog cotton, deer grass, dwarf shrubs and sphagnum moss – all underlaid by deep stores of peat, growing now for some 10,000 years. This wide-open blanket bog, about 6,000 acres in size, is known today as the Moine – from the Gaelic *a' mhoine*, meaning quite simply, 'the moss'. A kind of spongy, watery steppe or prairie, it is defined by the waters of Loch Eriboll to the west, the Kyle of Tongue to the east, and the Atlantic Ocean to the north. To the south, the base of the bog – and the whole peninsula – is formed by the mountainous ridgeline of Ben Hope.

In Alexander Bryce's mid-eighteenth-century *Map of the North Coast of Britain*, the area was called the Moan and annotated as 'a great morass'. This phonetic translation from the Gaelic was unintentionally appropriate. Most of the early visitors who came to the peninsula saw it as a desolate place, mentioning it purely to vent their frustrations at how hard it was to cross. Writing in the summer of 1760, Bishop Richard Pococke, an English churchman and traveller, said it was a 'morrasy' and 'impassable' country that could be navigated only by using the locals' 'little bog horses'. In his 1786 account of a journey through the Highlands, the philanthropist and passionate 'improver' John Knox described it as 'partly a deep moss floating on water. It has no traces of a path, is much cut up, and though no more than eight miles across in a direct line, whoever passes that way in October, must walk at least twenty miles of a most fatiguing journey.' For the minister at Durness, the Reverend Macdonald, who regularly had to cross it to deliver services at Tongue, it was 'tedious' and exhausting, the difficult conditions underfoot only made worse by the constant buffeting, whatever the season, of a 'boisterous wind'.

In 1830 work began on the construction of a road across the Moine. Paid for by the new landowner, the Duke of Sutherland, its foundations were formed out of bundles of cross-hatched timber logs that stretched out in an undulating line – winding to avoid innumerable lochs and pools – to run right through the middle of the peninsula. Raising the road surface above the level of the bog, the logs were then rolled with layers of turf, which were finally covered with compacted gravel. All along its course, ditches and culverts were dug out to drain the water down into the mossy peat. The result, as reported by George Anderson in his 1850 *Guide to the Highlands and Islands of Scotland*, was 'an excellent road . . . by which the traveller may proceed, without fear of broken bones, or the perils of bogs and pitfalls'. Crossing the Moine, 'which formerly was the laborious achievement of an entire day, may now be accompanied in an hour's time with ease and comfort'.

All the same, in recognition of the exposed sweep of this landscape, and the extremes of weather that frequently broke across it, the decision was taken to mark the halfway point of the journey with a shelter. A house – known as Moine House, literally the 'Moss House' – was constructed right by the roadside, to sit all alone at the exact dead centre of the vast peat bog.

I had approached the now roofless shell of Moine House along the modern A838, which lies, with one or two small diversions, almost exactly on top of the original road. As the house grew closer, the landscape beyond it, to the east, began to spool upwards out of the previously flat horizon. One by one, the four granite peaks that make up the mountain of Ben Loyal rose into view. Looking off to the south, I could see Ben Hope, sealing the base of the peninsula in a jagged wall. It was late autumn, and the mossy plain glowed a vibrant orange. A bank of huge, high rainclouds was advancing from the south-west, and the sky had turned an ominous shade of purple-blue.

There was a little gravel track leading off the main road towards the house, and I pulled into it and parked my car. Outside the wind tore at me: not so much 'boisterous' as full-on belligerent. The grass broke and swirled in ceaseless waves. A little stretch of the old road branched off to reappear here and run past the front of the house. Even with no roof or windows, the shelter it offered was welcome. When first built, a stone inscription had been added to the east gable which read, 'This house, erected for the refuge of the

Wild History

traveller, was to commemorate the construction of the road across the deep and dangerous morass of the Moin, impracticable to all but the hardy and active native; to him even it was a day of toil and labour.' Those words were now worn away to nothing, but in their place was a startling display of graffiti. All rendered in black and white were two giant portraits of a boy and a girl, the prone, dessicated figure of a ghoul or witch, and a vignette of two large hands gripping the waist and thigh of a naked woman.

Moine House had been constructed on the north side of the road, its doors and windows all orientated to face south. For a time in the later nineteenth century, it was even occupied by a family – an old forester called George Mackay, who lived there with his son and daughter, along with his son's wife and five children. I looked off through the bare windows towards Ben Hope.

Although those early travellers had written of no road crossing the Moine, this was not entirely true. Just three miles to the south, running directly parallel, was another path – quite possibly much older – that skirted the bog by sticking to the lower slopes of the mountain. It linked the southern end of Loch Hope to Kinloch at the very head of the Kyle of Tongue. It was said to have been walked by the people who lived here, and by their cattle. Until the Duke of Sutherland, the architect – or rather paymaster – of the new road, forcibly moved all of them off this land anyway, to replace them with sheep. According to local folklore, it wasn't just the people that left, but the deer too. There was a story told of a drover – known as An Dròbhair Bàn, the 'fair-haired drover' – walking on the Moine who suddenly encountered a long column of deer, maybe a thousand or more, marching out of the peninsula in what appeared to be a coordinated migration. Recounting this tale in their work *Sketches of the Romance of History*, the brothers John Sobieski and Charles Edward Stuart (who claimed to be direct descendants of Bonnie Prince Charlie) wrote that the deer 'disgusted by the invasion of the sheep and their dogs . . . had collected from all parts, and unable to find "clean ground" continued their course out of the country, dispersing into the most solitary glens. From these they never returned'.

It is a reminder that roads are not always about connection. And sometimes a landscape that is seen as empty, has become that way because it has been *emptied*.

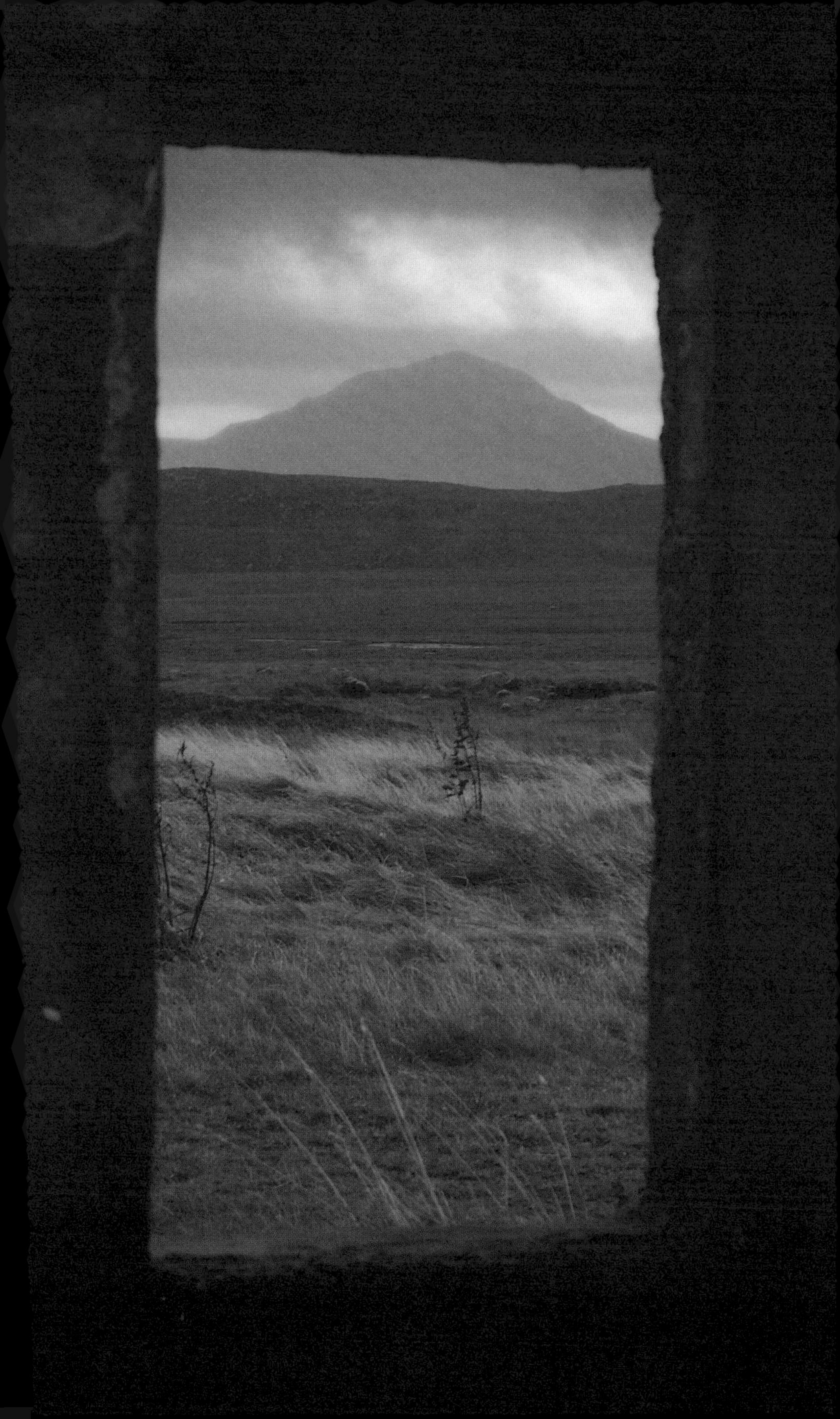

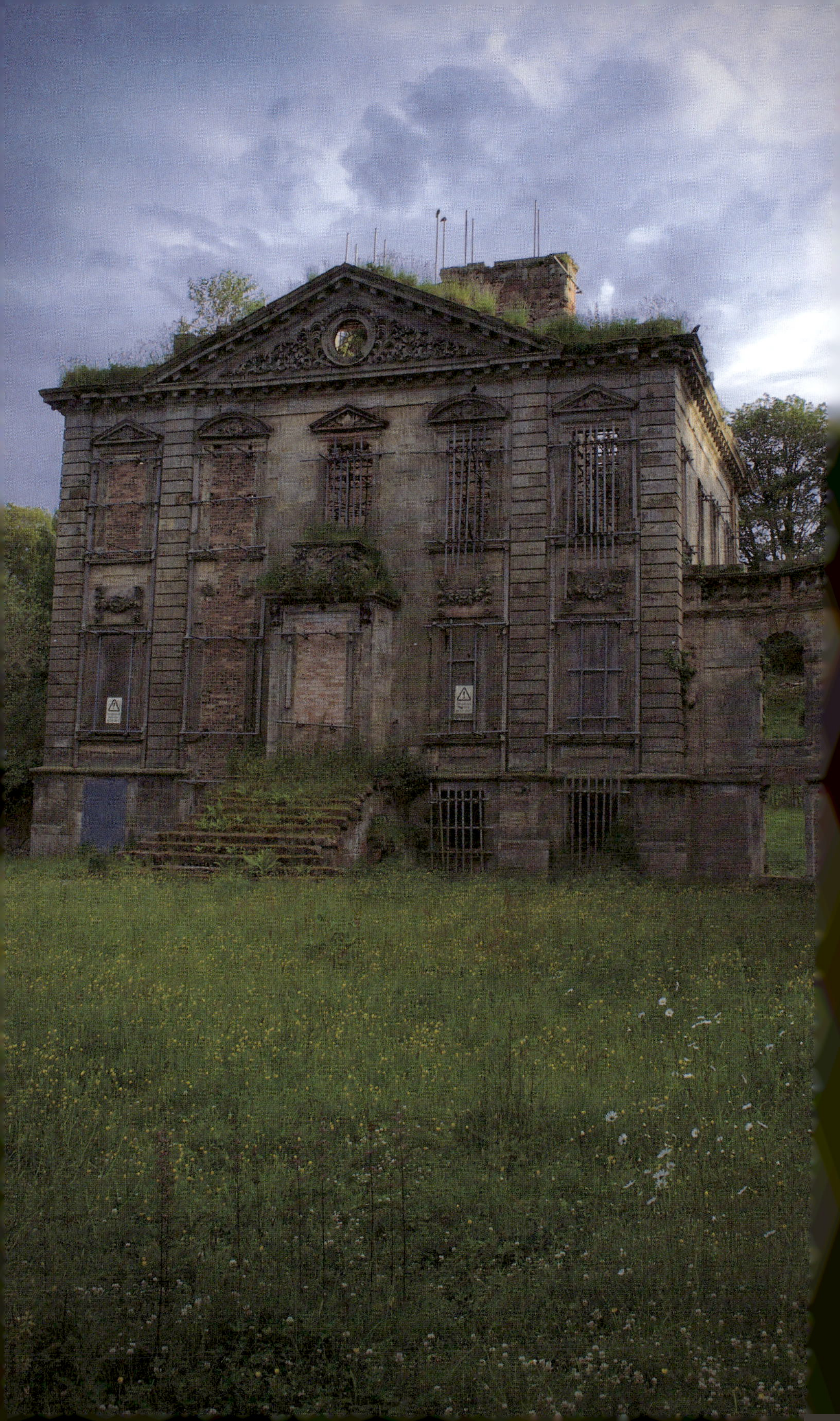

Mavisbank, Loanhead

NT 2880 6514

Outside Edinburgh, just to the south of the old mining village of Loanhead, the land falls away sharply into a narrow valley. The valley's slopes are very steep on either side of the river – the North Esk – that runs through it, although there is a thin strip of flat land stretching for around half a mile along the course of the northern bank. The modern houses of the towns of Bonnyrigg and Lasswade sprawl above the river to the south and east, but they are barely visible from down in the valley floor. Once, this place was the focal point for the whole surrounding landscape. Now it is abandoned and forgotten.

I had come in the evening, just a couple of days before midsummer, following a muddy path that hangs – in places slightly precariously – above the tree-lined river. A little way along, there was a break in the trees that led to a wide, tussocky meadow. I passed a small lake, much of it now colonised by tall banks of reeds, and an old oak tree, standing solitary near the centre of the meadow. Ahead of me was the western end of the valley. It was formed by a wall of tall trees running into a hill that rose back up towards Loanhead. At the foot of the hill, just visible through a small gap in the foliage, was Mavisbank House.

Backlit by the dipping sun, its sandstone façade glowed a warm, creamy red. It was two storeys tall, topped by the handsome triangle of a large pediment. Yet, even from a distance, the signs of decay were obvious. All the windows were bricked up or shored up with metal bars. Moss, long grass – and even a handful of saplings – sprouted from the stonework around the edge of the roof and ran up the slopes of the pediment. The main roof itself was entirely gone. More steel bars rose into its empty space, part of a lattice of supporting scaffolding filling the centre of the house and keeping its walls from collapsing. What remains today is a shell.

This house was built almost exactly 300 years ago, the vision of two men – William Adam, the head of Scotland's most famous architectural dynasty, and Mavisbank's owner, Sir John Clerk of Penicuik. Clerk's family was one of the first generation of Scotland's aristocrat-industrialists. They effectively owned – indeed, created – the village of Loanhead as a settlement for miners employed to work the abundant coal seams beneath this landscape. (And not just work – the miners were 'bonded' to the coal here – which meant that they had no rights to leave or find other employment; they just had to keep extracting until there was nothing left to extract). It was the money from the mines that helped to pay for the construction of the house. Indeed, Clerk built it in this valley, in theory, to keep a close eye on the coal works. But really, he had far greater ambitions for Mavisbank.

Clerk had left Scotland in 1694, aged eighteen, studying for three years at the University of Leiden – his subjects including mathematics, philosophy, history, divinity and law – and then travelling on to Rome, where he lived for another two years as the music pupil of the composer Bernardo Pasquini and the violin virtuoso Arcangelo Corelli. Few of Scotland's aristocratic class had had such a wide-ranging and cosmopolitan education. Clerk was a modern man, but with a deep love of the ancient past. When he finally came home, he wanted to change, fundamentally, the country of his birth; to improve it by transplanting the elegance and refinement of classical Europe, and Rome in particular, into the very soil of Scotland.

Mavisbank was intended as nothing less than a template, an architectural model for a new nation. Clerk worked on its designs with William Adam, at the same time commemorating and elaborating on the ideas that lay behind them in a 1,500-line poem, 'The Country Seat'. Although styled after the famous Roman poet Virgil, it was, in essence, a list-like treatise on what Clerk believed comprised the 'perfect' house. First, he said, you had to 'Choose not a Seat too lofty nor too low':

> But on a River's Bank or downy Plain
> That gently slopes to the meridian Sun.
> Let many lofty Trees with Spreading Tops

Defend you from the Cold of Northern Blasts.
Let here and there be seen some little Hills
Fit pasture for your harmless bleating Flocks
Let all the Fields in view be chequered round
With flowry meadows, Groves and plenteous Springs,
Or Rivulets descending from the higher Grounds

The little valley of the North Esk, of course, fit this description perfectly. The poem went on to advise on building materials, floor plans, heating, fireproofing and interior decoration, and even included the ideal dimensions for the rooms. The end result was a villa, at once grand and domestic, supplemented by two quadrant walls that reached out to visitors with what Clerk described as a 'kind embrace'. (He had long been disdainful of the artistic sensibilities of his Scottish contemporaries, and he admonished them for living in 'cold, unwholsome' old tower houses.) Mavisbank was the antidote, the way forward. The country had to modernise, he believed, or it would drift into crude obscurity.

Clerk was a man of contradictions. An arts student turned industrialist; a would-be poet who suddenly became a prominent politician – at a pivotal moment in Scotland's history. In 1706, at the age of just thirty, he was appointed to a group of thirty-one commissioners charged with drawing up the Treaty of Union between Scotland and England: a treaty that ultimately asked Scotland's parliament to vote itself out of existence. Clerk spent the rest of his life conflicted by what he had been a part of – arguing publicly with others, and with himself in his own writing, over the merits of union versus independence. 'Some are regretting the extreme poverty of the nation and scarcity of money,' he wrote, 'yet, notwithstanding, they exclaim against the Union as a thing that will ruin us; not considering how any condition of life we can fall into, can render us more miserable and poor than we are.'

Completed twenty years later, in 1727, Mavisbank was intended as a symbol of a brighter future. Clerk continually looked at Scotland and wanted it to be better. Basically, he wanted it to be more like *him*.

I had walked up the last curve of the old driveway, to stand right in front of the house. Or, at least, right in front of the looming spiked steel gate that now surrounds its ruin. Clerk died in 1755, and Mavisbank remained as the country retreat for generations of his family, until 1815, when it was bought by a retired surgeon of the East India Company, Graeme Mercer. When Mercer died unmarried, it passed on to another family – the Arbuthnotts – who sold it for £25,000 in 1877 for use as what was described as a 'Private Lunatic Asylum'. In 1907 it was renamed New Saughton Hall, and it stayed as a home for patients until the 1950s, when the company that owned it went into voluntary liquidation.

Various parts of the estate's lands were sold off, with the house itself purchased by a Mrs Willis Stevenson. Twenty years later, in 1973, a fire destroyed the house's interior, while its forecourt became a kind of ad-hoc scrapyard, filled with beat-up cars and a caravan used as a home by Stevenson's son. Then, in 1987, with British Coal having announced their intention to mine the seams lying directly underneath Mavisbank, Midlothian Council announced its intention to demolish the house. It was only a volunteer watch, who guarded it round the clock for eighteen days until the security fence could be erected, that prevented it from disappearing entirely. It is, of course, a rather sorry state for Clerk's 'perfect' house to find itself in. That one-time stamp of progressive, Enlightenment modernity ultimately gutted, portioned up and left in limbo by a post-modern world. Mavisbank still stands, but only just.

It was a warm, humid night, still and windless. The sky mixed patches of clear blue with stacks of high, rumpled clouds that threatened the possibility of thunder. A carpet of wildflowers – admittedly rather beautiful – ran from the fence all the way up to the walls of the house: tall daisies and yellow dandelions even climbed its front steps. I could hear the distant sound of music. A brass band had been playing in Loanhead's village square as I had passed through on my way here – right beside the memorial to the many miners who had lost their lives beneath this ground over the centuries. Their tune was carrying on the air, faint and elegiac, to settle down into the valley and fall on the house like a fine dust. There is no little irony that the coal that paid for Mavisbank is also one of the reasons for its current parlous state. So much was taken out of the seams below here that the land has become unstable, causing subsidence: quite literally undermining the house.

Some still dream of its restoration – that this lost valley might somehow be redeemed. It seems unlikely. And is it even desirable? You suspect that

Mavisbank, Loanhead

Clerk, that arch-moderniser, would have had little appetite for rebuilding a ruin. In many ways, this house – and this whole valley – is a monument to change and upheaval, to oppositions. It's all about new versus old, local versus global, industry versus art, the elite versus the common man, union versus independence. Mavisbank is an identity crisis in stone. A building that asks the question: what do you want Scotland to be? A question that Clerk could never quite answer in his own head. And a question that, three centuries on, we're still asking today.

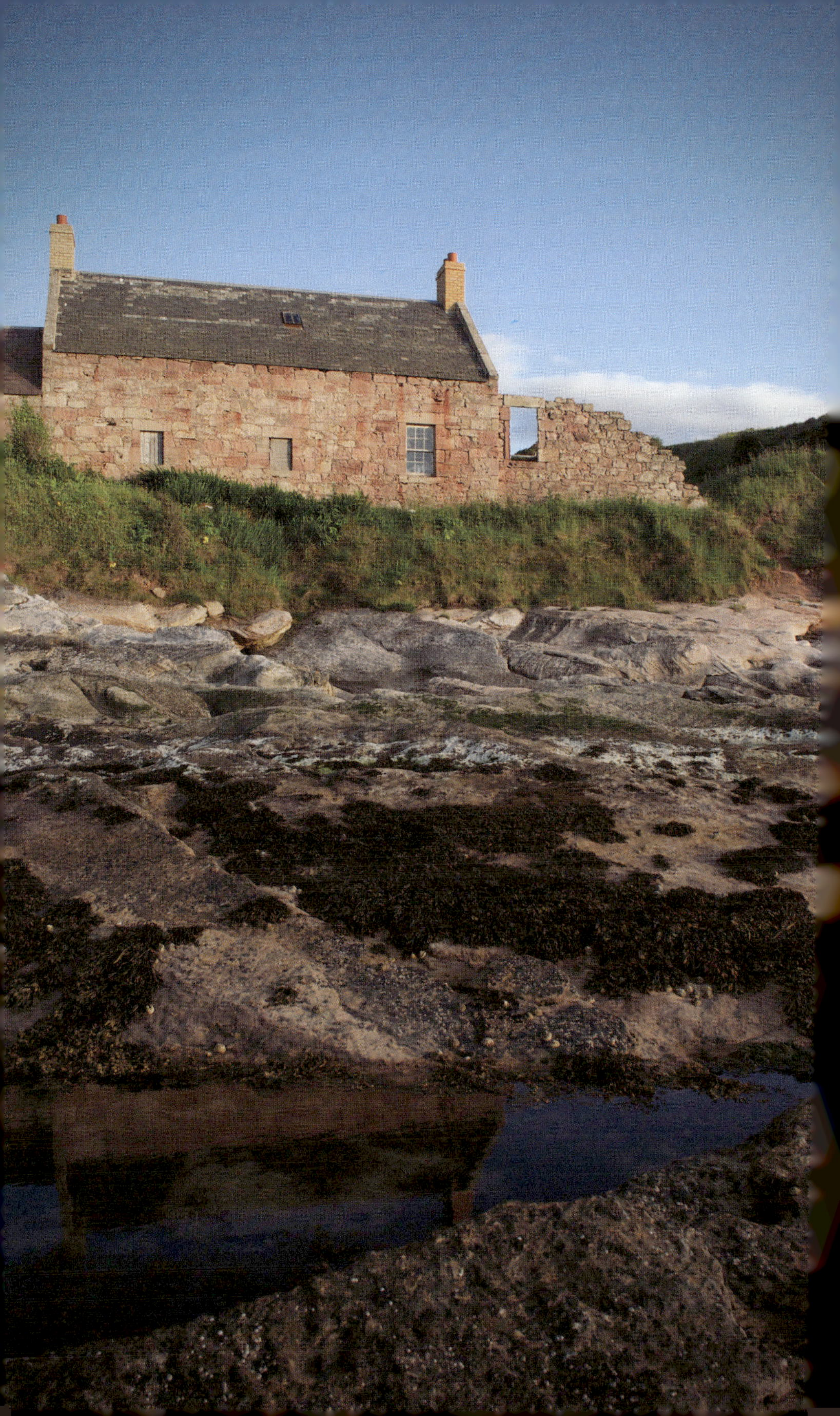

Cove Harbour, Berwickshire

NT 7850 7169

It was a little after eight o'clock in the evening, a week past midsummer, when I walked the long, sloping cliffside path leading from the tiny village of Cove down to the harbour. The tide was out, revealing a great, curved stretch of natural breakwater: sinuous terraces of rock that turned seaweed-black as they shelved into the North Sea. Sandstone makes up much of this stretch of coastline, and in the low sunlight, angling in from the west, it glowed a warm, blush pink. There was barely any wind to stir the waves, and the still, humid air was heavy with the scent of salt and wildflowers. Behind me, far out on the edge of Torness Point, was the hulking, boxy silhouette of a nuclear power station.

 At the foot of the path were two neat, stone cottages – attached to the ruined wall of a now-absent third. Ropes and lobster pots were piled up on what had once been its floor, and an empty rectangle of window perfectly framed a half-and-half view of sea and sky. The cottage walls were built from red sandstone and appeared to emerge, almost organically, from a red sandstone bluff, which had been smoothed by waves and weather into sweeping sculptural forms. Beyond them, the natural rock gave way to a stout, stone harbour wall.

 This wall was completed in 1831, one of two long, pincer-shaped piers, projecting towards each other from the north and south of the fifty-metre-high sandstone cliff which cradled Cove's small beach and tidal inlet. An itinerant labourer, Alexander Somerville, wrote of coming to Cove in the spring of 1830 to work on the harbour's construction, when he was just nineteen years old. He was part of a team tasked with laying the foundations of the quay head, which meant waiting for the lowest ebbs of the spring tides, and then climbing into 'strong boxes' sunk into the sand. Water had to be bailed out constantly, 'the sand and silt thrown out, and the rock beneath cut into form for receiving the lower course of stones'. Only two men could go into the confined space at one time, and always they were racing against the speed of the incoming sea, which lapped up against the side of their box until, just before it overflowed, boats would arrive to take them and their tools back to shore.

Somerville dug out the rock 'night time and day time, when the ebb tides served', mostly in tandem with the local fishermen, who 'had been used from babyhood to dabble in the sea, and thought nothing of it'. The rest of the crew were a 'motley assemblage of masons, quarrymen and labourers, from all parts of Scotland', and he soon found that, among them, 'drink at each pay day, and occasionally between pay days, was almost unavoidable'.

This was the third attempt at building a harbour at Cove. A decade earlier work had been abandoned as successive storms swept in from the North Sea, washing away everything down to the foundations. Another sixty years before that, in the mid eighteenth century, the original construction works had suffered the same fate. In General Roy's map of Scotland from the 1750s, the bay is marked as 'a new harbour' with a tiny sketch showing quays and an artificial breakwater. Yet, as the *Statistical Account of Scotland* from 1794 explained, 'The wall was considerably advanced when a strong wind from the north-east raised such a heavy sea as almost destroyed the work, and it was not again renewed.'

Although the piers were left in ruins, one unusual feature remained. A tunnel had been carved – and possibly blasted with gunpowder – right through the sandstone cliff. Running for some 180 feet, it joined the cliffside path to the beach, which was otherwise only accessible at low tide. Inside the tunnel were four cellars. Although local tradition has it that, after the works failed, they were used for smuggling whisky and rum, it is more likely that they simply remained empty until the harbour was finally finished in the 1830s, at which point they could serve their original purpose as a place for curing and storing hauls of cod and white fish.

In the summer of 1883, half a century after Alexander Somerville had come to Cove looking for work, another young man arrived on this coastline. Travelling by train, he disembarked at the tiny village station at Cock-

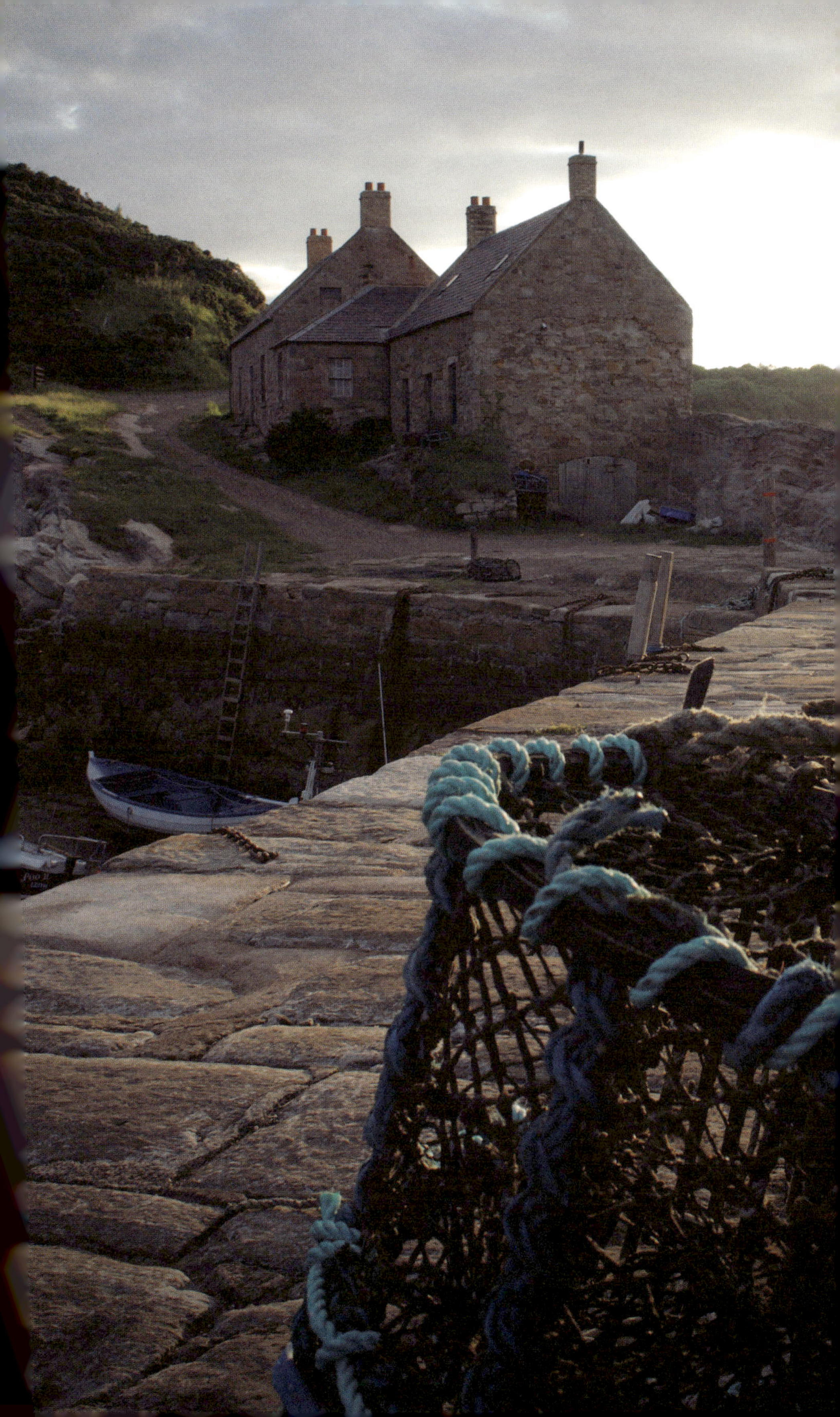

burnspath, just a couple of hundred metres from the bay. Twenty-four years old, a clergyman's son and a recent Glasgow Law School drop-out, he was here in search of inspiration. He took a cottage in the village and then began tramping out across the countryside, socks rolled over his trouser legs, carrying sketchbooks, pencils, paints and an easel.

His name was James Guthrie and, as the weeks passed, he was joined by two friends, Edward Arthur Walton and Joseph Crawhall. All three were artists, and all three were dissatisfied with traditional Scottish painting – sentimental, romanticised views of Highland landscapes, all ruined castles, sublime mountains and noble peasants. Influenced by the emerging naturalist painters of France and Holland, they wanted to show real people in their real environments, out in the open air, where they could be captured in light and shade with wide, free brushstrokes. In the autumn of 1883, in a field just above Cove, Guthrie painted *A Hind's Daughter*, an image of a young farm labourer, cabbage in one hand, cutting knife in the other, staring out of the picture as if interrupted from her work in a moment of surprise. The effect – as close to documentary photography as it is to painting – was startlingly radical for the time.

Soon, more young artists were coming to Cockburnspath – George Henry, Arthur Melville, Corsan Morton, Alexander Roche, Whitelaw Hamilton – either to stay with Guthrie in his cottage or to take their own lodgings. Collectively, they became known as the 'Glasgow Boys' – in part because they had all been trained in, or had close connections to, the city, and in part because they all railed against the traditional art establishment in Edinburgh. Theirs was a quiet radicalism, and it came with an inadvertent irony. They were largely ignoring the city of Glasgow itself, at that time one of the most industrialised places in the world, to seek out scenes of rural realism. Yet their paintings of farm workers – so natural and so modern in style – were recording the last days of a way of life that was dying out rapidly. The magnetic pull of the cities was drawing more and more people away from the countryside.

The fishermen of Cove lasted longer here than many of the labourers working the fields above; but gradually they, too, were squeezed out. As the years passed, the offshore herring vanished almost completely, and intensive, largely unregulated netting of cod, mackerel, sprat and sparling decimated sea stocks. A fleet of twenty boats at the beginning of the 1900s was down to three by the 1960s.

Nearly three centuries after it was first cut through the sandstone, Cove's tunnel remains in use. I walked down its cool darkness to arrive at the bay's narrow strip of cliff-enclosed beach. The ends of the two harbour walls were lit red-gold by the sun, and beyond was the flat horizon of the North Sea. For hundreds of years, people worked to turn this bay into a modern fishing station, and it barely lasted a century before it was all but obsolete. I could see five boats lying at odd angles down on the wet sands below me, waiting for the tide to turn and the inrushing water to raise them up into the sea. The harbour still does its job: offering moorings, giving shelter. But it is a relic of a different age, quiet and half forgotten. Its physical structure is still strong. It is its original purpose that is in ruins.

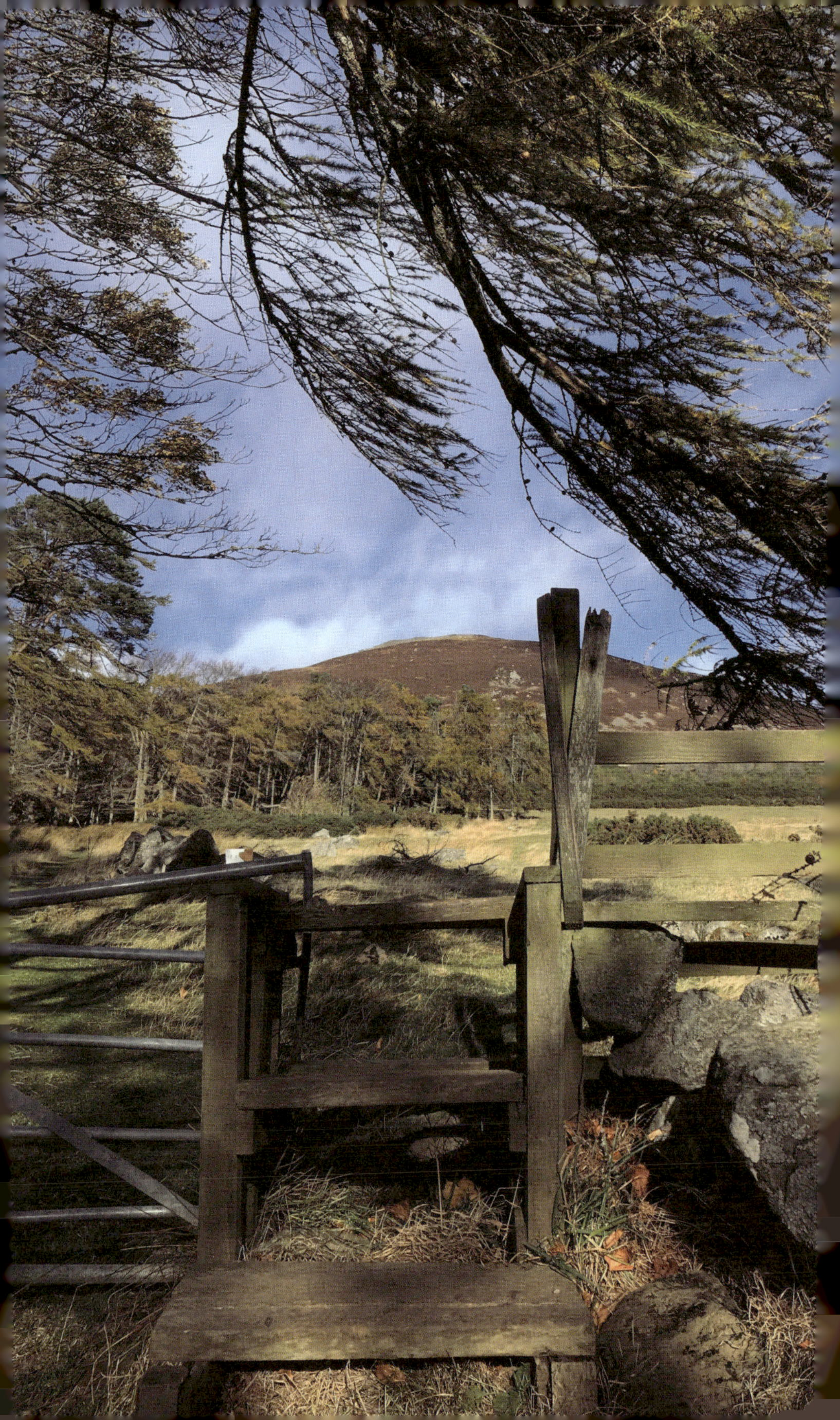

Tap O' Noth, Rhynie

NJ 4845 2930

The wind was relentless, blowing in from the south-west and shifting banks of clouds across the sky at terrific speed. Out on the moor, it felt like walking through a timelapse. The path had approached the great, solitary bulk of the Tap O' Noth from the south, passing between a thin line of trees for a few hundred metres before emerging onto the open ground of the lower slopes. From there, it kinked west to begin a long loop that traversed the rapidly steepening hillside to where I could see it finally winding its way up to the top. Everywhere was clad in dark-brown heather – apart from the summit itself, which was flat-topped, and surrounded by a massive crown of pale grey rock.

For a time in the eighteenth century, the prominent theory was that this rocky summit of the Tap O' Noth (along with a number of others like it throughout Scotland) was the remains of an extinct volcano. The Enlightenment farmer-scientist James Anderson explained the origins of this belief in a 1777 letter to the Society of Antiquaries of London – fragments of once-molten rock were 'usually first discovered by travellers around the bottom and on the sides of steep hills, frequently of a conical shape, terminating in a narrow apex, exactly resembling the hills that have been formed by the eruption of volcanoes'. Go even closer, he continued, on to the summit, and 'would not his former conjecture be much confirmed when, at the top, he should find himself in a circular hollow, surrounded on all sides by matter rising gradually higher to the very edge of the precipice . . . would he not be reckoned sceptical in the extreme if he should entertain the smallest doubt of the truth of this opinion, upon seeing the very opening itself in the centre of the hollow, through which the boiling lava had been ejected?'

The reasons for this conclusion were understandable, Anderson suggested, as he began to explain precisely why it was nevertheless wrong. Instead, he said, the melted heaps of rock had been created by the process of vitrification. 'Through all the northern parts of Scotland,' he wrote, there is 'a particular kind of earthy iron ore . . . much abounds. This ore might have been accidentally mixed with some stones at a place where a great fire was kindled, and being fused by the heat, would cement the stones into one solid mass.' For Anderson, however, this was likely *not* an accident, but a deliberate process, an ingenious part of the construction of a large fortification. Having chosen 'a proper place for their fort', he wrote, 'they would raise a wall all around the area' and then surround it with wood to 'kindle a fire . . . sufficiently intense to melt the vitrescible ore, and thus to cement the whole into one coherent mass'. Using that incredible heat, therefore, to fuse together all of the rock encircling the hilltop.

Anderson was right. Tap O' Noth was no volcano, and a huge fire had once consumed the summit, torching a circle of stones interlaced with a timber frame. What we still don't know, for sure, is why. If it was, as Anderson thought, a construction technique, then it was an inexact and extreme one that did not always strengthen the walls, sometimes making them broken and brittle instead. Was it arson, then? Or ritual? We know that the fort was in use around 2,500 years ago and that the fire happened in about 200 BC. The sight of it must have been tremendous. Tap O' Noth rises up some 560 metres above a great flattening plain that stretches all the way east to the North Sea. It would likely have burned for days, even weeks – a beacon of super-heated flame churning out huge clouds of black smoke. And then, as far as we can tell, after 100 BC the summit was never used again.

In more recent times, that halo of vitrified rock has been something of an archaeological eye-catcher too: drawing excavations to the top of the hill but distracting from the slopes that surround it. Lower down the flanks of Tap O' Noth, there is another ring of stones. Formed out of rough boulders, it runs for over a kilometre, although much of it is now lost or covered with heather. When originally constructed, however, it enclosed an area of some sixteen hectares of the upper slopes of the hill. Since at least the 1960s, those who have come to study the Tap O' Noth began noticing small depressions in the ground, scattered between the outer wall and the summit. Some contained their own little clusters of stones. These were the tell-tale signs of what are known as 'hut circles': the trace remains of ancient timber dwellings.

Over the years, the numbers of recorded hut circles slowly increased. A handful had become 154 by the 1980s. Another few decades on and it had risen to 234. Then, in 2020, a study run by Aberdeen University – which combined on-site excavations with airborne laser scanning – returned the staggering figure of over 800 hut circles. Samples of the soil buried beneath them turned up charcoal-rich fragments filled with the likes of burnt animal bones, teeth, slivers of metal, clay moulds and wheel-thrown pottery. Radiocarbon dating revealed that that the huts had been in use long after the fire on the summit – as much as five centuries after, spanning the period from the third to the sixth century AD, when this land was part of the kingdom of the Picts. Factor in that each hut would likely have been home to a family, and the possibility exists of a huge, early medieval community of upwards of 4,000 people. Which would make Tap O'Noth the largest post-Roman settlement in Scotland, and perhaps even in all of Britain.

It was strange to think, as I followed the path to enter the faint ring of outer stones about 470 metres up the side of the hill, that I was walking the long-abandoned high street of what might once have been the country's 'urban' centre – a Pictish 'city', if you like. People had built it in the literal shadow of that older fort on the summit, that burnt-out ring of rock. Did they remember the stories of the great fire that once flamed here? Or had they come to colonise someone else's ruins? Set their settlement sprawling just beneath the remnants of what they saw as some primitive or arcane acropolis?

The wind continued to tear at me, rifling across the thick, spongy heather. The lee of the hill offered no shelter, as the huge gusts just seemed to catapult around its slopes. I made my way, at last, to the top, almost blown off my feet as I entered the ring of burnt and broken stones. I watched a shower flash past just to the south, a misty column racing over the ground, the sun streaming through it and throwing out flickering rainbows. To the east was a vast patchwork of fields and farmlands, disappearing into the horizon. As ever, the passage of time has that unerring capacity to mix and subvert our landscapes. Below me, a picture-postcard of modern rural life unfurled beneath the great bulk of an old, long-forgotten, hilltop 'city'.

The Shepherd's House, Pentland Hills

NT 2120 6444

I could still see where the fire from the hearth had marked the stones. There was once a chimney on this spot, at the point where the broken walls met. It offered a blackened memory of heat – and of people. I sat on the collapsed gable end of the building and ate a sandwich. I was wearing gloves but the chill air seeped in. Off to the west the high, central spine of the Pentland Hills – Turnhouse Hill, Carnethy Hill, Scald Law, East Kip and West Kip – still held the snowfall from the previous week. Opposite was the pudding-bowl lump of Bell's Hill, its patches of near-black heather surrounded by masses of tawny, withered bracken. It was just after three in the afternoon in early January, and the sun was faltering behind a thin, grey gauze of cirrus clouds.

I had stopped to rest in the ruins of the shepherd's house. I often stop here. If you head south, away from Edinburgh, skirt west of the spruce-ringed oasis of Bonaly Reservoir and follow a narrow sheep track around the side of Harbour Hill, you meet the path that descends through Maiden's Cleugh. It's not much more than an hour's walk from where I live in Colinton. A halfway point for a tramp into the hills and back again. Had you made that journey a century ago, the occupants of this house would have greeted you and offered refreshment – a cool glass of water on a hot summer's day; tea – or maybe even a dram – and a place by that fire, in the cold of winter.

I had recently come across an old book called *The Pentland Hills*, first published in 1926. Its author, William Anderson, wrote of coming here – and to a second shepherd's cottage, found deeper in the hills, further up the course of the Logan Burn – where he had found 'shelter from wintry blasts, and enjoyed the kindly hospitality and racy conversation of its inmates'. That other cottage still stands. It was put up for sale on the open market in 2018

The Shepherd's House, Pentland Hills

– as a two-storeyed, three-bedroomed family house, coming with three acres of land and, if you wanted, option to buy a further two acres of hillside. 'A remarkable opportunity,' as the selling agent put it, 'to own a magical little piece of the Scottish landscape.'

This cottage has no such future. It is too far gone. Yes, some fragments of wall still rise up two or three metres – and they feel as sturdy as ancient standing stones, leaning out of the hillside from their massed cement foundations. But they, too, will fall. I wondered, as I sat there, if I would see it happen. One day, would I round the corner from Maiden's Cleugh, walk beneath the shadow of the tall, solitary oak tree on the brow of the hill, and find it all collapsed? Or will it occur by tiny increments? The weeds and grass and little trees that have taken hold in the stonework, pushing it all ever so gently apart; the elements working away, a slow but constant diminishing. It occurred to me that by passing this way so often, by always stopping a while in the remains, I am in some way thirling myself to this cottage. From this point on, which of us will better bear the passing of time? I'm not sure I want to know the answer to that.

This is not an old house. It was built in the 1850s, and its first resident was a shepherd called John Smith. Other shepherds followed until, at the turn of the century, a labourer at the nearby Kirkton Farm – which still sits today on the other side of the valley at the base of Bell's Hill – moved in here with his family. He extended the building with a small byre, probably used to shelter a single cow for the family's milk and butter. I've seen a photograph of the cottage taken in the 1920s that shows, in profile, a pleasant, sturdy-looking, rubble-faced house with chimneys at either end, punctuated here and there by patches of neat, dressed sandstone. You can still find lumps of that dark-pink sandstone scattered around the ruins today. In the photo, the sash window high up on the north-facing side of the house is open – although there's no sign of the people who lived there then.

Seeing that photo and comparing it to the cottage now, it seems almost inconceivable. The family left sometime in the middle of the last century. But there is no record of how this place collapsed so completely. The military still operate a firing range on Castle Law, the hill behind the cottage to the east. You could imagine a stray shell shattering this place. That, maybe, would be easier to accept than the reality: that this is what abandoned buildings do. Their stones feel the unyielding weight of gravity, and they are pulled, inexorably, back to the earth. It's always just a matter of time.

A little way up the hillside from the ruin of the cottage was something new – a wooden post fixed with a silver plaque. Beyond that, a high deer fence. I walked up to read the plaque. It explained that, beginning in 2017, trees had been planted all across the hillside behind the fence, in commemoration of those Scots who had fallen in the Great War. A new forest will slowly rise here. That forest will grow, while below it the cottage will continue to crumble. And I will watch them both, for as long as I can.

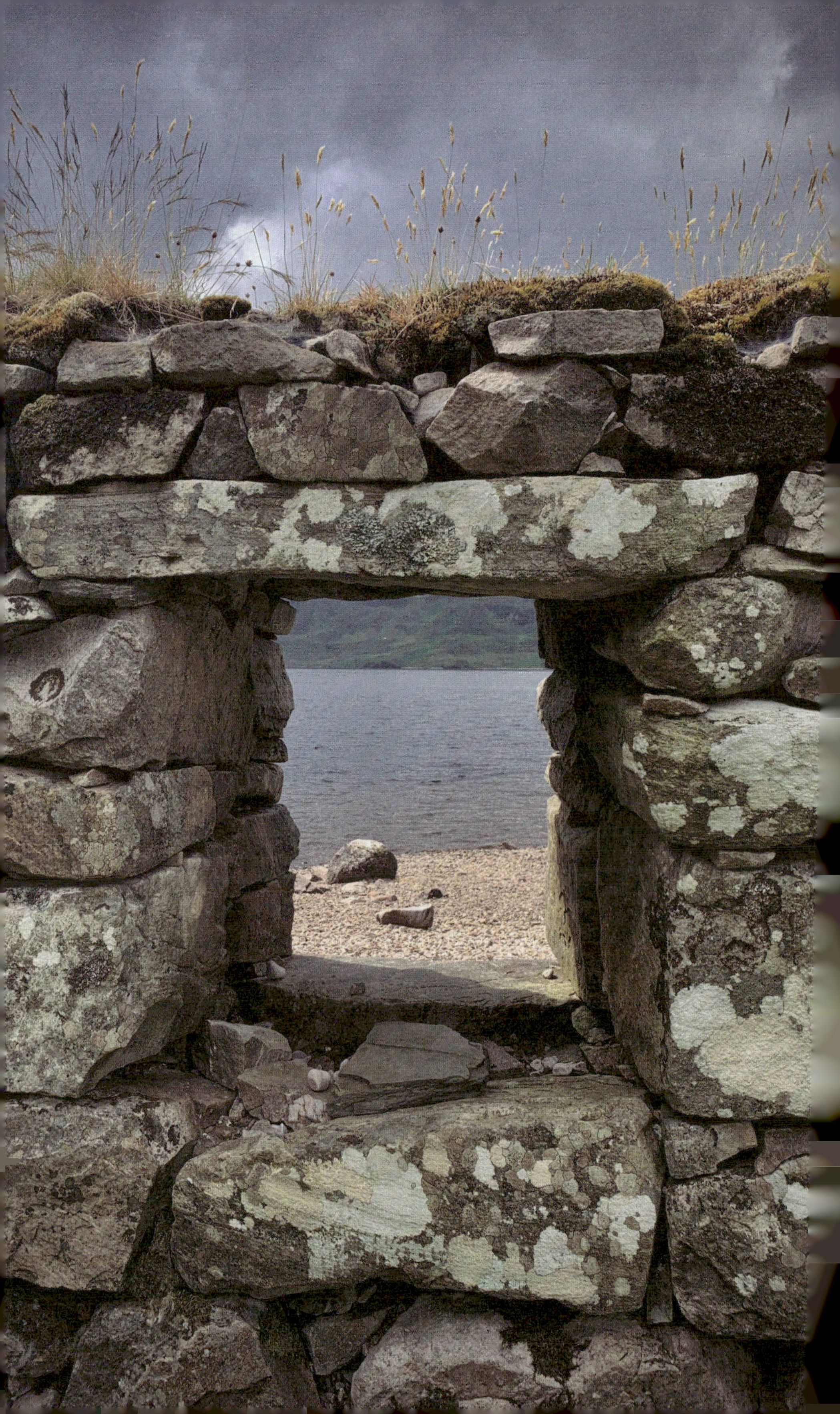

Postscript

Over the previous 300 pages, I have described my visits to 55 different sites all across Scotland. It could easily have been (time and distance notwithstanding) 105, 1,005 or even 10,005. In many respects, the point of this book is to demonstrate that the sheer amount of 'wild history' out there makes it impossible to be comprehensive. Whatever number you arrive at will only ever be a window onto a much larger 'lost' world. Partiality was always the intention in my final selection – to seek out places that I had discovered or heard about through anecdote, chance or circumstance. The joy of working in an archive for as long as I did was that it brought the obscure and the neglected to my attention in all sorts of ways – in a century-old survey drawing of a site visited once and all but neglected ever since; in an aerial photograph of a halo of intriguing stones in an otherwise empty stretch of rugged coastline; in the spidery, fading hand-writing of an antiquarian's leather-bound journal. These discoveries in the quiet gloom of an archival store planted the seed and ultimately compelled me to find the places for real.

But rather than produce a functional gazetteer, or reference guide, I wanted to give my accounts of visiting each site the space to breathe. To try, as best I could, to capture the atmosphere of *now* alongside the details of *then*. What I hope emerges through this process is the idea that every place – no matter how meagre or ruined or faded or diminished – contains the thread of a story. Think of this every time you go out into the landscape. One way or another, people have shaped everything you see. If you really start to interrogate your surroundings, then the questions quickly tumble out. Who arranged those boulders into a circle? Why does that stone dyke cut across that particular stretch of hillside? Who dug into that ground over there and what for? What are the origins, even, of the very path on which you are walking? The answers may be prosaic or may not necessarily seem to speak of grand histories – certainly not in the traditional sense. But they exist on the canvas of the wide sweep of human events, containing within them the traces of religion, or war, or politics, or industry, or even climate change. Evidence – real evidence you can still touch – of how the push and pull of a constantly shifting and changing world reverberates into the very fabric of the landscape. Evidence of how everything is connected.

Of course, it was inevitable that, in selecting sites for a book like this, I had to leave things out. There are, sadly, far too many to enumerate here, but I will offer some as inspiration for your own future journeys. Just north of Glasgow, for instance, on an otherwise empty stretch of heather plains at the foot of the Campsie Fells, sit three boulders bearing a series of carved heads, grotesque and eerie, that glower out of the rock. On the sparse Atlantic coastline of the Isle of Harris, a wide stone 'carcass ramp' leads up from the sea to a tall redbrick chimney – all that remains of a Norwegian whaling station established on the island in 1904. Scramble a little off the main path that takes you to the summit of Schiehallion and you can find the simple footprint of a bothy that played host to a remarkable eighteenth-century experiment – where the Astronomer Royal attempted to work out the mean density, and weight, of the entire earth (and then burnt the bothy to the ground in a whisky-fuelled celebration once the calculations were complete). Then there is the desolate moorland to the north of Glencoe where a rocky knoll is studded with the concrete grave slabs of the men, one woman – and one 'unknown' – who died while building the vast wall that overshadows their final resting place: the Blackwater Dam. Or the quiet, sandy bay of Glenbatrick near the mouth of Loch Tarbet on the Isle of Jura, site both of the discovery of a great cache of microliths left by a hunter-gatherer community who came to the island perhaps as long as 8,000 years ago, and also the house, set just above the shore, where George Orwell retreated to write his masterwork, *Nineteen Eighty-Four*.

The truth is that our landscapes are brim-full, even overflowing, with stories. Some are harder to find than others, faded with time and age; hidden or lost or buried. But make no mistake, they are still out there. It's just a question of perception, of looking at your surroundings with an open curiosity, with a commitment to *noticing*. And once you start, it becomes very hard to stop.

List of Illustrations

2: Glencoe, looking west past the snow-covered 'Three Sisters'.
18–19: The ruins of Fethaland at the northern tip of Shetland Mainland, looking east towards the North Sea.
20: Rusting remains of a steam-driven derrick crane above the abandoned quarry of Belnahua.
24: The path of the Cauldstane Slap, looking north to the pass between the hills of East and West Cairn
28: Fasagh, Loch Maree, looking east towards the mist-covered summit of Beinn a' Mhùinidh.
31: Crossing the Fasagh River in torrent as it runs out into the eastern end of Loch Maree
34: The top of the funnel of the Ard Nev deer trap, looking north across the sea to the Skye Cuillins.
40–1: The old 'fish road' emerging from beneath the waters of Loch Glascarnoch and running straight off into the western distance.
44: The end of the path leading to Loch Coire nam Mang, with Ben Griam Beg rising behind, to the east.
48: Looking south to the concrete square of the old Kirnie Law reservoir.
52: (Top) View from my boat looking inland towards the entrance to the Viking shipyard. (Bottom) View at low tide looking south down the ruins of the canal towards Rum.
56: Below the giant archways of the Ard Neackie limekiln.
60–1: View of the limekilns and pier, looking south towards the head of Loch Eriboll.
62: Looking east through the ruined doorway of a fisherman's cottage at Fethaland.
66: Rail tracks running south past the wall of the Ailsa Craig gasworks.
69: Collapsed bridge of the old walkway leading to Ailsa Craig's north foghorn.
72: Looking west over the beach of Sandwood Bay, past the sea stack Am Buacahille towards the Atlantic Ocean.
74–5: The ruins of a shepherd's cottage overlooking the still waters of Sandwood Loch.

78: The ruined curtain wall of the Salisbury Dam where it attempted to block the Kilmory River.
82: Looking north towards Charles Jencks' unfinished land art project – fashioned form the spoil heaps left behind by the St Ninian's opencast mine.
85: Tree planted in a ring of rubber tyres on the summit of one of the earth mounds
88–9: Na Clachan Aoraidh stone circle, looking north.
90: The lichen-covered upright of the Callanish XI standing stone.
94–5: Looking west past Callanish XI to the waters of the sea loch Rog an Ear.
96: Swordle Bay on the Ardnamurchan Peninsula, looking north towards the silhouettes of Canna, Eigg and Rum.
100: Archway of yew trees leading into the Glencruitten Tree Cathedral.
104: Looking west onto the shrine of the Cailleach in Glen Cailleach, with its family of stone statues standing outside.
107: (Top) Near the half-way point of the track running to the north of Loch Lyon, the route bends northwards towards Glen Cailleach. (Bottom) Looking west towards the head of Loch Lyon.
110: Looking up towards the cantilevered classroom block of Cardross Seminary.
113: View down from the top floor of the concrete shell of Cardross Seminary sanctuary block.
114; 116–17: View of the ground floor of the central sanctuary space of Cardross Seminary.
118: Posts and climbing ropes running over the cliff edge that leads down to the ruins of the early Christian sanctuary space of Sgorr nam Ban-Naomha.
122: Looking east along the one-time ramparts of Dun Deardil, across Glen Nevis towards the summit of Ben Nevis.
128–9: The ruined terracing at the west end of Cathkin Park.
132: Looking north past the one remaining upright stone of Na Clachan Aoraidh stone circle.
136: View of Buachaille Etive Mhor, foregrounded by the entrance door to Jacksonville Hut.
139: View across the River Coupall to Jacksonville and Buachaille Etive Mhor.
144–5: Looking west across the wet sands of Traigh Chlithe towards the dark silhouette of the Isle of Rum.
147: Sweeney's Bothy exterior (top) and interior (bottom) looking out on the Isle of Rum at sunset.
148: The central 'corridor' of the forest pitch hut, near Selkirk.
150–1: View of the forest pitch and its boundary fence.
152–3: The great boulder boundary marker of Clach na Briton, viewed looking south west down Glen Falloch.
154: Dere Street Roman Road, looking north west up the slope of Cow Hill.
156–7: The point by Whitton Edge where Dere Street merges with the modern road to run northwest past Jedburgh and towards St Boswells.
160: Section of the Culbin Sands poles, looking northwest across the dune system towards the Moray Firth.

List of Illustrations

164: View looking northeast up Glen Falloch, foregrounded by the great hulking boulders of Clach na Briton.
168: The rusting hull of one of two X-Craft Midget submarines on the tidal sands of Aberlady Bay.
172: The last stretch of path leading to Cairn Cul Ri Albainn, looking west towards the dark summit of Ben More.
174–5: View of the cairn looking back east, towards the valley of Loch Ba and the summit of Cruachan Dearg.
177: Foreground view of the cairn, looking south towards Glen More.
178: The entrance leading down into the Kinbrace nuclear shelter.
182: Path leading through the dense bracken that approaches Rubers Law from the east.
184: Gate in a drystone wall near to the summit of Rubers Law.
186: Drystone boundary wall cutting across the steep upper slopes of Rubers Law. Beyond, to the northwest, are the farmlands of the Teviot valley.
188: View down the length of the Atlantic Wall, looking out across Sheriffmuir. In the foreground is a shattered section sprouting tendrils of bent rebar.
192: View through the gates of the old coastguard house at the highest point of Inchkeith, looking south across the Firth of Forth towards Edinburgh.
195: View through workshop window towards Inchkeith's 19th-century lighthouse.
196–7: Looking west across the Inchkeith's military ruins towards the distant Forth Bridges.
199: A wartime observation tower – built on top of an older Victorian fort – rises up above a massed field of nettles.
200: View south from the concrete gun emplacement of the North Sutor Battery.
205: Waves breaking over the wrecked hull of *John Randolph* at Torrisdale Bay.
210–11: View south from the Cramond battery gun emplacement down the line of the causeway and its concrete obelisks.
214: The River Spey running beneath one of the two stone arches of General Wade's Garva Bridge.
220: Path leading away from Ardoch Fort, looking north-west towards the Grampian Mountains.
222–3: Path leading through the earthen ramparts of Ardoch Fort.
226–7: The ruin of Mavisbank House emerging from the summer undergrowth.
230–1: Looking out of the 'Fox's Den' cave westwards down the valley of Glen Dubh.
234: View through the ruined doorway of an old house at the township of Peanmeanach.
236–7: View of the stone track running on the high ridgeline of the Ardnish peninsula, looking north and west across the waters of Loch Nan Uamh.
239: (Top) Looking north across the ruins of Peanmeanch. (Bottom) The old post and schoolhouse repurposed and reroofed as an open access bothy.
240: Near the southern tip of Borgie Forest, on top of a lonely knoll, you can find the narrow entrance to Cracknie Souterrain.

Wild History

243: Stopping for a rest on the forestry track leading to Cracknie Souterrain. In the distance, shrouded by cloud, is Ben Loyal.

246: (Top) Looking south-west from the site of Staffa's bothy, over the 'Port of Refuge' bay towards the Atlantic Ocean. (Bottom) View of Staffa's distinctive hexagonal rock columns near the entrance to Fingal's Cave.

250: View from the entrance of Coire Gabhail, looking south.

253: (Top) View south from the floor of the 'lost valley'. (Bottom) Looking back north, across Glencoe, towards the ridgeline of Am Bodach and A' Chailleach.

258–9: Hermit's Castle at sunset, looking north and west.

260: Ruin of Shiaba's shepherd's cottage, the last building of the township to be abandoned.

262–3: Looking west over the ruins of Shiaba to the towering cliffs of the Ross of Mull.

266: An accidental 'cathedral of trees' created by felling a line in the planation above Portmore Reservoir.

270: Looking out over Village Bay, Mingulay, through the ruins of a doorway half-buried by wind-blown sands.

275: (Top and Bottom) View east over the roofless ruins of Village Bay.

276: Looking directly east, beyond a farmhouse to the summit of the Sgurr, Eigg.

279: (Top) View northwest from top of the Sgurr's ravine, over Loch Beinn Tighe towards the mountains of Rum. (Bottom) Looking up from below the western tip of the Sgurr.

284–5: The shell of Moine House frames a view south over the expanse of the peat bog to the silhouette of Ben Hope.

287: View looking east through the empty window frame of Moine House.

288: The overgrown façade of Mavisbank House in midsummer.

294: Looking in from the seaward side towards the Cove Harbour cottages.

297: View looking west from the end of the north pier of Cove Harbour.

300: View looking north of a style and woods framing the summit of Tap O' Noth.

306–07: The ruins of the shepherd's hut foregrounding the view south-west towards the high ridgeline of the Pentland Hills, with the peaks of Scald Law and East and West Kip visible in the distance.

308: Ruins of a chapel on the northern bank of Loch Morar.

Acknowledgements

No book is an island, and as ever, there are a whole host of people I have to thank for *Wild History*'s existence. Hugh Andrew and Andrew Simmons at my wonderful publishers Birlinn were hugely supportive of the idea from the outset and generously offered a significant degree of latitude on the delivery of the text when the small matter of a pandemic made travel impossible. Thanks also to Craig Hillsley for his astute copy-editing, Abigail Salvesen for her beautiful cover design, Mark Blackadder for the stunning internal layout, and everyone else on the team who has been involved in bringing this book out into the world.

Most of the journeys that feature in this book I made alone – but not all. So another huge thank you those who came with me to some of the more extreme locations (either in body or in spirit), including Andy Twaddle, Rachel Bell, Jamie Flynn, Alastair McCormick, Peter Keith, Colin Murray, Richard Downes, Jon Morrice, Andrew Thompson, Bertie Allison, Emma Burns, Jonah Jones, Billie Simmons and Willie Gorman.

Thank you to my great friend and former agent Maggie Hattersley: *Wild History* was one of the last books that she worked on with me before her well-deserved retirement. And thanks most of all to Hazel, Brodie and Nate, who were continually roped in to drives or trips to obscure locations, and endured my fiddling with various different camera lenses, and my need to 'wait for the right light' or 'get just one last photo'.

And a final thanks to Alexander Curle, first Secretary of the Royal Commission, whose beautifully mad idea to go out into the landscape to find and inspect every trace of Scotland's past inspired this book.

Index

abandonment *see* clearances; depopulation
Aberlady Bay 169–71
Achmelvich 256–9
Adomnán 175–6
Agricola 157, 224
Ailsa Craig 67–71, 105
Am Buachaille, Sandwood Bay 77
anchorites 121
Anderson, George 283
Anderson, James 59, 301–2
Anderson, William 304
anti-boat barriers 208–13
Arctic convoys 206
Ard Neackie 57–61
Ard Nev Deer Trap 35–7
Ardnamurchan 97–9
Ardnish Peninsula 235–8
Ardoch Roman Fort 221–5
Argyll, Duke of 261–2
Atlantic Wall, Sheriffmuir 189–91

Banks, Joseph 247
Bates, Professor Richard 91–5
batteries 193–4, 201–3, 208–13
Bay of Laig 142–6
Belnahua 21–3
Ben Griam Beg 45–7
Blaeu, Joan 77, 174, 268
blast furnaces 32
bloomeries 29, 32
boat burials, Viking 97–9

boats 54, 119–20, 205–7 *see also* shipwrecks; shipyards
Bone Caves 228–33
Borges, Jorge Luis 14
Borgie Forest 241–5
bothy, Isle of Staffa 247–9
boundaries 165–7, 173–6
Braco 221–5
British Fisheries Society, the 39
burials 97–9, 134–5, 143–6
Burt, Edmund 217–18

Cailleach, the 105–9
Cairn Cul Ri Albainn 173–6
cairns 98–9, 143–6, 173–6, 181
Callanish 91–5
Canna, Isle of 119–21
Cardross 111–17
Carroll, Lewis 14–15
Cathedral of Trees, Glencruitten 101–3
Cathkin Park 126–31
cattle 25–7, 174, 252–5
Cauldstane Slap 25–7
caves 229–33
charcoal production 29, 32
churches 111–12, 120–1
Clach na Briton 165–7
Cladh nan Sussanach 30
Clarke, Edward 36
clearances 37, 76, 79–80, 261–5, 268–9, 286 *see also* depopulation
Clerk, Sir John 290–3

Index

Cliffs of the Holy Women, Canna 119–21
climate change 46–7, 124–5
Cnoc na Craoibhe, Loch Tummel 133–5
Cockburnspath 296–8
Coire Gabhail 251–5
Cold War, the 180–1
Coles, Fred 133–4
collieries 83–6, 290
Columba, St 120, 175–6
convents 121
Corrieyairack Pass 216–19
Corryvreckan 105
Coulthard, Craig 149–50
Cove Harbour 295–9
Cracknie Souterrain 241–5
Craigallian fire 137–8
Cramond Island 208–13
Cramond lioness 212–13
Cranborne, Viscount 80
Creag Dhu Mountaineering Club 138–41
Cree, John 232
Cromarty Firth 201–3
Culbin Sand Poles 161–3
Cultural Olympiad 149–50
Cunningham, John 140–1
Curle, Alexander Ormiston 12–13, 184, 241–5
curling stones 68–71

D-Day 163, 170–1, 190
dams 42, 80–1
deer 80, 286
deer traps 35–7
depopulation 237–8, 271–2, 274, 298–9 *see also* clearances
Dere Street Roman Road 155–9
Dio, Cassius 159, 225
droving 25–7, 174
Drumalban 175–6
Dun Deardail 123–5

Eddleston 267–9

Eigg, Isle of 142–6, 277–81
enclosures, Ben Griam Beg 46–7
evictions *see* clearances

Fasagh Ironworks 29–33
Fethaland 63–5
Fife Earth Project 86
Fingal's Cave 247–8
fires 123–4, 125, 134, 137–8, 302–3
Firth of Clyde 67–71
Firth of Forth 193–8, 208–13
Firth of Lorn 21–3
Fish Road, Loch Glascarnoch 38–43
fisheries 38–9, 63–5, 273, 298–9
fog horns 70
football 126–31, 149–51
Forest Pitch 149–51
forestry 101–2, 162, 268–9
forests, commemorative 306–7
forts
    hillforts 12–13, 46, 123–5, 267–9, 280, 301–3
    Roman 221–5

Garnett, Thomas 248
Garva Bridge 215–19
giants 201
Gillespie, Kidd & Coia 111–12
Girvan family 68–70
Glascarnoch Dam 42
Glasgow 126–31
Glasgow Boys, the 298
Gleann Cailliche 108–9
Glen Falloch 165–7
Glen Lyon 105–9
Glen Nevis 123–5
Glencoe 251–5
Glencoe Massacre 254–5
Glencruitten, Cathedral of Trees 101–3
Gorman, Willie 137–41
granite 68–71
grave robbing 145–6
Great Depression, the 137–8
Great Sand Drift, the 161–2
gun emplacements 203, 208–13

Guthrie, James 296–8

haaf stations 63–5
Habchester 12–13
Haldane, A.R.B. 26
Hampden Park 126–31
harbours 295–9
Hay, Sir George 32
hermitages 120–1
Hermit's Castle 256–9
hillforts 12–13, 46, 123–5, 267–9, 280, 301–3
houses, shepherds' 76, 265, 304–7
hut circles 302–3
hydroelectric schemes 50–1

Ice Ages 228–33
Inchkeith Island 193–8
Inchnadamph 228–33
Innerleithen 49–51
Invergordon 202, 203
ironworks 29–33
isolation (quarantine) 196–8

Jacksonville Hut 137–41
James IV, King 194
Jameson, Professor Robert 277–8
Jencks, Charles 86
John Randolph 205–7
Johnson, Samuel 198, 247
Jolly, William 271

Kays of Mauchline 70, 71
Kerouac, Jack 187
Kinbrace 179–81
Kirnie Law 49–51
Knox, John (philanthropist) 38–9, 283

Laing, Malcolm 254
Lassodie 83–7
Leitch, Archibald 127
Liberty-class vessels 205–7
lighthouses 64, 70
lightning strikes 93–5

lime kilns 58–60
Loanhead 289–93
Loch Eriboll 57–61
Loch Glascarnoch 38–43
Loch Maree 29–33
Loch na h-Airde 53–5
Lost Valley, the 251–5

Macadam, William 29–30
MacCulloch, John 67–8, 142, 216, 277, 280
MacDonald, Neil 261–5
MacFadyen, David 54
Mackay, Alexander 102–3
Mackenzie, Colin 268–9
MacNeil, Angus 272
MacQueen, Nellie 238
Mavisbank 289–93
Mercer, Roger 47
Miller, Hugh 36–7, 277, 278–81
mills, textile 50–1
Mingulay Village 271–4
missionaries 119–20
Modernist architecture 111–17
Moine House 282–6
Moine, the 282–3
monitoring posts, Royal Observer Corps 179–81
Mons Graupius 224–5
Mountain Bothies Association 238
mountaineering 137–41
Mull, Isle of 173–6, 261–5
Munro, Neil 70, 218–19
Murtagh, Paul 130–1

Na Clachan Aoraidh 133–5
National Pride 87
North Sea Mine Barrage 202, 206
North Sutor Battery 201–3
Northshield Rings 267–9
nuclear attack 180–1
NVA 115–17

Oban, Glencruitten, Cathedral of Trees 101–3

Index

passes 25–7, 216–19
paths 215, 218, 286
Peanmeanach 235–8
peat bogs 91–5, 123–4, 282–3
Pentland Hills 304–7
Picts 143, 302–3
Pont, Timothy 76
Portmore Reservoir 268

quarantine 196–8
quarrying 22–3, 58, 70
Queen's Park FC 127–30

railways 67, 70, 235
reivers 27, 252–4
reservoirs 42–3, 49–51, 268
roads
    drove 25–7, 174
    improvements 38–43, 283–6
    Roman 155–9, 216
    Wade's military 215–19
Romans
    Cramond lioness 212–13
    forts 221–5
    roads 155–9, 216
    signal stations 183–7
Ross, Dr Anne 108
Royal Commission on the Ancient and Historical Monuments of Scotland 12–15
Royal Observer Corps Monitoring Post, Kinbrace 179–81
Rubers Law 183–7
Rubh' an Dunain 53–5
Rum, Isle of 35–7, 79–81, 119, 142–3

St Ninian's open-cast mine 86
St Peter's Seminary 111–17
Salisbury's Dam 79–81
salmon fishing 80
sand movement 161–2
sand poles, Culbin 161–3
Sandwood Bay 73–7
Scott, David 256–9
Scottish National Buildings Record 14

Selkirk 149–51
Severus, Septimius 159, 225
Sgorr nam Ban-Naomha 119–21
Sgurr, the 277–81
sheep farming 76, 255, 261–4
shepherds' houses 76, 265, 304–7
Sheriffmuir 189–91
Shetland 63–5
Shiaba 261–5
ships *see* boats
shipwrecks 119, 205–7
shipyards 53–5, 205
signal stations, Roman 183–7
Skene, William Forbes 175–6
Skye, Isle of 53–5
slate 21–3
Somerville, Alexander 295–6
souterrains 241–5
sporting estates 80
Square Cairn Cemetery, Isle of Eigg 142–6
Staffa, Isle of 247–9
stone circles 91–5, 133–5
Stuart, John Sobieski and Charles Edward 286
submarine nets 202, 209
submarines, X-Craft midget 169–71
surveying, geophysical 91–3
Sutherland, Duke of 283, 286
Sutors, North and South 201–3
Swordle Bay 97–9
syphilis 196–8

Tacitus 158, 224–5
Tap O' Noth 301–3
Telford, Thomas 39–42, 216
Third Lanark AC 130
Tigh na Cailleach 105–9
Tirpitz 170
Tolkien, J.R.R. 142
Torrisdale Bay 207
townships 76, 237–8, 252–5, 261–5, 271–4
Treaty of Union, the 291
tunnel, Cove Harbour 296, 299

Ullapool 39
US Mine Squadron 202

Vikings 53–5, 73, 97–9, 232
vitrification 123, 125, 302

Wade's military roads 215–19
war memorials 102, 146, 306–7
watch towers, Roman 183–7
Watters, Diane 116

wilderness 10–11, 76–7
World War I 102, 189–90, 202, 209
World War II
   defences 162–3, 189–90, 193, 203, 209
   ships and submarines 169–71, 205–7

X-Craft midget submarines 169–71